D0387975

Imagine Ourselves Richly

Imagine Ourselves Richly

Mythic Narratives of
North American Indians

Christopher Vecsey

HarperSanFrancisco

A Division of HarperCollins*Publishers*

IMAGINE OURSELVES RICHLY: *Mythic Narratives of North American Indians.* Copyright © 1991 by Christopher Vecsey. Printed in the United States of America. No part of this book may be used or reproduced in any manner whatsoever without written permission except in the case of brief quotations embodied in critical articles and reviews. For information address HarperCollins Publishers, 10 East 53rd Street, New York, NY 10022.

FIRST HARPERCOLLINS PAPERBACK EDITION PUBLISHED IN 1991.

Reprinted by arrangement with The Crossroad Publishing Co.

This edition is printed on acid-free paper that meets the American National Standards Institute Z39.48 Standard.

Library of Congress Cataloging-in-Publication Data

Vecsey, Christopher.
    Imagine ourselves richly : mythic narratives of North American
Indians / Christopher Vecsey. — 1st HarperCollins pbk. ed.
      p.   cm.
    Reprint. Originally published: New York : Crossroad, 1988.
    Includes bibliographical references and index.
    ISBN 0-06-250891-1
    1. Indians of North America—Religion and mythology.   I. Title.
[E98.R3V43   1991]
299'.72—dc20   90-20511
                                                   CIP

91 92 93 94 95 RRD 10 9 8 7 6 5 4 3 2 1

Contents

Illustrations

Acknowledgments

In writing the following book I have been fortunate in having two colleagues who have shared with me their corresponding interests. John F. Fisher and I collaborated on a project that is chapter 3 in this book, and Carol Ann Lorenz and I joined methods in creating part of what is here chapter 2. Both have made helpful suggestions regarding other chapters, but neither should bear any responsibility for any failures herein.

Colgate University has been generous in supporting my research, by grants through the Faculty Research Council, the Division of the Humanities, and the Native American Studies Program. In addition, the John Ben Snow Memorial Trust provided funds to further the project. I am indebted to these sources of money.

I am also grateful to Prof. Harold Turner and his staff at the Study Centre for New Religious Movements in Primal Societies at Selly Oak Colleges, Birmingham, England, for making their extensive archives available to me. The Colgate University Case Library, the Hobart and William Smith Library, the libraries at the American Philosophical Society, Columbia University, Northwestern University, and the University of Ibadan, as well as the Smithsonian Institution's National Anthropological Library, have all been helpful to my research.

I hope that the seven essays (and Preface) that comprise this book will prove useful to students of mythology and religion, and to those interested in American Indian traditions. Although each chapter contains an extensive bibliography representing a full array of sources for my information and ideas, I have reduced the number of parenthetical references to a minimum for the sake of readability. In so doing I am not pretending originality; indeed, I am wholly dependent upon my sources. The reader who wishes to see more thoroughly documented versions of these chapters can turn to earlier published versions (listed below), or may consult manuscripts in my possession at Colgate University.

The Preface first appeared as part of "Envision Ourselves Darkly, Imagine Ourselves Richly," in *The American Indian and The Problem of History*, ed. Calvin Martin (Oxford University Press, 1987): 120–27. Chapter 2 is composed of two articles: "The Emergence of the Hopi People," *American Indian Quarterly* 9 (1983): 69–92; and "Hopi Ritual Clowns and Values in the Hopi Life Span" (with Carol Ann Lorenz), in *Humor and Aging*, ed. Kathleen McCluskey et al. (Academic Press, 1986): 199–220. Chapter 3 appeared first as "The Ojibwa Creation Myth: An Analysis of Its Structure and Content" (with John F. Fisher), in *Temenos* 20 (1984): 66–100; and chapter 4, "The Story and Structure of the Iroquois Confederacy," was published in the *Journal of the American Academy of Religion* 54 (1986): 79–106. I appreciate the permission granted by these publishers to include the essays in the present book.

Preface

I am a historian with a special interest in American Indians and their religions. I began my studies examining the stories of American relations with Indians, and in time I concentrated on Indians themselves: their existence in relation to the environmental, human, and spiritual worlds. Finally, I have focused my attention on the means by which Indians have traditionally examined their lives—their own stories. In their stories American Indians have examined their lives in a way at least as valid as the discursive methods of academics. We often repeat Socrates' dictum that the unexamined life is not worth living, as though it meant that we Westerners (or, more exactly, we academics) are the only people who examine our lives and try to know ourselves. This is a misconception. American Indians have examined their lives, both discursively and narratively. They have been willing to enter metaphysical disputations (we have records of such encounters), but in the main they have relied on their storytelling for self-knowledge. And if we believe that an *unexamined* life is not worth living, their stories indicate that examining life's possibilities and problems accomplishes nothing if it takes place apart from the life-sustaining web of human, environmental, and spiritual relations. In Indian stories, I have found, it is the *rootless* life that is not only worthless but impossible.

In the winter of 1979 I visited the Grassy Narrows Reserve in western Ontario to gather information from the Ojibwa Indians there for their legal claims regarding a mercury despoliation case. I interviewed an old man, John Beaver, who answered many of my questions with seasoned Ojibwa stories. When I asked him what distinguished an Indian hunter from a white hunter, he replied that the difference lay in their differing attitudes toward the animals they hunt. He proceeded to narrate a lengthy story about a bear who adopts a boy. Taking the child into his den and calling him his grandson, the bear shows what happens when bears allow themselves to be killed by hunters. If the hunters perform the proper thanksgiving rituals for the fallen animal, the bear comes back to life and can give himself to another hunter. After having demonstrated also that bears live in societies similar to those of humans, with similar motives and emotions of sexuality, protectiveness, and belonging, and with laughable foolishness similar to that of humans, the bear gives himself up to another hunter, who turns out to be the boy's father. The man and his son are reunited. John Beaver taught me that to Indians (at least the Ojibwas), human life depends upon other-than-human persons who give up their lives so humans can live, and who deserve and demand human respect.

The following year at Hopiland I heard from Eugene Sekaquaptewa, and later from Thomas Banyacya, versions of the famous story of Hopi origins. At the invitation of the god, Masau'u, the ancestors of the Hopis emerge from the earth, trek across the body of the land, and establish what is now their homeland, becoming a people in the course of their journey and settlement. Through this story the Hopis define their human essence in terms of human community. Their story demonstrates that community networks are a matter of life and death; that human life depends on community cooperation; that disruptions, jealousy, and factionalism make human persistence impossible and, indeed, are pivotal factors in bringing death into the world. At its core the story is a declaration of dependence on community cooperation, just as the Ojibwa story is a declaration of dependence on the earth and its creatures.

Both stories indicate also that the spiritual world cares deeply about human life and promises to nurture it, if humans can live harmoniously with themselves and their fellow beings. These two stories epitomize for me the grand corpus of Indian stories that espouse a triplefold declaration of dependence on the surrounding world: of the individual on the community, of the community on nature, and of nature on the ultimately powerful world of spirit. It seems to me that the crucial matters of Indian stories—their thought-about-world—are crucial to us, too, just as our knowledge of their lived-in-world is important.

I have come to the conclusion that Indian stories can help us expand our concept of who we are. Too readily we think of ourselves as white Western moderns, belonging to a Judeo-Christian religion and a Greco-Roman polity. However, by seeing our humanity reflected and revealed in Indian stories, we can release ourselves from the repressed images of our full humanity. By retelling the stories of Indian lives, stories which are, I contend, our own stories, that is, *human* stories, and by imagining ourselves as *humans* instead of contemporary, white Americans, we can make manifest some crucial latencies of our human nature. Indian traditions have something to offer us non-Indians: values we have repressed or never known regarding environment, society, and the spiritual world. Their texts offer us insights concerning the possibility of human systems that we might recover or attain. The study of American Indians, I have found, challenges us in our Americanness and enriches us in our humanness, permitting us—as N. Scott Momaday has recommended (1980)—to "imagine ourselves richly," to know ourselves well.

1

Mythography

MYTHOLOGY AND FALSEHOOD

Contemporary common parlance speaks of a "myth" as a falsehood, a belief which does not accurately reflect reality. For most of us, "myths" are to realities what fictions are to facts. A person may *believe* a "myth," but when in proper possession of the facts, one *knows* reality, or a reasonable facsimile thereof. To most of us, "myth" is a matter of fallacious belief.

Even further, many think of "myth" as an escape from the reality of life, a delusion which people dwell upon in order to avoid the inescapable facts of existence. Some writers have charged that the makers of "myth," the believers in "myth," and the students of "myths" are escapists from the "powerhouse" of history and contemporary politics; romantics who want to recline in the passivity and unverifiable falsity of mythopoeic thought; gullible folk who will believe any old story they are told (Rahv 1953; Wiesel 1980).

Students of myth have fashioned definitions of the subject matter that differ little from common terminology. Hence: "A myth is an unverifiable and typically fantastic story that is nonetheless felt to be true and that deals, moreover, with a theme of some importance to the believer" (Bierhorst 1976:3). Or: "Mythology is the study of whatever religious or heroic legends are so foreign to a student's experience that he cannot believe them to be true," that is, "incredible" tales (Graves 1959:v). Whether we speak of a single narrative, a "myth"; or a corpus of mythic narratives, a "mythology" (e.g., Bulfinch 1967; Hamilton 1942); or even if we speak of the study of mythic narrative, "mythography" (Feldman and Richardson 1972:297; Kirk 1970:8; Spence 1931:13ff.), we encounter skepticism and opprobrium.

The use of "myth" or "mythology" as descriptive terms arouses difficulties with a reading audience. The layperson hears the terms and assumes that these false things are of no importance; myths are things to be destroyed, put aside, and scorned, certainly not to be studied inten-

1

sively and sympathetically. Even more troublesome, when addressing the people whose mythology we study—American Indians, for example— we find that they have heard the term used disparagingly for so long, by so many people, that the very use of it rankles and insults them. They prefer the terms "traditions" or "stories" or "sacred narratives," rather than the opprobrious term "mythology."

In this book we certainly do not mean to disparage the texts we are studying; indeed, our claim is that they are matters of crucial importance to the people who create and believe them, and although they may possess nonrational depths, in our present context they are not regarded as false-hoods. We prefer to use a description of the phenomenon of mythology similar to William G. Doty's (1980:533) complex definition:

> A mythological corpus consists of (1) a usually complex network of myths, which are (2) culturally important (3) imaginal (4) stories, conveying by means of (5) metaphoric and symbolic diction, (6) graphic imagery, and (7) emotional conviction and participation, (8) the primal, foundational accounts (9) of the real, experienced world, and (10) humankind's roles and relative statuses within it.

Maybe it is just authors' hubris to acclaim the subject matter close to their heart and scholarship; however, we regard the importance and va-lidity of these myths under study, and we mean to give them our fullest sense of appreciation as well as our fullest analytical skills. We wish to know about these myths, and enjoy them, too; appraise and prize them; both think about them and thank them for the insights they offer us. Our approach to myths and mythology is directly counterposed to the popular attitudes toward them.

Today's commonplace definition of myth began to take shape during the axial period of history in Greece as early as the sixth century B.C. At that time a contrast was developing between the folk and educated views toward the popular stories of Greek culture. While the uneducated pop-ulace continued to tell their tales in assorted attitudes of belief and ap-preciation, the intelligentsia began to rationalize the traditions, stepping back from them, seeing them in a critical manner, as things to be analyzed rather than heritage to be loved. Western philosophy arose in this Greek setting, encountering and overcoming myth. Philosophy forged its own being on the already existing crucible of folk mythology, as Ernst Cassirer has shown: "The images of mythology, it was held, must conceal a rational cognitive content which it is the task of reflection to discover" (Cassirer 1955:2).

Finding myths untruthful on their surface, Greek scholars explained the existence of mythology in various ways that have continued through the ages. Plato, Aristotle, other members of the Academy and their contemporaries recognized the philosophical, nature-allegorical, psychological, social, religious and historical origins of mythology. By pointing to these various causes of myths, the educated Greeks from Hellenic and Hellenistic periods hoped to demythologize their society. By showing how myths come into existence, they hoped to quench the popular need for myths' existence, in order to help establish a more organized, rational state. The first critics of myth in the century before Plato—Xenophanes of Colophon, Theagenes of Rhegium, Thales, and Pythagoras—disdained the polytheism of their people and the unbecoming depiction of deities contained in "the fables of old" (Spence 1931:40–41).

Since the gods of myth were nonexistent and their behavior distasteful, myths were said to be allegories of philosophical arguments, with various gods playing the roles of certain discursive positions. Plato perceived the moral import of such myths, and he wished to build his republic by ridding society of the poetic myths and espoused principles he found undesirable, replacing them with teachings and myths of his own making.

At the same time he followed Theagenes of Rhegium, who viewed the battling gods as warring elements of the universe: Apollo the Fire, Hera the Moon, Poseidon the Sea. In the interpretation of myths as nature-allegories, descriptions of seasonal activity, each god plays an aspect of the natural world, symbolizing its role in the universe and in the lives of humans. Since for Plato and his colleagues, the appreciation of material reality constituted a deflection of true philosophical progress, he wanted to deny these nature-myths their wide usage.

Both the philosophical and nature-allegorical interpretations of mythology implied to each myth a manifest and latent content, the former being the story itself, the latter being the message or meaning of the story lying behind the surface of narrated events. The flow of narrated events hints at the latent content, the meaning, but requires decoding in order to be more fully comprehended. Hence, while disparaging the myths of their day, Plato and his fellows lay the groundwork for all future myth-analyses, including the present work.

Plato and other Greeks also ascribed to myths a psychological cause and function. They said that fear of nature, fear of death, fear of exclusion from the group, are all influential in creating myths and in predisposing humans to respond favorably to them. According to this view, myths have a profoundly personal—as well as philosophical and natural—dimension that attempts to describe the human condition with its diseases of the soul, and that tries to remedy its ills. The Greek theorists did not admit to the validity of the mythic portrayals or prescriptions, but they did allow for the psychic depth of mythology.

Plato also spoke of inventing myths for the purpose of social control, and Aristotle surmised that priests, politicians, and rulers fabricate and employ myths in order to socialize their followers, instilling religious belief and piety, and fostering state control over behavior and loyalty that arise also from shared belief and shared way of life. In this view, those in power can manipulate myths as ideology, so as to move the populace to this or that action, suiting the design and needs of the authorities, religious or political. In short, social and religious systems are instrumental in producing mythology for the easily beguiled populace.

Hecataeus of Miletus and Epheus attempted to find historical, as well as social and religious, elements in myths. Then in the third century B.C., Euhemerus the Messanian wrote *The Sacred Record,* lost to modernity, in which he theorized that the gods of mythology are deified dead men whose stories are told by their followers in order to perpetuate their hegemony. In this opinion, for example, Zeus was a vain ruler who attempted to persist after death in the same way that Egyptian pharaohs glorified themselves with monumental architecture. The euhemeristic view of myths, therefore, is essentially historical, positing that myths derive from distorted biographies of great persons. In this way mythology becomes a type of ancestor veneration carried to a point of deification. Also associated with the euhemeristic position is the theory that rituals and myths are intimately connected. The death of a king, thus, occasions his people to hold a grand ceremony to commemorate and glorify him. At that time his followers recount his deeds, and periodically through the years his descendants codify and heighten the rites and praises until his tales become myths of gods and his commemorations become sacred ceremonies. The claims of Euhemerus found repetition among the later Christian church fathers, including Augustine, as attacks upon pagan religions. To the Christians—whose deified object of worship best proved Euhemerus's theory—euhemerism demonstrated that all pagan gods were false and powerless; hence Clement of Alexandria belittled the heathens: "the gods you worship were once men" (Ruthven 1976:6–7).

All the ancient theories for explaining myths have endured to our day, and in more sophisticated versions carry considerable weight. Indeed, they constitute the intellectual baggage of modern mythography, including this book. It was the temper of the interpretations, however, rather than their insights, that pressed on most vigorously through the centuries. The overriding purpose of these explanations was to disparage the ancient mythological traditions by rationalizing their origins and functions. If a story about a god is in reality a mere and fanciful portrayal of nature, or a king, or a moral tenet, why not dispense with the fancy and state one's case directly, rationally, and unambiguously? If one can encounter psychological fears more directly by simple description, why succumb to metaphorical fables? The lines between the two—myth and reality— were strictly drawn in antiquity, and have continued to color opinion, informed and uninformed, on the subject of mythology into modern times.

Despite attacks by Greek intelligentsia, however, the myths persisted through Mediterranean antiquity. In addition, the spread of Greco-Roman culture to the wilds of Europe meant renewed contact with mythmakers and their flourishing myths. At the same time that early Christian apologists were increasing the attack on pagan myths (while borrowing their motifs, as the Stoics and later Neoplatonists pointed out), a new, thriving world of mythology was facing the rationalized Mediterraneans.

Roman expansion, barbarian conquests, and Christian missions to Western Europe meant the intermingling of Christian and heathen myths. Throughout the Middle Ages, Christian folk continued to tell their old traditions, although intertwining them with Christian motifs and personages.

The educated portion of the medieval world developed no new persisting theory of myth-analysis, but a new, syncretistic corpus of myths sprouted in the tangle of European folk religion and expanding Christianity. The prevailing official attitude toward tribal myths was one of disapproval and scorn. There might be some truths contained in the tales, perhaps parallels to Christian ideas, but according to the Christian hierarchy they were probably plagiarized from Christian or Hebrew sources and had no validity outside the structure of Christendom. Savage myths were certainly not worthy of study and analysis, for they pointed away from and defied the one true God.

In the Renaissance, Europeans rediscovered the Greco-Roman myths, prizing them as beautiful stories, inspirations for poetry, art, and song. But as confirmed Christians with over a millennium of mythophobic heritage, they puzzled how to interpret the ancient stories. Certainly they could not appreciate the myths as true stories, since ostensibly they recounted the imaginary deeds of pagan gods. Surely they were not factual or divine revelation, although they unveiled beauties and truths in titillating, obscure fashions. The Renaissance and the seventeenth century proliferated classical images, iconographic and erotic guidebooks to classical myths, but eschewed probing analysis of the pagan myths they enjoyed, preferring to dwell on them as euhemeristic tales or poetic masterpieces of imagic, allegorical literature.

Europeans discovered new myths as well as old ones when in the age of commercial expansion and conquest they engaged the peoples of Africa, Asia, and the Americas. These continents were replete with their own bodies of lore, their own accumulated traditions that sometimes mirrored, sometimes challenged the scriptures and strictures of European Christianity. Christian explorers were bewildered, for instance, by the similarities between Aztec and Christian systems of myth and ritual. The same martyric heroism, the same eschatalogical hopes, the same cult of the virgin, the same emphasis on communal sacrifice and love feasts, seemed to exist in both "savage" and "civilized" worlds.

Anti-Christians in Europe seized upon the similarities to prove the falsehood not only of paganism, but of all religious beliefs. In its encounter with the world religions, Christianity came under attack in the eighteenth century, the Enlightenment, as simply another myth-laden, superstitious complex, no better—and possibly worse—than equally distorted traditions of heathens. The study of comparative religion grew up alongside the desire to debunk the authority of all religions—primitive, ancient, and modern—or even to show that primitive religions, for all their mythic superstitions, were less corrupted than Christianity. In order to avoid persecution, most Enlightenment thinkers made only the most subtle references to Christianity in their debunking of mythology and religion worldwide.

Among the literate eighteenth-century despisers of mythology like Voltaire and Pierre Bayle, Bernard Fontenelle published his *Discours sur l'origine des fables* (1724), the first full-scale treatment of narrative folklore, which set slowly into motion the scattered, and then systematic, collecting of world folk traditions. Fontenelle treated myths as documents that reflect the minds of primitives and ancients, relatively undeveloped mentalities that fantasize, fabricating exaggerated, distorted tales. The myths of these primitives, always amazed like children at the living wonder of the dangerous world, are not sources of wisdom, but rather mistakes of perception and glorifications of power. "So let us not look," he said, "for anything in the fables except the history of the errors of the human mind" (in Feldman and Richardson 1972:18). In his view, primitives create myths in their fumbling attempt to describe the real world, and thus mythology is an imperfect form of science, a faulty intellectual exercise in seeking causes by primitive peoples whose technological simplicity leaves them at the mercy of natural forces. Interestingly, while including Christianity implicitly in the mythic folly of all people, a folly that should "make us tremble" (in Feldman and Richardson 1972:18), Fontenelle suppressed his anti-Christian feelings and placed the Bible outside the category of fable.

His contemporary Voltaire was not so gracious to the established European religion of his day. He repeated the ancient charges that mythology arises from fear and misunderstanding on the part of uneducated persons, and he claimed that Hebrew and Christian texts are laden with foolishness, fostered by religious establishments for their own power and benefit. In his writings he expressed the idea that religion and mythology are constructions of priests, fostered upon a foolish populace; superstitions promoted by the manipulative ideology of ruling classes (in Feldman and Richardson 1972:151–56).

In Voltaire the modern scorn of mythology as religious nonsense is most baldly expressed, but one could equally as well turn to the nineteenth or twentieth centuries, to the scientific positivists like Karl Marx or Sigmund Freud, in order to find the same dislike for things mythical and religious. Marx based his understanding of incorrect economic and political theory on the model of religious fetishism. He wrote that people who are not in touch with the real world turn to mythology and obscurantism in order to explain what they do not really know. Alienated from themselves and their world, they attribute powers to imaginary and inanimate entities—the gods of myth—and thereby live in delusion. For Marx, people must destroy their myths to redeem themselves in this world (Feldman and Richardson 1972:488–94; Marx 1977:165ff.; Tucker 1972:77–78, 118, 129). Freud saw the origin of religion and mythology in the dreamwork and repression of neurotic mentalities, and although he believed that a study of myths might enlighten us regarding the human psyche, he was in no way interested in encouraging mythmaking as a means of plumbing the depths of human being. A psychoanalyst may interpret folktales, but he has no desire to perpetuate them (Freud 1927:49–50). With Marx and Freud, as with most post-Enlightenment Westerners, mythology has been synonymous with falsehood. Christian theologians such as Rudolf Bultmann, seeking to escape the scrutiny of the skeptics, have tried to rid their religion of its mythology, seeking to abandon the stories whose truths seem undecipherable (Bultmann 1958; Jaspers and Bultmann 1958), in order to accommodate scientific impulses.

Even nineteenth- and twentieth-century students of myth, people who devoted their careers to the examination of world folklore and comparative religion, scholars like Sir James Frazer, held to the denigrative view of myths first set forth in ancient Greece, referring to them as

mistaken explanations of phenomena, whether of human life or of external nature. Such explanations originate in that instinctive curiosity concerning the causes of things which at a more advanced state of knowledge seeks satisfaction in philosophy and science, but being founded on ignorance and

misapprehension they are always false, for were they true, they would cease
to be myths. [in Hyman 1974:275–76]

Until quite recently, "this, then, was common and official doctrine. . . .
To study myths, it was believed, was to review the errors and follies of
man, at times a distracting business, at times mournful, like leafing through
an album of pictures of a bygone age" (Grimal 1965:9). The popular
Western mind to this day equates myth with falsehood, stupidly believed
and foolishly studied.

TYPES OF MYTHOGRAPHY

At the same time that Fontenelle and Voltaire were lambasting myth
and religion, new types of mythography arose that drew upon ancient
modes of analysis and which prefigured all of the modern schools of
myth-analysis. In the eighteenth century, after fifteen centuries of ban-
ishment, the pagan images and stories made their reappearance, and their
interpreters attempted in a spirit of investigation a unified view of mythology as a human phenomenon. The theories of David Hume and Giovanni Battista Vico best illustrated the new approaches to the study of
mythology, approaches which we have inherited.

Hume was the first modern philosopher of religion: an empiricist and
skeptic who shook the religious establishment even though he hid his
atheism from the authorities. He had the audacity in 1757 to publish his
Natural History of Religion in which he described religion as one would
any natural organism or created institution; that is, he stated that religion
has natural—not supernatural—causes and origins. In brief, for Hume,
religion is a creation by humans, certainly not a primary human activity
like sex or eating, but a creation that serves human needs. Religion's
origins are in human life, in the human desire to continue and persist,
in human fears, hopes, imagination, and unreason. At the beginning of
human history, humans had a terror of death, a thirst for revenge, a dread
of future misery, and religion served to ease these anxieties. In the face
of the unknown causes, early humans projected their humanity onto gods
and turned natural forces into gods, in order to turn anxiety about themselves and their world into manageable fear. Because of the many dangers
in the world and in society, early people believed in many gods, and in
the same way different societies in different settings developed different
religious complexes.

Hume showed that myths, the central texts of belief and tradition in
religious systems, aim to be pragmatic as well as speculative. They describe

the universe in order to adapt to it and control it. For Hume's religious people, religion is a crucial element in their lives, positing through myths a supernatural order which powerfully affects human lives and which can be appealed to in times of need and crisis. Hence myths may promote human life as well as religious life, no matter how imperfect they may be as scientific observations. Hume pointed to the active, imaginative process of humans in inventing their myths from their own experiences, and in turning to them in periodic, crucial, religious situations. Myths may not be rationally true, he stated, but they have a purpose and function in the lives of people who believe them, and since people persist in creating and using their myths, the texts must be of some value. From Hume developed a sympathetic, critical study of comparative religion and mythology as parts of practical human culture (Hume 1947; 1956).

When Vico published his *New Science* in 1725, he was derided by the philosophers of his day, but as much as Hume, Vico lay the groundwork for the modern appreciation, study, and discovery of mythology. Vico is regarded as the proto-founder of anthropology, sociology, psychology, even historiography, because his "new science" of self-knowledge was based on the minute observation of human individuals and cultures as a means of ascertaining the structure of the human mind in its changing conditions and manifestations. Vico believed that if students are to understand the profound realities of the human condition, they must first and foremost study the myths produced by human societies. He saw myths as the most useful of human inventions, the most human of human inventions, holding the most searching, least disguised expressions of human being, and he asserted that no study of humans can be complete (even begun!) without an extensive examination of mythology. For Vico, myths are the primary agents of human communication, reflecting the means by which primeval humans created their civil and social institutions and formed their consciousness. Taking seriously the idea that people believe in, and try to live by, the myths they tell, Vico described mythology as an accurate and deep reflection of human cognition and condition. If we study myths, the most spontaneous and honest parts of human expressive culture, we shall come to know human essence and existence (Vico 1968).

Not until a century later did European scholars begin to accept Vico's advances. It took Romanticism and postindustrial alienation, a thirst for mythmaking espoused by Johann Gottfried von Herder and Friedrich Nietzsche, as well as the rise of universities and their academic disciplines to produce an atmosphere in which scholars might study myths with methodological prowess and openminded respect.

The German Romantics like Herder lamented modern man's dearth of mythology. In an attempt to revive the Neoplatonic appreciation for myths as mainsprings of human culture, and as a reaction against an Enlightenment that did not take myths seriously, Herder wrote in a spirit of myth appreciation that reverberates to the present day. Comparing the ancient Greeks to American Indians, Africans, and European folk, Herder saw that each Volk responds to its particular environment—its Klima—with awe and wonder. In each case, people create bonds with their world, finding goodness and godliness in it as well as in themselves. Their mythology affirms the life in every being of the world, in humans, nature, and supernature. For Herder, myth is a form of nature-devotion that will help us discover the ground of our being, a profound and secret language of the universe whose revelations we should seek to unearth (in Feldman and Richardson 1972:224–40). If Hume taught the modern world that myths function as critical elements of practical human culture, and if Vico affirmed myths as reflections of human mind and culture, it is Herder who encouraged us to regard myths as significant lessons for human survival and sanity. All three, writing in the eighteenth century, put forward unified theories of mythology and human existence that continue to transcend the findings of most modern academic disciplines.

In the nineteenth century, the budding fields of anthropology and folklore paid close attention to the myths of tribal peoples, with an eye toward discovering a universal mythmaking process. While folklorists concentrated on collecting and cataloguing folk narratives and their distinctive patterns, anthropologists built elaborate theories of human development based on their findings. Following their work, "the last century and a half has seen a frenetic scholarly search in the West for the meaning of myths" (Waardenburg 1980:60).

E. B. Tylor founded the first of many schools of myth-analysis current during the past century when he published *Primitive Culture* in 1871, becoming the "official" Victorian ethnologist (Chase 1969:50–53), even though he did not devote his sharpest attention to myths themselves. Following the discoveries of Charles Darwin, Tylor tried to create a scientific model of natural, human progress, claiming that the human mind—like a mollusk or a primate—has evolved from earlier forms. It was the bent of Tylor and his cohorts to see phenomena in evolutionary terms; he viewed myth as a reflection and indication of a certain stage of human thought which he termed "animistic," belonging to a stage of human development called "primitive." To the primitives who tell their myths, the world is alive and personal; each tree and star and cloud possesses an animating soul, and thus in their myths primitives represent natural entities as if they were persons with wills, abilities, and feelings. For Tylor, myths are stories of nature-experiences and the causes of natural events, stories told by people who resemble children in their naiveté and simplicity. In Tylor's mind, primitives are primal, not only in the sense of being throwbacks to past ages and stages along the evolutionary scale but also in the sense of being essential. Here are people, still relatively close to their original condition, in which the basic qualities of human phenomena are simple, unadorned, unsophisticated, and thus more easily isolated and examined. Tylor and the other early anthropologists also felt that only primitives maintain a working mythopoeic ability; civilized races may contain vestiges of primitive mentality in aspects of superstition, but, by and large, mythmaking is to be found only among the primitives. To Tylor, this mythic animism is irrational, childlike, and doomed to extinction in the face of expanding science and civilization; it should be studied before the last primitives disappear (Tylor 1958).

Tylor's evolutionary school swooned before the primitives did. Another approach even more quickly outdated was that of the etymological-semantic "solar" school of myth-analysis espoused by F. Max Müller that reigned from around 1860 to 1880. Like the evolutionists, Müller believed in a mythological age, when people were "inventing absurd tales about gods and other nondescript beings . . . , a period of temporary insanity, through which the human mind had to pass" (Müller 1867:10–11). At that time language differed from its present state. Whereas today we speak of the sun arising at dawn, formerly they could say only that the sun loved and embraced the dawn. Sunset was the sun growing old and dying; sunrise was night giving birth to a brilliant child. This was the age of poesy. Through processes like polyonomy (in which one word takes on many meanings, and thus the true, original meaning is obscured) and homonymy (in which many words express one idea, and thus the connection between word and idea is obscured), the original meaning of these poetic utterings was disguised, until at a later date people like the Greeks were bewildered about the etymologies surrounding their celestial phenomena. Müller asked himself how the Greeks, those founders of logic and democracy, could have formulated and believed in such foolish gods as are seen in their myths. His answer was that they had inherited indecipherable portions of their language from the earlier Aryans, the mythopoeic people, and in their "intellectual vivacity" had created myths as etymological explanations. Providing his own etymological tales, Müller demonstrated that the ancient Aryan words for dawn, sun, moon, and so on became the words of the Greeks' major deities. In short, through a "disease of language" the Greeks took literally what the mythopoeic Aryans had meant metaphorically, and myths came into being (Müller 1867:63–64, 77, 85–88, 94–95; 1885, 2).

In arguing that the original meaning of myths are found in words that describe celestial beings, in fact asserting that almost all myths are about celestial phenomena, Müller the linguist reduced mythology to an absurdity, and he became an erudite fool whose star faded after his death in 1900, allowing for the dawn of the modern age of mythography. Nevertheless, like Tylor he understood the fascination that the natural world has for nature-folk. They are obsessed with natural phenomena because of their direct dependence upon the elements, and they are impressed by the regularity and powerful display of celestial entities in particular, because they constitute symbols of eternality. Therefore, for Müller, myths about the sun, moon, storms, and stars are reflections of human dependency on nature for survival as well as a contemplation (however diseased) of immortality (Müller 1867:97; 1885, 2:565).

Underlying Müller's assertions was the assumption that all original myths describe celestial phenomena. This theory gained some credence and then received deserved abuse, particularly from a rival, related school headed by Sir James Frazer and Andrew Lang. Lang admitted myth to be a pseudoscience by primitives in mystic communion with nature, and he agreed that most myths are animistic nature-allegories; however, he and Frazer recognized the multifaceted character of myths—their magical goal of influencing as well as describing nature, and their moral ideas. Both men used a comparative method in studying world mythology and religion, separating the mythic-religious phenomena from their cultural environment. Both were, at various times in their careers, evolutionists, ritualists, cognitionists, and euhemerists. Both garnered immense popular praise. Both emphasized the irrational elements in mythology, but stated that mythmakers possess their own form of logic, not as fully developed as that of a modern Westerner, but valid in its own terms. Above all, both recalled the ancient Greek theories regarding the allegorical purpose of myth. Frazer in particular in *The Golden Bough,* published first as two volumes in 1890 and expanded to twelve volumes between 1911 and 1915, stated over and again that myth-tellers are attempting to describe nature—the change of seasons, the cycle of the moon, the growth of vegetation—by means of narrative metaphors. At the same time myths describe human events and situations, using the imagery of the natural environment. Lang accused Frazer of overemphasizing the nature-allegorical aspects of myth (referring to Frazer and his followers as the "Covent Garden School," after London's famous farmers' market), but in fact Frazer's ideas about myths were more complex, perceiving allegories not simply as enjoyable tales of explanation and description, but rather as magical means of influencing the natural and supernatural worlds in order to aid human survival. Frazer showed that primitive people's mythology and religion concentrate on nature and the dead—both deified—which are active, powerful forces which people must know and control in order to foster life's continuation. For Frazer, and also for Lang, myth is the philosophy and magic, the science and religion, of tribal peoples (Frazer 1913:9–86; 1926; 1927:16–17, 23–25, 37–38, 300–302, 392–95; 1930:v; 1933; 1964; Lang 1887).

The evolutionists, the solar-semanticists, and the nature-allegorists all shared conclusions regarding mythology that merit our attention. They all agreed that mythmakers devote a great deal of their narratives to the observation of the nonhuman environment; that their observations play important roles in their relations with the world around them; and that their myths about their lived-in universe convey and transmit a consciousness concerning nature, a palpable world view.

Inspired by Vico, the Romantics, and Kant, and drawing on the early anthropologists and students of comparative mythology, while reinterpreting their evolutionary line, Ernst Cassirer and his followers constituted a smaller, lesser known school that characterized myth as a special form of symbolic expression. Seeing myth as a type of language, a peculiar mode of consciousness and communication, this "symbolist" school compared myth to music, art, and mathematics, each of which contains its own purposes, grammar, and logic, apart from discursive expression. Just as music is not a failed form of science, myth is not a failed form of logic. It has its own mode of expression, and is valid on its own terms. Myth is, to Cassirer, "a particular way of seeing, and carries within itself its particular and proper source of light" (Cassirer 1953:11). As an expression of human feeling, myth is a special type of thought-communication, using symbols as points of reference between humans and their world. The symbolists did not posit a mythopoeic mentality for tribal people; instead they argued that in every culture the need exists for mythic expression, just as there is the need for pragmatic, scientific description and musical composition. For the symbolists, myth and science are simply two different ways of knowing the world and preparing us for action in the world. Both are necessary and good for life; to do without one or the other would be a sad loss. Cassirer resented Müller's contention that mythology is a "disease of language," saying rather that "true mythology arises out of something independent of all invention" (Cassirer 1955:5–6), spontaneously and signficantly. Like Vico two centuries previous, Cassirer, Susanne Langer, and other symbolists regarded mythography as a primal tool for understanding human needs and consciousness.

Although dealing with individual cases, the psychoanalytic approaches to myth have also stressed the universal quality of mythmaking. For centuries before Freud theorists had been discussing the psychological origins and functions of folktales and myths, particularly in association with fears and with the mechanisms of projection, and in the years right before Freud, with dreams. Under the scrutiny of Freud, Karl Abraham, Carl Gustav Jung, Theodor Reik, Géza Róheim, and Bruno Bettelheim, among others, twentieth-century psychoanalysts have tried to show that myths are projections and indications of subconscious patterns of human thought. Although recognizing the differences between public, social myths and private, personal dreams, the psychoanalytic school has shown the relations between myth and dream as revelations of human depth and irrationality, reflecting individual, local cultural, and universal forms of human consciousness. They have stressed the problem-solving and cathartic quality of myths, both for cultures and individuals, and they have analyzed folk narratives as moral tales that face predicaments of childhood development, separation anxieties, interpersonal relations, and oedipal conflicts, illuminating healthy models of growing up for children to emulate. The diverse psychological school has shown the function of myth in keeping at bay feelings of guilt and anxiety, adapting individuals to reality; in offering possible solutions for life-crises acceptable within a cultural framework; in establishing mechanisms of ego defense; in symbolizing man's evil for himself; in solving problems concerning castration and death. Psychologists have looked at myths as complicated but useful ways of probing the profound content and structure of the human psyche, and their work has been so associated with the study of mythology that its code words—narcissism, oedipal complex, and so on—derive from mythological characters. Whatever their particular inclination, all agree that myths, like dreams and jokes, lie close to the primary process of human cognition and consciousness, expressing the deep, paradoxical, impossible desires of humans.

The builder of the movement, Freud, laid the foundation for all psychoanalytic interpretations that followed him. By comparing religious rituals to obsessive acts of neurotics, by illuminating daydreams and myths as ill-disguised glorifications of the self, by comparing the motifs in dreams and folktales, by equating the mechanisms of dreamwork and mythmaking, by looking at the expressions of the superego in the myths of Jesus Christ, Freud encouraged and inspired his students to build upon his work (Freud 1931; 1962:89ff.; 1970:17–26, 34–43, 59–66; 1977:158–72, 389).

Freud's prize pupil had other ideas. Whereas Freud saw aspects of dream in myth and theorized about universals in human thought, using the data of individual clients, Jung found myth—universal, archetypical myth— in dreams. For him, myth is produced by a collective as well as an individual unconscious, propelled by archetypes such as that of the wise old man, the mother, the maiden, the hero-child, the shadow, and the anima-animus, and expressed through symbols and images. Mythmaking is a universal, natural phenomenon that reveals the consciousness of humankind, past and present, without which we lack psychic wholeness. Influenced by the idea that the evolution of the race is repeated in each individual, he took up the notion that the consciousness developed by primitive folk continues within us moderns, appearing as dreams and fantasies and as myths. Telling a myth, then, serves the purpose of bringing to the surface of consciousness the deep and often renegade elements of the psyche, things that we did not know were there, and integrating them with the conscious self (Jung 1963; 1964; 1969; Jung and Kerényi 1969).

Both the symbolists and the psychoanalysts have been interested in understanding universal phenomena of human cognition through the study of mythology. They have been "intellectualist" in their emphasizing the powerful and creative role of mythic models in influencing behavior of persons and cultures worldwide, and they have attempted to formulate broad conclusions regarding global mythmaking and consciousness based on their limited case studies. As such, they have tended to downplay the cultural bases for mythic invention, and they themselves have been accused of being culture bound in their prescriptions. Still, both schools of myth-analysis have added a great deal to mythography by searching behind the surface of narrative content for latent meanings and signification.

The twentieth-century schools in the social sciences—anthropology and sociology—while asserting the universality of their theoretical findings, have been more concerned with the specific relations between myths and the cultural-societal matrices that produce them. By taking special account of the social functions of mythology, the social scientists have rejoined the issues raised by Plato, Aristotle, Hume, and Vico.

Franz Boas, Bronislaw Malinowski, and other social scientists undercut the universality of Freud's findings by showing that different types of society have different psychic reactions, producing different folklore and mythology. More "materialist" in their approach than the psychoanalysts and symbolists, they have tried to indicate empirically the specific ways in which myths fit their cultural environment. In attempting to refute the view of myth as nature-contemplation, Boas and his legion of followers showed the cultural reflections in myths. He argued that myths are human stories reflecting human situations and problems of community life, "particularly those that stir the emotions of the people" (Boas 1966:405; see Boas 1905; 1912). Early in his career he claimed that the culture of each people will be reflected and refracted in the stories they tell, and his students set out to prove him right with scores of myth-analyses that linked social life, kinship, and personality to mythic image.

Malinowski and other social "functionalists" went beyond Boas in documenting not only social reflections in myths but also the societal use of myths in maintaining authority and equilibrium. Malinowski (1925; 1954) showed that the particular contexts of a myth—in his case, the Trobriand Island milieu—produces the specific content of the myth. He found that Freudian categories are too broad to be useful as analyses of specific myths, and that "an intimate connection exists between the word, the mythos, the sacred tales of a tribe, on the one hand, and their ritual acts, their moral deeds, their social organization, and even their practical activities, on the other" (Malinowski 1954:96). Like Émile Durkheim who said that myths and rituals express and maintain solidarity through categorizing functions (Durkheim 1915:419ff.), Malinowski characterized myths as charters for acceptable social behavior and as sanctions against lawlessness within the community, thereby showing people how to act, enforcing group solidarity, and sublimating antisocial tendencies within a given population. The functionalists have attempted to prove that myths serve to legitimize social institutions, even acting as ideology for societal rules and rulers. And because myths are concerned with society, they reflect everyday life, the material bases of social existence, as Boas said, even though they also exaggerate cultural and societal elements.

Therefore, the social-scientific study of tribal myths has revealed much about the cultures of mythmakers and the social functions of mythology. In so doing, twentieth-century social scientists have brought myth-analysis into a more minutely particularistic and materialist framework than either the symbolists or psychoanalysts had with their universalistic and intellectualist tendencies. The anthropologists and sociologists have kept in clear view the fact that myths are the creations of particular people with their own environmental and social relations, and hence they have contextualized mythmaking as a social process. They have argued against the idea of the mythopoeic culture and said that common folk produce their myths as part of their practical, expressive culture.

Structural anthropology, however, concerned with particular cultures, has been far more interested in returning to the earlier search for universal themes in mythology, the attempt to grasp the essential workings of the human mind by analyzing myths. Structuralism has arisen as a special form of semiotics, viewing every aspect of human culture as a mode of communication, carrying a message and revealing the structure of human intellect. In the structuralists' vision, myths constitute the most rewarding mode of communication, because they are found in such abundance, particularly among tribal peoples, and because their primary purpose is to communicate important cultural ideas from generation to generation. Claude Lévi-Strauss, Edmund Leach, and other structuralists have enraged more orthodox social scientists by discussing the ramifications of their data beyond the limits of particular cultural contexts; they have dared to "philosophize" about mythology. They have sought to discover the meaning and logic underlying mythical invention, the diffusion of conceptual systems, and the symbolism of nature and consciousness in narrative folklore (see Lévi-Strauss 1962; 1963; 1975; Leach 1976b).

Rather than looking at the narratives themselves, however, structuralists have tried to cut up the myths into their smallest units of analysis, called "mythemes," each mytheme representing one action in the text. By placing each mytheme on index and computer cards, and by comparing large numbers of related myths, the structuralists have found numerous repetitions and inversions of equivalent mythemes, inferring that these emphasized elements contain the essential messages of the myths. While making comprehensive use of other modes of analysis, structuralists have claimed that narrative content is but the surface of mythic reality; the deep meaning exists in the structure of the stories, the repetition and inversion of the basic blocks of narrative. Rather than examining the high points and sequences of the texts, and ignoring the poetic language for its own potential significance, the structuralists have focused their attention on the harmony of equivalent mythemes, wherein lie the latent meanings of the myths (Leach 1976a:25; Lévi-Strauss 1963:203ff.; 1967; 1969; 1971; 1974; 1976).

Structuralists have come to certain conclusions regarding myths. First, they have viewed myths as conveyances of cognitive categories, the human intellect's way of grasping and bringing into relation enigmatic phenomena in the world and in society. They have shown that myths pay special attention to boundaries between opposites; the mythemes point repeatedly to the problem areas experienced by people, the situations where individuals and cultures feel uncertainty, ambiguity, tension, and fear: the relations between in-laws, the paradox of human animality, the role of divinities in human affairs, and so on.

More importantly, however, the structuralists have said that myths seek to resolve the paradoxes and tensions felt by a people, bringing into closer contact the seemingly irreconcilable elements of human life. Myths make numerous binary distinctions; they counterpose phenomena with their opposites—reflecting the basic binary structure of the mind—and then serve to bring the oppositions into relation. The result of such mediation is a syzygy, in which the two irreconcilable elements of human life are brought into harmonic tension (Maranda and Maranda 1971b:27). In this view, myths are functional (structuralists *are* social scientists, after all), both psychologically and societally, indicating to individuals and groups through symbol, metaphor, and inversion the ways in which paradoxes can be understood and life can be made less difficult and complex. Relationship between seeming opposites is the result of mythic creation, thereby promoting a fuller consciousness of life's possibilities through the formal structure of myth.

All of the modern methods of mythography we have surveyed so far have been interested in the mythic texts for what they can tell us about human lived-in and thought-about worlds: evolutionary categories, symbolic behavior, mental or social structure, and the like. They have seen myths as aspects of practical, expressive culture. They have used myths as tools for analysis, rather than appreciating them simply as aesthetic devices to enjoy for their own sake. Folklorists and students of comparative literature, on the other hand, have not only taken on the massive task of collecting myths and other types of oral traditions, but they have attempted to catalogue the varieties of mythic elements and plot their worldwide distribution and dissemination. They have studied the forms and histories of myths in order to understand the global phenomena of oral literature.

Antecedent to the structuralists by a century, the folklorists tried to reduce myths to their basic units of narration, calling them "catch-words" (Kroeber 1908; Lowie 1908a), "motifs," or "functions," while at the same time placing myths into the context of folklore, connected to songs, proverbs, riddles, poems, and other forms of oral tradition. The result of such cataloguing was the enormous *Motif-Index* compiled by Antti Aarne and Stith Thompson (Aarne and Thompson 1964; Thompson 1955–58; cf. Thompson 1968:271–367), which ignores all matters of cultural context and interpretation in order to organize the hundreds of basic plot elements from all peoples. Another formal exercise of the folklorists has been the attempt to identify the universal structure of oral narratives, the general plots that all myths follow.

In addition, folklorists have tried to trace the development of specific folk motifs in myths, showing the extent to which a tale can be carried from one people to another, and suggesting the geographical and historical origins of certain stories. Their interest has not been to shed light on history by examining mythic texts, but by tracing the movement of the texts themselves, they have looked for the history *of* myths, rather than the history *in* myths.

Finally, folklorists have allied themselves with a multiplicity of other approaches: evolutionary, diffusionist, psychological, functionalist, and structuralist, among others. They have tackled the problems of translation; they have examined the context of performance in which a myth takes shape; and they have acted as erstwhile critics of all other schools of mythography.

Unlike folklorists, mainstream historians have ignored myths by and large as sources of factual evidence, using them only in ethnohistorical studies as indications of world view or as underdeveloped, circular contrasts to documented, linear history. Until recently it has been the conclusion of most historians, anthropologists, and folklorists alike that myths are useless in the reconstruction of tribal histories.

In the last two decades, however, Africanist Jan Vansina has attempted to develop a systematic method of evaluating and employing tribal myths and other oral traditions in Africa as historical data. By examining the minutiae of oral testimony: the context in which a myth is told, the manner of testifying, the variants of texts, the mnemonic devices and social control over recital; by taking into account the failure of memory and the purposes of oral transmission, Vansina has made evaluations of oral traditions as vehicles for historical knowledge, and he has found them useful (Vansina 1965; 1970; 1978).

FORM, CONTEXT, AND FUNCTION OF MYTHOLOGY

Having reviewed the history of mythology's disrepute, and having surveyed the major schools of mythography, we shall now look frontally at the phenomenon of myth. Lauri Honko (1972) has provided a concise set of criteria by which we can define and analyze mythology systematically, and we shall follow him in this regard, examining the form, context, function, and content of tribal myths.

Myths are part of the oral traditions of people, part of expressive folk culture. They are cultural inventions, artifices through which people communicate personal and cultural messages. As a genre of folklore, myths are set off in time from ordinary communication; everyone in a community knows the difference between a narrated myth and an ordinary conversation. The myth, like other forms of folklore, has recognizable openings and closings which mark it off as a special event with something special to say. The style and language of narration also distinguish myths from mundane discussion among people; the myth's performance directs attention to the messages to be communicated.

Myths are formal narratives, using prose and sometimes verse in a symbolic manner, which are passed down as a tradition. They are not eyewitness accounts of events, but rather secondhand at least. They are narratives, but with extensions and inclusions of song, dance, art, and other elements of expressive culture. They are an art form, in addition to being types of consciousness and messages to be communicated.

Myths are dramatic narratives rather than static cosmologies. They are driven forward by difficulties encountered by the characters within the stories; therefore they have suspense and plot, motivations and dualities, inherent in their form. Characters oppose and aid one another in their attempt to ameliorate their condition; conflicts and resolutions are the formal requirements of the mythic narratives.

Furthermore, myths are performances, examples of "verbal art" (Bascom 1955) in face-to-face communities. Researchers have great difficulty remembering this fact if their only contact with myths is through written texts; however, myths are almost without exception oral presentations involving narrator and audience. Performed myths are more akin to plays and concerts than to written literature; they are lived, vivid experiences where narrator and audience meet face to face. Reading a myth, divorced from its setting, is often like reading a musical score. It sags without the facial and bodily expressions, the intonations that are essential to myths as verbal art. Myths are performative acts, an outlet for the performer and the audience alike. Myth-telling is social. It is born of interrelationships and tends to enforce bonds of ethnicity, religion, occupation, age, and kinship. The performance takes place before an audience, and thus myths must entertain as well as communicate. Even though they may contain crucial lessons, they cannot be entirely didactic, since they must hold the audience's attention. Perhaps to the philosopher the entertaining aspects of myths are less interesting, maybe even distracting, in contrast to the inner messages; nevertheless, the myth is a spoken narrative that must entertain in order to communicate. Hence it is essential to note the connection between the performative context of the myth and its form as dramatic narrative.

Anthropologists and folklorists once expressed the opinion that myths are rigid repetitions by people who are at heart mindless conservatives. These observers saw tribal people, mythmakers, as "children" of culture, trapped in a mold created by a tyrannical "parent"; hence the tribal folk have been said to repeat the same myths verbatim, year after year, without altering their form or content (Greenway 1964:150–51).

But Albert Lord's pathbreaking *Singer of Tales* (1973) and other astute studies have proven this contention invalid. Describing Serbian storytellers, Lord demonstrated the performative aspects of folklore, showing how the singers actively shape their performance to suit the mood of their audiences on particular nights. Other researchers have found audiences correcting the narrator in regard to details, and thereby taking part in mythic creation, making each version unique, even though the same motifs may be repeated. Lord and other folklorists have shown that storytellers have freedom to change their stories within limits. Even Navajo and Polynesian mythic traditions, long said to be word-for-word recitations, vary considerably from telling to telling. Thus imagination, pragmatic expediency, and memory work together to create each myth performance, and variations occur both over an area within a certain culture, and over time. Two brothers may tell very different versions of the same story; the same storyteller may vary his repertoire considerably depending on audience and situation. At Isleta Pueblo, for instance, Esther Goldfrank (1926) found ten versions of the same story, all different from one another. She concluded that flexibility exists for the storyteller: characters and incidents may change, although core items must remain constant for the myth to still be regarded as itself. The most central motifs are present in all the versions of the same story. Thus a single story exists, but with no absolutely fixed text from which others vary. On the contrary, all variants are equally valid, each a new performance reflecting the storyteller's style, talent, and interest.

In a sense, the narrator is a stage director who is given a script, a mythical story. There are set acts; he must deliver them in his own way. He has license to use his techniques to organize and present the basic constituent elements. The mythmaker is also like a bricoleur; he can reorganize materials from eclectic, diverse sources to create a new, syncretic story of old elements in order to suit the situation he is addressing. Without seeming too mechanistic, we can say that the mythmaker has a storehouse of used, available motifs, episodes, characterizations, and so on. He stores, retrieves, and transmits them as he sees fit, recombining them to meet his and his audience's needs. The context in which a myth is performed has direct bearing on its form, and we should not regard one printed version of a myth as the only authoritative model; instead we should search for many versions to see the fullness of the mythic form.

Despite the variations of form that occur in the mythic performances, each myth contains core elements that remain relatively stable. What we find is a process of marginal elaboration. The core of the myth remains consistent, but the periphery changes considerably with each performance, each product. It is safe to say that the essential form of the myth, that which is considered by narrator and audience and culture to be more significant and important, is what remains relatively constant despite variations of marginal features. Hence, in examining myths the student should be able to locate and distinguish core and periphery.

More difficult, however, is the job of translating the form of a myth, with its texture and metaphor, poetry and gesture, from the vernacular into written English so that we cultural outsiders can know the myth's beauty as well as its meanings. It is hard enough to translate individual words, much less the style and ornamentation of the performance. As one translator has commented, translations of tribal myths too often appear stilted or childish, and very often they are downright unreadable. The best we can do is be true to the texture, as well as the text and context of the myth, without adding metaphors that the native narrators would not use, or placing moralistic endings on stories that do not express their messages so baldly. Moreover, the translator should try to capture the literary devices of the mythmaker. Unfortunately, however, translations can never convey the full formal beauty of the mythic texts, even though they can accurately convey the drama and import of the narratives.

We have been describing myths formally as performed, dramatic narratives; such a formal description can equally apply to tribal folktales or legends, two other types of narrative folklore normally distinguished from myths. From the time of Herder, folklorists and anthropologists have contrasted myths (true, sacred, serious stories about the gods, stories that take place in primordial time) with legends (true, serious stories about humans and gods set in historical time) and folktales (entertaining, fantastic fictions set in another time and not considered true, although they may contain important lessons). However, it is our purpose *not* to make a formal distinction between myth and other types of oral narrative, because if any hard and fast distinctions can be made, they must come from the people whose oral traditions we are studying. Each people has its own categories of oral literature, based not only on the content of the stories but, even more importantly, on the attitude which the community holds regarding a particular narrative. A myth and a folktale can have the same form, even the same subject matter, the same diffused motifs and style, but one community may distinguish between the two while another community will not. As we shall see, a myth becomes a myth because it is perceived as such by the community that tells and hears it.

As we have seen already, the myth's performative context is closely involved with its form. Throughout the twentieth century, mythographers like Sir James Frazer, Jane Harrison, and Lewis Spence have written about the ritual nature of mythology, going so far as to say that "myth . . . is in the strict sense of the term, the description of a rite, its story, the narrative linked with it" (Spence 1961:15). Some, like Harrison (1969) and her Cambridge school, have said that ancient people uttered magical incantations during their rituals in order to influence the gods; in time, the magical utterances provided a life-history for the supposed source of supernatural power, until eventually the mythic life-history separated from the ritual. Others, like Ruth Underhill (1965:38), have given equal primacy to ritual, saying that primitives make up myths to explain the rituals they have always performed without understanding why. Further research has shown the opposite to be true in many cases, for example, in Christianity where the myth of Jesus Christ has given rise to the ritual Mass. Few mythographers will deny the "intricate interdependence" (Kluckhohn 1968:147), the "interpenetration" (Gaster 1966:24) between ritual and myth, and in many cases rituals will carry out the ideals, make actual the promises, of mythic texts. As a result, we take cognizance of the ritual context of mythology and the mythological context of ritual.

Furthermore, the performance of a myth—apart from more elaborate ceremonialism—constitutes a ritual in its own right. As an event that takes place ritually before a community audience, a myth is well known by members of the society. Myths are not esoteric; they must be familiar to the adult population at the least. These are not priestly secrets, muttered in private; rather, they are the domain of the entire community. Even if their narration is proscribed to a certain few, they embody the whole community's consciousness. Although people of different age groups and different temperaments may understand a myth on various levels, even though one clan may hold special knowledge about its parts, the core of the myth is public knowledge. Therefore the mythic context is the community itself. Divorced from the community, a myth loses its essential power. A myth is a myth because a people regard it as such; its persistence depends on a community to repeat it, listen to it, manipulate its form, share it, believe in it, and act upon it.

The community invents a myth by believing it to be true; indeed, the primary difference between a myth and a folktale is that the community judges the former to be an accurate narration of real events, whereas the latter is admittedly fictional. Whether all members of the community place the same degree and kind of trust in the texts is impossible to tell; in fact, the community may not believe a myth to be literally true, only metaphorically. Nevertheless, the community's belief in the myth's truth is the sustaining context for the myth's continuance.

Often myths contain logical contradictions that are as readily apparent to the people who believe in them as they are to cultural outsiders. Myths are surely paradoxical, both to us and to the tribal people who tell them. It may even be that myths are expressly contradictory to test the community's faith in the mysteries of common and religious life. Like Roman Catholics who take pride in saying they believe in a virgin who gave birth to a god, because it is a mystery of their faith, the believer states that there are forms of logic and meaning that transcend ordinary ways of knowing, and which are revealed through the impossible paradoxes of myth. The paradoxes push the people's consciousness to its borders of perception. They describe events that seem impossible, but are believed as the foundations of community truth. If myths are impossibilities, they are to be believed with fervor in no small part due to their quality of impossibility. It would be as remiss to doubt a people's belief in its mythic traditions as it would to doubt Christian sincerity regarding the virginal origin of its deity. The context for myths is a community of belief, a community with a shared consciousness regarding myths, and partially created by myths.

Myths rely on the community's willingness to perpetuate them, just as they depend on the community's will to believe them. Because a community passes down its traditions orally, depending on limited memory, the most important stories and messages of the cultural heritage are (ideally) preserved for posterity, while trivial aspects become lost over the years. The needs of community life and of individuals within the community find their reflection in the myths that are recalled, told, and retold, thereby enveloping the myths in the context of community life: often a life of face-to-face contact with kinsfolk, of firsthand economy and shared subsistence activities, a life that is grounded in its shared mythology.

When we ask ourselves why these stories have survived the centuries, why have people perpetuated them, we are asking a question about their function. What does the repetition of myth do that people find it enjoyable and useful enough to persist in the repetition?

We cannot recount every possible function of mythology in society and individual life; we can only mention the most salient functions to which people have put their myths. Myths tend to anchor the present generations in a meaningful, significant past, functioning as eternal and ideal models for human behavior and goals. They can teach moral lessons to children and adults alike, communicating cultural messages and representing the community's philosophical positions to its own members through a revered vehicle of tradition. Myths can bind a community in a knot of belief and common consciousness, glorifying ancestors and heroes of the recent and distant past, imaginary and historical, who can serve as paradigms for conduct. They can authorize institutions or call for their alteration, marking off a culture as an accepted way of life. They can contemplate unsatisfactory compromises in social life, provide safe outlets for deviant desires, and serve as ideological weapons by one portion of the population against another.

For individuals, myths can aid in child development and guide people of all ages in their relations with the human and nonhuman environments. They can both allay fears regarding the known and unknown, and stir pangs of conscience and anxiety in order to enforce social mores. They can mediate moral and amoral needs, what is necessary and what is right, physical survival and ethical values. They can give voice to impossible wishes and also reduce wishes to their limits of possibility, helping to preserve the mental health of individuals and society as a whole. They tend to express inner feelings of people in safe, artificial ways, where more direct expression might embarrass the auditors and threaten society, and in such a way they serve as outlets for repressed emotions.

Cognitively, myths describe the world in living terms in order for people to know and possibly control it, while pleasing the esthetic sensibilities of storytellers and audiences with their style, emotions, and power. They serve as models and bases for societal versions of reality, upon which individuals can situate their lives. They can make narrative sense of a world full and paradoxical, thereby adapting the individual to society and society to the larger universe. They help define what humanity is, and what it is not, facing people to the aspects of life which are felt to be most threatening. They can repeat over and over again the essential ingredients of proper human life, indicating the means by which such a life can be achieved, and the mortal dangers in swerving from the correct path. In short, the functions of mythology are as full, varied, and contradictory as life is full, varied, and contradictory, and our ability to enumerate a complete list of functions is limited only by our limited perspectives. Myths contain whatever functions humans, particularly humans in society, wish them to have. They function as they are used, each function augmenting the others, although it would be unrealistic to think that they always function perfectly or even adequately.

In laying out the salient theories regarding the functions of mythology, we have meant not to favor one over others; indeed, our survey to this point has reflected the panoply of academic disciplines, the humanities and social sciences, each with its own bailiwick and methods, which attempt to understand humanity, its being, conditions, and products. But we have neglected to declare what has been most obvious to many observers: that myths function commonly—but not exclusively—as part of the complex known as religion. As Durkheim said of mythology, it "is one of the essential elements of the religious life" (Durkheim 1915:100–101).

In effect, we have neglected our own field of interest and training, the comparative study of religions, their history and literature. Partially, we have demurred to this point because comparative religion or religious studies is not a discipline in its own right with a method peculiar to itself; rather, it is a subject matter which is studied from many different perspectives. Mircea Eliade (1957; 1959a and b; 1961; 1963; 1969; 1970) and many others have all contributed to the academic study of religion and myth, but each has applied very different methods of study. There are as many approaches to the understanding of religion as there are approaches to mythology.

It is impossible to discuss either the function or content of mythology without considering the connections between myth and religion. Clearly myths have religious functions, just as they have social, political, psychological, or cognitive ramifications. Myths instruct a community regarding traditional beliefs in supernatural beings, using palpable, concrete symbols to signify the numinous. Myths are the major intellectual means by which religious heritage is passed down; they help a people to know about the gods in order to enhance communication with them. They validate priestly duties and reveal the origins of religious paraphernalia.

Myths possess religious functions in their association with rituals. Whether a myth can be described as a text accompanying a ritual, a permutated conceptual equivalency in which the uncompleted mediations of myth are acted upon and further resolved, a justification for a ritual's existence, or the underpinnings for ritual communication with the supernatural, the connections between myth, ritual, and religion are tightly bound. Myths can even be said to be preeminently religious phenomena, in their context, function, and content. We need, then, to define more carefully what we mean by "religious." In so doing, we shall take up the fourth criterion—content—in defining and analyzing mythology, without leaving aside the question of function.

THE LIFE-AND-DEATH CONTENT OF MYTHOLOGY

Mythographers have often described the content of myth by saying that it "is an account of the deeds of a god or supernatural being" (Spence 1931:11), adding that "the myth must have a religious background in that its principal actor or actors are deities" (Voegelin 1950:778). The supernatural content of myths binds mythology closer to religion, since—on the most minimal level—religion is essentially concerned with the supernatural. Religion consists of knowledge about and communication with the supernatural. Particularly in its ritual aspects, religion is communication *with* the supernatural; in this context, mythology is communication *about* the supernatural; its content is religious.

But for most of the peoples whom we are studying, there exists no native terminology to indicate religion as a distinct category of life activity or experience. American Indian religion cannot be so easily defined as communication with the supernatural—although such communication lies at its heart—for it is part of the fullness of life's complex, the economic, political, social, and mental life of the tribal community. American Indian religion is interwoven with every part of tribal existence, personal and communal.

More than that, however, Indian religion seems to have for its function not the mere communication with the supernatural for its own sake, but for the sake of the human community. Indian religion is a creation of the Indian community in response to the supernatural with the community's existence and well-being in view. In previous books (Vecsey 1980:1–2; 1983:3–5) I have defined religion as beliefs in, attitudes toward, and relations with the ultimate sources of existence, because I have wished to emphasize the function of religion to promote the life of the community that creates and lives it. I wish to employ this definition once again in this study of Indian myths, although I shall expand the definition throughout this work.

The content of myths includes the supernaturals; however, to at least an equal degree they are about the fullness of humanity in its community context. Myths are like histories in that they are stories about the human past, stories that are considered significant and true. The line between myth and history is not all that distinct; indeed, documented histories often contain significant aspects that we consider mythical. To say that myths are stories about the supernaturals is not sufficient. They are, more inclusively, stories about human beings and their ultimate sources of existence—supernaturals, if you will, but supernaturals in ultimate and intimate contact with human destiny.

Like religions, myths are creations of human beings. Each myth, therefore, points to the humanity that produces it. As narratives of symbolic communication, myths point to and signify the supernatural, the human, and the crucial relations between the two. While seeming to point away from humanity to the supernatural—humanity's opposite—myths point to and illumine humanity and its ultimate concerns, in all their diversity of content and function. Myths are fully and wholly about and concerned for human existence: human relations, subsistence, medicine, sexuality, and death. There is one origin of myths: humans. There is also one central subject matter of myths: humans. In mythology a human becomes a symbol to himself, the most symbolic of symbols, with extensions reaching into every corner of the known universe: external and internal, natural and supernatural. Myths are rational and irrational, moral and amoral, conscious and subconsious, individualistic and societal; they are polysemous. Their surface subject matter—their content— can include anything conceived of by humans that the community thinks of as vitally important, worth recalling and communicating in specialized, dramatic narratives. Through their myths the community puts on display for itself the fullness of itself: the multitude of human emotions and situations in all their contradictory complexity.

No single myth covers all the bases of community life, but just as each community creates a language that suits the diverse needs of the people, each community also develops its own corpus of myths, its own mythology, to meet its essential life needs. And like language, mythology helps shape people's needs and expectations and behavior. Mythology becomes an active force by which people shape and integrate their lives. It is a form of consciousness that arises from life activity, and which in turn influences life activity.

Whatever method of myth-analysis we have employed, whatever our hermeneutics for learning the content of mythology—what it says, what it intends, what it means, and what it implies; whether we read our texts literally, symbolically, culturally, or as universal messages; whether we examine the most powerful themes or the most persistent ones, the descriptions or prescriptions, we discover that myths are about life-and-death matters, matters that define humanity for the storytellers, and perhaps for us.

One mytholographer has said that "A mythic event is 'important' . . . mostly because it is or has been critical and consequential to the welfare of a society as a whole or of most of the individual members of a special cult or a great religion" (Murray 1969:327). A scholar of religions has noted:

> In its original form the sacred story has taken shape mainly around certain crucial events of permanent significance, such as the creation of the world, the loss of immortality, the destiny of man, the sequence of the seasons and the struggle between good and evil. [James 1957:476]

Myths often deal with origins, causes, crucial relationships, and changes. They point to differences that have made a difference to the people who tell about them; they describe the boundary situations of humankind. The events of the story point beyond themselves to the impact that they have had on the present community. They tell stories of events that have had a significant effect and continue to have effect. So they often point to creations, transformations in the world or in nature or in human capacity and relations. They represent situations in which boundaries have been crossed—from unconsciousness to consciousness, innocence to experience, natural to cultural, chaos to order—not just any liminal crossings, however, but of thresholds that have made a life-and-death difference to humanity. Through its mythology humanity speaks of its life-and-death matters. For this reason—more than for the reason that myths tell about gods—we say that the content of mythology is religious.

A religious situation is a life-and-death situation perceived as such, a situation of ultimately crucial importance. If religions consist of beliefs in, attitudes toward, and relations with the ultimate sources of life, we see that myths reveal not only the sources of existence, the supernaturals, upon whom all life depends, but also the crucial events, the life-and-death matters, that the community must understand in order to survive. Myths reveal the essential characteristics of human life: the raw edges, the festers, the sufferings, triumphs, and deaths, the crucial concerns in all corners of community existence. They tell of extinction and survival, decay and renewal, glory and humiliation, submission and defiance, good and evil in all their manifestations. Myths seem to correlate life's multiplicity by representing the most critical matters of human concern. They leap from one extreme of human experience to another, lingering on the thresholds, the boundaries of life. They express all sorts of contradictory human impulses and emotions, from the momentous to the ludicrous, and thereby serve to integrate the wholeness of human adaptation to life. Myths are a means by which humans attempt to integrate themselves with all the contradictions of their human, natural, and supernatural worlds. By concentrating on the life-and-death matters, myths help humans become graceful enough to dance, to leap, and to linger in ritual meant to promote life.

Myths face the supernatural and natural matrices of life; they also face death. Like Orpheus, they travel to the world's rim, face death, and tell the community about the encounter. Myths incorporate death into life, facing life in its fullness, and find meaning in the realization of life's limitations. The content of mythology is a life-and-death matter, where humans realize, face, and communicate the furthest reaches of their potential, incorporating emptiness into fullness, struggle into solidarity, limitation into completeness, death into life.

Myths do not always accept death, certainly not as final. Instead they extend life into afterlife, masking death's reality as well as facing it. Every person and every society are concerned with their existence, conscious of their tenuous hold on permanence. Religion and mythology consist of recognizing mortality and simultaneously denying its finality. By revealing the supernatural sources of life while revealing the limitations of life, myths teach that life exists beyond life. They are stories with meaningful ramifications for human life in all its fullness.

More than this, however, they are means to confer life, promote life. The lessons they teach tell not only how the world came into being, but also how humans can survive in the present order of life. They are pragmatic as well as expressive narratives that people use in their everyday lives.

Describing mythology in terms of its form, context, function, and content, we have emphasized the essential quality of myth as a life-and-death matter, a matter that arises from and is about the crucial thresholds of full human life. Because each myth is full, and each image has a multitude of potential meanings beneath its surface content, mythology can be interpreted validly from a number of perspectives. Indeed, we have tried to survey the rich means by which mythology can be studied. Humans mean myths to integrate the contradictory, polysemous fullness of their lives. By analyzing myths from all angles, the student can gain a full perspective into the lives of the storytellers. Therefore we favor in the following chapters a multidisciplinary analysis of the cross-disciplinary phenomenon of tribal mythology.

We follow Percy Cohen (1969) in this regard. In his brilliant article, Cohen exhorts the students of mythology to attempt cross-disciplinary, multiperspective analyses of mythology. He argues convincingly that any one method we use tends to limit the full import and significance of the myth under observation. If we choose a solely psychoanalytic viewpoint, we tend to lose sight of the religious dimension. If we emphasize too stringently the mythic reflection of social life, we may neglect the reflections of the natural world. Cohen encourages us to attempt every type of analysis in a more or less simultaneous way, building up a many-leveled structure of meaning from the narrative of myth.

He is suggesting a type of "cubist" (Reinitz 1969) view of mythology, in which we illustrate our findings about a body of myths from as many angles as possible. The cubist manifesto was that any one perspective robs the viewer of other views; it is our aim to provide in the following chapters as many perspectives on tribal myths as we can muster, in order to present a polysemous picture of a polysemous phenomenon.

We evoke here not only the advice of Cohen but also the original insights of Hume when he characterized mythology as a religious phenomenon, religious in the sense that it is concerned with the most serious aspects of human life, in order to promote life. And so, we call up, exhume Hume, who first saw the life-and-death content and function of mythology.

Equally we evoke Vico, the multidisciplinary founder of human sciences, who recognized mythology as the most fully symbolic of human creations, the product that reflects most about humanity, the subject that can reveal most about human life in its totality, because its topic is the totality of human life. We emulate Vico in using myths to know humanity in its humanness and variation through holistic analysis.

Rather than applying every method within our grasp to each myth, we plan to employ different modes of analysis through a sequence of myths and rituals from Indians across North America. Although each analysis can stand on its own, we mean for the reader to absorb the chapters as they appear, in order.

We begin with the Hopi myth of emergence and clan migrations, which defines humanity in terms of community existence. The Ojibwa myth of Nanabozho emphasizes the ultimate dependence of humans on their environment, a dependence in hunting cultures of life upon the death of animal persons. The Iroquois myth of the Confederacy delineates civil institutions as a cumulative response to human death, in order to ameliorate both killing callousness and vengeful mourning. In the myth, society is seen as a mode of ritualized condolence. The Navajo "Orpheus" tradition establishes the irreversible power of death, but a Navajo hero myth promises a life of medical rejuvenation, to be obtained through ritual. The common feature of all these myths is that they face death and find meaning in the encounter, thereby facing life in its broadest context. At the close of the Hopi study, we address the question of myth-ritual connections by examining Hopi ritual clowns. These clowns bring myth into the realm of ritual, acting out creation and recreation in the Pueblo plazas, to affirm Hopi life in the face of drought, outside intimidation, and death. As ritualized tricksters, the clowns reveal the rich blend of humor and seriousness, divinity and humanity. In the numerous myths of peyotism's origin we find an American Indian monomyth—a myth that incorporates a vast corpus of other myths—that is grounded not only in the aboriginal cultures of Western Indians, but also in the historical circumstances of the past century. This set of pan-Indian narratives helps us to understand the multifaceted nature not only of the peyote religion, but of religious life in general. Finally, we look at a contemporary sweat lodge ceremony conducted by a Muskogee-Creek spiritual leader, the late Phillip Deere. We find in this ritual not only the yearnings of modern Indians, but also the mythological traditions of Southeastern Indians, traditions that are centuries old.

We have chosen these studies not only for their range of mythological possibilities, but also because they derive from a range of American Indian culture areas (see map on page 32), thus illustrating a range of environments and social networks. The Southwestern Hopis and Navajos (distinctly dissimilar peoples), the Northeastern Iroquois, the Ojibwas of the Subarctic, the peyotists of the Plains and beyond, and the Southeastern Creeks all offer rich images through which we can perceive Indian mythology and envision ourselves.

We hope that the range of myths and interpretations can serve students as a handbook in mythography. But more important, we hope to illuminate the texts because we think that their matters are crucial not only to the people who produce them but also to us. In this way our studies are the result of search and research, both, evoking Herder who overcame the unfeeling criticism of mythology in order to appreciate its meanings.

We have said that "mythology" can mean a particular set of myths, or

TRIBAL LOCATIONS

OJIBWAS
(Subarctic)

PEYOTISTS
(Northern
Plains)

IROQUOIS
(Northeast)

NAVAJOS
HOPIS
(Southwest)

CREEKS
(Southeast)

PEYOTISTS
(Southern
Plains)

it can refer to the study of myths, their mythography. In saying that mythology is a life-and-death matter, we have implied the former usage, meaning that the myths people create and tell are *to them* a matter of life-and-death importance. However, we are also implying by writing this book as we have that the study of myths might be of survival importance *to us,* the people who make an attempt to understand the myths of tribal and other people. The lessons they teach—community harmony, natural reciprocity, realism in facing death, yet hope and striving to better the human condition, a laughing sense of life's absurdity, and yet acceptance despite it all—these are healthy, eminently health-promoting ideas that we can hardly afford to ignore. Mythography, understanding crucial texts of others and embracing ones of our own culture, critically and lovingly, is an important matter to us, a means of facing our humanness, a basic human endeavor that we would be poorer without.

We do not offer this series of analyses as a definitive work on American Indian mythology, even though we have tried to make them, and the book as a whole, as comprehensive as possible. The reader should realize from this introduction and from the format of the chapters, that we consider no one method applicable to all myths. Each method offers insights into human ways of life and thought, and no single method of analysis can possibly exhaust all the meanings inherent in any myth.

We recognize that we are outsiders to the cultures of these peoples, and our interpretations can be halting, just as when a foreign language is first encountered. Like languages, myths do not say everything explicitly; very often they are cryptic, even purposefully deceiving. Like masks, they conceal as well as reveal, and each of their images holds many meanings and possibilities of analysis. They contain both message and noise, and so our task of conveying the meanings of the myths to others of our culture is difficult. We do not intend to tell the respective Indian peoples what the myths mean; they have known these myths far better than we, at least traditionally.

Nevertheless, we have dared to take apart the myths as they stand as narrative performances, and put them together into analyses for outsiders like ourselves to understand and learn from at least a part of their meanings. In the process we have made every attempt to avoid—and we hope we have avoided—doing violence to the traditional myths we have studied. We begin our mythography with some trepidation; however, we take courage from Sherlock Holmes who declared, "What one man can invent another can discover" (Doyle 1930:525). We hope for the validity and usefulness of our discoveries.

2

The Emergence and Maintenance of the Hopi People

In this, our opening analysis, we wish to begin simply, by recounting one prominent myth from the Hopi people of Arizona, and providing a relatively uncomplicated, generally unified analysis. Then we will try to build a more intricate structure of interpretation upon this foundation, by interpreting the behavior of Hopi ritual clowns.

We have chosen the myth that recalls the emergence, wandering, and settling of the Hopis' ancestors following the world's creation, a myth through which the Hopis define their identity as a people. Out of many possible versions (e.g., Courlander 1971; Cushing 1923; Nequatewa 1967:7–41; Sekaquaptewa 1981:224–28; Stephen 1923:3–13; Titiev 1944:73–74; Wallis 1936:2–20; see further, Goldfrank 1948:242), we have chosen one for our narrative (Voth 1905:16–26; cf. 10–15), although we will use material from other versions to illuminate our analysis.

We think that the myth manifests the Hopi people's past to themselves, placing them in their chosen land and their chosen way of life. The myth tells how the Hopis chose to become themselves, how they made a project of their tribal identity, how they struggled against their own social disequilibrium and its dreadful consequences, and how through language, clans, and rituals they cohered to each other as a people, a discrete portion of humanity. It validates the Hopis in their historical element. In addition, the myth extends the community to include both the dead and nonhuman environment, while at the same time reflecting the context of political strife, exacerbated by white intrusions, at the time when the myths were recorded.

Consisting of world view and ethos, description and prescription, the myth functions in helping control recurrent tensions in community life.

This chapter has been written with Carol Ann Lorenz.

It helps explain the sources of disruption, and reinforces social sentiment against attack both from within and without Hopi society.

The myth is one of many Hopi narratives that have been collected and published over the last century. It typifies the emergence and migration legends that abound in Southwestern America. Following this story chronologically, although not necessarily connected to it at any one telling, are stories of the origin of Hopi clans, in which the events of the emergence and wandering are correlated with the specific episodes of clan history, interweaving individual family stories with the fabric of Hopi tradition. For the purposes of this study, however, we shall concentrate on the more encompassing history, even though the details of the clan origin myths could fill out our conclusions. Each Hopi clan possesses its own versions of the tribal traditions, each version containing episodes especially germane to the clan members' historical and contemporary experiences. The Hopis have numerous priesthoods; they have no central hierarchy or dogmatic theology; moreover, any Hopi adult can tell a myth at any time of day or year as he or she wishes. Therefore the versions differ in diverse details, reflecting the particular circumstances of narration; however, in essence the variants of the Hopi myth bear marked similarity to one another.

From Oraibi, on the third mesa in the Hopiland desert, comes the story, "The Wanderings of the Hopi," recorded around the turn of the century. It begins: "A very long time ago they were living down below." Down there everything was good; rain and fertility flourished. But because the chiefs grew bad, the rain stopped, the people became sick. Sorcery and adultery were practiced increasingly, until "by and by it was like it is here and now."

The chiefs responded to these events. They planned both a revenge upon the evildoers and an escape from their deteriorating condition. They heard sounds up above them, footsteps. Someone was walking up there. The village chief, Kik-mongwi, wanted to investigate. The chiefs, therefore, made a bird through song, sending it up with instructions to tell whoever was above that they, the people, wanted to come up. They planted a fir tree that failed to reach the surface, but a reed they planted alongside reached the top successfully.

The bird flew in spirals around the two ladders—the fir and the reed—up through the hole, but could find no one in the darkness above, and returned exhausted. The chiefs made another bird messenger, hummingbird, small but swift and strong. They gave him instructions to see who lived up there, if he was "kind" and "good" and "gentle." If so, they wished to come up. But hummingbird also failed and returned, exhausted.

The chiefs then created hawk, but he, too, could find no one above to tell of the conditions below—the bad hearts of the chiefs' "children"—and he came back equally exhausted. The chiefs revived each of these birds in sequence.

So they made a fourth bird, Motsni, a northern shrike, giving him the same message. He was stronger than the others, and he found the place where Oraibi is today, although "there were no houses there yet." Someone was sitting there, and he moved his head to the side, telling the bird to sit down and inform him of his reason for coming. It was Masau'u, the Skeleton, who listened to Motsni's report from the chiefs. Masau'u told the bird, "Now this is the way I am living here. I am living here in poverty. I have not anything; this is the way I am living here. Now, if you are willing to live here that way, too, with me and share this life, why come, you are welcome." The bird returned to the chiefs with this message.

Living below were all sorts of people—the White Man, the Paiute, most of the Pueblo Indians. The better of these heard the message, although some very bad ones heard it, too. The chiefs announced that in four days they would leave.

At that time many people gathered, and the chiefs led them up the reed ladder—the Kik-mongwi, who was also the Soyal chief; the Flute chief; Horn chief; Agave chief; Singer chief; Wuwuchim chief; Rattlesnake chief; Antelope chief; Marau chief; Lagon chief; and the Warrior chief. The people followed, and when the news got around, everyone was clamoring to climb the reed. But fearing that too many two-hearts (sorcerers) would come to the surface, the village chief pulled up the reed, leaving a great number to fall back below the earth's surface.

The large number who had surfaced gathered by the rim of the opening, where the village chief told them that from then on they were to live good, single-hearted lives. They should follow Motsni wherever he instructed.

Before long, however, the boy-child of the village chief became sick and died. Suspecting sorcery, the chief made a ball of fine meal, threw it in the air, and when it landed on a maiden, he began to throw her back down below. He feared that the people would return to their old ways with a two-heart amongst them. In order to save herself, she promised to be always on the chief's side in any village dispute; furthermore, she showed him that his son was alive down below. " 'That is the way it will be,' the maiden said to the chief; 'if any one dies, he will go down there and he will remain there only four days, and after four days he will come back again to live with his people.' " The chief relented, allowing her to remain.

The Warrior chief noticed that it was cold and still dark. With Flute priest's help, Spider Woman made the moon and sun, respectively, out of native cloth and buckskin. They drew on them, rubbed egg yolks over the sun, and put them in position in the sky. Everyone was happy because now it was light and warm.

The chiefs then made blossoms and plants, and the people prepared to scatter. The Hopi chief wanted to keep his cherished language for his own group; so he asked Mocking Bird to instruct the other people in various languages other than the original Hopi common to them all. Then there was a common meal where the chief laid out the various types of corn ears from the underworld, from which different groups could choose. In the contention for the choice ears, the Navajos, Utes, and Apaches got the longest ones; the Hopis waited and received the short corn ears. The chief said, "Thanks, that you have left this for me. Upon this we are going to live." The short ears were true corn, but the long ears he turned into seed grasses like wheat.

The chief's elder brother selected some good tasting foods and led a party toward the sunrise, where he touched the sun with his forehead and lived there, but he always remembered his brethren. He agreed that if the Hopis should get into the same trouble they had in the underworld, he would come back, seek out the two-hearts and cut off their heads. The elder brother's party became the "White Men."

The chief and his people took a southern route, as each group dispersed, taking with it a grandmother and a special stone. The two-hearted maiden, Powak-mana, followed at a distance behind the chief's group.

And so, each party, each with its chief, became separate, all traveling eastward. They stopped here and there, settling, leaving the ruins that can be found throughout Hopiland. "White Men" had Spider Woman with them, and they fared well, with horses and burros. The party that took along Powak-mana lived at Palatkwapi for a while without a clan name. Each group would stay for a year or so wherever they found good springs and fields. On their wanderings they took foodstuff. Sometimes, when they found fields without water, they buried a small, perforated vessel filled with stones, shells, prayer-sticks, and the like. From this spot a spring would rise a year later. If they moved on, they took their magic package with them.

Before they finally reached the place where they are now, they were already becoming as bad as they had been below. They were squabbling and fighting with one another, attacking each other to steal possessions. Some built their villages on cliffs and mesas for protection.

Finally, some arrived at Moenkopi—the Bear clan, Spider clan, Hide strap clan, Blue-bird clan and the Fat cavity clan—"all of which had derived their names from a dead bear upon which these different parties had come as they were traveling along."

A short time after, another Bear Clan, different from the one at Moenkopi, settled at Shongopovi, just east of the present village. It was the first village to be started, of those remaining. At this time Skeleton was still living where Oraibi is now. The group that had settled near Moenkopi moved to where Moenkopi is now, but the Bear clan, Hide strap clan, and Blue-bird clan moved toward Oraibi. When Spider clan reached Moenkopi, they made marks on a nearby bluff, claiming the land always for the Hopis, because water existed in that location for planting.

Soon after, the Snake clan arrived, and wanting the same land, they wrote the same marks on the bluff. Burrowing owl clan did likewise when they arrived. Then they all journeyed to where Skeleton was staying. Skeleton met the Bear clan members, just northwest of Oraibi. They asked him to be their chief, to share land with them; but he refused, saying that they had brought two-hearts with them and would make no improvement over their behavior in the underworld. Not until White Brother should return to kill the sorcerers would Skeleton be their chief. He gave the Bear clan land, distinctly outlined, and he told them to settle what is now Oraibi.

The Bear clan brought with them the Soyal cult, the Aototo, and the Soyal kachinas. Other clans arrived, asked for permission to establish themselves. If they knew some ceremony "to produce rain and good crops," they were permitted to stay—Hide strap clan, Blue-bird clan, Spider clan, and more. Other clans were settling Walpi and Mishongovi. In the same way, if they knew fertility ceremonies, they were given land to cultivate. In this manner the fields were distributed.

One of the first was the Bow clan, bringing the Shaalako kachinas, the Tangik kachinas, the Tukwunang kachina, and Whawiki kachina, very powerful bringers of rain. These kachinas danced and caused a great downpour, filling the desert washes. This was the origin of the Wuwuchim ceremony, the first Hopi ritual to take place in Hopiland.

Then came the Soyal ceremony under the direction of the village chief, and then in the prayer-stick month, the Snake and Flute ceremonies, alternating each year. Snake clan brought the Snake cult, Blue-bird clan brought the Antelope cult, and Spider clan brought the Flute cult. Lizard brought the Marau cult, Parrot clan the Lagon cult, and still others came. Small bands heard about the growing settlement, and they asked for permission to join. The villages grew slowly on the mesas.

Thus the people lived, bringing rain with their few and simple rituals. People were happy and good. But at Palatkwapi, Powak-mana, the two-hearted maiden, had taught others her sorcery, until the town was destroyed by water delivered upon them by the great water serpents. Almost all died, but a few were saved.

These few found their way to Walpi, where they spread their evil art to other villages, causing disease and death among the people. They also turned the Utes, Navajos, and Apaches into Hopi enemies. "And then the White Men came and made demands of the Hopi." The Whites were brought to Hopiland by the sorcerers, "and now the White Men are worrying the Hopi also."

The Hopis continue to look to their Elder Brother in the east, according to the promise of the old men and the ancestors. The present White Men are not the same as the Elder Brother. These people try to take away Hopi children, baptize the Hopis, and threaten the people with beatings and even death. "But we should not listen to them, we should continue to live like the Hopi." But there are two-hearts among the people who speak for the White Men, who tell Hopis to obey the Whites. The ancestors prophesied this. "We are now in trouble," the narration concludes, "Our children are taken away from us, and we are being harassed and worried."

UNDERSTANDING THE MYTH

Before discussing the content of the myth, we need to examine two of its contexts, one obvious and political, the other conceptual and more subtle. Then we can proceed to analyze the narrative of Hopi origins.

Clearly, the myth is a description of Hopi tribal existence. Equally apparent, the myth concentrates not only on Hopi past but also Hopi present, the contemporary context in which the myth is recorded. And that context is overwhelmingly political.

The story ends with a supposedly ancient prophecy regarding the troubles that Whites will deliver unto the Hopi people. The intruders, it is foretold, will attempt to take away the bulwarks of Hopi existence. They will try to destroy Hopi religion and language and kinship structure; they will try to alter Hopi habits regarding food and dress. They will turn one Hopi against another, disrupting the cohesiveness of the community. That time, the document states, has come to the Hopi people. Past events, past oracles, and present events are now running concurrently and merging into one crucial history and contemporary account. In addressing the present situation, the text stresses the continuity of Hopi tradition, warning strenuously against the changes that whites preach. The myth stands as a manifesto not only against the white intruders but also against the Hopis who would accept white ways. Thus the myth is as much about the present as about the past, as it guards against corrupting forces, both from without and within Hopi society.

Therefore we must see the myth in the context of white incursions and their political ramifications. During the last few decades of the nineteenth century, Anglo invasions crowned the centuries of white disruptions among the Pueblos, disruptions that the Hopis had until then been able to withstand. The coming of American troops and missionaries created intense factionalism among the tribe; gossip, hatred, family disputes, and clan rivalries flared chronically; witchcraft accusations mounted, one Hopi against another, under the stress of white demands that Hopis deliver up their children for white indoctrination, both secular and religious, in schools away from the Hopi villages.

The societal tensions are reflected in the myth, with its repeated references to adultery, corruption among chiefs, sorcery, theft, battle, and contention. Esther Goldfrank (1948) has shown that Hopi myths collected between 1883 and 1932 show concern for immediate political situations. Goldfrank traced Oraibi factionalism to the early 1700s, but indicated that Americans exacerbated the problems by demanding that children be indoctrinated to white standards. The crucial event during this political strife was a dispute in Oraibi from 1905 to 1906 which literally split asunder the entire community over the issue of accommodation to white demands. The factions "hostile" and "friendly" to white coercion could no longer live with one another in Oraibi, the oldest of the Hopi villages, dating back to the middle of the twelfth century. In 1906 its population was under enough pressure, with tight quarters, no central leadership, and political strife, that the two major factions held a decisive pushing match to determine which group should remain in their home. The conservative faction lost the symbolic fight, and removed itself to Hotevilla, providing an opening for whites to enforce their will over the Hopis. Factionalism did not cease, however, and today two Hopi parties still contend both with each other and white intruders to determine the Hopi future. Significantly, Hopi conservatives like Tom Banyacya still turn to Hopi myths and prophecies, traditional ideological weapons, against the devastating offenses of coal and oil companies, greedy for Hopi resources. Now as then, Hopi myths bend to meet the needs of the political winds, as Goldfrank suggested.

In particular, Goldfrank traced the rivalries between the Spider and Bear clans from the same kinship group. The Bear clan held political power in the late nineteenth century, maintaining control at Oraibi, but the Spider clan brandished the Flute and Antelope ceremonies, and the Bears resented the conservative Spider upstarts, including Spider Woman herself, one of the most beloved of traditional Hopi deities. The push-of-war in 1906 concerned mainly opponents from the Bear and Spider clans, the accommodationist Bears emerging victorious. When Frank Cushing recorded another version of the same emergence myth in 1883 (Cushing 1923), a Spider clan member narrated it. Bear clan kinsmen threatened to throw Cushing off a cliff, calling him "shit" to be evacuated from the mesa (Goldfrank 1948:243–45). Although the Hopis had persisted in peaceful traditions for centuries, the societal stresses had upset them sufficiently enough that Cushing took their threat seriously. Violence was already erupting within Hopi society, including beheadings of those accused of witchcraft. Cushing defended himself with a pistol and recorded the myth.

In short, the political context in which the myth was recorded helped create a tone of intensity and feud in the myth itself, far at odds with the image of peaceful Pueblos promulgated by Ruth Benedict (1959:esp. 78–79) and espoused as an ideal by the Hopis themselves. It could even be said that the myth is *about* the contemporary struggle, using narratives of a mythical past as ideological armaments against both outsiders and fellow Hopis.

In addressing the contemporary issues of Hopi existence, the myth of Hopi origins means to be authoritative through its great age. For the traditional Hopis the myth represents the most ancient and persisting of Hopi heritages. One version of the myth begins, "My grandfather, and my father also, told me this story" (Wallis 1936:2), placing it beyond the limitations and fallible contentions of the present storyteller, stamping it with a seal of reverence due to elders and ancestors. It is a story to be believed implicitly, and by which to judge the honesty of other traditions and accounts.

Politically, the myth grounds present difficulties in past verities; however, according to Hopi conceptions concerning time, the distinction between past and present disappears. Thus we must take account of the Hopi conceptual context—as well as the political context—for the myth.

Benjamin Whorf (1975; cf. Whorf 1956:51–56, 102–24) has claimed that the Hopis' language conceives not of past, present, and future tenses, but rather "manifested" and "unmanifested" phenomena, events that have entered conscious awareness and those that have not. According to Whorf, the Hopis distinguish between things that are apparent and things that are hidden, waiting to spring up and be discovered, rather than placing events along the Western axes of time and space. Events in the future and in the forgotten past take an expective mode of verb; present situations require inceptive tense. Thus an event taking place in another place, but at the same time as the present, is unmanifest, expective, unconscious, hidden; once a person hears of the event, however, it becomes manifest, inceptive, apparent, conscious. For the Hopis the supernatural is generally referred to in unmanifest modes with an implication of inevitability that it will spring into view, whereas nature is obvious, manifestly objective, before the Hopis' eyes at all times.

In this context, the Hopi myth does not tell of a past event, even though it must be translated as such into English, but the myth becomes manifest, it takes place, it occurs, as it is being recounted, as the storyteller narrates its events to the listeners. In Western terms, the distant, primordial events of the myth become present realities during the narration of the myth; in Hopi terms the expective becomes inceptive, and thus the past and present (so-called) merge into one meaningful continuity. In the telling the myth bridges the gap between aspects of manifest and unmanifest existence. The troubles of the past and present become merged in a conscious, controllable, palpable form. Therefore to say that the myth of Hopi origins reveals both Hopi past and present, simultaneously, is to recognize not only the political but also the conceptual contexts for the myth.

Just as in Hopi dreams in which mythic elements are incorporated (and, as we shall see in this chapter, in Hopi rituals as well), the myth contextualizes serious concerns of the Hopis through the artifice of folklore. General anxieties are made specific, societal problems are made individual, with the function of reducing the individual and society's anxieties through the manifest mode. If unmanifest anxieties can be named and imaged, through dream, ritual, or myth, they are better handled by individuals and by the community at large.

The myth exists in the context of the Hopi community's political disputes and in the context of Hopi linguistic conceptions. Moreover, the myth is *about* Hopi politics and conceptions; it is a narrative *about* Hopi tribalism and the Hopi conception of the community, a story *about* the Hopi "us." Hence it is fitting that at the end of the myth the narrator refers repeatedly to "we" and "our" and "us," in order to emphasize the subject matter of the myth being concluded. The myth recounts the emergence and origin of the Hopi people, and defines a Hopi person as someone living in community with others of the same origin, language, history, and customs. Furthermore, the myth proclaims the necessity of community for the continuation of Hopi life. It defines humans as social beings, and states that human life exists by virtue of its community. The myth does this by demonstrating both the rewards of tribal consciousness and the mortal dangers of community disequilibrium, both describing and prescribing the way of tribal life.

In the first paragraph of the myth, societal woes have occurred. Sexual license, adultery, and wife stealing are rife. The children disobey authority and the chiefs bemoan that their "children won't listen to us." From the opening of the story, with its edenic quality, the people tear their social harmony into disarray. The story shifts quickly to a situation of dis-ease, famine, and conflict, presenting contemporary Hopi problems as recurring events in Hopi history.

When the people grow bad, the rains stop and sickness comes. In this Hopi tradition, as in other American Indian myths, human evils affect the whole of nature, creating a disastrous effect on human wrongdoers. The myth projects the past events forward to serve as lessons to present Hopis, while projecting present warnings back into the past, to show the fatal results of social contention. If people are evil, the clouds will withhold their waters, the crops will die, and humans will perish; it has happened before and it can happen again, the myth implies.

The chiefs and their people emerge from the wasted underground in order to save themselves from their own misfortune. When they emerge, the village chief exhorts the people to social cohesion. He reminds them that they have emerged as a group, as one people, and although they will separate, they must continue to think of one another as a people. In order that they should not forget their essential ties of kinship, they share a grand feast, becoming companions in food as they are relatives by blood. As Elder Brother prepares to leave, he, too, reasserts his kin relations by vowing to remember always his younger brothers, the Hopis. The emergence as members of a tribal community precedes the various migrations, and the chief's speech reaffirms kinship as an ontological and economic necessity by which human existence can endure.

But at the same time the antithesis of community rears its persistently ugly head. Immediately following emergence, a witch causes the first death in the present world. In other versions of the same myth, the finality of the first death is blamed on the trickster, Coyote, a character regarded as the most antisocial of beings, the most uncharacteristic of Hopi personages; and on jealousy, the most disruptive of social sentiments, especially among the Hopis who caution their children against trying to compete with their tribesmen. Hopi excellence should exist for the group, not for one individual in competition with another. Thus, in three versions of the myth, death is said to be the result of antisocial behavior, symbolized by witchcraft, a trickster, and jealousy. As the village chief is proclaiming community as a life-promoting force, the myth equates death with social disharmony, symbolized in this version by witchcraft.

There is a special concern for witchcraft in the myth, a concern that belies the tensions in Hopi society during the recording of the myth as well as in tribal life in general. In a society where tensions were mounting uncontrollably, a need existed to designate blame. It was easy enough to call the invading whites evil (despite their possible connection with the departed Elder Brother), but how could the Hopis explain the evil of their own people?

Lévi-Strauss (1963:172–75) and others have shown that witchcraft accusations actually serve the community in which they are made by singling out a coherent cause for evil. For people who believe that their nature is essentially good and their society is essentially kin related, as the Hopis do, the belief in witchcraft explains how aberrant evil can come about. For the Hopis, witches are beings at direct cross-purposes to community standards. They are greedy, jealous, aggressive, acquisitive, beguiling, and argumentative; in brief, they are *kahopi*, un-Hopi individualists. They reverse community ideals and undermine community life. In this myth, they bring death into the world.

In this way the Hopis make an internal problem—social disharmony, evil within the tribe—seem like an external intrusion, for the witches are perceived as persons beyond the pale of society, as foreign to Hopi regularity (however ever-present) as invading Anglos. Those who cause evil are not really Hopis; they are outsiders, aliens, witches who have insinuated themselves into Hopi life.

In the myth the village chief instructs the witch-maiden to follow behind the migrating clans, ostracizing her from the clan communities; however, she finds her way back into their midst, contaminating the rest of the people, and ultimately creating the present political battles by passing on her evil seed. Witchcraft inserts itself into the healthy community and rots it, the myth says. It causes death to the chief's son, and disintegration to the Hopi community.

As with American Indian theory regarding disease, in which foreign elements cause disease by getting into the human body and shattering its cohesiveness—requiring a doctor to exorcise it from the ailing body by sucking or other means—the witch causes societal sickness, and even death, by injecting her malevolence into community structures. Later in the myth, greed is said to be the cause of strife, greed activated by contagious sorcery, a disease of greed infecting the body politic.

It would be cozy to conclude that the myth makes concise equations: witchcraft, antisociality, and death versus community bonds and life. Surely the equations exist; however, the placement of death as an antithesis of tribal society is too simple.

In our version of the myth, the chief accepts the death of his son when shown that the child continues to live in the underworld and will rejoin his people after some time. In other versions either the witch or the chief makes speeches in praise of death: its transitory nature, its necessity, or the pleasantness of the afterworld. In addition, all versions state the belief that the dead and living will continue to relate, one to the other. Death is said to be not an end, but rather a metamorphosis, and communication can continue between living humans and their departed, ghostly forms, despite the work of sorcery or trickish Coyote. Mischa Titiev seems correct in saying that "perhaps the most fundamental concept of Hopi religion is a belief in the continuity of life after death" (Titiev 1950:369). As a Hopi woman has said regarding the first death at the emergence place, "Thus they learned that you must pass from this world to achieve immortality," and, as a result, the witch-maiden was saved (Sekaquaptewa 1981:226–27).

In fact the Hopis—like other Pueblos—believe their ancestors to be fertilizing clouds, bringers of rain who will nourish the crops upon which the living subsist. The necessity of death in the myth becomes even more accentuated, therefore, since the first death sets into motion a cycle of nourishment, growth, and decay that is to the Hopis life itself. Death brings into existence the ancestors, who turn into clouds and kachinas that bring rain; moisture feeds the corn and other foods that in turn nourish the Hopi people themselves, and in the eternal cycle, death feeds life (Tyler 1964:74–79; Marriott and Rachlin 1972:232–37; for a more explicit statement of this cycle, see the parallel Zuni myth of emergence in Marriott and Rachlin 1972:123–27). Death is incorporated into life, making it richer and more permanent. It is no surprise, then, that the Hopis consider visits by the living to the land of the dead to be sources of mental health and strength.

The gods of Hopiland, the kachinas who control the environmental forces, who bring rain and food and animals and community existence—who are invoked toward the end of the myth, when the clans are setting up their lodgings and system of life-bring ceremonials—are by and large the ancestors themselves, the creations of death, the products of the first death in the present world brought about by the two-hearted maiden. Thus the episode of the first death sets the stage for the appearance of the kachinas near the conclusion of the narrative.

Masau'u himself, the skeleton god who beckons the Hopi people to share his life in the upper world, is the Hopi deity of death. Masau'u is central to the myth, and he is sometimes reported to be the chief of all Pueblo deities. Pictured as a skeleton with a mask that points both to living and deathly realms, he possesses mastery over war, fertility, fire, jokes, and boundaries, as well as death. He stands at the entrance to the underworld, the land from which the people emerged, guarding its threshold and mediating between the living and the dead. As god of boundaries, he has the power to change anything into its opposite, making mockery of appearances and broadening Hopi consciousness regarding the possibilities in themselves and the world around them. In the course of the emergence myth the Hopi ancients follow his tracks to their promised land. "Hence," they say, "Death is our greatest father and master (God), for we followed his tracks from the exit of the cave worlds, and he was the only being that awaited us on the great world of waters where now is the world" (Cushing 1923:166).

Why were the Hopi ancients drawn to Skeleton's territory and to his leadership? Why should the god of death serve as their master? Hamilton Tyler suggests,

> Because his touch causes change the god has . . . taken on a broader attribute which is the important link between the forces of death and the forces of life. Masau'u has the power of causing all the metamorphoses of nature, a factor which sets him apart from many other Pueblo gods. . . . [He] alone provides the vital elements which keep in motion the Hopi cosmic drama. [Tyler 1964:14]

It is Skeleton's epiphany as god of death that makes him crucial both to the story and to the Hopis themselves. In his person the various episodes and lessons regarding death are epitomized. He reminds them, with his life of simple poverty, of the overabundance and overcrowding of human life in the underworld. As god of death he evokes the opposite of a Hopi's most prized value—fertility—showing that illicit and redundant fertility can result in great danger. He reminds the Hopis how it was in the underworld, overstuffed through adultery and other forms of rampant, misguided fertility, so that the people were covered with snot and spit and contagious diseases because of their tight quarters.

In addition, like the common American Indian myths of the origin of death, Masau'u, the spare, stark skeleton, shows that it would be worse if people lived forever, for the overcrowding they would bring on themselves and their fellow immortals. As well as the two-hearted maiden, Masau'u helps the Hopis face death.

But he, like the myth itself, also masks the finality of death by pointing beyond death to an afterlife, an existence for the ghosts both in the world below and in the sky as clouds. He turns a deficit into a credit, creating more out of less, by implying how the greater number in the community will be served by the continuing dead, his helpers the kachinas. Like Masau'u, the pivotal scene of the dead child of the chief serves to defy and define the categories of life and death, demonstrating them to be mutually supporting. For a myth that turns on the axis of the first human death, Masau'u makes a fitting crucial character, and for the Hopis he makes a suitable central deity.

From the underworld emerged the various people familiar to the Hopis;

they arose as a single group, and after emerging they shared in a common meal. Not only the different Hopi clans but also their Indian neighbors (friends and enemies alike), and possibly the whites, climbed the sacred ladders together. Despite later accreted differences in language, technology, staples, and style, the myth portrays a kinship more ranging than the Hopi tribe itself. Indeed, the myth emphasizes at this early point the greater connections of all humanity, the physical companionship symbolized by the shared feast, before the dispersal and migration.

However, during the course of the narrative, following the axial first death, the Hopis establish themselves as a distinct tribe, made up of the wandering clans who initially lived as one folk in the underworld. All people enjoy equally the effects of the first death, the creation of the sun and moon, and the agricultural innovations that precede dispersal; but the Hopis distinguish themselves through their choices of language, staple crop, peaceful poverty, ceremonial prowess, and eventual site for habitation.

The village chief holds his native tongue in such loving regard that he instructs Mocking Bird to teach all the non-Hopis other languages. The chief signals the Hopi identity first through its common and distinct means of verbal communication. The importance of language in this context is informative, since language is necessary for human culture to exist. Without the use of communication, the vital messages of a people cannot be transmitted, including the myths themselves. Since myth is a form of cultural communication which uses language as its medium, it is interesting that the myth points directly and proudly to the Hopi language as a special trait and prized reserve of the Hopi people. Through the episode of choosing a language, the myth defines the Hopis as a separate people from their related neighbors, set off by their common means of cultural communication.

The Hopis choose to accept death and they choose a god of death as their guide. They choose for themselves their native tongue, and they choose a life of peaceful poverty, symbolized by the short ears of corn, their staple crop. Their choice of the corn takes place in a suitably Hopi way. Rather than pushing their way aggressively to demand certain ears of corn, they hold back and accept what is left them. They eschew the forceful acquisitiveness of the other Indians, and as a result they are rewarded with "real" corn, whereas the more aggressive people find themselves in possession of wheat and other seed grasses, that is, crops brought by whites to the New World. Through this episode, the myth further identifies the Hopis through their traditional food crop. The myth distinguishes the Hopis not only through their common language but also through their common source of nourishment.

The short ears of corn, less grand but more consistently nourishing than the large ones, serve to represent the life of poverty that Masau'u describes to them through Motsni, when the people are still below. The god warns that their chosen life with him will be hard, and the people accept the offer. Their chosen life is difficult, but it is a good life for them, and they are proud of it. They must sacrifice luxuries for the solidity of community existence in the desert, where rainfall averages about ten inches each year, where each drop of rain is a precious commodity to be hoarded by the group and channeled to its proper goal of fertilizing the corn. Through their choice of common poverty the Hopis further identify themselves as a tribe.

Finally, the Hopis establish themselves as a people, following their years of migratory search, in a common home, a chosen land, where they still live today. When they were in the underworld, the people knew of their eventual home through Motsni's mission to Masau'u. After arriving in the present world, it is their task to find the place of Masau'u, which will be their territory. Even though they find other locations, other fields for growing crops, other sources of water; even though they possess the ability during their travels to create magically the life-giving springs, the clans push on to their destined spot for settlement, where their community will coalesce. They seem irresistibly drawn in their variegated clan-forms to a single spot where their life should take place.

As they journey to their chosen land, they stop at various sites that are still remembered by name and ruin. The mention of these place-names serves to acquaint the Hopi audience with their world, reaffirming the Hopi claims to a territory larger than their immediate dwellings, and placing them in the milieu of their past events. The ancients who made the migration to their eventual homeland continue to manifest themselves through their ruins around Hopiland, and the ruins give visible credence to the accuracy of the narrative as a historical account of ancestral travels. Indeed, one researcher (Fewkes 1900) has shown that the Hopi migration legends find verification through archaeological data, indicating that the Hopis did move, for example, to protective mesas as a means of defense. Since the myth aims to anchor the present Hopi life in the past, the manifest world in the unmanifest, the frequent mention of ancient place-names where visible ruins remain serves its purpose admirably.

Despite their commonality of emergence, language, food, customs, poverty, and eventually land, the Hopis are not thoroughly unified in the myth. Through the dramatic sequences—the exploration of the world above, the emergence, the crisis of the first death, the migratory search for their promised land—the leitmotif of strife and contention punctuates the narrative. The adulterous unions with their concomitant jealousies;

the separation of the Hopi people into clans, later to be reunited; the squabbling, fighting, and stealing that drive the clans up onto their defensive positions on the mesas; the contention for watery sites in present Hopiland; the existence of sorcerers in their midst—all of these factors illustrate the mythical awareness of disunity, just as the concluding references to intratribal factionalism reflect accurately the historical context in which the myth was narrated, when kinship was giving way to ideology and a struggle for power.

The myth points out that intratribal dissension has its roots in ancient Hopi tradition. The people may have emerged as a group, but they have never enjoyed perfect harmony as a tribal unit. The existence of the clans serves as a reminder of the separate clan histories within the larger Hopi whole, a fact further evidenced by the distinct clan myths of migration and the localization of clans within each Hopi village. The Hopi myth recognizes both the ideal of community oneness and the reality of long-lived Hopi disjunctures.

The myth records a series of factional episodes; other versions tell about the separations, not only of clans but also of the sexes. One version relates how the women become dance crazed so that they neglect their community duties. Following an argument with the complaining men, the sexes separate. After a long period of disunion, they can no longer stand the alienation and they reunite (Cushing 1923:165; cf. Stephen 1929:3–4). In a sense, the episode mirrors the whole of the migration myth, in that it recalls a tribal split and eventual reintegration. It teaches that all Hopis—the various clans as well as the sexes—must work together in order for their life to flourish. Just as the beginning of the myth shows the dire effects of adultery and other forms of societal dysfunction, the episode of sexual separation indicates the foolishness of sexual disunity. It is interesting in this regard that the initial dysfunction results in an overabundance of fecundity, whereas the separation of the sexes results in an undermining of fecundity. Both point out the perversions of normal, social relations between the sexes that make up the community, and thereby guide the Hopis to a middle path.

The myth upholds the ideal of community cooperation, while recognizing the inherent discontents of society life. Freud (1962) was not the first person to see the interconnections between security, sexuality, and discontent in human society. Indeed, this issue seems to be a central concern of the Hopi myth of emergence. Even more than Freud, the myth seems to argue for the sacrifice of rampant individualism in exchange for the life-giving security of a community in union. The myth even suggests that real freedom—from economic peril brought by drought and fighting, jealousy and sorcery—can take place only in a community of united kinsmen who are willing to forego the illusion of personal achievement for the more palpable benefit of the group. The myth is a declaration of dependence on the community.

In this regard, interesting work has been done on certain human communities that require cooperative work in order to control and regulate either scarce, unpredictable, or dangerous water sources. Called "waterworks" societies (Wittfogel and Goldfrank 1943:19–28), these communities tend toward cooperative forms of infrastructure, favoring a life of sharing to no life at all.

The Hopis fit this description. Their traditional life has depended on irrigation cooperation, working at the rivulets, springs, and arroyos, channeling the scarce water in order to fertilize their cornfields. Their communal cleaning of springs was a sacred societal ritual that required cooperation from all clans and both sexes. In the myth, the procurement of fertilizing water is a major concern during the migrations and in the choice of specific sites in the eventual Hopi homeland. Different clans are allocated water supplies sufficient for their needs, and each clan must recognize the others' claims if their society is to persist peacefully.

The concern for fertilizing water, and in fact of fertility in general, permeates both the myth and Hopi life itself. Fertility has been shown to be the focal morphological image in all of Pueblo—including Hopi—ceremonialism, a veritable obsession in dreams, myths, rituals, and technological organization. In the Hopi mind, fertility and community survival are synonymous.

The emergence itself is a symbolic representation of the crucial acts of fertility: gestation and birth. The people who climb their vegetal ladders from the earth into the air and seek sunlight and rain are akin to plants growing from the soil. In a way, the myth equates the origin and growth of the Hopi people with the origin and growth of their foodstuffs, particularly corn. The proper fertility of one promotes the fertility of the other. Imbalance in one can bring about disease in the other. Thus, when adultery creates an illicit fertility, the rains and crops cease to supply the people with their requirements for nourishment. The misguided, maldirected fertility in the underworld indicates that fertility by itself is not an unmitigated blessing. Instead human fertility must be organized and controlled, channeled like irrigated water for the life-promoting good of all.

Once in the upper world, the Hopi clans seek the most fertile, watery places, and create water through magical means. When they come to their promised land, each clan is permitted to settle only if it can demonstrate its rapport with the rain-bringing ancestors, the kachinas, through their ceremonials that now mark the seasons of the Hopi year, the cermonials that were first designated before the dispersion of the clans from the emergence place. In order to join the tribal community, each clan must show its willingness and ability to bring rain and fertility to the whole community.

The first and most vividly portrayed of these ceremonies is the Wuwuchim, a November ritual that welcomes the kachinas, the Hopi ancestors, into the villages of the living. At the Wuwuchim ceremony Hopi boys undergo initiation to the Hopi secret societies. The masked kachinas thrust them into the adult world of understanding and participation; at the same time Masau'u serves as chief host to the dead. The first Wuwuchim ceremony causes not only a great downpour of rain but also a reintegration of the living and the dead, with Masau'u—symbol of death and fertility—in the mediating role.

The parade of ceremonials, each under the direciton of a certain clan, represents in effect the whole ceremomial year of the Hopis. In this way the myth validates the Hopi ceremomial calendar with its panoply of chiefs who received their powers after ascending from the womb of the earth. The clans, which were signs of Hopi factions during the migrations, become the effective building stones of Hopi society through their life-giving ceremonials.

The Hopi clans arrive slowly, one by one, and they need to be reincorporated into the fullness of Hopi life. Through the centuries they have maintained their traditional clan loyalties, but through the ceremonial system with its conjoining secret societies (whose membership cuts across clan ties), as well as through the emergence myth's message, they have worked for unity in theory and practice. The clans may historically have been different ethnic groups, but according to the message of solidarity explicit in the myth, and carried out through the ceremonials, they are all one people. They remember their separate histories, and they will not be ruled by one clan; they persist in factional disputes, but they are all Hopis, kernels on a single ear of corn.

The mythic narrative thus relates the dramatic episodes through which the Hopis—part of a primordial population beneath the earth's surface—becomes a community of people. The Hopis cross the threshold from lower to upper worlds; more importantly, they cross the threshold from related but divided fellows, through separated, wandering clans, to reunited, reintegrated, tribal kinsmen. As the Hopi people reunite at Oraibi and the other Hopi towns, they begin the community life that continues to the twentieth century, where it is once again threatened by the invasion of coercive whites.

These migrating clans were ultimately all the same people who separated at the emergence hole. They all came up the same reed from the same underground womb. They are all kinspeople. Yet they persist in squabbling; disunity seems part of their being. Thus the myth recognizes a basic contradiction. The Hopis are all one people, closely related, and yet civil strife exists even in the most cooperative of communities. Therefore the Hopis must be active in promoting their general welfare, their common weal, against the threat of factionalists and invaders. They must accept their life, and protect it, too.

But the myth does more than place the Hopi individuals and clans in a tribal context. In addition, it places the community in the setting of a nurturing, nonhuman environment, to which humans must be conjoined if they are to live. The myth classifies humans as social beings, certainly but their society lives in relation with nature.

The myth opens with an edenic paradise in the earth, an underground womb from where the Hopis emerge. It is more than poetic metaphor for the Hopis to refer to the earth as their mother who gave them birth and who continues to provide them with nurturing gifts. All the races of humanity were housed together in the earth's body, and thus they are co-related by the earth. Moreover, the people grow like plants from the soil, and are thereby equated with crops that they farm. The earth is mother of plants and animals, humans and nonhumans.

When they emerge from the earth, the Hopis are not disassociated irrevocably from their mother. Instead their kivas—called "wombs" by many of the Pueblos—and rituals tend to orient the people to the earth from which all life springs. The place of emergence, the sipapu—often said to be the Grand Canyon—is the gateway to the underworld, the Hopis' ground of being, where communication with the dead, Masau'u, and the other fertilizing agents of the earth is most possible. The fir tree and reed ladders symbolize the communication between the two worlds, an *axis mundi* in the Hopi world view. In addition, each village has at least one representation of the sipapu and the earth womb—the partially underground kivas where the society gathers, climbing down ladders, retracing their steps into the womb—to celebrate the fertility of the earth and kachinas. Furthermore, all sorts of earthly orifices are types of sipapu, earth navels, which constantly remind the Hopis of their earthly origins.

After emerging from the earth in the myth, the Hopis help to put the present world in order, creating the sun and moon and plants, choosing a staple food, finding their home, and establishing a socioreligious organization whose primary goal is to foster fertility of the human and non-human community. Through the course of the myth, the Hopis take shape through their evolving environment, upon which they depend for subsistence.

Throughout the myth, when humans perform evil deeds, nature responds by delivering punishment on the people, either by undercutting the basis of fertility by withholding rain, or by overwhelming the clans with devastating floods. Thus the myth demonstrates human dependence on nature and the consequences of offending the natural world through antisocial behavior.

In the end, the Hopis settle in their chosen land. They set into effective motion their ceremonial system. By so doing, they not only classify themselves historically through their various clan functions, but they also classify their world around them through an intricate, totemic web of associations. Their totemic system provides an emotional attachment to nature, incorporating their clan and ceremonial patterns—that is, their culture—into nature. They project themselves into nature and introject nature to themselves, using the mythic text as primary model. They take the material of the myth—the descriptions of clan origins and associations—and form it into an enduring institutional format, in which seasons and clans and ceremonies, animals and vegetation and colors are all intertwined, crosscutting clan allegiances like a spider's web to touch as many Hopis to one another and to their nonhuman environment as possible. All this the myth sets into motion for the benefit of the Hopi tribal community.

HOPI CEREMONIAL CLOWNS

The Hopi myth of emergence and migration—the myth of Hopi origins—defines humans as social beings, whose existence depends on cooperation in community. In their most sacred rituals, and in their determination to persist as a people, the Hopis send in their clowns. As among other Pueblo groups, and indeed among American Indian tribes in general, clowning is an integrating element in Hopi ceremonialism. Clowns are part of the bulwark of Hopi society, promoting the Hopis' very existence.

The generic Hopi term for clown is *Chukuwimkiya*, which might derive from a term meaning "to spring up from a concealed place" (Fewkes 1892a:156). There are various types of Hopi clowns, identifiable by their costumes and body paintings (see figures 1–4 on page 54).

The *Chuku*—sometimes called "true" Hopi clowns (Fewkes 1892a:6, n.2)—have two distinct appearances. The *Sikya Chuku* paint their body yellow or yellow and red, with red stripes across their eyes and mouth; they wear sheepskin wigs and red-dyed rabbit fur ear pendants. *Nasomta Chuku* are smeared with whitish clay, *chuku* (Parsons 1936:332), and blackened around the eyes and mouth. Their hair is dressed up into bunches on either side of the head and may also be covered with mud.

Figure 1 *Nasomta Chuku* clown with hair tied up into bunches.

Figure 2 *Paiyakyamu* clown with alternating black and white stripes and banded horns (adapted from Roediger 1941, plate 39).

Figure 3 *Tachuktu* or Mudhead clown with cloth mask and black kilt (adapted from Roediger 1941, plate 40).

Figure 4 *Piptuku* clown with white face mask, dressed to parody a Mexican.

A second type of clown, *Paiyakyamu,* has black and white horizontal stripes painted the length of its body, with blackened eyes and mouth. These clowns wear tight-fitted headdresses with tall, similarly banded horns. Like the *Chuku,* they perform naked, except for a breechcloth or blanket. Their organization—long gone now— is said at some mesas to date from the time of emergence.

Tachuktu, or Mudheads, are painted all over with pinkish clay, and wear a sacklike cloth mask with knobs containing seeds and cotton. They wear a black cloth from a woman's discarded dress as a kilt or over one shoulder, woman-style. They also wear a black cloth around their neck, concealing additional packets of seeds.

Piptuku usually wear white face masks and sheepskin wigs, but their costumes include various forms of motley, ragged, and ephemeral bricolages. They burlesque foreigners, wearing Navajo dress, nuns' habits, garish bermuda shorts, or whatever they can lay their hands on.

Some of these clowns wear sexual insignia. Some carry food, such as melons, corn, *piki* bread, and gourds. Most of the clowns are men, although clowning is not restricted to males. Indeed, it is not even restricted to the clowns themselves.

In addition to the *Chukuwimkiya,* there are kachinas and sodalities who perform clowning acts. During the New Fire ceremonial, members of the men's society interrupt a solemn procession to joke and laugh hysterically before continuing their procession in silence. In another important processional at the end of the Bean ceremonial, certain kachinas pretend that their lightweight baskets of young bean plants are heavy, as a form of prayer for a successful harvest. Their staggering under the "weight" of the baskets causes much amusement among the Hopi spectators. Other kachinas are known to jitterbug, or play madcap hopscotch and basketball, as a respite from their more serious duties. Clowning pervades Hopi ritual.

Although there is debate about whether the clowns are truly kachinas, the *Chukuwimkiya* appear when the kachinas are in force, approximately from the winter to summer solstices which divide the Hopi year. They no longer possess the formal organization that they had a century ago. Over the past decades the clowns have lost many of their official functions, and some types are defunct at certain villages. Under white intrusions the clowns have subdued some of their scatological, sexual, and violent antics, but the clowns persist against white intimidation.

Every visitor to Hopiland has a favorite story describing the clowns. Their performances are deservedly celebrated. They arrive at the plaza via rooftops rather than taking normal paths. After jumping up and down on the roofs, they descend the ladders head first, amusing the crowds with their contrary behavior. They frequently do the opposite of whatever the kachinas are doing. While the kachinas dance, the clowns may stand motionless or sit on the ground. If the kachinas dance slowly in single file, the clowns race around them in a wide circle. The clowns often dance backward, stand on their heads, and use inverted speech, saying the opposite of what they mean. They build a "house" in the plaza, using ashes which they refer to as logs and clay.

The clowns act incompetent, frequently trying in vain to imitate the dance steps of the kachinas. They fall down, eat the wrong foods, walk the wrong way; they limp, stagger, and beg for food. Hopi clowns some-times ridicule deformed or crippled persons in the audience, as well as widows and orphans, and they are not above stealing the crutches from a paralyzed spectator.

The clowns also satirize personal and group foibles and eccentricities, like tippling, philandering, and arguing. It is interesting that today the Hopi newspaper at New Oraibi, *Qua'toqti,* uses images of striped clowns to deliver social commentary in their editorial page cartoons. Both in print and in the plaza, the clowns jibe their fellow Hopis.

Foreigners are special targets for the clowns' pranks. The *Chuku-wimkiya* mimic foreign speech and wear foreign clothing in their skits. Curly hair is exotic to the Hopis, and therefore something to satirize. Often the clowns wear woolly wigs, including some black wigs to imitate black Americans. The clowns impersonate white traders and shopkeepers, soldiers, and a variety of government attachees, including teachers, social workers, and administrators of the Bureau of Indian Affairs. The clowns comically mime anthropologists, priests, and hippies, and actively taunt student groups, forcing White youths to race them in rigged contests. A clown at Old Oraibi recently grabbed a student's *Time* magazine and magically pulled a *Penthouse* centerfold from it, lasciviously displaying it to the appreciative Hopi audience. Hopi clowns mock not only whites but also Mexicans, other Pueblo Indians, Navajos, Utes, and Apaches, and even Hopis from other mesas.

Neither the Hopis' own religious leaders, sacred ceremonials, nor the kachinas themselves are immune from the clowns' jokes. Clowns have mocked an old priest who officiated at kachina dances the year before. Clowns with large gourd penises simulate copulation with impersonators of old women on a sacred altar. Clowns also perform comic dramatizations of Hopi myths, and will even grab a kachina and imitate copulation with him. Such are their excesses.

The clowns are sexually excessive. Some wear outlandish false penises and vulvas. They may display their natural genitals in public, snatching each other's loincloths, pulling each other around the plaza by the penis, plastering their genitals with food and medicine. The clowns copulate after mock weddings, often with inappropriate partners, for example, old women with young boys, or with animals. Sex reversals are also common. Transvestitism, as well as bawdy songs, indecent suggestions, and other pornographic excesses occur regularly. The clowns' sexuality is as often anal and oral as it is genital.

Furthermore, the clowns have been known to drink urine and eat excrement and other filth. They douse each other and other Hopis with feces and urine, and at one ceremonial seven clowns drank two to three gallons of urine. This scatology has long disgusted and intrigued prudish whites, and has been moderated lately in public performances.

Clowns' eating habits are excessive as well as scatological. Gluttony is a universal trait among Pueblo clowns, and the Hopi *Chukuwimkiya* in particular. The clowns are supplied with huge quantities of food, which they stash at their plaza "house" and consume ravenously during the ceremonials. They are excessive, too, in their loud, babbling talk and puns, their fast-paced races and games, and in their rowdy actions and exaggerated costumes.

The clowns' violence is equally excessive, reminding us of their similarity and historical relationship to Hopi military orders of the past. They rough up spectators and kachinas and sometimes cut white youths' hair or try to strip them. In former days the clowns would stun and devour a live dog during a plaza ceremonial; this dog represented an "enemy," for example, a Navajo. Today the clowns may attack a watermelon, reveling like warriors in its red pulp as they once did the red blood and entrails of dogs, and in 1987 they slaughtered a pig in the plaza, smearing Anglos with the entrails.

But the clowns get their share of abuse in return. Sometimes they beat each other with yucca whips or sticks. At other times the impersonators of their Indian "enemies" thrash the clowns. Even more commonly, the Hopi kachinas administer brutal beatings to the clowns, pummeling them with whips, sticks, and wooden saws, flogging them unmercifully. At the end of each ceremonial, however, there is reconciliation among all the parties.

In light of all the excesses of clown performance, it is important to note that the clowns also serve nonclowning duties. They often play the role of leaders of the kachina dancers, as the chiefs once led their people from the underworld, and as organizers of the performances; some are known as "fathers of the kachinas." The Mudheads are the first "kachinas" to return to the pueblos at the winter solstice. They likewise precede the kachinas at various ceremonials, and they announce upcoming performances or the arrival of the kachina dancers. Clowns also arrange for a supply of food to be prepared for a ritual, and they are responsible for keeping spectators in line; in addition, they serve as valets to the dancers, freeing tangled hair or adjusting fallen rattles.

They have other solemn and sacred functions. They sprinkle sacred cornmeal on the kachinas, and are blessed with meal in return by the chiefs or other leaders. They make prayer-sticks and deposit them at shrines. They distribute prayer-feathers to the kachinas at the close of ceremonials, and they join the elders in thanking the kachinas for their performance and praying for rains to follow. Often clowns simply sing, dance, and drum in a serious manner. In this sense the clowns are "priests" (Fewkes 1892a:10; Fewkes 1894a:70), ritually important intermediaries to the gods. Their images on sacred objects such as prayer meal bowls and fetish vessels, and on kiva walls in conjunction with corn, clouds, rain and lightning symbols, bear this sacrality out. Even with declining duties, the clowns have a profound effect on their fellow Hopis.

Hopis respond to the clowns' buffoonery with genuine, profound laughter. It is what the clowns want. As they are heading for the plaza to perform, they say, "May I gain at least one smile" (in Sekaquaptewa 1979:7). The laughs do not signify disrespect for the clowns' roles; indeed, the clowns are highly respected for their powers of fertility, life, and death. The clowns are also loved because they are humorous and they amuse people, and because their labors are recognized as a sacrifice for the good of the entire community. They are subject to dietary and sexual restrictions and their acts are physically taxing. They must endure a variety of indignities, some of them painful. These hardships bring blessings to the community.

In particular, the clowns bring rain. The *Chuku* wear their hair in two bunches representing clouds. The *Tachukti* knobs are stuffed with cotton which also symbolizes clouds, as well as snow and rain. The cornsmut used as a black body pigment is a pictorial prayer for rain, since cornsmut thrives on moisture. In general, the clowns are associated with watery places, springs, and wells. They are bringers of rain and fertility. When they jump up and down on the rooftops before entering the plaza, they symbolize rainclouds. All their urine and water play tries to provide rain. Their erotic activities also aid fertility of crops, animals, and humans alike. This illustrates the prayer of all Hopi ceremonialism: to promote rain, fertility, and life.

While the Hopis are grateful for the rain and agricultural bounty which the clowns bring, and despite the love and esteem which they feel for the clowns, there is nonetheless an element of tension in the Hopi reactions to many of the clown antics. Some of this is generated by the caustic commentary and physical violence employed by the clowns in their social control function. Sometimes this tension goes deeper than the obvious fear of being ridiculed in public. For example, clowns' mock arguments remind the Hopis of the dangers of rupture in their society, dangers that are as old as the emergence of Hopi society in mythic times. In many ways the clowns are disquieting because they are the antithesis of the ideal Hopi. They are disagreeable, uncooperative, and unpredictable. They are tricksters in the public plaza. They are *kahopi*, or un-Hopi. The Hopis think of themselves as members of a group, as we have seen—kernels on an ear of corn, they say—and the clowns are unbridled individualists and eccentrics, akin to witches. And even though the clowns are only actors, and even though their eccentricities are laughable, they are also perceived as potential dangers to the established Hopi way.

The *Chukuwimkiya* are somewhat like the dead, whom the Hopis regard with ambivalence. It is said that the striped clown bodies represent the bones of the dead, and their cloud symbolism refers to the ancestors, who are fertilizing clouds. The clowns are also identified with Masau'u, the god of death, metamorphosis, tricks, opposites, war and blood, as well as the deity who beckoned the Hopi ancestors from the underworld in the emergence myth. Like the dead and like Masau'u, the clowns are fertilizing agents, germinators, sources of existence, yet they are the opposite of living Hopi ways, of normal routine. And so the clowns, like the dead, are helpful and frightful, both.

In their priestly, joking, fertilizing, military, pornographic, scatological, and excessive connections, the clowns touch base with all extensions of the Hopi universe, including death and the dead. Each clown performance is a polysemous act that touches the bases of Hopi existence in all its contrariness and variety.

It is the polysemous nature of the clowns—like that of mythology—that makes them so fascinating and so difficult to interpret simply. They express so many meanings that almost anything we can say about them can be negated with a contrary, equally valid contention. Their impact has a trickish fullness that is as broad as their excesses.

Even the laughter that greets them is more than a simple indication of humor. People laugh in a variety of situations: when they succeed, fail, or feel threatened; out of joy, embarrassment, and nervousness; at the unexpected and the familiar. So the laughter of the Hopis points to a many-faceted response to a many-faceted phenomenon. Hopis are laughing at the forbidden, the indecent, the incongruous, and the inappropriate, at false pretenses, nonsense, paradox, surprise, and breaches of the usual order. Indeed, the closer we look at the clowns and the laughter they produce, the more we can tell about the Hopis, their religion and life, and about laughter itself. As we shall soon discuss, their laughter is both biological—a physical response to a situation which implies satisfaction with the status quo—and cultural, as a patterned Hopi response to things found culturally risible.

We have described how the Hopi people became manifest as a people, how they sprang up from the earth and emerged into the world that has been theirs for centuries. The clowns, we wish to show, symbolize all of Hopi existence—they make manifest the entirety of that existence—when they "spring up from a concealed place" into the Hopi plaza. The *Chukuwimkiya* elicit the fullness of Hopi laughter and thereby integrate the fullness of Hopi existence. We come to this conclusion whether we look at Hopi clowning from psychological, religious, cognitive, or anthropological viewpoints.

The *Chukuwimkiya* spring up from the subconscious and integrate Hopi personality, by bringing to a conscious level renegade, troublesome, subliminal elements. The Hopis witness these elements, recognize them, and assimilate them into their consciousness. Thus the clowns bring about a more complete Hopi self, just as dreams help integrate portions of the subliminal into the whole person.

In this regard the clowns are not heroes, but underside figures; not egos, but a collective id. Because the clowns reveal subliminal human nature, they are dangerous and worrisome. Their shit and sex, violence and transformations are disturbing. On the other hand, they offer a release from this ambiguous aspect of human personality by exposing it in a controlled, ritual setting.

The clowns not only manifest the wellsprings of the Hopi self but also put the Hopis in touch with their primordial, earthy origins. The Hopi clowns represent primeval, unformed matter, a throwback to a time when humans had not fully emerged from nature. Covered from head to toe in clay, Hopi clowns dramatically illustrate the bridging of humans and the earth. They reunite the Hopis with their ground of being, the earth from which they emerged in mythic times, and also to their animal nature.

If Hopi clowns may be seen as precultural in terms of mythic age, they may also be seen as precultural in their infantility. Clowns are like unsocialized children. They frisk, run, cavort, and play. They are socially inept. Their gluttony is like the unchecked appetite of small children at meals, or in-between meals. Their nakedness also evokes the child in Hopi society. Even their mockery of unfortunates may be likened to the brand of cruelty often practiced by children. Their sexuality, too, is infantile: uncontrolled, omni-directional, polymorphously perverse, and simulated. They are simultaneously anal, oral, and genital. They will hump or suck a burro, an old woman, a little boy, a transvestite, a kachina, an aunt, or a spectator, whoever is available for their simulated gratification. Theirs is sexuality without sex, eroticism without adult libido.

Because they are infantile, they are free from restrictions which adults must honor. Hopi society is permissive to them and vicariously shares the freedom from restraint and responsibility which the clowns enjoy. On the other hand, clowns suffer punishment for their misbehavior, accepting it without resistance like children who know the proper authority. They threaten but they do not overthrow. They test the limits of their infantile freedom, but they do not destroy the rules. Rather, they integrate ruled and unruled realms, adult and childish prerogatives.

In addition to integrating Hopi libidinous, archaic, and infantile impulses, the clowns also serve Hopi religion. First, they make the religion digestible, working like catalysts to break down difficult abstractions and mysteries. They offer comic relief during awesome rituals, burlesquing the gods and thus bringing the mighty ones down to earthly proportions. Grabbing them down by the throat, they make the kachina-divinities more accessible to their human relatives.

Even though the onlookers know what to expect from the *Chukuwimkiya*, the jokers always surprise them. This element of surprise acts as an intensifier—in this case, to the ceremonial emotion—thus heightening the whole of the religious experience. They do not relax their audience; they put the Hopis on alert. They open them up for revelation. They heighten the sublime by comparison with the ridiculous, just as the audience is elevated in status by contrast with the fools before them.

Almost by accident, almost by design, the clowns reveal to the Hopis crucial incongruities which they then integrate. As in William James's definition of religion, they offer a feeling of disquiet, followed by its resolution (James 1958:383). Through the craziness of their performances they reveal.

Their revelations are cognitive, surely. They reveal contradictions between the subliminal and the conscious, the ideal and the real, the adult and the infantile, between rules and disorder. They bring together within their costumes and actions the contrasting elements of their world. Like jokes, they bind together incongruous elements, showing both their similarities and dissimilarities. Through the clowns, oppositions like religion and humor, phallicism and infantility, gods and excrement, are attracted and connected. The clowns marry elements which are normally considered mutually exclusive. Their motley costumes, their muddy lumpishness, and their stripes highlight the contradictory, ambiguous, polysemous nature of the world from which they spring. They are walking contradictions, living examples of interbanded dualisms, brought together in the plaza for all the Hopis to see. They contradict themselves—by being serious and ridiculous simultaneously—as well as the mundane world around them, and their incongruity serves to integrate Hopi religious elements, Hopi culture, and Hopi personality, as well as Hopi logic.

Clowns will not be tied down to one category. They are liminal as well as subliminal. They perform in the plaza crossroads and at the village border, often at the changing of seasons. They move between and around the dancers, and their clowning takes place during intermissions of kachina dancing. One often finds them between buildings, amidst the lines of cultural texture and architecture. As liminal figures they join the categories that they cross: nature and culture, fertility and death, funny and frightening, gods and men. They serve to conjoin the many apparent dichotomies of life. The *Chukuwimkiya* give formlessness to structure, parody to piety, and thus they rebalance the Hopi humors, as well as the bodies religious and politic, in ritual settings of intense seriousness. Hopi clowns act as physicians, therapists for personality, ritual, and society, integrating diverse elements through their ribaldry.

On an anthropological level, the *Chukuwimkiya* attack the restrictions and repressions of ordinary society. They personify vitality attacking rigidity. They are the epitome of freedom in a community-minded tribal society, calling into question cultural categories. They are ids in a community of strong superegos. But they are obviously no more destroyers of traditions, leaders of revolt against the order of society and the world, than the Hopis who tell the story of emergence.

They defy order, but to make the Hopis laugh the clowns must produce a properly improper inversion. Their nonsense must make cultural sense to the Hopis. As performers, clowns are not outside the cultural system, because they are playing a role designated to them. They question; they attack order; they offer freedom, but only within the ritual event. Like folkloric tricksters, they are cultural creations who help regulate symbolic representations of deviancy and make themselves laughable and safe. They offer vicarious revolt, subverting the probability of real ones. They offer catharsis for complaint and actually reinforce Hopi commitment to normal behavior by pointing out what is wrong. The *Chukuwimkiya* probe and improve the rules of Hopi society.

The clowns are not only radicals who question the order of things, who cross every conceivable Hopi boundary, but they are also conservatives who question the ability to ask a sensible question of the establishments of tribal life. They are cynics and skeptics alike, who reduce to an absurd level the claims against society, thus exposing the foolishness of innovation and revolt. They do not offer radical syllogisms, but rather revelatory "sillygisms" that muddy up all logic.

Not only are the clowns ultimately harmless because the threats they pose can be laughed off, but they are frequently punished for their misdeeds. The audience that laughed uproariously at their misbehavior laughs again at their chastisement. The *Chukuwimkiya* are both escape and scapegoat. They offer relief from order, then relief from freedom, thereby integrating the two: order and freedom.

In the process they make the Hopis laugh. At their performances the Hopi audience—the descendants of the people who once emerged from beneath the ground and wandered over the body of the earth in search of themselves as a people—laughs together like members of a societal chorale. That harmonic laughter is a praise song to everything they know, in all its contrariness. Their laughter points to and participates in a shared world view, a consensus, a mutal acceptance of Hopi life. Their laughter is a socially (as well as psychologically, religiously, and cognitively) integrating phenomenon; it strengthens their bonds on every level of existence. They share their laughter and criticism like allies sharing tobacco, like intimate companions sharing a meal.

What is this laughter that they share, which the clowns evoke? It is a physiological and cultural act which helps create, sustain, and express a state of satisfaction. On a biological level, respiration, circulation, and blood pressure increase during laughter, producing a sort of euphoria, an interruption of breathing which confers a soaring sense of breadth, where no reform is necessary. Tribally, the Hopis' clowns produce integrative laughter which symbolizes contentment with their way of life, which they have defended against white encroachments. By joining together the manifest and unmanifest into one recreated fullness, the clowns foster a tribal state of satisfaction. Even though their myths remind them that total integration and contentment is impossible, their clowning recreation in the plaza helps re-create and celebrate the Hopi existence defined in their mythology and experienced in their everyday lives.

3

The Ojibwa Creation Myth

The Ojibwa Creation myth presents the major actions of Nanabozho, culture-hero and trickster, from his birth through his creation of a new world following a deluge. The myth is familiar to students of American Indian folklore and religion. It traditionally provided the Ojibwas—Subarctic hunters of the Great Lakes region—with a means of knowing what the universe looked like, how it came to be that way, what the vital principles of life were, what hierarchy there was for the world's living beings, what to expect from living beings, how to test reality, and how societal customs came into being. For the religious specialists in Ojibwa society, members of the Midé Society, the myth formed the base on which they placed their esoteric addenda. In short, the myth helped construct the Ojibwa world view.

For those outside the Ojibwa society who wish to understand the traditional Ojibwas, the myth provides stunning insights and valuable verifications. It is surprising, therefore, that only a few modern scholars have attempted analyses of the myth. One saw it as a lunar-matriarchal-agricultural expression (Schmidt 1948); another used it to describe Ojibwa personality (Barnouw 1955); a third made a cursory look at Ojibwa motivation through the myth (Parker 1962); a fourth used the myth in evaluating a theory on taboo (Makarius 1973). Despite these attempts at unraveling, and despite the wealth of available material, both published and unpublished, the myth remains an enigma.

In this study we are analyzing the structure and content of the myth in order to understand its message and meaning. We are examining closely forty-eight versions of the myth from seventeen different sources (see table 1 at the end of this chapter). In addition, we have consulted versions of the myth contained in over two dozen sources, ranging from Schoolcraft 1839 to Leekley 1965, and including manuscripts as well as published texts.

The Ojibwas spent their winters in family units, hunting for food. During this season, certain old persons in each family unit would recount

This chapter has been written with John F. Fisher.

the legends of the tribe. One Ojibwa attested to the large number of legends; he stated: "I have known some Indians who would commence to narrate legends and stories in the month of October and not end until quite late in the spring, sometimes not till quite late in the month of May, and on every evening of this long term tell a new story" (Copway 1858:98).

This body of approximately two hundred legends was divided by the Ojibwas into two basic categories: (1) stories relating to human beings, connoting "news" or "tidings," called *tabatcamowin* or *tibadjimowin;* and (2) myths, tales about the manitos—the deities—and past living humans, called *atisokanak* or *atisokan* (Hallowell 1960:28; Chamberlain 1906:346–47; Redsky 1972:66). The Ojibwas considered both the tidings and the myths to be true; they had no category of fiction.

The myths could be told only in the winter. When asked why, Ojibwas responded that legend telling was a winter occupation because of economy, environment, or entertainment, but "the reason that seemed uppermost in the mind of the old Ojibwa was the strong, traditional belief that if stories were told in the summer, the animal manitos ... would then hear themselves spoken of. Frogs, toads, and snakes were feared particularly" (Coleman, Frogner, Eich 1962:5).

Aiding the storytellers were pictographs, employing natural and invented symbols, which recalled to the storyteller's mind the essential events in the tales. These mnemonic writings were similar to those used in the Midé Society, only these could be understood by all, whereas the Midé writings were esoteric; both were simply memory devices, not means of communicating entirely new information, except the most rudimentary. A series of pictographs describing the Creation myth is in Kohl (1860:387–91).

The tales were similar in many of their motifs, themes, and underlying concepts to the tales of other American Indians, as the folklore of native North Americans was remarkably constant from area to area. Furthermore, within the Northeast-Woodland Algonkian culture area the Ojibwa folklore had more similarities with other peoples' folklore than did that of any other Algonkian tribe. The Ojibwa language was spoken over a huge area and understood beyond that, so that Ojibwa oral traditions were widespread.

On the other hand, there were distinctive Ojibwa traits (shared by Ojibwas, Chippewas, and Saulteaux, the three subdivisions of Ojibwas proper; thus it is correct to view the three as one people with local differences rather than as three similar but basically distinct peoples), which were not shared by neighbors. For example, Gluskabe of the Eastern Algonkians was similar to Nanabozho of the Ojibwas but their relationships with their wolf brothers were completely different, and Gluskabe had few of the "trickster" traits which were basic to Nanabozho. Most important, the legends carried certain meanings to the Ojibwas. Whether or not the same legends had the same meanings to other tribes is an interesting topic, but one that does not concern us here. We are interested in what the Ojibwa myth told the Ojibwas, and what it tells us about the Ojibwas.

Simply understanding the Ojibwa Creation myth in the Ojibwa cultural context is a difficult enough task because even within that context there was (and under Christian missionary influence, there is even more) a wide variance of opinion about the central character, Nanabozho. He was known as a model, an ideal for customs, a true culture-hero, yet he was also known as a buffoon, a sorcerer, a breaker of laws. The Ojibwas viewed him as human, as a manito, a hare, a wolf; some christianized Ojibwas today think of him as the devil. He was known to take on many forms and many personalities within a single myth. In short, he was a composite figure with contradictory and complex characteristics, a transformer.

The many versions of the collected myths exhibited wide variations. No two myths were exactly alike. Some devoted much time to Nanabozho's adventures while traveling around the earth; others omitted these aspects completely and told only of the deluge and recreation of the earth. Some described Nanabozho's travels with the wolves or his battles with his brothers at great length; others summarized these events in a sentence or two. This variability was due to many factors.

Ojibwa society tended toward atomism; each family spent much of the year separated from other families, giving it an opportunity to diverge from the mainstream. Versions of myths told by members of different families, especially in different communities, contained many contradictory elements. This societal atomism was even more accentuated because individual Ojibwas drew major inspiration from individual visions, creating an even greater chance for divergence. One folklorist heard six versions of the deluge narrative in 1946 on the Upper Peninsula of Michigan; all varied from each other, including two told by brothers (Dorson 1952:48).

In addition, in the historical period the members of the Midé Society possessed esoteric knowledge, much of which centered on Nanabozho and the giving of Midéwiwin to the Ojibwas. In versions of the Creation myth told by Midés there was a greater emphasis given to Nanabozho's actions after the flood than to his early life, and there were elements present which were not usually told or known by Ojibwa lay persons.

Furthermore, as oral tradition these myths were subject to the variations due to the aesthetic preferences of the storyteller and the situation in which the stories were told and recorded. If a storyteller had a willing or receptive audience, he or she might extend the myth, adding details, artistic flourishes, and illustrative addenda. Myths told to ethnologists and other strangers to the storyteller most likely differed from those told to family members sitting around the winter campfire. It seems unlikely that Dorson collected a complete myth when he approached an Ojibwa man tinkering with his car in the rain (Dorson 1952:19). The deluge narrative told by an Ojibwa at a mission fund-raising garden party in England (Wilson 1886:107–8) or tales recorded through bribes of hats, groceries, clothes, rides, and other presents (Walker 1959:203–4) probably differed from the traditional legends. Many collectors of myths were interested in different aspects of the myth or in particular elements. Many wanted only to hear about the deluge because it appeared to parallel the biblical deluge myth. The myth recorded would vary according to the questions asked by the collector.

Moreover, we must be aware that there were foreign elements in the Ojibwa legends; there were Eastern Siouan and Iroquoian influences, and in historical times the Ojibwas used the Creation myth to justify their traditional way of viewing the world and their traditional religious behavior, as an argument against Christian critics. As Ojibwas became defensive about their traditions, they might alter them or refuse to tell them in full. Finally, as their culture disintegrated, the Ojibwa storytellers no longer passed down the entire corpus of myths. By the twentieth century many storytellers no longer knew all the episodes of this very lengthy myth; others added Christian elements.

As a result, we must be wary of additions through time as well as divergences due to culture atomism, geographical diffusion, and individual preference. Despite these difficulties, however, we believe that most versions shared an underlying unity which makes it possible to understand what was essential to the Creation myth.

STRUCTURAL RECAPITULATION

In this section we will attempt to analyze the Ojibwa Creation myth utilizing a structural method. We cannot discuss at length the various methodological problems involved in this type of analysis; however, we must clarify some of our assumptions. Although we recognize Claude Lévi-Strauss as a pioneer in this area of myth studies, we cannot accept wholeheartedly his assumptions or methodology. The reader should not consider the present study a "Lévi-Straussian" analysis; it is a structural analysis which takes into account the various component elements in the myths and their relationships to each other. We are attempting to discover the overall message which the myths imparted to their traditional listeners in order to understand the myth and the Ojibwa people themselves.

Given the wide variance in the recorded myths, we might have conducted our analysis in several ways. We might have taken the most complete version and used it as a standard by which all the others could be evaluated. We could have tried to reconstruct the "original" myth from all the available components. Instead we chose to gather all the versions available from printed sources and manuscripts, breaking them down into component parts in order to see what elements stood out as the most logical (from an Ojibwa point of view) and interesting (from our point of view).

Because of the length of many of the myths, we limited our investigation primarily to eight episodes, the core of the myth: A. the birth of Nanabozho; B. the theft of fire; C. Nanabozho and his brothers; D. Nanabozho and the wolves; E. the death of Nanabozho's hunting companion; F. the shooting of the underwater manitos by Nanabozho involving the stump episode; G. the killing of these manitos involving the toad woman episode; H. the deluge, earth divers and recreation of the earth.

We shall examine each of these episodes, giving an outline of the events and an interpretation. Then we shall look at the combined effect of these episodes and try to interpret the overall message of the structure of the myth and how it offers insights into Ojibwa culture.

A. Birth of Nanabozho

In the majority of versions which contained this episode (see table 2 at the end of this chapter) Nanabozho's mother was living with her mother; in V6 she was living with her parents and in V35 she lived with her father. The most consistent element seems to be that she was a virgin or unmarried woman (V43). Where there was only a vague reference to Nanabozho's early life as in V12, the myth may have stated that his parents were killed by some monster; however, the more detailed versions stated that his mother was an unattached maiden.

She was cautioned by her mother not to sit facing a certain direction, for example, west, south, or any of the four cardinal points (V23). She did not follow her mother's advice and became impregnated by the wind in most cases (V1, 7, 14, 16, 17, 26, 46). She then gave birth to several beings, the first of which was invariably Nanabozho (in V3a and V19 Nanabozho had an older brother). In most cases the mother died in childbirth. Her death was later attributed to someone (usually the flint brother) upon whom Nanabozho later sought revenge. In some of the more sparse versions the one responsible for the death of Nanabozho's mother was not his brother but the underwater manito. In the course of the myth Nanabozho had several enemies whom he held responsible for the death of a relative. He always sought revenge upon these enemies and many of the stories parallel one another in specific ways. One interesting exception is V13 in which Nanabozho's mother was stolen from her husband by an underwater manito and placed in a cave. The underwater manito ate Nanabozho because he was afraid Nanabozho would kill him but Nanabozho eventually did kill him and rescued his mother. This version took elements from the myth in which Nanabozho was swallowed by a fish or whale and managed to kill him from inside (cf. V16, 23).

The most stable components of this episode were an initial situation (IS) in which a marriageable female was given advice by her mother. She disobeyed this advice and as a result became pregnant with supernatural beings and died. A structural diagram for this episode looks like this:

IS	Advice	Action	Result
unwed	dangerous	doesn't heed	birth (+)
female	direction	advice	death (−)
(+ −)	(+)	(−)	

B. Theft of Fire

This somewhat independent episode appears in only three of the versions surveyed (V1, 15, 23). It related how Nanabozho in the form of a rabbit stole fire from neighboring peoples and gave it to his grandmother with whom he lived after his mother's death. The concept of Nanabozho as a culture-hero who gave various aspects of culture to the people first comes to the fore in this episode. He and his grandmother lived alone; he decided they should have fire and against his grandmother's wishes traveled to another place where people had fire. He stole the fire and brought it back. It is interesting to note here that the myth began with a negative situation, that is, the lack of fire. Nanabozho proceeded to obtain this fire. His grandmother warned him but he went ahead with his plan and brought mankind a positive element. In episode A we noticed that the mother's advice to her daughter was not heeded and a positive situation resulted, the birth of Nanabozho (although the mother's death resulted too). In this episode the advice was again unheeded and the result was positive. From this we can observe that the real progress in humanity's condition, according to the Ojibwa world view, was brought about by broken taboos and disregard of respected advice.

Note, however, that from the point of view of the people from whom fire was stolen, the situation was entirely in reverse. When Nanabozho reached them, the maiden took him close to the fire against the wishes of her father who warned that even a tiny rabbit might be a manito and should be treated cautiously. The diagram of this episode shows the opposite pattern clearly:

IS	Advice	Action	Result
no	danger (V1);	N. seeks	N. gets
fire	fire doesn't	fire	fire
(−)	exist (V23)	(+)	(+)
	(−)		
fire	danger from	daughter	N. gets
(+)	rabbit	doesn't heed	fire
	(+)	advice (−)	(−)

By ignoring his grandmother's warning, Nanabozho obtained fire; by ignoring her father's warning, the daughter was responsible for Nanabozho's theft.

C. Nanabozho and His Brothers

In this episode Nanabozho sought revenge for the death of his mother. While living with his grandmother he wanted to know about his family. He asked if he had a mother, and when told of the account of his birth, he decided to seek vengeance upon those responsible. In several versions (V1, 3, 17, 23, 37, 38, 46) he held his flint brother responsible; in other versions (V13, 22, 26) a sea manito or fish killed the mother. In any event, Nanabozho—again against the wishes of his grandmother—went off to kill the monster. In many of the versions the monster lived on an island surrounded by obstacles such as pitch on the water, mountains, or various sentry animals. In V1 Nanabozho had two brothers; first, he did battle with a brother who apparently could not be killed. He was then told by a weasel that he must shoot at the antagonist's hair-knot in order to kill him. Nanabozho did this and as a result all people were to die. The brother then departed to become the leader of the land of the dead. In order to justify the action, Nanabozho gave a speech on the necessity of death. He then battled with his flint brother, and again could not kill him. Informed by a woodpecker that this brother's death spot was also his hair-knot, Nanabozho killed him. He then beheaded the brother and took the head to a nearby village where he instructed the people on the proper rituals to perform after an enemy is killed. When he returned home, his grandmother scolded him for originating war and strife.

In several versions a bird told Nanabozho how to kill his brother (V1, 12, 22, 31) and in V3a it was a "voice from above." V1 and V16 had the information coming from a weasel and in the rest of the versions Nanabozho alone killed the monster. The idea of aid from above becomes more important to V43, episode F, in which Nanabozho initiated a battle between the thunderbirds and the underwater manitos who killed his hunting companion. In many ways the killing of Nanabozho's hunting companion paralleled the killing of his mother. In both cases he sought revenge upon dangerous creatures and did so with the help of animals, mostly birds.

Some variations take place in V7 in which Nanabozho killed his flint brother because he limited Nanabozho's mobility. Later, in the same myth, Nanabozho killed his other brother for the same reason. In the end, Nanabozho was free to roam all over the earth "wherever he wanted to go." In V20 the evil being was not his brother and he did not kill Nanabozho's mother, but the actions are strikingly similar. Nanabozho's grandmother dreamed that he should kill a strong man who lived on an island across the great sea. After a struggle the strong man gave up and revealed that he was a corn man. He then gave Nanabozho some of his body and taught him how to plant corn. In V23 there are three parallel episodes in which Nanabozho killed two brothers and a great whale. Next he killed the first brother and the whale out of revenge for the death of his mother and grandfather respectively; however, he killed the second brother for power rather than for revenge. After killing the brother Nanabozho declared that now no one could kill him, for there was no one with more supernatural power than he. No revenge motive for the killings existed in V18 or V19; rather, Nanabozho and the brothers were always fighting (V18), or Nanabozho wanted to kill his older brother (V19). The diagram of this episode shows once again the idea of advice, given not only by the grandmother but also by animals. The revenge motive serves to extend the diagram, which usually ends on a positive note except for the origination of death and war.

IS	Advice	Action	Journey	Battle	Result
revenge (+ −)	grandmother warns (+) danger (−)	prep. for war on grandmother's advice (+)	over water (−)	N. and flint (−)	
	bird (above) (+)	N. knows death spot (+)			N. kills flint (+) war (−) death (−)

D. Nanabozho and the Wolves

In this episode we find that Nanabozho desired to travel with a pack of wolves. He wanted to join them because of the onset of winter; V44, 45, 47 state this explicitly, while V3, 24 state that he met the wolves on an ice-covered lake. In V1, 2, 3 the wolves said they were going to find some food hidden in the summer. They usually did not want Nanabozho to join them, but he persuaded them and they began to travel together. In the course of their travels Nanabozho and the wolves had several misunderstandings which eventually led to the wolves' expelling Nanabozho; however, they gave him one wolf to be his hunting companion for the winter.

As they traveled, Nanabozho and the chief wolf saw some feces; the chief wolf told Nanabozho to pick it up but he refused. The chief wolf then picked it up and it became a blanket (V1, 2) or a wolf skin (V24). They saw stuck in a tree a tooth that became an arrow (V1, 2, 3, 7). When they camped for the night the wolves wanted to camp in what Nanabozho thought were cold, unsuitable campsites (V1, 2, 21, 32). During the night Nanabozho became cold and the wolves covered him with their tails (V1, 2, 3, 21, 32, 44); however, he then became too hot and cursed them for putting their tails over him. The final misunderstanding occurred when one of the wolves decided to make grease from the bones of the animals they killed. The wolf told Nanabozho and the others not to look while the process took place; however, Nanabozho looked and as a result was struck by a bone. Nanabozho then decided to try making grease and deliberately hit the wolf whose bone had magically hit him before. In V1, 3, 26 Nanabozho killed the wolf but then brought him back to life. A curious episode occurs in V26 in which Nanabozho joined a group of feathers. At night they twisted themselves and prohibited Nanabozho from looking; he did and was hit. He then deliberately hit one of the feathers, killing it, but later brought it back to life and took it for his son. Our diagram shows that the episode begins with a somewhat negative situation, that is, Nanabozho alone at the onset of winter. He then tries the possibility of joining with wolves; however, this proves unsuccessful so he tries living with only one wolf:

IS	Advice	Action	Journey	(Battle) Problems	Result
N. alone in winter (−)		N. joins wolves (+ −)	on land (+)		
	chief wolf offers advice (+)	N. doesn't understand (−)		N. gets angry kills wolf (−)	N. leaves wolves (−) takes one wolf as companion (+)

E. Death of Nanabozho's Hunting Companion

Most of the versions relate that Nanabozho's hunting companion was a wolf (a fox in V28); however, V34 says that it was his grandson and V8 says it was his son. In several versions the companion was Nanabozho's brother who changed into a wolf to hunt. In almost all cases the companion was a great hunter who provided all the food for the pair. V10 has Nanabozho living with Wissekedjak, who was the Cree and Northern Saulteaux "equivalent" of Nanabozho. In this particular version Nanabozho was killed by the underwater manitos and Wissekedjak sought revenge upon them.

Structurally this episode parallels episode A in several ways. First, we observe Nanabozho living alone with the wolf; then Nanabozho had a dream or simply advised the wolf to beware of streams. In some versions (V1, 2, 3, 23, 32) Nanabozho told the wolf to throw a small stick across any stream or dry bed he might want to jump over. The wolf did this for a while, then forgot once and was carried away by a river which appeared magically. This seems confusing until we look at some other versions. In V12 Nanabozho told the wolf to cut down a tree and use it as a bridge to cross the stream. This seems more sensible, but still very impractical for a hunter. V35 and V47 seem to hold the answer: they say that the wolf fell through the ice covering a river or lake. This would account for the ringing in the wolf's ears in V1 and V2; it was the sound of the ice breaking. It would then seem logical for Nanabozho to tell his wolf to throw a stick where it looked as if a river might be, that is, a dry bed, or if he could tell it was a stream, he could throw a stick out to see if the ice would hold his weight before crossing. If we remember that this part of the myth supposedly took place during the winter or the onset of spring, then the advice makes more sense. In any event, the wolf did not obey the advice and as a result drowned in the water.

A note to this episode concerns the idea of protecting one's hunting grounds. Each time the wolf was killed he was about to kill some game, a moose or deer, near the water. It could be that the underwater manitos did not like the wolf hunting in or near their "territory" and thus killed him. Whether or not the prehistorical Ojibwas had hunting territories, by the time the myths were collected, "the law was that anyone found hunting and killing game in a territory belonging to another tribe was to forfeit his life" (Blackwood 1929:322–23). This might be stretching the point a bit, but during winter when survival was difficult, one had to be careful not to endanger someone else's life by wasteful or improper hunting practices.

By placing this episode in our diagram we can see how it relates to the rest of the myth, and, in particular, episode A. This time the advice was given by Nanabozho to his companion. When the wolf did not listen to the advice, he lost his life, just as the maiden, Nanabozho's mother, lost her life when she disobeyed her mother's advice.

IS	Advice	Action	Journey	Battle	Result
N. and wolf $(+ \ -)$	beware of ice (water) $(+)$	doesn't heed N.'s advice $(-)$	land $(+)$ water $(-)$	wolf falls in water $(-)$	death of wolf $(-)$

From the viewpoint of the underwater manitos the end result of this episode was positive because the wolf, who was killing game, died. In this connection, V33 becomes interesting in that the animals held a council in order to kill the wolf because he was such a good hunter that he was killing them all. We can see here the aid given Nanabozho previously by animals, which was always positive, became inverted. An animal now lured the wolf to his death rather than saving Nanabozho's life. This seems to indicate that some animals could be trusted for advice (especially birds), while others could not always be trusted—especially those hunted for food.

F. Nanabozho's Shooting of the Underwater Manito(s)—Stump Episode

After the death of his companion, Nanabozho sought revenge as he did after the death of his mother. In this episode he transformed himself into a stump in order to kill the manitos; however, he usually did not succeed in killing them. Rather, he wounded them, leaving the actual killing to episode G.

Some of the versions told of a flood after Nanabozho wounded the manitos, which receded in a very short time (V1, 2, 3, 12, 21, 22, 43). Other versions move from this episode directly to the deluge, indicating that the manitos had been killed (V10, 11, 27, 32, 34, 37). The remaining versions containing this episode omit the flood at this time and go directly to episode G or possibly interject some other episodes before proceeding with episode G. The advice given Nanabozho in this episode always came from birds. The kingfisher usually gave the advice, but in V10 the advice came from a crane, while in V3 the advice came from both a kingfisher and a loon. Advice of any kind was absent in V6, 7, 11, 18, 30, 37, 44, 45, and 47. In V43 birds did not give Nanabozho advice, but the thunderbirds did play a ball game with the manitos in order to distract them while Nanabozho wounded the chief manitos. The most constant element of this episode was Nanabozho's transformation into a stump in order to shoot the manitos. This element is absent in only two of the versions: V11, which is very brief, and V34, in which Nanabozho snuck up on the sleeping manitos and killed them with a club.

In two versions (V6, 32) Nanabozho did not transform himself into a stump, but made a stump from bark (V6) or hid in an existing stump (V32). By hiding in an existing stump, Nanabozho did not create a suspicious situation as he did in the rest of the versions. The manitos, especially the chiefs, suspected some foul play when they spied the stump which had not previously existed. They usually sent animals over to the stump to test it. A snake coiled around the stump trying to crush it, and a bear clawed at the stump in order to see if it might be Nanabozho. They were always convinced of the authenticity of the stump after these tests and fell asleep thinking they were safe.

The bird had advised Nanabozho not to shoot the manitos in their bodies, rather to shoot their shadows; however, in several versions he insisted on shooting them in the body first. When nothing happened, he then remembered that he should shoot their shadows. Thus wounded, the manitos slipped back into the safety of the water.

From the diagram we can see the parallels with episode B. The motivation for both episodes was revenge for the death of a "relative." In both episodes Nanabozho was given advice regarding his "relative's" killer and how best to seek revenge. The only major difference lies in the battle; in episode B Nanabozho killed the brother or monster, but in this episode he only wounded the underwater manitos. Nevertheless, Nanabozho always succeeded in killing the manitos eventually, so that the death of his "relative" was avenged.

IS	Advice	Action	Journey	Battle	Result
revenge (+ −)			near water (+ −)		
	bird tells who killed wolf and how to shoot shadow (+)	N. turns into stump (+)			
	manito(s) suspect stump (−)	animals test stump (+)		N. shoots sleeping manito(s) (+)	partial revenge (+ −) flood (−)

G. Nanabozho's Killing of the Underwater Manito(s)—Toad Woman Episode

After wounding the underwater manito(s), Nanabozho met an old woman in the woods. She usually carried a load of basswood on her back and sang medicine songs. In most of the versions the old woman was a toad; she was simply an old woman in V9, 24, 30, 36, 43, 44, 45; in V7 and V32 she was a relative of the manitos (a mother or wife). From her Nanabozho learned that he had only wounded the manito(s), and that she was on her way to cure them. He then learned her medicine songs and sometimes even the curing ritual. After gaining that information he killed her, skinned her and put on her skin as a disguise in order to penetrate the camp of the manitos. The toad woman played an important part in this episode; she allowed Nanabozho to enter the manito camp in such a way that he could finish the killing successfully. In V33 Nanabozho did not don the toad's skin (a male in this case); rather, he transformed himself into a toad and dove down into the lake to the manito camp. In V36 Nanabozho killed an old woman and then was guided by a frog to the manito who lived in the water. After reaching the camp of the manito, Nanabozho pretended to cure him; however, he actually killed him, causing the deluge.

By placing the episode in the diagram we can see that the motivation for this action was again revenge. Nanabozho received crucial, unwitting, advice from the toad woman. He then traveled in the water to the manito camp where he killed the one(s) responsible for the death of his wolf companion.

IS	Advice	Action	Journey	Battle	Result
revenge	N. learns	disguise as	in water	N. kills	revenge (+)
(+ −)	songs from	toad	to enemy	manito(s)	death of manito (+)
	toad (+)	(+)	camp (−)	(+)	(deluge) (−)

H. Deluge, Earth Divers, Creation of New Earth

Because of the parallel with the biblical deluge, this episode of the myth has been collected in more variants than any other episode. The earth diver sequence is possibly the most widely found American Indian mythological motif, and is found on other continents as well. The entire complex is found in thirty-one of the forty-eight versions surveyed in this part of the analysis.

In this episode Nanabozho did not actually battle with a manito but he had to prevail over the flood caused by the death of the underwater manito(s). Most of the versions tell of Nanabozho's either having a raft ready on the advice of the kingfisher in episode F, or making a raft before the water reached the tops of the trees. In V25 and V43 he did not have a raft; instead he simply struggled in the water, or the water reached up to his mouth. In several versions (V7, 36, 44, 45) Nanabozho raced to the top of a mountain or high hill to escape the water. When the deluge reached him, he climbed a tall tree and then commanded it to stretch itself as the water got higher. Finally, the water stopped and Nanabozho was on top of the now-extended tree with water up to his head.

At this point Nanabozho decided to create a new earth, so he told several animals—the beaver, loon, otter, and muskrat—who were on the raft or swimming nearby to dive into the water for a piece of the old earth. The muskrat always succeeded while the others failed. Nanabozho then proceeded to create a new earth from the small pieces collected by the muskrat. He usually blew on the dirt, causing it to expand into the present land areas. Sometimes he placed it out to dry and then it expanded on its own. Three of the versions (V39, 40, 41) had him shaping the earth in the manner of a muskrat house on the water. An interesting variation occurred in V37, in which Nanabozho tied the earth in a pouch on the neck of a raven who then flew around the world, spreading the earth.

After the first act of creation, Nanabozho sent an animal out to see if the earth was large enough for all the people and animals. In most cases, the earth was too small and he had to continue the creation. This second creation appeared in all but nine of the versions (V28, 32, 33, 37, 39, 40, 41, 43, 45). After the creation of the earth, Nanabozho often set about to create various aspects of culture. He named the animals (V3), created laws (V8, 45), placed trees, lakes, mountains, and valleys on the newly created earth (V11, 12, 22, 33) and even created man and woman (V30) in an apparent borrowing from the biblical myth. By placing this episode in our diagram, we can see how it ends the myth on a positive note. Nanabozho created a new earth and gave mankind various means of survival by giving a certain amount of order to the new world. Then he went off again to hunt for food.

IS	Advice (Aid)	Action	Journey	Battle	Result
onset of flood (−)				flood (+ −)	
			on water (−)		
earth divers (+)		creation of new earth (+ −) second creation (+)			new earth (+) order (+)

An episode occurred in V35 which we should mention here. After the death of his twin brother, Nanabozho mourned so much that all nature sympathized with him. In response, the Great Spirit returned Nanabozho's brother. Nanabozho then sent the brother to the land of sunset, that is, the land of the dead. Nanabozho continued to mourn and the Great Spirit sent various animals down from heaven to get Nanabozho. After others had failed, the otter finally succeeded in bringing Nanabozho up to heaven where he lived for some time, returning to earth in order to instruct mankind in various cultural aspects. This episode has played an important role in the myth of Midewiwin's origin. How it was altered and refashioned to fit the Midé needs and beliefs would make a fascinating study in itself but we cannot concern ourselves with such a topic here.

Structurally this episode is strikingly similar to episode H. Because of some cataclysmic event, the flood or Nanabozho's lamentation, someone sent various animals *down* in order to restore order. Nanabozho sent the earth divers for a piece of the old world, and the Great Spirit sent animals down for Nanabozho. As a result of this action, the earth was made more suitable for existence.

We have completed our structural examination of the episodes contained in the various versions of the Creation myth; now we shall look at the myth as a structural whole. By doing this, we can begin to see the overall effect of the myth rather than concentrating on the specific elements and variations.

First, the idea of death permeated every aspect of this myth. A death of some kind was contained in each episode, except the theft of fire, B; however, each death led to a benefit of some kind. In episode A the death of the mother resulted in the birth of the culture hero. The death of the flint brother produced the small pieces of flint which the Ojibwa used to start fires and make various tools. Even the death of the chief wolf in episode D resulted in a hunting companion for Nanabozho. The death of the hunting companion eventually led to the death of the underwater manito(s), which after the flood led to the creation of the new earth. The death of Nanabozho's mother and the death of the wolf seem to have been primary elements in the myth. The mother's death resulted from "supernatural" beings' entering her body because she ignored the advice of her mother. The death of the wolf came about by "supernatural" beings because he did not listen to Nanabozho's advice. Both of these deaths led to Nanabozho's seeking revenge against the beings who caused the deaths. Nanabozho killed at least two beings in the course of the myth in order to avenge deaths.

Seen from the viewpoint of the myth, existence seemed to be a struggle between factional "families," represented most specifically by Nanabozho and his "relatives" in opposition to the underwater manitos. In this struggle death seemed necessary for the continuation of life (and here we should not forget the vital and ontological importance of intertribal revenge raids: deaths of relatives had to be avenged to continue the spiritual vitality of tribal members).

That death was necessary for life can be seen most clearly in the earth diver episode in which the animals who dove for the earth usually died in the attempt. Even the muskrat, who succeeded in getting a piece of earth, died before he could return to the raft. Although Nanabozho usually brought the dead animals immediately back to life, their deaths seem to have been essential preconditions for their success, as death was for success through the different episodes.

Indeed, Nanabozho himself was responsible for originating death. In

V1 he was in the process of killing his brother when the latter told him that his action would have severe consequences for those "who in the future are to live" (Jones 1917:21), that is, the Ojibwas. His brother's argument had no effect on Nanabozho, who later defended his action by saying:

> Yea, overmuch (and) too soon will this earth fill up. Where will live the people who in after time are to be born? Now, therefore, this is what shall come to pass, that people are to die. So, therefore, this is why I have brought it about that they should die who in times to come will fill up this earth, this earth which I have created. Although we could bring it to pass that not till they have reached old age they should die, yet nowhere would they have room if this should take place. Therefore this is how it shall come to pass that while they are yet in infancy they shall die. Such, therefore, is what I now see. It is the same thing that will happen to them who in the future are to live, and like unto what is now happening to you. It is only a change of going from one earth to another. To you where you are shall come they who shall cease to live (here). [Jones 1917:22–23]

The myth plainly informed the Ojibwas that death was essential to progress of life.

Second, the myth pointed out a fundamental communication gap between humans and animals in the world view of the Ojibwas. In episode D Nanabozho lived with wolves. They appeared similar to men in several ways; for example, they hunted animals for food and they camped for the night like hunting parties, and even stored up food in the summer for the winter. Nevertheless, animals saw reality differently and acted differently from humans. The chief wolf pointed out some feces to Nanabozho and told him to pick it up. Nanabozho refused and the old wolf picked up the feces which turned into a blanket or skin. The same kind of misunderstanding occurred when the wolves made some grease from the bones of the animals they had killed. They told Nanabozho not to watch, but he did and a bone hit him in the eye. The wolf did not hit Nanabozho; rather, Nanabozho caused the damage himself. Nevertheless, Nanabozho held the wolf responsible and later killed or hurt him. This act caused the expulsion of Nanabozho from the wolf pack.

Although animals were different from human beings, they were not seen as a totally separate order of creation. Their reality differed from, but could be of use to, humans. In the myth, most animals gave aid to Nanabozho in some way or other. The only animals which were not helpful were the moose and deer who lured the wolf to his doom, and the "family" of underwater manitos. Small animals like the otter, beaver, and muskrat were helpful to humans as earth divers, and birds seemed especially valuable as allies.

Taken as a structural whole, the myth represented some aspects of the Ojibwa world view. It seems to have functioned as a heuristic device which allowed the Ojibwas to function in their frequently hostile environment. The two main lessons of the myth, as indicated by a structural analysis, concerned death and animal-human relationships. It taught the Ojibwas the beneficial importance of death, a vital lesson as we shall see in a hunting culture in which the death of animals was necessary for the continuation of human life. It also taught the Ojibwas the proper human place and role in what we call "Nature," especially in the animal world of hunters and hunted. The question now remains: What was the primary concern of the myth, that is, what was the myth about?

CONTENT ANALYSIS

In this section we shall examine the content of the Ojibwa Creation myth with the goal of defining the major, if not the ultimate, concern of the traditional Ojibwas. It is our thesis that the myth's content essentially related how the world became ordered so that humans could physically survive through hunting. In other words, the primary concern, the most important if not the determining factor in almost every major decision in Ojibwa life and society, was simply physical survival, nourishment by food made available by hunting. This thesis should come as a surprise to no one, considering the millennia during which Ojibwa ancestors were hunters, but it is remarkable, that is, noteworthy, how such a concern was expressed in and through the myth.

It is our purpose here to analyze the content of the myth in three ways: (1) what it told the Ojibwas; (2) what it tells the outsider about the Ojibwa person and society; (3) what the primary concern-and-meaning of the myth was.

First, the Creation myth described the world to the Ojibwas. It was a flat island with another beneath, with water separating the two. There were four winds residing in the four cardinal directions, and a sun which revolved around the earth. This cosmology came into being as a result of the birth of Nanabozho's four brothers and Nanabozho's subsequent fashioning of the present island earth from a bit of the earth beneath.

Beneath the surface lies an ideology established by the earth divers. This sequence is an exact obverse of the Hopi emergence, in which four birds are sent up to the surface. They match each other perfectly: the exhaustion, the magical revival, and all. One moves from below to make contact with the earth's body surface; the other dives to make contact with the earth's submerged, muddy crust. Both make blatant reference to the earthly origins of human creativity and life. Just as the Hopis maintain contact with their Mother Earth, Nanabozho needs to touch the old earth in order to create a new world surface for the successful continuance of human life. Both myths present life emerging from the earth, the concrete ground of being.

In the universe there were numerous animated entities: the sun, winds, animals, feathers, birds, giants, stones, trees, manitos, humans, and so forth. Each entity had a vital force, the soul, which was contained in the heart, although the heart could be located in various parts of the body; thus in the myth Nanabozho had to locate the heart of his adversaries in order to kill them. Sometimes the heart was in the toe, or in the back of the neck, or outside the body entirely. Once it was found, it could be destroyed and the person died. Another animating part of the body was the shadow, which often operated apart from the body and soul. In many of the texts, Nanabozho was told to aim for the shadow of the underwater manito(s), in order to kill. The distinction between shadow and soul was ambiguous, although some Ojibwas have defined the soul as perception and the shadow as sensation. What is important here was that not only did humans have these animating forces; so, too, did all aspects of Nature. There is a distinction in Ojibwa grammar between animate and inanimate nouns; all natural objects, including shells and stones, can be considered animate. In the myth entities like the sun were considered as persons; they did not act mechanically and they could not be depended on to act in a certain way at a certain time, at least no more than could humans or animals. In general, "any concept of impersonal 'natural' forces is totally foreign to Ojibwa thought" (Hallowell 1960:29). In fact, the Western idea of a person being a human was entirely too confining to the Ojibwas. They related to "supernatural" beings, animals, and all aspects of Nature in basically the same way that they related to other humans, despite the lack of total communication between the various realms. This was, we think, partially because the myths and particularly the Creation myth presented Nature as a living collection of persons. The individual Ojibwa, thus informed, interpreted the universe in a like manner.

The world view of the Creation myth was one which did not make a sharp dichotomy between the "supernatural" and "Nature." There was a hierarchy and an interdependence within the universe, based on the amount and type of power possessed by the individual entity. Nanabozho proved himself more powerful than the winds or the underwater manitos, yet he needed the advice and assistance of animals, birds, and trees. The wolves had the ability to work magic and they were better hunters than

Nanabozho. In all of his battles Nanabozho needed the knowledge of birds, especially the kingfisher. When Nanabozho fought with his rivals, each antagonist was endowed with power from other beings who were considered more powerful than the two antagonists themselves. In general, Nanabozho was successful only to the extent that he had the cooperation of other entities.

The myth, then, presented two complementary views of the universe's structure. First, there was conflict between entities in the universe, in which some proved themselves more powerful than others. Second, success was based not on individual prowess but on aid given by friendly entities. This accurately portrayed Ojibwa world view and society. Individual Ojibwas did attempt to attain aid from manitos and were constantly in rivalry with each other. This was especially true of the shamans, who were not so much religious specialists as they were persons with a great degree of assistance from manitos and other beings. Nanabozho was a shaman par excellence, in conflict with other endowed beings.

Nanabozho's power as a shaman was particularly illustrated by his ability to transform himself and appear in various disguises, most particularly by his transformation into a stump. The myth informed the Ojibwas that beings could take the form of other entities; metamorphosis was a fact of life. Indeed, it might be said that one of the characteristics of life was the ability to change; specifically, "metamorphosis to the Ojibwa mind is an earmark of 'power' " (Hallowell 1960:39). In the myth the wolves had the power of transformation and Nanabozho had to beg them to transform him into a wolf. Such a view presupposes the idea that there was no qualitative difference between humans and animals, despite their different points of view. Men stood in active relationship to animals, hunters and hunted alike. One observer has written that the Ojibwa appeared "more concerned about his relationship with the animal world than with the social world of every day life" (Sieber 1950:99). We can see that the Creation myth presented a coherent cosmology and ontology to the Ojibwas.

The myth also provided means by which to judge reality. These means were observation, dreams, and divination. When the mysterious stump appeared, the underwater manitos were suspicious, knowing as they did the ability of Nanabozho to transform himself. They decided to test the stump empirically, by feeling it, watching it carefully to see if it moved; a snake wrapped around it and a bear clawed it. In one version, they waited to see if it remained motionless for four days. Only after empirical testing were their suspicions allayed.

In the myth dreams were used as means of receiving warnings and information. For example, Nanabozho's grandmother dreamed that her daughter would become impregnated by the wind or sun, and Nanabozho dreamed that his wolf brother would drown if he tried to cross the illusory river or lake. Dreams were valid bases on which to act.

The third means of gaining knowledge presented in the myth was divination, for example, through a whetstone. It is curious that there was no description of a shake lodge in the myth, considering how important the institution was to the traditional Ojibwa system of divination. It is also curious that fasting for visions and power played such a small role. Perhaps it was felt that in Nanabozho's time there was no need for fasting or shake lodge divination since there was such constant communication with the manitos; perhaps the myth as a whole presented a type of vision quest for power in which Nanabozho traveled and encountered various and powerful beings who gave him their aid, making him a powerful being in the process. On the other hand, there is no reason why any one myth should illustrate every cultural element.

What is important here is that the myth provided the means by which its own information could be validated. The Ojibwas were keen observers of the world around them; they had to be to survive. If the myth were not consistent with their empirical knowledge, they would have been hard pressed to believe it as they did, but since they interpreted events around them employing the means provided by the myth itself, the myth was constantly validated. As Hallowell stated:

> Experience and belief must be harmonized if beliefs are to be believed. The Indian is no fool. He employs the same common sense reasoning processes as ourselves, so that if he firmly holds to certain beliefs, we may be sure that they are supported in some degree by an empirical foundation. Thus experience is obviously the crux of religious rationalization. But dogma furnishes the leverage which makes the reconciliation of experience with belief possible. [1934:393]

It is clear that myth influenced personality, society, and action, just as they influenced myth; which came first is not important. Dozens of examples could be given of Ojibwas acting like characters in myth; let one suffice. An old Ojibwa couple lived by a lake. One day a moose entered the lake to escape from wolves. As it crossed the water, it was forced to swim. In such a position, up to its head in water, it was helpless to prevent attack by human hunters. The old couple got in their boat and gave chase. As they approached it, the man said in a style uncannily reminiscent of Nanabozho's hunting procedure: " 'Bo-zhoo! moose, you are always afraid of an Indian. Don't hurry, we want to get acquainted with you' " (Armstrong 1892:171). All the while the woman was telling her husband to slit its throat and hamstring before it escaped to shallow water. As it turns out, the moose did escape. Nanabozho always addressed his victims as brothers and pretended friendship with them. The old man in the story was acting exactly like the mythical model.

We have been discussing the ways in which the Ojibwa Creation myth provided the Ojibwas with a knowledge of cosmology, cosmogony, the vital principles of life, the hierarchy of life, the ability of living beings to transform themselves, and the means of testing reality. It should be noted here that the myth also validated certain societal customs by describing either their origin or their use by Nanabozho and others. An informative study of the societal customs validated by myths could be made, using all the Ojibwa mythological material. For now we wish only to list some of the more salient customs mentioned in the Creation myth. There was positive validation of funerary rites, Midewiwin, the sweat bath, fasting and fasting feasts, revenge, tobacco offerings, and curing. There were also explanations of the origin of work, hunting territories, and clans. These items not only informed the Ojibwas of the origin and importance of their customs, but they also reveal to us some aspects of traditional Ojibwa life.

We are given hints by the myth regarding Ojibwa personality and history, although this information is difficult to evaluate, especially since Nanabozho was both an ideal person and an example of what not to be. His behavior was not exactly indicative of Ojibwa behavior; neither was the behavior of his companions and rivals.

For argument's sake we shall demonstrate that even when personality traits were evidenced which we know were actual Ojibwa traits, the correlation was ambiguous. First, there were examples of suspicion in the myth and we know that the Ojibwas were suspicious of each other, of shamans, of the unfamiliar, of other Indians. This suspicion was an outgrowth of their fears of sorcery, joined to their belief that appearances were deceiving. In the myth, however, suspicion seems like common sense. For instance, the underwater manitos were suspicious of the newly appeared stump. Considering the fact that they had just killed Nanabozho's hunting companion and they knew Nanabozho's powers, their suspicions were justified and don't appear at all excessive.

Second, we know that the Ojibwas were relatively individualistic. They spent the long winters alone, hunting, and their acquisition of power was for personal benefit. It is instructive to note that the Ojibwa myth is about a single person, acting in conjunction with other actors—human, divine, and animal. Contrast this individual emphasis to the Hopi myth, which describes the actions of clans, groups of people firmly bound to each other by kinship. This is not to say that the Ojibwas had weak kinship ties, but their emphasis, perhaps based on a hunting economy which necessitated individual skills, was on the individual rather than on the group.

Despite this tendency, however, Nanabozho's individualism was tempered. He did travel alone but yearned for the companionship of the wolves, and he had great affection for his adopted wolf brother. Both Nanabozho and his enemies demonstrated group solidarity and concern for "relatives" and "family." Nanabozho's solitary nature was pitied by other characters in the myth and by the Ojibwa storytellers themselves who always made the point that Nanabozho was always hungry, always traveling alone. We do not wish to belabor the point; what we do want to warn against are depictions of tribal personality as illustrated by the content of a people's myths.

Of more practical value are the historical uses of the myth, although these, too, are merely indicators of data already known. For example, we can easily see Iroquois influences in the flint brother episode, and there were southern influences in the origin of corn. We can also discern the growth of pan-Indian ideas and Christian intrusions. We know that in some locations Ojibwas have amalgamated biblical and traditional characters of myth, for example, Noah and Nanabozho. One example of the myth's being used in defending traditional Ojibwa beliefs and practices can be found in Kohl (1860:201), in which the Devil offered the newly created Ojibwa couple a heavy book. They rejected it. Then the Supreme Being offered them birchbark scrolls, which could be carried around and which contained sacred knowledge. The Ojibwas traditionally had no concept of a Devil, yet they were willing to use the Christian concept against Christianity by showing in the myth that the Bible was a gift from the Devil and birchbark scrolls were a gift of the Supreme Being. The myth tells us something of Ojibwa religious development in historical times.

The question still remains, however, regarding the essential meaning of the Creation myth to the Ojibwas. Our intention now is to offer evidence to support our theory that the primary concern of the myth was the alleviation of hunger through successful hunting.

The Ojibwa life cycle was devoted mainly to sustaining subsistence. In the nineteenth century one observer commented that among the Ojibwas "the satisfaction of hunger is here the standing question the year through. They are almost always in a state of want" (Kohl 1860:72). A modern scholar noted that "getting a living by hunting dominated the waking thoughts as well as the dreams of these people" (Flannery 1946: 265). Certain studies have shown that fishing rather than hunting has been in historical times the chief Ojibwa means of obtaining food, and in the Lake Superior area "fish were the Indians' mainstay" (Osborn 1942: 54). Traditionally, however, the Ojibwas were primarily hunters. Fishing played a role, too, but in life as well as in the myth, hunting dominated.

When an Ojibwa boy was old enough to walk, he was given a bow and arrow and he practiced hunting. When he killed his first animal, usually a bird, he was given a feast; for each subsequent kill of the first of a species, another feast was given. At his puberty vision fast, he sought help primarily for future hunting. His status among his people was determined chiefly on his being known as a good hunter, a position which rested on both his natural skills and his assistance from manitos gained in the fast. Each hunter was a shaman whose manipulations were aimed at successful hunting and maintaining health in order to hunt.

It is worth noting that cultural forms common and distinct to the Northeastern Indians included certain divination techniques, charms, taboos, and ceremonialism, all of which were concerned with hunting. Magical rites and observances among the Ojibwas were directed almost entirely to the hunting of large animals and furbearers; there were few rituals or taboos associated with berry picking, canoe making, or other pursuits, although there were some fishing taboos. Even the puberty seclusion of girls was associated with hunting luck.

In short, hunting was considered a sacred activity and carried with it certain rules and a most certain emotional attachment with religious significance. The Supreme Being was known as the giver of game for food (as well as giver of life and giver of death), and thanksgivings were offered for nourishment. The most extreme emotional fears of the Ojibwas were associated directly with possible starvation, that is, the belief in windigos, who were starved Indians who practiced cannibalism. Insults were made to other people's totems mainly by saying or insinuating that they were hungry.

The Ojibwa myths themselves were referred to as "stories of the olden days, of how the Indians eked out their existence, and of how they tried to keep in good health" (United States Works Progress Administration 1936–40; 1942: Envelope 12, no. 9). Nanabozho was described as always hungry, always searching for food, and throughout the Creation myth were interspersed tales relating how he searched for food. As a youth he was a little hunter, always killing birds with his bow and arrow.

When he contended with his brother wind(s), it was for the expressed purpose of providing good hunting and fishing for the Indians. The controlling of the winds was a very important factor of winter hunting success for the Ojibwas. During the late winter a strong, cold north wind was needed to crust the snow to enable hunters to overtake large game.

During the summer heavy winds would make it impossible for fishing on the lakes. In the myth Nanabozho controlled the winds to make hunting and fishing possible. It is interesting to note that the Ojibwas attempted to control the north winter wind by making the impression of a hare or man, probably representing Nanabozho, in the snow, facing north. They were trying to control the wind by evoking Nanabozho's image.

In the Creation myth, Nanabozho's success against his enemies was due to his ability to locate their vital spot, a hunting necessity. Ojibwa hunters employed a technique called *mussin-ne-neen,* which consisted of drawing outlines of animals like bears, deer, and birds, indicating the position of the heart. The "x-ray style" of shamanistic art is a widely known and widely used technique for successful hunting; what is important here is that Nanabozho demonstrated to the Ojibwas the necessary hunting practice in overcoming his adversaries.

As good a hunter as he was, Nanabozho was no match for the wolves with whom he ran. They not only were fast but also worked magic, thus they were extraordinary hunters. When Nanabozho separated from them, he took with him a wolf to be his brother. They were a hunting pair, a theme which was distinct to the Ojibwa culture-hero cycle. They were so successful and were killing so much game that the underwater manitos sought revenge or the animals of the world complained of their depleting numbers. The motivation for the underwater manitos' killing of the wolf was explicit: he was too good a hunter; he was killing too many animals. The battle between Nanabozho and the manitos was clearly over the issue of hunting: Where and how much could Nanabozho and his "relatives" hunt for food? Nanabozho's subsequent revenge and victory over the underwater manitos was his successful assertion of the right to hunt successfully. His theft of fire made the cooking of food possible. Each episode in the myth was directed toward hunting from one angle or another.

This fact is made more apparent when we observe that a hunting narrative mirrors exactly the killing of the underwater manitos. In another version Nanabozho ate the underwater manito after killing him. Finally, Nanabozho's first act after creating the new earth was to release animals to roam the world, after which he immediately went hunting and successfully captured a flock of ducks (or other game).

Nanabozho's two main acts of revenge in the myth were against the winds and against the underwater manitos. The former was to make conditions conducive to hunting (and fishing); the latter was to assert the rights of hunting. Thus in the course of the myth Nanabozho overcame two sets of adversaries, the winds and the underwater manitos, both for the expressed purpose of providing for and maintaining successful hunting to alleviate hunger.

What is especially intriguing about this interpretation is that it reveals an implicit duality of the universe: sky and underwater (water, underground). In the course of the myth Nanabozho controlled the masters of the sky and the masters of the underwater.

We approach the topic of duality with some reluctance. The categories seem too preconceived, too universal to have any real meaning in the Ojibwa context; however, as much as we attempt to discount the dualism, it apparently existed and was related to the achievement of successful hunting. We don't wish to impose our Western dualisms on the Ojibwas. On the other hand, we don't wish to ignore Ojibwa realities simply because they appear too much like our own.

It should be remembered that the Ojibwas had no moieties; neither did the Ottawa or Potawatomi, although other Algonkians did and their categories were invariably earth and sky. The Ojibwas in some locations divided the eight degrees of the Midé Society into four earth and four sky degrees, the latter being more powerful and advanced degrees.

To the Ojibwas the sky beings, the thunderbirds, winds, birds, sun, were generally helpful to humans, although they were not always predictable. Sky imagery meant power, for example, horns indicated a shaman whose power was directed to the sky. (We should note, however, that the underwater manitos were called horned serpents or lions.) The thunderbirds were created by Nanabozho to control the cardinal directions and the "evil" gods, presumably the underwater manitos, and the Ojibwas thought of lightning as arrows thrown by the thunderbirds at the great snakes of the water and ground. Nanabozho's kinship was with the winds; he was sometimes thought of as the northwest wind or the east wind.

Throughout the myth Nanabozho was assisted primarily by birds; they usually gave him information which led to the death of his adversaries. To the traditional Ojibwas, birds were both signs of spring and the first food of spring; they were literally a godsend for the starving Ojibwa in late winter. Thunderbirds themselves were truly thought of as birds, especially since thunder and lightning seemed to migrate with other birds— appearing in the spring and disappearing in the fall. These thunderbirds which fed on the giant serpents and punished the wicked were greatly revered. One Ojibwa commented: "We were taught to show respect for the Thunder; we were told to sit down and to be quiet until the storm had passed over. It was just like God going by" (Hilger 1951:61). Dreams in which birds, thunder, sun, and lightning appeared were considered favorable to the dreamer; those of water and snakes were considered ominous. As much as possible, "the Indians were careful to avoid snake dreams, as it was considered an evil omen to dream about these creatures" (United States Works Progress Administration 1936–40; 1942: Envelope 6, no. 1).

Serpents were intimately associated with all meat, as evidenced by the Eagle Feather Belt Grace Dance: "In ceremonial pow-wows, the serving of any kind of food to the participants is forbidden. An imitation of the thunder birds must first be given before serving the meat, as meat of any kind is regarded as reptilian in nature" (United States Works Progress Administration 1936–40; 1942: "Types of Dances"). That is not to say that the underwater manitos were considered entirely evil; this seems to be a Christian influence and interpretation, especially since the Christians associated the underwater serpent with the Devil. More correctly, the underwater manitos were dangerous but potentially helpful powers who had influence over game, fish, and curing herbs. Allouez noted in the seventeenth century that the underwater manito was offered sacrifices to obtain good fishing (Kinietz 1940:286). They helped in controlling the seasons, were beneficiaries of the Midé Society and punishers of those who mocked its teachings, usually by drowning them, and they were helpful in the creation of physical attributes of the world. In the Creation myth they simply had to be controlled by Nanabozho to ensure the continuation of bountiful hunting.

The duality of the universe was not an explicit or major theme of the myth. Nanabozho did not create the duality; he was born into it. The antagonism between the two sides of the world—sky and underwater—was not even emphasized in the myth. Rather, Nanabozho dealt with the world as the Ojibwas perceived it. First he battled with his "relatives," the winds; then he battled his "enemies," the underwater manitos. Instead of presenting a disjointed duality, the myth demonstrated that both aspects of the world had to be controlled for the sake of successful hunting.

Our structural analysis indicated two major messages of the myth. The first was that death was essential to the continuation of life. As shown by the content of the myth, the most elementary example of this message was the continuation of human life through the hunting of animals for food. The death of animals was essential for the continuation of human life.

The second structural message was that humans and animals, although ontologically similar, had different realities, different roles, and a difficulty in intercommunication. The myth's content illustrated man's place in Ojibwa "Nature," as hunter of animals, whose ability and right to hunt were established by Nanabozho.

Nanabozho is a transformer and thus plays a crucial role in helping the Ojibwas cross a formative threshold on their way to becoming, through myth. Before the time of Nanabozho's creative acts, the animal-human connections were close and firm, but through the myth he breaks the solid kinship with the animals, gaining for himself and implicitly for other Indians to follow the right to hunt and kill animals for human needs. Animals and humans are still in a covenant, but it is an unequal one in which humans have the upper hand; relative equivalence is lost in the process. The Ojibwa Creation myth thereby concludes with a syzygy of progress and loss.

Table 1

Versions of Creation Myth—Location and Sources

V1	Bois Fort, Minnesota	(Jones 1917:3–159)
V2	Bois Fort, Minnesota	(Jones 1917:159–279)
V3	Ft. William, Ontario	(Jones 1917:373–435)
V3a	Ft. William, Ontario	(Jones 1917:437–501)
V4	Bois Fort, Minnesota	(Jones 1919:531–47)
V5	Bois Fort, Minnesota	(Jones 1919:547–59)
V6	Timagami Ojibwa	(Speck 1915:28–38)
V7	Northern Wisconsin	(Barnouw 1955:73–85)
V8	Great Lakes Region	(Kohl 1860:387–91)
V9	Sarnia, Ontario	(Radin and Reagan 1928:62)
V10	Dinorwic, Ontario	(Radin and Reagan 1928:63–67)
V11	Nett Lake, Minnesota	(Radin and Reagan 1928:67–70)
V12	Nett Lake, Minnesota	(Radin and Reagan 1928:70–76)
V13	Cross Lake, Minnesota	(Radin and Reagan 1928:102–3)
V14	Nett Lake, Minnesota	(Radin and Reagan 1928:106–8)
V15	Fond du Lac, Minnesota	(Coleman, Frogner, Eich 1962:62)
V16	Leech Lake, Minnesota	(Coleman, Frogner, Eich 1962:63–65)
V17	Leech Lake, Minnesota	(Coleman, Frogner, Eich 1962:65–66)
V18	Nett Lake, Minnesota	(Coleman, Frogner, Eich 1962:66)
V19	Fond du Lac, Minnesota	(Coleman, Frogner, Eich 1962:66–67)
V20	Leech Lake, Minnesota	(Coleman, Frogner, Eich 1962:67–68)
V21	Nett Lake, Minnesota	(Coleman, Frogner, Eich 1962:70–72)
V22	Unspecified Ojibwa	(Reagan 1921:347–52)
V23	Red Lake, Minnesota	(Josselin de Jong 1913:5–16)
V24	Lac Court d'Oreilles, Wisconsin	(Gilfillan 1908–9:2–6)
V25	Lac Court d'Oreilles, Wisconsin	(Gilfillan 1908–9:7–8)
V26	Birch Island, Ontario	(Radin 1914:12–13)
V27	Rama, Ontario	(Radin 1914:19–22)
V28	Georgina Island, Ontario	(Radin 1914:22–23)

V29	Unspecified Ojibwa	(Blackwood 1929:321–23)
V30	Unspecified Ojibwa	(Blackwood 1929:323–29)
V31	Unspecified Ojibwa	(Blackwood 1929:329–33)
V32	Western Ontario	(Carson 1917:491–93)
V33	Ontario	(Chamberlain 1891:196–98)
V34	Sault Ste. Marie, Ontario	(Chamberlain 1891:198–99)
V35	French Bay, Ontario	(Chamberlain 1891:200–201)
V36	French Bay, Ontario	(Chamberlain 1891:201–3)
V37	Michigan	(Chamberlain 1891:204–5)
V38	Potawatomi	(Chamberlain 1891:206–7)
V39	Cree	(Chamberlain 1891:207–8)
V40	Cree	(Chamberlain 1891:208)
V41	Fort Cumberland, Saskatchewan	(Chamberlain 1891:208)
V42	Canada	(Chamberlain 1891:208–9)
V43	Menomini	(Chamberlain 1891:210–13)
V44	Long Plains, Manitoba	(Skinner 1919:283–88)
V45	Garden River, Ontario	(Gabaoosa 1921:i–xxvii)
V46	Garden River, Ontario	(Gabaoosa 1900:1–7)
V47	Unspecified Ojibwa	(Miscogeon 1900b:1–25)

Table 2

Episodes

A. Birth of Nanabozho:
   V1, 6, 7, (12), (13), 14, 16, 17, 23, 26, 35, 37, 38, (43), 46

B. Theft of Fire:
   V1, 15, 23

C. Nanabozho and His Brothers:
   V1, (3a), 7, (12), (16), 17, 18, 19, 20, 23, (26), (30), (31), 37, 38, 46

D. Nanabozho and the Wolves:
   V1, 2, 3, 7, 12, 21, 23, 24, (26), 32, 44, 45, 47

E. Death of Nanabozho's Hunting Companion:
   V1, 2, 3, 7, 8, (10), 12, 21, 23, 24, 27, 28, 32, 33, (34), 35, (36), 37, 43, 44, 45, 47

F. Shooting of Underwater Manito(s)—Stump Episode:
   V1, 2, 3, 6, 7, (10), (11), 12, 21, 23, 24, 27, 28, 30, 32, 33, 34, 36, 37, 43, 44, 45, 47

G. Killing of Underwater Manito(s)—Toad Woman Episode:
   V1, 2, 3, 6, 7, 9, (10), 12, 21, 23, 24, 28, 30, 32, 33, 36, 43, 44, 45

H. Deluge, Earth Divers, Creation of New Earth:
   V1, 2, 3, 4, 5, 6, 7, 8, 9, (10), 11, 12, 21, 23, 25, 27, 28, 30, 32, 33, 34, 36, 37, (39), (40), (41), (42), 43, 44, 45

(Note: the numbers in parentheses indicate versions in which the episodes did not exactly conform to the majority of versions; however, their similarity was striking enough to include them here.)

4

The Story and Structure of the Iroquois Confederacy

In previous chapters we have described mythology and analyzed the myths of two Indian groups, the Hopis and the Ojibwas. We have stated that myths communicate cultural messages; they are ritual acts of shared community consciousness, set in dramatic narratives, the basic formula of which is conflict and resolution. Furthermore, tribal myths focus community attention on decisive events with crucial import to the tribe: threshold situations which we have called life-and-death matters.

The Hopi and Ojibwa myths concentrate on thresholds particularly crucial for peoples living at a primary stage of social subsistence, although their lessons are soundly applicable to any community. The myths which we shall analyze in this chapter have even further reaching universality, highlighting as they do the ultimate question of human death in relation to the "state."

The Hopi myth of emergence, we have seen, is an attempt to describe and prescribe the conditions of tribal life, especially the problems concerning cooperation and conformity, factionalism and witchcraft, in villages of concentrated population density and limited natural resources. The myth defines for the Hopis what their social life is and what it should be. In the course of the narrative, the Hopi ancients cross the crucial threshold from primordial seekers to kinsmen in their chosen land; that is, the narrative portrays the coming into being of the Hopi people as a people. The myth dramatizes their emergence from the underground and their migrations across the body of the land in search of themselves. In their process of becoming, the characters in the myth try to mediate the difficulties between individual and societal requirements, placing emphasis on the vital necessity of interpersonal harmony and mutual sharing. The myth presents us, therefore, with our first definition of human being: it takes place in a human community.

The Ojibwa story of Nanabozho elaborates a theme raised in the Hopi myth: the dependence of humans on their natural environment for survival. In particular, the Ojibwa myth emphasizes the ethical dilemma of subsistence by hunting. We have seen that for the Ojibwas hunting carries a special emotional load because the animals necessary for the continuation of human life are thought of as persons, relatives of humans. The hunter needs to justify his killing of animal kinfolk, the deaths of whom are essential for the continued life of the Ojibwas, as individuals and as a people.

The threshold of the Ojibwa myth occurs as humans, represented by the culture-hero Nanabozho, win the right and power to hunt for their food. By such right and prowess the Ojibwas can subsist, as long as they do not kill more animals than they need for survival. In the course of crossing this threshold, a mediation is enacted between the hunters and hunted; an uneasy peace is established, and the rules of hunting behavior are set forth. In such a way, the myth puts before us a second definition of human existence: humans depend ultimately on the living environment for survival; human life is vitally and intimately attached to nonhuman life.

We see, then, that both myths highlight life-and-death resolutions, the first that supports human existence through human community, the second which supports human existence through the nonhuman environment. In both cases, the myths point directly to sources of human life. At the same time, they focus attention dramatically on decisive deaths: that of the chief's son in the first, that of Nanabozho's brother and the underwater adversaries in the second. Both myths justify these deaths, both implicitly and explicitly in their different versions, by saying that death is absolutely essential for the continuation of human life. Death is the food upon which life feeds. At least in one version of each myth, a major character delivers a speech that rationalizes death in no uncertain terms. In the same speeches, moreover, exponents not only point to death but also point away from its finality, by revealing the existence of an afterlife, an obliquely immortal existence after death.

The Iroquois myths we shall now observe make no promises about such a future world. They are concerned completely with the foundations of a civil society, based on universal principles, natural law, and divine intervention, as a means of overcoming death. Not death in the abstract, but deaths of Iroquois caused by other Iroquois, deaths created by a fatal cycle of mourning and revenge. The myths define political, civil society as a means to comfort mourners and cleanse the mind of vengeance.

Between 1400 and 1600 five Iroquoian nations—the Senecas, Cayugas, Onondagas, Oneidas, and Mohawks—established a Confederacy or League, a "state" built upon kinship loyalties and national alliances that reached its peak of military, economic, and diplomatic power in the seventeenth and eighteenth centuries. The Confederacy functions today, but is weakened in relation to the United States and Canada, which are its neighbors and sometimes its adversaries.

The aim of this chapter is to examine the stories that describe the founding of the Iroquois Confederacy and to discern the pervasive messages communicated through their narrative structure. Numerous versions of these stories derive from sources that date from the beginning of the nineteenth century to the present day, but a core consistency is readily identifiable and best represented by a manuscript recorded in 1899 (Gibson 1899).

Behind the dozens of episodes that comprise the stories, and behind the many dimensions that various academic approaches can uncover in the stories, there exists a unity. The stories define and express the teleology of Iroquois *national* life: its grounding in human nature and human problems; its rules of ritual propriety; its incorporation of seemingly conflicting forces; its hope of transforming individuals and groups. These are stories—I should say, this is a story—of nation-formation, with its infrastructure, transcending loyalties, reciprocal duties, and principles for promoting human life according to divine models and accomplished through supernatural intervention and power. An analysis of such a story can help to illuminate the relationships among myth, religion, and national identity.

Since there is no original or perfect version of the story, my method is to gather every version—including many fragments—in order to determine the normal form of the narrative and discriminate the central elements from the peripheral or idiosyncratic. The League legend "is known from fragments as early as the eighteenth century" (Fenton 1975: 134)—the Moravian missionary Pyrlaeus, who learned some Mohawk stories in 1743, but whose manuscripts disappeared and come down to us only through the reports of others (Beauchamp 1921:7); Canassatego, a Seneca chief who gave a brief and vague account in 1763 (Beauchamp 1921:8)—but the earliest identifiable account is from the Mohawk statesman-soldier, Joseph Brant, in 1801 (Boyce 1973:288). Since then, around two dozen sources—some published, some still in manuscript form—have appeared (see Versions at the end of this chapter). Some are a page or two in length; others contain hundreds of episodes. Some are written by Iroquois with direct access to tribal records; others are filtered through non-Iroquois translators and editors. Some are unimpeachable in their authenticity; others are suspect (e.g., parts of Clark 1849 and Schoolcraft 1847) or clearly bogus (Canfield). Some are original tellings; others are distillations, syntheses, and retellings of other versions in the corpus. Most are told by Iroquois from the three elder nations—the Mohawks, Onondagas, and Senecas—although there is one important version from a Tuscarora, David Cusick (Beauchamp 1892), a member of the Indian nation admitted as the sixth participant in the League in the eighteenth century.

The versions of some Iroquois storytellers can be scrutinized for ideological biases. For example, Seth Newhouse, an Onondaga of Six Nations Reserve, Ontario, a speaker of fluent Mohawk (his father was probably Mohawk), was deeply involved in the struggle between the Warriors Party and the Council of Life Chiefs on his reserve, and his texts (Newhouse 1885, 1897; Parker 1968) tend to represent his position in the debate. He was also a strong advocate of Iroquois political autonomy against Canadian intrusions. Thus he wrote at the outset of one story, "We are now upholding our *Ancient Government* which was *Established* by the *Heavenly Messenger 'De-ka-na-wi-dah'* centuries before our friendly en[e]mies the Columbians (The Palefaces) came to this continent" (Newhouse 1885:1, emphases his). In addition, he emphasized the leadership role played by Mohawks in the Confederacy's founding, at the expense of the other Iroquois nations. Many examples in Iroquois history indicate how Mohawks and Onondagas in particular have often vied for prominence in the League, and the storytellers of these nations tend to validate their political claims against one another, as they have done for centuries. Enough is known of the scholars who have collected, translated, edited, and sometimes altered the Iroquois texts that adjustments can be made for their biases. J. N. B. Hewitt, for instance, was not above "revising" some of the legends in his search for "a consistent historical background" to the founding of the League (1931:175). For their part, Goldenweiser, Parker, and Fenton have all become embroiled in the debate about the possibility of aboriginal Iroquois constitutionality, and their disagreement has colored their work. All of these factors have been taken into consideration in evaluating the versions of the League legends.

This analysis of the Iroquois stories also takes into account the published interpretations of the texts. For the wealth of versions, there are only a few creative exegeses of the narrative. Some studies have indulged in honorifics for the Confederacy. Other scholars, such as Hewitt and Beauchamp, have made numerous and excellent observations about the stories without conducting a full fledged interpretation. Hertzberg performs a very useful service in relating the legend to the structure of Iroquois society and polity; Anthony Wallace (1958b) probes the story's presentation of cultural change and revitalization. Other observers have made helpful remarks, but a systematic analysis of the full complement of versions is still lacking.

The Iroquois have three genres of narrative: (1) fictional tales (e.g., of tricksters); (2) recent human adventures; and (3) stories of true events that took place long ago, and which are believed by the narrators. The story of the Confederacy is part of the third category, which might be called a "myth." There are three great myths of the Iroquois: (1) the Creation, in which a woman falls from the sky, lands on a newly formed earth, and her grandsons, Tarenyawagon (the good creator) and Tawiskaron (the contrary-minded) give shape to the present world; (2) the Founding of the League; and (3) the Good News revealed to Handsome Lake in 1800 and the years following. Although the last event took place less than two centuries ago, the Iroquois consider it an ancient event because it established the third era of history, following the eras of the Creation and the League.

It is said by some that the Iroquois regard the League legend as a "gospel" (Fenton 1975:132) or a "Bible" (Wallace 1946:5). They treat it with reverence reserved for sacred texts that express ultimate and normative values. They think of its characters and events as having formed the present civil order with the authority and power of the "supernatural"—called *orenda*, a supramundane, qualitatively superior force that permeates and empowers all special being. They tell it in a highly metaphorical language with rhetorical, legal, and ritual phrases that are absent from ordinary Iroquois speech and unintelligible to most Iroquois. For these reasons, we can speak of it as a "myth," a foundational, preternatural, ritualized, religious narrative.

We should note, however, that as long as a century ago Iroquois storytellers were demythologizing the text. Horatio Hale commented that the Canadian Iroquois he encountered "only smile with good-natured derision" when extraordinary events in the story were mentioned (1883: 21). Seth Newhouse, it is said, "no longer believed in the mythology" of the League (Fenton 1949a:156). In a more recent Mohawk text (Akweks 1948:10–12), the narrator has rationalized the magical disappearance of lake water by asserting that a beaver dam must have given out and the water run dry. If the story serves as scripture to the Iroquois, at least a few of them interpret it figuratively, rationalistically, and perhaps with an emphasis on its philosophical principles. For many Iroquois the narrative is a "legend" about human heroes sanctioned by *orenda*, or a "story" expressing commendable ideas and values. Hence we use the terms "myth," "legend," and "story" interchangeably in this study.

THE STORY

There is no one way to catalogue all the episodes, motifs, or mythemes that make up the legend of the League. To present the story fully but concisely, we have separated the narrative into twenty-two sections. In so doing, it has been necessary to reorganize the chronology of many versions to fit the prevailing model. No one version contains every episode, although Gibson's 1899 manuscript comes the closest to completeness (see Versions at the end of this chapter).

I. The Migration and Separation of the People

Tarenyawagon saved the five nations from Stonish Giants. He destroyed monsters and put the world in order, establishing principles for humans to follow, thus setting the stage for the later Constitution. He gave the five families the art of war, the right of expansion. He cleared waters of obstructions and pointed out good fishing. But a disagreement arose, and the five bands went their separate ways, with separate tongues. As they migrated, they established temporary, local leagues.

II. The Birth and Growth of Deganawida

In the ancient times of the ancestors, a mother and daughter lived alone among the Hurons near the Bay of Quinte. The daughter was a virgin, but became pregnant. When she would not confess to her mother of sexual relations, her mother became depressed at the shame and deception. But Tarenyawagon visited the mother in a dream and told her that the child, born of a virgin, would do the work of the divinities on earth. He was an incarnation of Tarenyawagon with a great mission. He was born, and the grandmother unsuccessfully tried to drown him three times, for fear of the calamity he would bring. He grew up honest, good, generous, beautiful, and peaceful. Animals loved him, but he was misunderstood and persecuted by his people. He grew very rapidly.

III. The Journey to the Mohawks, the Situation, and the Mission Explained

Deganawida left on his mission in a white (stone) canoe. He told his grandmother: If a tree runs blood, I have died; if not, I am successful. He crossed Lake Ontario and found hunters whose village had been destroyed. They told of intertribal warfare; of sorrow, destruction, starvation, and death; of feuding factions, lawlessness, warmongering, the slaughter of innocents, and cannibalism. The people had forgotten the Creator's ways. Deganawida told them, "The Great Creator from whom we all are descended sent me to establish the Great Peace among you. No longer shall you kill one another and nations shall cease warring upon each other"

(Parker 1968:15). He promised to protect against invasion and establish government.

IV. The Mother of Nations Accepts Deganawida's Message

Deganawida visited a woman, Djigonsasa, the Mother of Nations, who fed warriors along the road. She fed him; they ate together, and he explained his message, telling her to cease supplying the war parties. He needed to explain to her the three double-faceted principles—Righteousness, Peace, Power—upon which his message was based, and the physical symbols of his message: the Extended House and the Great Law. She accepted his message, the first to do so, thus giving clan mothers priority.

V. The Cannibal Converts

In Gibson (1899:34–60) the cannibal is Hiawatha. In Parker (1968: 69–70) the cannibal is Tadadaho. Deganawida found an empty house. He climbed onto the roof to the smokehole. The owner returned, carrying a human corpse. He boiled the body in a kettle, and when it was ready he looked into the pot. He saw a man looking up "from the depths of the standing pot" (Gibson 1899:37). At first he thought he was being tricked, then he said, "So then it is really I myself that is looking up from the depths of the pot. My personal appearance is most amazing. So, on the contrary, perhaps my manner of doing is not so beautiful, that thus it should continue to be my purpose to keep killing people and eating their flesh" (Gibson 1899:39). He hoped that someone would tell him how "to compensate for the number of human beings whom I have made to suffer, in order that peace may prevail" (ibid.). Deganawida met him as he threw away the body, and they shared a meal of venison, which the Ruler has ordained as a food for humans. Its antlers shall be worn on the head, as a sign of authority. Together they buried the body, saying that from then on each person will be responsible "to care for the body of man" (Gibson 1899:57). Deganawida explained his message, and the cannibal accepted it. He gave him the name of Hiawatha.

VI. The Prophets Prove Their Power

Deganawida went among the Mohawks, preaching his message. He had to prove his power by sitting in a tree that was chopped down into a precipice. He emerged unharmed. In Gibson (1899:74–82), Hiawatha exchanged places with him and was thought to be Deganawida. He married the favorite youngest daughter of the chief and became a chief himself. The chief accepted the message.

VII. Tadadaho the Wizard Prevents Peace

A wizard was the chief of the Onondagas. He had snakes for hair, a snake for a penis, wrapping around his body. He had turtle claws the size of bear paws for hands and feet, seven crooks in his body, and a club in his fist. In youth he had been normal, the half-brother of Hiawatha, but now he was twisted in body and mind, hated but feared. He was a tyrant who blocked all attempts at peace by killing and spying on his fellows. Hiawatha tried to organize chiefs against him for peace by holding councils, but Tadadaho stifled every attempt. As Hiawatha's delegation approached him by canoe at his isolated nest, he drowned most of them with wind and waves. One version presents Tadadaho as a great chief without any evil. Another describes his hostility but asserts that he requested that his people transform him. One says that he was associated with Tawiskaron.

VIII. Hiawatha's Relatives Are Killed

A. Osinoh the Witch Kills Hiawatha's Daughters
A visionary learned that Hiawatha would be able to conquer Tadadaho if Hiawatha would leave Onondaga and join forces with Deganawida. Yet with his daughters still alive in Onondaga, Hiawatha would not leave. "With the daughters dead they knew the crushing sorrow would sever every tie that bound him to Onondaga. Then would he be free to leave and in thinking of the welfare of the people forget his own sorrow" (Parker 1968: 18). So they hired Osinoh the witch, who transformed into an owl and killed the daughters when they refused marriage. Despite attempts at revenge by his family, Hiawatha was shattered.

B. Tadadaho Kills Hiawatha's Relatives with a Great Plunging Bird
As Hiawatha was planning for another council, his pregnant daughter (or other female relative) was gathering water or firewood. A great, beautiful bird (an eagle, vulture, or wampum bird) plunged down to earth where she was. A great crowd trampled her to death, in curiosity, fear, or greed for its feathers.

IX. Hiawatha Mourns and Quits Onondaga

No one comforted Hiawatha in his grief. His people had become so used to fighting that they were inured to each other's bereavement and to death itself. Therefore Hiawatha left Onondaga; he "split the sky," that is, went south, wandering.

X. Hiawatha Invents Wampum

A. Hiawatha Uses Elderberry Twigs
As Hiawatha wandered, he found elderberry rushes. He cut them into lengths and strung them into three pieces, saying, "This would I do if I found anyone burdened with grief even as I am. I would console them" (Parker 1968:20).

B. Hiawatha Uses Shells
Hiawatha came to a lake, or group of small lakes, where ducks were thick on the water. He startled them, and as they flew up, they carried all the water with them. Hiawatha gathered shells along the lake bottom and strung them into beads, making a speech about consoling and other uses of wampum. Or, he walked to the bottom of the lake and found the wampum beads among the weeds. Or, Hiawatha or Deganawida found shells on the paddle of a canoe, and planned to represent their plan pictorially through the beads.

C. Hiawatha Uses Bird Quills
Hiawatha strung eagle or wampum bird quills as he traveled.

XI. Hiawatha Gives the Mohawks Lessons in Protocol

Hiawatha traveled to a Mohawk town. He found a hut in a cornfield outside the village and sat there by a fire, making wampum. A female saw him and reported his presence to the chief, who sent messengers to invite him in. Hiawatha taught them the proper way to deliver messages with wampum. When he entered the village, they asked him why such a chief should be wandering. He said that he wandered because Tadadaho killed his family: "I don't care what shall become of me now" (Newhouse 1885: 7). The chief promised to place him at an honored seat at council and consult him; however, these promises were broken, so he continued to travel, searching for consolation.

XII. Deganawida Consoles Hiawatha

Hiawatha met Deganawida, who proceeded to console him using eight of the thirteen strings of wampum beads gathered by Hiawatha. Hiawatha's bereavement and depression were relieved, and now his mind was capable of judgment, so that he could help create law. Deganawida took the wampum, saying, *"This* is the *thing* that will *accomplish* our *undertakings"* (Newhouse 1885:10). From then on, this is how mourners would be consoled.

XIII. Scouts Travel to Tadadaho

Deganawida sent scouts, sometimes as crows, sometimes as bear and deer, to find Tadadaho's column of smoke. They passed through Oneida and found Tadadaho, whom they described in horrible detail when they returned.

XIV. Deganawida and Hiawatha Join Oneidas, Cayugas, and Senecas to Mohawks

Interspersed with visits to Tadadaho, the two prophets brought their message to the other Iroquois nations, and each in turn accepted the message, including the two chiefs of the Senecas. Each nation took its name from Deganawida. Now the two had the power of unity behind their words and could approach Tadadaho in order to transform him.

XV. The Nations March to Tadadaho, Singing the Peace Hymn

Led by Deganawida, the nations marched in procession to Tadadaho, singing the Peace Hymn, which Deganawida taught and which could "soothe the angry feelings" (Norton 1970:103) of Tadadaho, reconstructing his mind "so that he may again have the mind of a human being" (Hewitt 1892:135). If the song was sung without error, it could straighten and transform Tadadaho. The song thanked the League, Peace, the Ancestors, the Warriors, the Women, the Kindred; it was a song to be sung for all time, especially at Condolences. All the while, Tadadaho's voice could be heard, shouting: It has not yet occurred, or when will it occur?

XVI. Deganawida and Hiawatha Transform Tadadaho

The procession reached Onondaga and performed ceremonies at the edge of the woods, while Tadadaho continued in his impatience. They met him and explained their message to him. He agreed to their plan after they promised to make him the firekeeper, the main chief, with Onondaga as capital and with veto power in his hands. Then they combed the snakes from his hair; they placated him; they gave him new clothes and shoes; they sang the song to him; they reduced his penis or made it harmless; they rubbed him with wampum; and after some false tries, he "became perfect. Harmless. Peac[e]able. And calm minded man . . . and his evil spirit left him completely" (Newhouse 1885:64–65).

XVII. Deganawida and Hiawatha Establish Iroquois Unity and Law

After curing Tadadaho, the two were able to establish national "peace and tranquility" (Hewitt 1892:140). They created one people, united, "one great family" (Converse 1974:189), "brothers again" (Akweks 1972: 29), with "filial love" (Boyce 1973:289), "a vast sisterhood of all the tribes of men" (Hewitt 1915:322). They created unanimity among the chiefs, and "If any one of these nations was attacked, the injury was felt by all of the Five Nations" (Akweks 1972:29). They created a permanent confederate government with local autonomy, a constitution, civic order, law, means of perpetuation, and unchanging customs, with each item of law represented by wampum. Such was the commonwealth, the Great Law. Underlying the entire structure were three principles, each with a double application: health and peace; righteousness and justice; authority and spiritual power.

XVIII. Deganawida and Hiawatha Establish League Chiefs and Council Polity

In order to ensure the future generations' lives, they established permanent chieftaincies. The chiefs were protectors and guides for the people, and should never consider themselves before others. They should be patient, long-suffering, thick-skinned, generous, and fearless in pursuing justice. The founders made a roll call of the fifty League chiefs, naming them by nation and clan. There were rules for installing chiefs, protocol at council, relations with the clan mothers and the warriors, and dire warnings should the chiefs fail in their duties. After providing the chiefs with deer antlers as symbols of authority, a seagull wing to sweep away dirt from the council fire, and an emergency pole to flick crawling creatures (i.e., propositions that might undermine the League) into the fire, Deganawida said, "So now we have finished that which in future days to pass shall be the protection of our grandchildren" (Gibson 1899:300).

XIX. The Confederacy Takes Symbolic Images

Deganawida established symbolic representations of the League: the Longhouse, with five fireplaces but one family; wampum belts picturing five nations, Onondaga being a great tree or heart at its center, or five brothers holding hands; the Great Pine Tree, high to the sky so all can see it, broad so all can find protection beneath its branches; the Eagle atop the tree, keeping watch for enemies; the Four White Roots of the tree, stretching out to other nations to lead them in; the weapons buried beneath the tree, where an underground stream carries them out of sight; a common meal of beaver tail, with no sharp utensils in the common dish; five arrows, tied together into a bundle to make them strong; the council fire and pillar of smoke that touches the sky; the antlers of office; five corn stalks coming from one stalk, built upon four roots. All of these symbolize the unity and power of the League.

XX. The League Declares Its Sovereignty

After setting up its internal structure, the League regarded foreign policy. It created laws of adoption, emigration, and laws regarding the rights of foreign nations. The League shall be a place of refuge for other nations, and delegations were sent out to Cherokees, Ojibways, and other Indians. Foreign aggressors would be given warnings, then war would be fought. The League reserved the right to battle any "obstinate opposing nation that has refused to accept the Great Peace" (Parker 1968:52).

XXI. The Condolence Maintains the Confederacy

The final effective symbol of the League was the Condolence ceremony, a reenactment of the rite performed by Deganawida for Hiawatha and repeated by them both for the cleansing of Tadadaho. The clearminded will speak kind words of consolation to mourners. One moiety will console another, when someone—especially a chief—has died. The Condolence will stop the mourner from incessant, destructive grief, and will reaffirm life and "mental equipoise" (Hewitt 1927:238–39). The living become "reconciled" (Parker 1968:58) with death and with one another. The thirteen wampum strings of Requickening will help maintain the stability and mental health of the League's officials and of the League itself.

XXII. Deganawida Departs

Having completed his business, Deganawida left, promising to come again in time of crisis. In some versions (Clark 1849:30; Henning 1898: 480) it is Hiawatha who went in his canoe up to the heavens after the League was formed. Deganawida either buried himself or simply disappeared, determining that his name not be included on the chiefs' roll; indeed, his name should not be used except at Condolence or when talking of the Good Tidings he brought. For this reason he is often referred to simply as "the Peacemaker" (Howard 1971:435).

THE STRUCTURE

Who were these heroes who created the Iroquois Confederacy? The three main characters, Deganawida, Hiawatha, and Tadadaho, exhibit some fixed characteristics that suggest connections to historical persons: Deganawida the healer, Hiawatha the mourner, Tadadaho the wizard chief who is cured. Nevertheless, the processes of folkloric storytelling have produced some interchangeable roles (both Hiawatha and Tadadaho are portrayed as the cannibal who is converted) and some twinning (Deganawida and Hiawatha are described as identical twins in some versions); Hiawatha and Tadadaho are presented as half-brothers in other sources. Among the Onondagas, Hiawatha plays the prominent role; the Mohawks favor Deganawida. It appears that local stories about separate persons combined as the nations combined into the Confederacy. If we look at early sources, for example, Colden's 1727 and 1747 history of the Iroquois, there is no mention of the three. Lewis Henry Morgan, as late as 1851, states (3–8) that there is no history of the League's origin, although he later refers to Deganawida as "the founder of the confederacy" and Hiawatha as "his speaker" (101, n. 1). It is only in the nineteenth century that one encounters any of the three names: 1801 for Deganawida (Boyce 1973), and 1816 for the three in the combination of roles familiar to the League legend (Norton 1970). Beauchamp commented (1892:137) regarding Hiawatha: "It is rather odd that what is now the most famous of Iroquois names was almost unknown but little over half a century ago." Hewitt noted (1920:537–39) that Hiawatha is really two different persons in Iroquois myth: the converted cannibal and the mourner. The fourth prominent personage, the Peace Woman Djigonsasa, was little known in traditional Iroquois mythology. She may represent an ancient chieftainness of the Neutrals, although her name is passed down among the Iroquois as a title. In the legend she plays the roles both of the Peace Woman and Deganawida's mother (Hewitt 1931:175–78).

The story's importance seems to be other than in the identification of the main characters. On the contrary, the legend does not concern itself with these characters' biographical data, but rather with their roles in founding the League. We note that there is no biographical record of Hiawatha after the League is founded; rather, he is merely a function of the Confederacy's formation. As Hale says, "The records of the Iroquois are historical, and not biographical" (1883:34). The story delineates the lives of its heroes, but against a background of egalitarian ideals and decisions by councils who act according to ritual rules of propriety.

The story establishes patterns of activity to regulate and inspire contemporary Iroquois behavior. The manuscript left by Seth Newhouse (1885) contains editorial changes—the changing of verb tenses, the addition and deletion of words—that show he was penning not only a description of what Deganawida did to convert Tadadaho, but a prescription for present Condolence ceremony. He even writes: "Note. The above part of the ceremony is always to be performed accordingly, afterwards when '*De-ka-na-wi-dah*' completely Established the confederacy" (62). When the Peacemaker speaks in Newhouse's text, he addresses "you" the listener, telling "you" what to do and how to live "your" life. There is then a clear connection between the myth and Iroquois ritual life. It is especially evident in the Condolence (the Peace Hymn, the Ritual at the Edge of the Woods, the Requickening) but is also apparent in the protocol of political diplomacy and alliance. We see, for instance, Hiawatha's insistence on ritual decorum, typical of Iroquois concern for form. He refuses to enter a village or attend a conference because he has not been invited properly or officially. We can find matching examples from Iroquois history. For example, in 1664 the Mohawks insisted upon French propriety in sending invitations before the Iroquois would attend a diplomatic meeting. The League legend prescribes ritual as a proper and effective mode of behavior.

One of the effective uses of ritual in the story is its ability to transform individuals and societies. Implied in this view is the Iroquois notion that every being is double-faceted, and even in the worst of creatures there exists a worthiness that can reveal itself. Paul Wallace (1948:393) is perceptive in seeing the central importance of episode V, the cannibal's conversion upon viewing Deganawida's (and his own) reflection in the kettle. The wretch sees what he thinks is his own face, but it is a face of "beauty," "wisdom," and "strength." Thus he sees "the possibilities of human nature, and of his own nature" (Wallace 1948:393). The story reveals a basic trust in human nature to heal itself, and to heal itself through ritual. As we shall see, the League legend—the League itself—is grounded in a view of human nature as salvagable, in part through ritual, propriety, and moral principles.

In Iroquois cosmology the salvagable human exists in the context of opposing dualities. The world is created by brothers who oppose one another in every activity, in their very being. In the League legend these forces of opposition are prevalent and significant, particularly in the struggle between Hiawatha and Tadadaho, the supposed half-brothers who carry out the cosmic drama of Tarenyawagon and Tawiskaron.

But if siblings fight one another in Iroquois folklore, twins are lucky and creative. Hiawatha and Deganawida are a case in point. These two are like right and left hands, both necessary for a successful life activity, both necessary for the mission to be accomplished.

The apparent oppositions in Iroquois world view do not oppose one another endlessly. Although there is dual antagonism in the folklore, there is also the common motif of incorporation of one's adversary. For example, in the Creation story, Tarenyawagon defeats his foe, Twisted Face, who then becomes a helpful curer through the Society of Faces. In the League legend the cannibal is first incorporated into Deganawida's mission, and then Tadadaho is incorporated into the League. Thus even the most wicked enemy can be part of the forces of good; indeed, he may even want to convert, as Tadadaho impatiently does. He wants to be cured, co-opted by promises of chieftaincy in the League, and incorporated into the new political order.

In this we see the more complex nature of Iroquois dualism, even between good and evil. Opposing forces are also complementary forces throughout the Iroquois cosmology, and reciprocity of design and responsibility abounds in Iroquois culture. Men and women, younger and older brothers, the forest and the clearing, hunting and farming: these examples only begin to suggest the wealth of reciprocal principles that fill Iroquois life. In the legend of the Confederacy we see actors working together, each with his own role, serving one another and serving a larger purpose of establishing the moiety structure of the universe in human institutions. We see the recognition of the victim as the other part of oneself; we see the adversary as the potential ally; we see the reciprocal responsibility in consoling the bereaved. In short, we see complementary, reciprocal dualisms as the metaphysical foundations for the founding of the Iroquois League.

The League legend begins with the metaphysical groundwork of a sal-vageable human nature within the context of complementary dualisms, and it ends with a Confederacy based on this foundation. The story describes the process by which kinship villages with their local systems of mutuality are able to combine into a kinship state with larger and more complex systems of mutuality. The story is, after all, one of state formation: the transcendence of village kinship loyalties; the creation of leadership beyond the local, lineage chiefs, the setting up of a central place of authority, a capital; the extension of the kinship longhouse to the larger kinship state. Compromise is essential to such a process, and the legend describes compromise and incorporation as viable political modes. Indeed, the very reciprocal arrangements that make up village life become the methods of state formation and the working principles of the state thus established. Not only kinship terminology, but the spirit of kinship, fills the story and the structure of the Confederacy. It makes the Iroquois state different from modern national systems, with regimentation of rights and duties through institutional, legal structures. The Iroquois expect humans to help one another as part of a kinship system. People even have the responsibility to provide one another the desires of their dreams. The Iroquois regard humans as salvageable; thus the story recounts the attempt to maximize human potential for mutual benefit through state formation.

In order for the Iroquois to help one another, there must be an infrastructure that promotes connectedness. In this regard, we can see the significance of Hiawatha (or Tarenyawagon) as the clearer of streams, who allows canoe traffic among the nations. Similarly, we note the symbolic importance of the Mother of Nations, who stops feeding warriors along the warrior road and transforms that byway into the Iroquois trail of unity. We also observe that Tadadaho is called "he who obstructs the road." It is necessary for the heroes of the story to clear all paths of obstructions along the great Iroquois trail. This trail helped hold the League together; it stretched like a belt from the Hudson River to Niagara Falls and was the means of communication over three hundred miles of territory.

Even more important to the infrastructure of communication is wampum. Just as Hiawatha helps clear the streams of obstructions and Tadadaho stops obstructing the path, Hiawatha's wampum clears the way for the Confederacy to occur. Wampum belts are the chains that bind nations of the League in alliance. They establish a means to send messages and record agreements, to make peace among the villages. In the seventeenth century, Iroquois symbolized their peace agreements by wrapping themselves in wampum; the action is reminiscent of Hiawatha, who wrapped wampum strings around his head while on his journey to the Mohawks.

A Mohawk in Albany in 1688 made such a gesture with wampum, recalling that such was the expression of alliance established "when the first covenant was made" (Snyderman, 1954:477).

Wampum is more than a means of communication or of exacting etiquette in invitations and diplomatic exchanges. It is a device that symbolically assures the truth of one's communication, a compulsive method of exacting truth from people's words. The Iroquois vow by wampum as one might swear on the Bible in our culture. Furthermore, using wampum provides one's words with their effectiveness, their power to cure. Wampum has metaphysical and supernatural properties that "could be used to restore to the body the powers necessary for clear thinking— only then would tempers be unruffled so that man could focus his attention on good, peaceful, and calm thoughts. Wampum thus became a medicine—a sedative to be administered to the contentious and injured; a healing agent which would enable the sick and wronged to forget injuries" (Snyderman 1954:475). When Hiawatha creates wampum, he creates the means by which he can be consoled, Tadadaho can be healed, blood feuds can be cooled, and mourning can be alleviated.

Wampum is also the means by which the principles and agreements of the League can be recalled and passed down to future generations. Before alphabetic writing among the Iroquois, wampum had the potential of creating a kind of constitutionality in Iroquois polity. Today, for those who can read them, the wampum belts can serve as reminders of Iroquois foundations. Wampum is a means of making and maintaining the Iroquois peace through a codification of Iroquois law. It is part of the infrastructure of the Confederacy.

The story of the Confederacy is one of peaceful purpose and peaceful means. Although it would be sanguine to conclude, as others have done, that the League is some sort of "primitive forerunner of the United Nations to promote peace" (Snyderman 1979:34), the section (XX) on foreign policy shows that warfare and imperial design are not foreign to the League's purposes. The cannibalism so condemned in the myth was practiced by the Iroquois against their enemies in elaborate and cruel ceremonies. The League thus provides a system to regulate feuds and revenge as well as to provide for a common defense. Warfare against others is explicitly allowed for just cause. However, "The dominant motive for the establishment of the League of the Five Iroquois Tribes was the impelling necessity to stop the shedding of human blood by violence through the making and ratifying of a universal peace by all the known tribes of men, to safeguard human life and health and welfare" (Hewitt 1920:541). The League comes about not through warfare but through comforting, curing, moral regeneration, converting, and compromising. The peaceful intentions of the peacemakers are matched by their peaceful methods of creating an Iroquois state.

In order for peaceful nationalism to occur, the myth states, it is necessary to see the other, the outsider, as one sees oneself. The cannibal looks into the pot and sees himself in the depths. He sees himself as the victim in the pot as well as the beautiful human paradigm. The cannibal must see his victim as a person reflected in himself. It is also necessary for the Mohawk to see the Onondaga as an extension of his own kinship group. Thus it is significant that Deganawida is born outside the nations that make up the eventual League. He is born among the Hurons and therefore is an outsider to League structure. Yet he creates the League, and the members that make up the League welcome him in. Even more, among his own people he is a "social cripple" (Chodowiec in Fenton 1975:140), an outcast without father and without acceptance. As an outsider, with no firm ties of kinship, he has all the potential in his nature to create a nation that transcends (and yet builds upon) tribal kin loyalties. As Hewitt states regarding Deganawida, "Tradition ascribes his lineage to no tribe, lest his personality be limited thereby" (1920:537). Paradoxically, other traditions suggest that Deganawida's father did exist and took three successive wives among the Mohawks, one from each of the three Mohawk clans. Therefore Deganawida was related to every person in the Mohawk nation and, through clan ties, to everyone in the League.

In Hiawatha we can see a similar pattern. His family is destroyed, and only because he is without family can he join Deganawida's mission to create a greater family of all Iroquois people. The pathos of his daughters' deaths and his subsequent mourning (and consolation) is balanced by the boon the deaths bring to the League's founding. He must be set free of kinship in order for the Confederacy to exist. Both heroes are liminal culture-brokers, going back and forth among the tribes, because they are tribeless.

The two heroes are travelers who cover the entirety of the Confederacy territory, naming locations, meeting with chiefs, creating clans and methods of communication. They are paradigmatic outsiders who move from one nation to another; they are links in the chain of the League. In their travels, touching base with all the local bases of Iroquois village life, they find adoption among the Mohawks. Adoption thus is crucial to the Confederacy and to the story. Historically, Iroquois clans and nations adopted outsiders—defeated enemies, displaced persons, and others—in order to fill the ranks of the League. Ironically, adoption became both a means of maintaining Iroquois membership in times of war losses, and a motive for war as clan mothers demanded more sons and nephews. In the story adoption is a means by which the League produces trans-tribal affiliations.

In some cases Hiawatha marries his way into tribal networks; in other cases the tribes adopt him and Deganawida, thus denying the categorical otherness of the perpetual outsider in the story.

The transformation of the outsider into the peacemaker and chief is matched by the three parallel transformations, boundary-crossings, that are the heart of the legend. First, the cannibal—whether it is Hiawatha or Tadadaho does not matter—is transformed into the messenger of peace and power. The figure moves from the most depraved form of human activity to the work of nation-building, from chaotic immorality to the moral project of making political order. Second, the transformation of Hiawatha from grieving wanderer to powerful lawgiver and chief is a replication of the first. In both cases Deganawida cures a sick person— sick from killing too much, sick from too much killing, sick as aggressor, sick as victim—and transforms him into an upholder of moral order. Third, the straightening of Tadadaho's mind and body repeats once again the pattern of curing and transformation in order to create an orderly state. The message of peace is repeated in these episodes and underscores the point that the Iroquois Confederacy exists in order to stop wanton killing and the mourning that produces a desire for revenge and more killing.

The myth replicates its message through these transformations. The person of Hiawatha (as cannibal and as mourner) is cured twice, but it is essentially the same cure for the same disease: the disease of killing. The person of Tadadaho is cured twice (as cannibal and as monster) for the same reason. In order to stop the cycle of killing and mourning, and revenge and killing, Deganawida must cure those caught in the cycle. He must cure the cannibal from his monstrously excessive disregard for human life, and he must cure the mourner of his disastrously excessive attachment to his lost family members. The cannibal undervalues, the mourner overvalues, human life, and Deganawida must cure them both. To the cannibal he says, stop killing and form a social order. To the mourner he says, stop mourning and form a social order. The structure of the Confederacy is revealed in these transformational cures. The League exists to stop killing and to comfort the bereaved.

Consolation and peacemaking are the bases for the League. Hiawatha's wild melancholy at his daughters' death needs to be relieved. He over-mourns; therefore he must, and the Iroquois must, learn to accept death. The ritual of Condolence, taught by Deganawida, helps the Iroquois face death, and the League is a mechanism and extension of the Condolence ceremony. The Feast of the Dead, witnessed in the early seventeenth century and still practiced among the Iroquois is perpetuated through a political organization, the Confederacy, that sees as its duty the comforting of mourners in the face of death. It is significant, then, that the procession of chiefs approaches Tadadaho singing songs of consolation, as if he were a mourner just as Hiawatha was. Those songs remember the dead, console the living, and cure society of its killing ills. It is in the best interest of Iroquois society to soothe the kind of mourners like Hiawatha and straighten the mind of killers like Tadadaho so they may think straight and well and act intelligently.

Condolence ceremonies became part of peace negotiations for the Iroquois. It was understood that there might be a grievance between other nations and the League, and before talking with them, the Iroquois delegates must soothe and comfort them. Alliance came to mean condolence, and thus the revenge warfare ("mourning war") that plagued the Iroquois and its neighbors could come to an end, as it did by 1800. In the League legend, Condolence is portrayed as a device for creating and maintaining the state. It stops the cycle of mourning wars, and it maintains the state when a chief dies and needs to be replaced. For the Iroquois, then, the Law is something that exists because there is death. Hertzberg (1966: 93) states that the legend faces death and law, but a causal relationship exists between the two. The Iroquois need law to prevent unnecessary deaths, to control mourning at times of death, and to provide for continuity when chiefs die and need to be replaced. If myths are ways of facing death, as they often are, the League legend states that individual deaths are mitigated by the eternality of the Confederacy and its Law. Significantly, Deganawida summarizes what he has created: the Dead Feast, or Condolence, and the Great Law (Gibson 1899:361). They are his perpetual gifts to the Iroquois.

It is not surprising that the Iroquois conceive their Law as an extension of eternal principles that reflect the will and intervention of the divine. As Hewitt says, Deganawida "knew and sought to do the will of the Master of Life [Tarenyawagon]" (1920:536). This deity put the world in order and established the principles by which humans live. But when famine, warfare, cannibalism all undermined the human order, there was a need for a practical plan, a restatement of the principles of good will. This was brought by Deganawida. We should see the League and its legend as particular manifestations of Iroquois religious principles, which the Iroquois say are grounded in natural law and ultimately in divine law.

The six principles that Deganawida explains to the Mother of Nations in episode IV reveal the Iroquois conception of divine law and its application in the League, as well as in each individual human:

1. *Ne Skenno.* (a) This means health, soundness, and normal functional condition, when used to describe a human person. It is what is achieved after the transformations of Hiawatha and Tadadaho. It is sanity of mind. (b) It is also peace, tranquility, between individuals, between groups like

men and women, and between nations, when describing the body politic. It is what the League promotes. Disease, illness, obsession, and possession through witchcraft are the antitheses of the first meaning. War, strife, and contention are the antitheses of the second. Deganawida finds these negative conditions when he first visits the Iroquois, and his mission is to produce *Ne Skenno* among the people.

2. *Ne Gaiihwiyo.* (a) This is a kind of gospel, a wholesome doctrine to persons, good to be heard, that denotes ethics, values, and righteousness in conduct, thought, and attitude. It is righteousness not only in action but also in advocating it in other people. Deganawida acts well and he also encourages others to act well. He is his own message, the peaceful promoter of peace, the orderly promoter of order. He embodies *Ne Gaiihwiyo.* (b) In addition, it denotes justice and right, as formulated in custom, manners, religion, ritual, and tradition. It points to equity or justice, rights and obligations in society; it is the mutuality epitomized by Deganawida when he takes it upon himself and the chiefs to cure Tadadaho of his monstrosities.

3. *Ne Gashedenza.* (a) This is the force, authority, or power of a people, the physical strength contained in civil chiefs or military power. It is necessary for defense of a nation. (b) It is also the underlying supernatural power, the *orenda,* of a people's institutions. It is the spiritual power that underlies physical power. The League depends on this power because all human life, the Iroquois say, depends on divine help as well as divine guidance.

As we might expect, the story of the Iroquois Confederacy is also a story about the intervention of the divine in human life. Tarenyawagon, the sender of dreams, communicates his will to Deganawida's grandmother and mother about the hero's mission, which is also a divine mission. In Iroquois culture dreams compel fulfillment because they are messages from the supernatural world. The story of the League portrays the fulfillment of Tarenyawagon's desires.

In addition, the legend manifests supernatural power *(orenda)* through the heroes. These men, thought by some Iroquois to be embodiments or incarnations of Tarenyawagon, are at the least messengers from the divine, and the institutions they create possess the power that derives from the supernatural. Perhaps only some Iroquois "thought their deities visited them in human form" (Beauchamp 1892:139); all traditional Iroquois regard their Confederacy as a direct reflection of divine law and the result of divine intervention.

For this reason, Deganawida instructed his chiefs, present and future, to give thanks to the Creator, "the source and ruler of your lives" (Newhouse 1885:22). Thus, when the Confederacy's council meets every year at Onondaga, there are prayers to the Creator similar to those given at other, more purely religious, rituals and festivals. The wampum created by Hiawatha is regarded by Iroquois as a medium of "communion with the Great Spirit" (Snyderman 1982:323), and the Great Tree of the League, like the column of smoke that symbolically rises from Onondaga, reaches from earth to the heavens. The Great Tree pierces the sky, from which Tarenyawagon's grandmother fell at the beginning of earthly time, and continues to furnish symbolic rapport between the Iroquois and the world above, the supernatural.

The Iroquois Confederacy does not constitute the whole of Iroquois religious life. Its meetings do not constitute the whole of religious rituals. Its story is but a part of the whole corpus of Iroquois religious narrative. One scholar states: "The founders of the League of the Iroquois did not aim to establish a religion, but rather a system of government" (Hewitt 1937:84). Nevertheless, "Behind the machinery of the League lay a religious motive" (Wallace 1948:391), and transcending the League is the supernatural world that created and continues to sanction both the story and structure of the Iroquois Confederacy.

Versions of the Iroquois Confederacy Legend Episodes

I.   The Migration and Separation of the People. Akweks 1972:2–25; Beauchamp 1892:10, 16; Brant-Sero 1901:166; Clark 1849:21–23; Hale 1883:18; Henning 1898:480; Henry 1955:28; Hewitt 1892:131; Howard 1971:437; Norton 1970:91, 98–99; Schoolcraft 1847:272.

II.   The Birth and Growth of Deganawida. Akweks 1948:3, 5, 6; Dunlap 1839:29; Fenton 1975:136–37; Gibson 1899:1–9; Henry 1955:30–32; Newhouse 1885:1, 169–72; Parker 1968:14, 65, 66.

III.   The Journey of the Mohawks, the Situation, and the Mission Explained. Akweks 1948:3, 6–9; Beauchamp 1892:16; Brant-Sero 1901:166–67; Clark 1849:24; Dunlap 1839:29; Fenton 1975:136–37; Gibson 1899:10–24; Hale 1883:18; Henry 1955:28–29; Hewitt 1917:436; Newhouse 1885:173; Parker 1968:15–17, 61–63, 67–69.

IV.   The Mother of Nations Accepts Deganawida's Message. Brant-Sero 1901:167–70; Fenton 1975:137; Gibson 1899:25–32; Hale 1883:29; Parker 1968:70–71.

V.   The Cannibal Converts. Gibson 1899:34–60; Parker 1968:69–70.

VI.   The Prophets Prove Their Power. Akweks 1948:7–8; Gibson 1899:74–105; Parker 1968:15–16, 71–73.

VII.   Tadadaho the Wizard Prevents Peace. Akweks 1948:8–9; Beauchamp
        1892:17; 1921:20; Clark 1849:24; Converse 1974:117; Dunlap
        1839:29; Gibson 1899:65–73; Hale 1883:20; Henry 1955:36; Hewitt
        1892:132, 136; 1920:538; Newhouse 1885:3–4; Norton 1970:100;
        Parker 1968:17–18, 69; Schoolcraft 1846:74–75.

VIII.   Hiawatha's Relatives Are Killed. A. Osinoh the Witch Kills Hiawatha's
        Daughters. Akweks 1948:9–10; Beauchamp 1926:31; Newhouse
        1885:4–5; Parker 1968:18–19. B. Tadadaho Kills Hiawatha's Relatives
        with a Great Plunging Bird. Akweks 1948:9; Beauchamp 1926:31;
        Gibson 1899:106–19; Henning 1898:477; Hewitt 1892:132–35;
        Newhouse 1885:6; Norton 1970:100; Parker 1968:17–18, 74–76.

IX.   Hiawatha Mourns and Quits Onondaga. Akweks 1948:10; Beauchamp
        1926:32; Hewitt 1892:133; Newhouse 1885:6; Norton 1970:100;
        Parker 1968:18–19, 114–15.

X.   Hiawatha Invents Wampum. A. Hiawatha Uses Elderberry Twigs.
        Akweks 1948:10; Parker 1968:20, 77. B. Hiawatha Uses Shells. Akweks
        1948:10; Beauchamp 1921:16; 1926:31; Gibson 1899:264–68; Hale
        1883:24; Henning 1898:478; Hewitt 1892:133; Parker 1968:20, 116;
        Snyderman 1961:581; 1982:323; Converse 1974:139–40, 187. C.
        Hiawatha Uses Bird Quills. Beauchamp 1892:64; 1921:17.

XI.   Hiawatha Gives the Mohawks Lessons in Protocol. Akweks 1948:11–
        12; Beauchamp 1926:32; Converse 1974:188–89; Gibson 1899:121–
        41; Henning 1898:477–78; Hewitt 1892:134; Newhouse 1885:7;
        Norton 1970:101; Parker 1968:20–22, 76–79, 117.

XII.   Deganawida Consoles Hiawatha. Akweks 1948:12–13; Fenton
        1975:137; Hewitt 1892:135; Newhouse 1885:10; Parker 1968:22–24.

XIII.   Scouts Travel to Tadadaho. Akweks 1948:15–16; Converse 1974:189;
        Hewitt 1892:136; Newhouse 1885:13–17; Parker 1968:26–27.

XIV.   Deganawida and Hiawatha Join Oneidas, Cayugas, and Senecas to
        Mohawks. Akweks 1948:14–15; Boyce 1973:288–89; Gibson
        1899:142–217; Hale 1883:29; Newhouse 1885:76–130, 175–76;
        Norton 1970:103–5; Parker 1968:25–26, 85, 96–97.

XV.   The Nations March to Tadadaho, Singing the Peace Hymn. Akweks
        1948:13; Beauchamp 1921:20–21; Hertzberg 1966:105; Hewitt
        1892:135, 137–40; Newhouse 1885:28–52; Norton 1970:103; Parker
        1968:27–28, 79–91.

XVI.   Deganawida and Hiawatha Transform Tadadaho. Boyce 1973:288–89;
        Converse 1974:118; Dunlap 1839:3; Gibson 1899:244–52; Hale
        1883:27–29; Hewitt 1892:140; Newhouse 1885:64–65; Norton
        1970:104–5; Parker 1968:27–28, 80–91.

XVII. Deganawida and Hiawatha Establish Iroquois Unity and Law. Akweks 1948:26–27; 1972:29; Boyce 1973:289; Converse 1974:189; Fenton 1975:136–38; Gibson 1899:253; Hale 1883:21–22; Henry 1955:32–33; Hewitt 1915:322; Newhouse 1885:9, 17, 65; Parker 1968:29.

XVIII. Deganawida and Hiawatha Establish League Chiefs and Council Polity. Akweks 1948:14, 18, 21–26; Gibson 1899:218–43, 266–300, 307–11, 322–41, 344, 350–57; Hale 1883:30–31; Hewitt 1892:140–44; Newhouse 1885:9, 17–28; Parker 1968:24, 91–92.

XIX. The Confederacy Takes Symbolic Images. Akweks 1948:5, 18; 1972:29, 31; Beauchamp 1921:19; Dunlap 1839:30; Fenton 1960:3–7; 1975:141–43; Gibson 1899:301–6, 312–21; Hewitt 1892:140–44; 1915:323–25; Newhouse 1885:24–25; Parker 1968:30, 44–49, 100–102, 116; Wallace 1946:7, 8.

XX. The League Declares Its Sovereignty. Akweks 1972:32; Fenton 1949a:150–51; Hale 1883:32–33; Parker 1968:49–55.

XXI. The Condolence Maintains the Confederacy. Fenton 1975:138; Gibson 1899:345–48, 365–67; Hewitt 1927:238–39; Newhouse 1885:11–13; Parker 1968:36–60.

XXII. Deganawida Departs. Gibson 1899:360–64; Hale 1883:31; Howard 1971:435; Newhouse 1885:130; Parker 1968:105.

5

A Navajo Heroic

DEATH, DISEASE, MEDICINE, AND RITUAL

In the previous chapter we viewed the Iroquois attempt to ameliorate death's effects. Unless we wish to interpret Iroquois political society as a symbolic transcendence of personal, individual death, we should observe that the Iroquois myths face without blinking the finality of human death. Numerous American Indian myths proclaim death's irreversible nature and warn against futile attempts to bring back the dead to life. A particularly widespread tradition occurs, which denies categorically and dramatically all human attempts to escape death's finality. Åke Hultkrantz (1957) has documented these "Orpheus" stories throughout the continent in a masterful study, which includes examples from the Navajos of the Southwest.

In its Navajo form, the Orpheus tradition relates how a man mourned the death of his wife. He

waited four nights at his wife's grave. Then something departed from it which he followed four days; during the day it disappeared in cracks in the rocks. In the afterworld the dead were found dancing: the woman was welcome, the man called a "ghost." Counter to instructions he built a fire during the day and saw skeletons lying about with torn blankets. Terrified, the man ran home pursued by his wife. A ceremony was made by animals during which the man was not to look at his wife. He broke the tabu and saw her as a skeleton once more. [Gayton 1935:271, from W. W. Hill's Navajo field notes]

In another Navajo version, at the world's beginning, when the Navajos had just emerged from below the earth (Haile 1942:411–14), a husband followed his dead wife, bloodied by witchery, to the emergence place and leaped down after her. With the help of Spider Man and Woman, he slept with his wife once again in an underground chamber with magic stones, which the husband was ordered not to move. Upon breaking the interdiction, he saw the reality of his wife's death, surrounded by skulls, rags, and crawling mice. Only with the help of two protecting gods was he able to escape, bringing back with him medicines against witchcraft, plus the ability to interpret symptoms of imminent death that "if heeded, would 'prevent bad things to come' meaning, that death and entry into 'this (emergence) place' " referred to as "nobody's home," where all dead people must go, "could be deferred." However, his wife made a lasting pronouncement, that " 'you that die shall return to this place one after another' " (cf. Wyman and Bailey 1943b:6–10). In a parallel tradition, Coyote seals the fate of the first person to die, a hermaphrodite, saying that death is necessary to prevent overcrowding in the world (Reichard 1974:40–2).

Of course the Orpheus tradition exists beyond the range of American Indians; indeed, it is one of the most common myths worldwide, in various manifestations, indicating its universal appeal. Western audiences know best its Greek variant and its cultic complex. Among North American Indians, as Hultkrantz has demonstrated, the Orpheus myth is a source of religious revelation, a paradigm for shamanistic behavior, a vehicle for prophecy, and a text of ultimate significance par excellence. Orpheus, the traveler to the land of the dead, crosses the boundary of human, earthly existence, and returns intact, although eventually without his goal. His story is a narrative of transcending, and yet reinforcing, the most crucially ontological threshold, a timeless and perpetually timeful tale that describes the ultimate and ultimately impossible aspects of human life. It is a myth intimately and directly concerned with human life-and-death matters.

In a concrete, personally appealing, even romantic narrative, the hero attempts the impossible of human life: to fetch his loved one from the afterworld, and to recover the fullness of kinship relations on earth, conquering death in the process. He attempts to deny death's supremacy while proclaiming his everliving love, but his quest is doomed to failure. Whereas the storyteller and audience may not accept gladly the fate of the moribund beloved, the destiny of all humans, they share the message of Orpheus's failure and must admit its truth. At heart the myth teaches the futility of all attempts to overcome death. In addition, the story cautions against excesses of mourning. The dead should be grieved, but life must continue. The living must concern themselves with daily matters while facing bravely the loss of their beloved companions.

Furthermore, most Orpheus texts bring the living community into focus by emphasizing the gifts brought back from the afterworld: dances that recall the celebratory movements of the dead in the afterworld, medicines, or agricultural benefits. That is, the story remembers the origin of human institutions, the cultural stuff of this world that must console us in our disappointed search for immortality.

At the same time, the myth reassures Indians regarding their immortal afterlife. In the other world the dead live happily, enjoying their tribal kinship bonds much as the living do on earth (with significant inversions, of course). The dead dance together at night, share meals, and enjoy each other's company so much that the departed wife does not wish to leave to return to earth. Hence the Orpheus tradition seems to herald an optimistic eschatology. The dead are seen for the most part (although not in the Navajo case) as happy creatures, content in their new mode of existence; so the Orpheus tradition softens the finality of death with a promise of joyous afterlife.

If it is a story of death, afterlife, and societal institutions, the Orpheus myth also heralds family love. It describes Eros as well as Thanatos, and although it teaches that the dead and living are divorced from one another, it emphasizes equally the importance of kinship emotion and loyalty. Active kinship ceases in death—Orpheus's attachment to his dead wife is excessive—but ties among the living are normal and healthy. Orpheus exhibits an ennobling heroism in struggling for love against invincible death; his failure does not diminish his nobility. Like other heroes, as we shall soon see, Orpheus's goal is ultimately eternal life—some other Orpheus myths state this goal directly—and his failure makes the reality of his impossible venture more convincing.

Hultkrantz's central theory regarding Orpheus in North America illustrates the mythic concern for simultaneously facing death and life, recognizing the reality of death and the reality of living life fully. Hultkrantz states that the Orpheus tradition is a shamanistic text, on a continent where shamanism has been democratized through almost universal vision quests. The myth sketches the technique by which a shaman can enter a trance at will, attain ecstacy, use imitative magic to emulate a dead person, and with the help of guardian spirits travel to the land of the dead in order to restore the lost or stolen or diseased souls of moribund individuals. Out of love for their community—a love like that of Orpheus for his wife—a desire to perpetuate healthy human life through mastery over souls, shamans are said to attempt the impossible: they undergo ritual death and rebirth (as Orpheus does) in order to promote life.

The shaman's special concern is combating disease and disharmony. In his guise as a shaman, the Indian Orpheus aims to heal the sick, even if he can not revive the dead. Our second Navajo story illuminates the stop-gap effect of shamanistic (and all other types of) medicine: it cannot prevent death, but for the living shamanism offers the hope of health and harmony in this life. It offers medicine, which is the concern of this chapter.

It is our purpose to concentrate here on one Navajo myth that describes the origin of a medicinal ritual, Prostitution (or Excess) Way. In the context of a heritage—the Orpheus tradition—that assumes the reality of death, the impossibility of immortality, the following myth stresses the power that humans have to ameliorate their own conditions, to forestall diminishment and death as long as humanly possible through ceremonial compulsion and catharsis. If the Orpheus tradition accepts death's power, the next myth from the same people celebrates human powers, within limits, in this life.

The existence of two Orpheus variants among the Navajos arouses curiosity, because the Navajos have precious little affection for their dead. The poignancy of the Navajo Orpheus's mission is increased when we realize that the Navajos loathe their dead, including their closest relations, from the moment of demise. To overcome his cultural fear, the Navajo Orpheus would have required astounding love and desire for reunification with his spouse.

For the traditional Navajos, it is this life that matters; the afterworld, "nobody's home," is of little or no concern. They posit no heaven or hell, and they possess no mortuary celebration. Some Navajos believe in a shadowy afterworld; others think there is no afterlife, despite the promise of their Orpheus tradition. For those who believe, the world of ghosts exists just below the surface of the earth, as we have seen, possibly to the north of Navajoland. The journey there takes four days, and at the entrance the ghost must undergo tests to prove it is indeed dead.

Whether or not they conceive of a specific afterland, all traditional Navajos hold similar beliefs regarding ghosts. No matter how good a person might be during lifetime, at death a malignant force is released—a dangerous ghost capable of returning to earth as an apparition and causing sickness and misfortune. The only persons who do not release such harmful entities are senile elders and newborn infants, both said to be "raw" and incapable of maleficence. A good spirit is also released at death, but it does not return to earth, perhaps remaining in the afterworld. Ghosts, on the contrary, come back after dark in the shapes of animals or humans, changing appearance and leaving ominous tracks. Their aim is to avenge slights made against them during their lifespan. They are beyond the control of humans, and indeed are the very opposite of humans.

The function of such beliefs might be to improve conduct toward the living, so as not to incur their wrath after death. Nevertheless, the immediate effect of Navajo eschatological beliefs seems to be thoroughgoing avoidance of all things associated with the deceased. Dreams about the dead cause great anxiety and require ritual ministrations to offset the potential dangers. News of a relative or close friend's death will postpone any major undertaking, including a ceremonial, since such news is regarded as ominous to life activity.

When a person is nearing certain death, the traditional Navajo relatives may move him or her from the home to a distant site to save the hogan from contamination. If someone dies in a hogan, it is abandoned forever, its door fastened with a conspicuous death-knot.

The burial itself is immediate, unceremonious, and hasty. Simply, the body is deposited in the ground, away from normal places of human activity, with the shovel or spade retired from future use. Those who perform the odious task of burial undergo ritual purification. Neither they nor anyone else will speak the name of the deceased, and every attempt is made to avoid the gravesite or mention of the deceased's name. Most of the dead person's possessions are buried with the corpse; no Navajo would wear the contaminated clothing of a late relative. Pregnant women take special care to avoid seeing a cadaver. If a person should die while being treated for disease, the implements being used can never again be employed to cure the illness from which the deceased suffered.

Historically, Navajo fear of the dead has affected their attitudes toward religious movements. For examples, their longstanding aversion to Christianity was conditioned by a disgust regarding any cult that promised the second coming to earth of a dead man, Jesus. And in 1890 the Navajos eschewed any association with the pan-Indian, nativistic Ghost Dance, because its major goal was reunification with the dead on earth. In recent years, however, Navajo mortuary practices and beliefs have begun to change.

It should be noted that the Navajos have no especially morbid fear of death itself; it is only the dead that produce such dread. The Navajos do not look to their ancestors for worldly aid. Rather, they emphasize their own power and control over events in their lives, particularly over disease.

In the shadow of death, and with no hope of help from their shadowy departed, the Navajos continue to proclaim their ability and will to put death off. The vast complex of Navajo rituals conveys the Navajo preoccupation with health and curing.

In brief, Navajo ritual, *nahaya* (Haile 1938:639), is regarded as concerted activity on the part of knowledgeable, effective humans to influence the course of events in a dangerous world. As a form of stylized behavior, Navajo ritual has a goal, to maintain—or more important, to restore—harmony between the individual and the universe. Gladys Reichard has remarked that "to the Navajo religion means ritual" (1974:3). Most prominently, Navajo rituals mean to cure patients of diseases.

Underlying assumptions both inform and propel these Navajo curing rituals that are said to be the central features of their social and religious lives. Most broadly stated, the Navajos believe in their own power of will and knowledge. Created from the skin of Changing Woman—perhaps their most powerful and revered deity—and living on a universe composed of one, monistic nature, the Navajos regard themselves as greatly competent in controlling events around them. Not alienated in essence from either the gods or the nonhuman environment, the Navajos possess the potential to know, to name, and thereby to direct events near to them, if they follow certain principles of perception and action: if they maintain orderliness, moderation, and control in all activities; if they are wary of strangers and nonrelatives; if they avoid excesses and respect the complementarity of male and female principles, maintaining balance in the world; if they respect nature's power and the individual's integrity; if they take literally what is said; and if they turn their attention to living this life without hope of future rewards.

Perhaps better than any other non-Navajo, Gary Witherspoon has explained (1977; cf. Witherspoon 1975) the high Navajo estimation of their own prowess. In a powerful, dangerous universe, the Navajos conceive of themselves as superior beings belonging to the same linguistic category as the gods themselves. No natural entity or force, no abstraction, can overwhelm a conscious, willful Navajo. By knowing, naming, and acting willfully, Navajos can coerce even the gods to share their potency, especially for the purpose of alleviating illness.

Humans, therefore, wish to know and thus bring under control all the parts of the integral universe. They seek to know not only the details of being (the properties of plants, the behavior of animals) but also the universal rules of existence (that like produces like; that the part stands for and can influence the whole; that association of entities is based on similarity of function; that all things are ultimately associated in defined hierarchies; that proper ritual grounded in proper knowledge can coerce all things). This Navajo ontology aims for more than understanding. It is the baseline for Navajo ritual action, seeking to cure human ailments and to prolong human life. Clyde Kluckhohn and Dorothea Leighton (1962:221) have described this Navajo notion, "that the universe works according to rules. If one can discover the rules and follow them, he may remain safe or be restored to safety—and more. The divinities must themselves bow to the compulsion of ritual formulas." In effect, the Navajos hope to achieve the impossible: to attain virtual human eternity and harmony through heroic willpower and knowledge, employing the ultimate powers of the gods.

It is beyond the scope of this chapter to catalogue the array of Navajo deities. For our purposes it is sufficient to note that the Navajo polytheism embraces a multitude of gods with overlapping functions, powers, characteristics, and lineages. Whether using the native categories of divinity or some schema composed by observers, the Navajos hold distinctive attitudes toward human relations with their divinities. Although humans "smell bad" to the holy people and must purify themselves before coming into contact with the gods, humans are said to have powers only slightly less potent than those of the supernaturals. Most significantly, of course, humans die and the gods do not. But in practice, humans can attain temporary equality—if the gods can be persuaded—by tapping divine power through informed, expert ritual. In the system of reciprocity between humans and gods, in which the divinities hold the ultimate trump card of immortality, humans possess the effectual tools of rituals. They can coerce the gods through ritual. Without humility or arrogance, but rather with knowledge and confidence, Navajos can call on their gods—including the Christian deity these days among Navajo pentecostals—to help cure diseases that plague and constitute human life.

Classifications of Navajo rituals divide conveniently between the prophylactic, ever-present Blessingways and the curative Chantways (and their subcategories: holyways, evilways, and lifeways). All ceremonials are derived from or center around Blessingway, the explanatory core of which is the Navajo origin myth. Blessingway is the backbone of Navajo ceremonialism, entering all aspects of ritual life, including blessings throughout the agricultural cycle, salt gathering, war and hunting rites, divination rites, and rites of passage.

The focus of this chapter is one of the Chantways, or rather a myth that commemorates the origin of a specific Chantway. Nearly two-thirds of the collected Navajo mythology consists of Chantway myths, each devoted to the cure of a specific type of disease, catalogued by its cause. The three major types of Chantways, holyways, evilways, and lifeways, deal with diseases caused, respectively, by supernaturals, foreign or native ghosts, and bodily injuries of mundane origin.

Behind this simple formulation, however, is a more complex set of theories regarding cause and cure of disease. In general, traditional Navajos think that their diseases come about through a lack of human awareness, consciousness, and control. When humans become unwillful, in a sense they will their own loss of mastery and allow dangerous beings and forces to molest and harm them. They present to their maleficent foes—ghosts, witches, monsters, malicious deities, other holy people who hold grudges for taboos broken—a visage of weakness and incapacity, vulnerability to sickness. When Navajos lose control over their surroundings, they fall ill.

Navajo ceremonialism is directed largely toward the cure of disease;

for the Navajos, therapy is the ritual norm. Studies in the 1940s found that Navajo men spent up to one-third of their waking hours in such rituals, women being slightly less involved but still devoting as much as a fifth of their productive time in rites of health (see Kluckhohn 1938b). It was also estimated at that time that 20 percent of family money supported the curing ceremonials, paying the specialists for their skills. If anything, the number of such rituals per year has increased as of late (even though the percentages per capita have fallen), due to the increase of Navajo wealth. Studies have shown that Navajo anxiety centers primarily around health and disease. The individual Navajo worries about his or her personal health, although in the greater context of universal harmony (Kluckhohn and Leighton 1962:238–40; Leighton and Leighton 1942:202–5). It is the job of Navajo Chantways to find the specific cause of a disease, and reestablish health by reasserting human mastery over the universe. This task is achieved in large part by identifying the patient with the immortal gods, by tapping divine power through ritual willpower.

Curing requires that first a proper diagnosis be made. Diagnosticians are trained for this job, as stargazers, hand-tremblers, and listeners. By perceiving significant signs, they can point to the possible causes of a patient's disease. For each disease there is a cause, and for each cause a ceremonial cure. In order to secure the proper cure, in order to turn to the proper singer-physician *(hatali)* with specialization in a certain ceremonial, the exact cause must be accurately determined.

Two examples can illustrate the difficulty and opacity of association in pinpointing a disease's cause. Beautyway, for one, cures diseases caused primarily by snakes. Sleeping in a snake bed, killing snakes, bad dreams about snakes, and snakebites can all bring about sickness that only Beautyway can heal (Wyman 1957:16–17). Windway, for another, cures diseases caused by winds: sleeping in a bed hollowed out by the wind, eating food cooked on a fire made with wood of a tree felled by wind, the connection to wind can be extremely oblique (Wyman 1962:20–22). In most cases, the patient is entirely unconscious of his or her tainted connection; indeed, it is the patient's lack of conscious perception of his or her actions that let the disease enter the body. It is the duty of the diagnostician, and then of the curer, to make the patient conscious, aware, in cognitive mastery of the disease and its cause, in order for the healing to take place.

From the start, the curing specialists must reduce the patient's bewilderment, his or her lack of control over emotions, and turn one's undirected anxieties about the potential causes of the disease into a knowledgeable appreciation of the disease's nature. By reducing panicky anxiety to responsible fear, and then eliminating that fear and reestablishing the patient's confident control over the situation, the cure can take place. To effect these beneficial changes, the singer, in combination with the patient's friends, family, and relatives, assures the patient of his or her latent potency and the efficacy of the ritual healing. All attention is focused on a cure constructed of confidence.

In many cases the patient has violated some taboo and must be made aware of—he or she must admit—the cause of the sickness. Those present at a cure—the patient, co-patient, sponsor, family, relatives, friendly spectators, intermediaries and practitioners such as the singer, his apprentice and assistants, an herbalist, and a diagnostician—all join their collective will for a safe recovery. They must share a consensus regarding the disease's nature and the procedure of healing. Such mutual realization is healing knowledge and brings on control. The commonly focused willpower is held by the Navajos to be supremely effective. If the curers devote their desire and energy in ritually accurate forms—if they pronounce their prayers correctly, if the prayer-sticks are properly bound, if the sand paintings are right in every detail, and if their wills are strong and in unison—a cure will occur. The compulsive, irresistible power of these ceremonials undergirds Navajo belief. The Navajos try to will themselves to harmony and health.

Through songs, prayers, and the ritual manipulation of sacred symbols—the wearing of masks impersonating the gods, the exorcism of evil from effigies, the unraveling of woollen strings, the laying out of prayer-sticks, the emetics and baths in steam and water—the singer and his numerous cohorts work to purify the patient and everything associated with him or her, adding new rites and paraphernalia when feasible. For a number of days, from one to nine, the patient is thereby instructed in the art of control, of clarification of the mind and will, in order for the ultimate act of healing. To this end the singer has devoted a lifetime of apprenticeship, memory, and will. Each singer, working on his own without an organized society of curers, is expert in one or a small number of these ceremonials, each of which requires immense concentration.

The apotheosis of each Chantway is the creation of a design made of sand, pollen, and ashes that symbolizes and invokes the immortal divinity ultimately responsible for this disease's cause and cure. With the help of assistants, the singer constructs the sandpainting on the ground to represence accurately the identity of the efficacious deity: perhaps the source of the disease, surely the source of its cure. Then the patient is made to wash and immerse the body in the sand patterns, to identify with the powers pictured in the images, to will the holy person's potence, in order to wrest control over the disease's cause. In effect, the patient undergoes a transubstantiation and becomes—for the practical purpose of the cure—the healing deity in the flesh. Through the mediatory aid of the singer and the others, through the sand painting especially, the patient challenges weakness, attains proper realization, and wills a transformation into a healthy being once more.

To an outsider the exercise smacks of psychic hubris; to the Navajos the cure is their lifeline, a manifesto of their heroic desire to live long and healthy lives, even in the face of eventual death and diminishment. Unable to span the fullest sphere around which revolves life and death in their most extreme polarity—unable to hope realistically for immortality, as we have seen demonstrated in the Orpheus myth, and unable even to hope for everlasting communion with the living after death— the Navajos devote their ceremonial life to achieving and reachieving a healthy existence. They try to revive themselves periodically and eternally, like Changing Woman, who restores herself seasonally.

CHANTWAY MYTHOLOGY

Through their mythology the Navajos lay the groundwork for their medical beliefs and ceremonial cures. The valorous conduct of their compulsive rituals finds its counterpart in the narratives that describe the ceremonial origins. Navajos refer readily to their myths to answer life's questions, and they seem to draw on the bravado of their storied heroes of the Chantway myths for their own courage in combating disease.

Each Chantway has its myth of origin, in which a hero encounters dangers while on a journey. He is struck ill or is destroyed or stranded. He obtains aid of holy people, learns a curing ritual and is healed, returns to his people to teach the ritual, or brings agricultural secrets, and finally leaves the people for life among the divinities or elsewhere. The myths are familiar to most Navajos, at least in outline form, and a singer of a certain Chantway should be able (but is not required) to recite the origin myth of a particular ceremonial. All of these Chantway origin myths are connected at least tangentially to the Navajo creation and origin myth, but each Chantway myth can stand on its own as a significant narrative. Often the Navajos tell them as part of winter night entertainment, apparently isolated from the rituals to which they are bound. Each Chantway can have more than one origin myth, although in their general outlines all the hero myths are markedly similar to (and structurally interchangeable with) one another.

To illustrate the heroic pattern, we have selected "The Story of San′ hode′di′begaeye, the Beggar's Son," the origin myth for the *Ajiłee* Chantway. *Ajiłee* is a five-day holyway, of minor importance in the past century and virtually defunct today, of the Mountain Chant subgroup, along with Mountaintop Way, Moth Way, Beauty Way, and the Way to Remove Somebody's Paralysis (Spencer 1957:13). The myth itself has overlapping episodes with Moth Way and Water Way, and is related in its mythology to Enemyway and Coyoteway. *Ajiłee* stresses the exorcism of evil, concentrating on the individual patient rather than tribal welfare, and it is also considered a rite of instruction with no sand paintings known to researchers.

Ajiłee has been translated most frequently as Prostitution Way, perhaps because the rakish hero of the myth pays for his brides. Its etymology is closely related to prostitutes and lewdness, as well as to lighthearted and reckless creatures like Coyote, and it is used "to cure inveterate prostitutes, as well as men who have patronized them" of their excessive sexuality (Haile 1978:149). The myth's main characters, the Sun, Butterfly, Coyote, as well as the hero himself, are all sexual copulators of obsessive proportions. The Chantway, then, "refers to the passionate reproductive behavior among all sexual beings on Earth—to all the possibilities and excesses of their excitement" (Haile 1978:2).

Its main feature, despite its being a holyway, is to counteract Frenzy Witchcraft, an attack which makes men or women uncontrollably lustful; however, in the late nineteenth century, the ceremonial fell into disrepute because it was thought to be used as a charm to seduce as often as it was to undo seduction. As a result, the myth and the Chantway are obsolescent.

As a ceremonial that attempts to treat symptoms of general insanity—sexual excesses, prostitution, divorce, wildness, shyness, disorientation, hallucination, drunkedness, restlessness, roaming, and malaise of Anglo-American mobility—*Ajiłee* should perhaps be called more accurately Excess, Recklessness, or Rashness Way, since at heart it "seeks to undo the effects of any kind of recklessness" (Reichard 1974:139). But whether we refer to *Ajiłee* as Prostitution or Excess Way, it promises most of all to dissipate sickness associated with lustful evil.

Rather than discuss the multitude of minute variations in versions of this myth alone, not to mention the fullest possibilities within the heroic Navajo archetype, we shall concentrate instead on one version of one myth (O'Bryan 1956:143–66), a version that has been overlooked by students of the Chantway. It opens with reference to the Navajo Creation Story.

The Story of San'hode'di'begaeye, the Beggar's Son

Now after the Great Gambler had been sent up into the sky, the Sun wanted the people to know about the medicine that the Gambler had used and had taken up into the sky with him. So he made a plan.

At the foot of Mount Taylor lived a poor woman who worked hard for her living. The Sun visited this woman secretly, and she brought forth a baby boy. When he was ten or twelve, he ran a race each morning around Mount Taylor. He thus became a great runner.

The woman and boy went to live at Pueblo Bonito. The people there made many turquoise offerings in the cliff rocks. Discovering these offerings, the woman took the pieces of turquoise and exchanged them for food with the people. They wondered where this poor beggar woman got the stones, and they guessed their origin. They tracked her, discovered her ploy, and the chief decided to kill her and her son; however, the two heard of the plan and fled.

They went to a place opposite Farmington. Some of the people there gave them food; others drove them away and were cruel to them. Again she discovered and gathered stone offerings, trading them for food. Again she was found out, but she and her son escaped before they could be killed.

They stopped opposite Fruitland and built a little home there, gathering seeds, killing a rabbit, a rat. When the people discovered them, they were no longer safe, so they went to Hog Back Mountains, built a little house, made grass mats and robes of rabbit and rat fur. By the time the robes were large in size, the boy had grown into a youth.

They were discovered again, fled past Shiprock, to the other side of the Carrizos; today you can still see a ruin of the house the boy built for his mother. He was a good builder by then. But when seeds ran out, they moved once more, to Kiet Seel.

Along the way they frightened the chief of Kiet Seel, who then gave them each a bundle of wood, telling them to burn the wood that night. Doing so, they ate and slept. No sooner were they asleep when some boys, men, and women came and threw sticks and stones at them, mud, water, and ashes, too, bothering them all night. Preparing to leave the next day, they brought the remainder of the wood to the chief, thinking him kind; but the food they received at his house was meager. So, the next night they camped further away. Still they were bothered, and when they brought more wood the next morning, they received only one morsel each. After another night of torment, they brought more wood, and received nothing for their work.

They traveled to Yakin, where the pattern was repeated: the man with wood, the nightly torture, the diminishing returns for their labor. After four days, they went to another spot where the pattern occurred once again. Fortunately the wickedness lasted but a short time. Then they went to Tala hogan, where they lived in a bark shelter. Young girls teased them, saying, "We want a husband to gather wood for us." Mocking the pair's poverty, they pretended to argue for the boy's hand as husband.

To avoid them, he hunted rabbits and rats early each morning. One day when he returned, his mother told him:

I was sitting here today when all of a sudden everything inside our shelter turned white. I looked and someone stood out there. It was a man who asked about you. I told him that you stay away all day because the girls come and tease you. He asked me about our food and about our bedding. I had baked four little seed cakes. I showed him the woven grass mats which we use for bed and cover. The man then took a piece of the bread and ate it and said: "This is my food also." I turned my head for a moment, and the man was gone. But there was only one track outside. The piece of seed cake he bit into is here.

The boy did not believe this story: "It is foolish to think that any people as poor as we are would be visited by a Holy Being."

The next day she repeated her story of the handsome Holy Person, who left two tracks this time. Again the boy did not believe her, and accused her of making the tracks and eating the seed cake. For four days the man returned, each day eating more of the cake and leaving an additional track. On the fourth day, the mother reported: "He wants you to wash your hair in the morning and to bathe your whole body, drying yourself with cornmeal and pollen. Then you are to get some water in the jar, and sit beside it in the shelter. You are to sit there and keep looking into the water."

He followed her instructions, and at noon, all turned white, and the young Holy Being appeared, announcing that he was going to take "his younger brother," and return. Four times the mother protested, saying he was her only support: "I would starve to death without him." However, after the fourth time, her son reminded her that he would be returned, and she relented.

A white rainbow flashed to the youth's feet, and the Holy Being told him to raise his right foot. They took four steps, on four different mountains, and reached a room filled with trash. In a second room someone spoke: "Um-m-m, I smell earthly people. . . . The fool-hearted youth must be bringing someone home." In a fourth room they saw a man, woman, and girl—People of the Mountain, the man, wife, and daughter. They washed the youth four times, dried him four times with corn pollen, and the girl gave him four baskets, of white bead, turquoise, white shell, and black jet. Then he was trimmed and formed like the maiden herself. She put her head beside his and he was formed like her, all except the feet. He had big feet.

Then the Sun came. The man and woman wanted to dress the youth, but the Sun said, "No, he is my son, and I will dress him myself." Then the White Bead Woman came and said, "If he is the son of the Sun he is my son also. I will dress him myself," which she did, accompanied by a chant:

The White Bead Woman's Chant

She dressed me with her white bead moccasins.
She dressed me with her white bead leggings.

She dressed me with her white bead garment.
She dressed me with her white bead bracelets.
She dressed me with her white bead earrings.
She dressed me with the perfect white bead called ha'da tehe which she
    had on her forehead.
She dressed me with the perfect crystals of pollen, the beautiful goods
    pollen, which were her words
And with which I can call for beautiful goods and pollen and they will
    come at my word.
She dressed me with the turquoise feather
On top of which sat the blue bird with his beautiful song.
I am dressed like the Most High Power Whose Ways Are Beautiful.
All is beautiful before me.
All is beautiful behind me.
All is beautiful around me.
All is beautiful everywhere.

[sung twice]

I am all dressed with her white bead moccasins. . . .

[sung twice]

After this the Sun and the White Bead Woman returned to their home.

The Man of the Mountain gave the youth blue gum and four herbs for his
medicine: from the East a plant with black flowers; from the South a plant
with white flowers; from the West a medicine of the mind, a very poisonous
medicine herb which is said to make them insane, like locoweed. The plant
from the North had yellow flowers with their mouths open; if touched, they
laughed. These were medicines the Gambler had used. The boy learned the
Gambler's chants, and he received from the man a bundle full of all the beautiful
goods of the mountain. That which had been trash was now beauty and food.
As payment for the chants and medicine, he was instructed to climb Red Side
Mountain, shoot arrows into four bushes eaten by deer, withdraw the arrows,
and return them to the place from which he had come.

When he returned by rainbow to his mother's doorway, she grabbed him
and said, "What have you done with my son? ... Where is he?" Four times
she asked, and four times he told her, "Mother, it is I." But he had changed,
he was different. His hair fell to his ankles.

He chanted the chants he had learned, chewed the blue gum, and blew to
East, South, West and North; they found themselves in a home like that of the
Mountain Man. When the girls came for their wood, he opened the door and
blew blue gum at them. They fell back and whispered about all the beautiful
things they had seen therein. Then he led them to the forest, cut wood for
them all. They took the wood home, ashamed of themselves, but also glad of
his help.

The chief had two daughters, maidens well guarded. The elder went to a
spring early one morning for water. He asked for a drink from her jar, then

tossed some of it on her. Four times she filled the jar, and he tipped it over with a blow of blue gum. After he showed her the secret of his power, she let the young man become her husband.

When she got 'home, her father told her to make water. He saw that she had been visited by a man, and he measured his footprint. None of the men in the village had a foot that big; neither did any men in the neighboring village. With the advice of Little Breeze, the young man charmed the chief into remembering him and his poor mother. After finding the young man and measuring his foot, the chief said, "My son-in-law, do you know that you are an expectant father?"

A baby boy was born, and the people sang birthing chants as they carried the infant to his father. They wrestled with each other and laughed. They gave him gifts and brought his wife, and also her younger sister to be his second wife. He received a longhouse from his father-in-law, but his mother remained in their house, with their beautiful goods. Over the next four days he killed one, two, three, and four antelopes for each household in the village, and with each day he received another longhouse. All the people said, "Our son-in-law is very great. We will have plenty of meat."

On the fifth day, while hunting antelope, a coyote hit him with his hide and blew four times upon him. The coyote took the man's antelope headdress and placed it on his own head; off he went, hunting antelope, leaving San'hode'di', the beggar's son, in the form of a skinny coyote. The coyote was unable to kill even one antelope, so he turned discharge from his eye into fat and took it to the two wives. Nevertheless, the younger one told her sister that this man was not their husband.

For four days the beggar's son ate berries under bushes in the four directions, but he was almost dead at this time. A person reported to the Mountain People what had befallen the young man, and the Holy Man who had first summoned him found the dying, skinny coyote. "What are you doing here?" he asked, but the coyote could only howl. Then his "brother" made a ring of cedar, and pushed the coyote through it, ripping the skin from the young man's head. Three more rings of three different kinds of wood worked to wrench the skin from the beggar's son; he was freed.

Now all this took place in order that the people might have medicine for another wrong that they would do. The beggar's son was instructed about this thing. In cases where a brother and sister cohabit, one or both of them will sicken. They usually become mad. It was necessary for the beggar's son to go through this black magic transformation so that he could make known the medicine. There is a certain kind of plant, with pretty flowers, that attracts both moths and butterflies. They fall dead if they light on it.

The coyote showed up while the young man was being cured. The young man, following instructions, hit the coyote with his own hide, and the animal resumed his true form. The antelope headdress was spoiled in the process, but the young man managed to kill one antelope before going home.

On the way home, the young man met a little creature who took him into his underground hole, in order to teach him an additional ceremony. The creature smoked the young man's sweet tobacco and brought little animals back to life. In return, the young man gave him an antelope hide, which became the creature's coat; he became the ground squirrel and was very pleased. The ceremony he taught was to be used for any young man or woman who became mad over drink, gambling, or sex, and it used the medicines that the Great Gambler had used against the people.

Then the beggar's son went to another place to go through another prayer ceremony, the prayer of the Turquoise Boy. Then the young man was made so that nothing in heaven or on earth could harm him, and he was ready to return to his home.

He was greeted by his wives and father-in-law. The younger wife and her father repeated the suspicions they had voiced about the coyote, and they called for the children of the coyote to be destroyed. The young man would not let them, but instead took them to a place where they became little animals, somewhat like a coyote, but with black faces, short tails, webbed feet, and they climbed trees. They lived along the water and were called "along-the-shore or water-edged coyote."

By this time San'hode'di's firstborn was a youth. His father sent him to live at Taho Chee Mountain, to be the master of game, providing the People of the Earth with game forever. Following the path of the Sun, the youth went, and the antelopes followed, disappearing into the mountain.

The beggar's son then went to his mother's home, telling his wives to remain behind; however, they followed him. They observed as the beggar woman and her son visited all the places where they had received bad treatment. In every village the beggar's son took the wives of the men and boys who had tormented him, to get even with them. When the four reached Sage Canyon, the two wives had worn out their moccasins, so their husband transported them back to their home on a flute, which returned to him.

Now he built a house for himself and his mother, a house with white bands, as it is called. At first he called his mother, "Mother," but as he was a Holy Being and remained young and she grew old, he called her, "Grandmother." The woman said, "My son," and then "My grandson." While they lived in their house together, San'hode'di visited the wives of the men who had been cruel to them. While traveling, he met a little dog, who lured him to a lake, Tqo ˈ del tqo ˈ, where the water rose in the air and almost engulfed the young man. Only by reaching the summit of a hill was he able to escape. He returned to his mother and told her about this episode of cruel water.

They traveled to other places, and at Beavers' Eyes another lake (where lived the Water Buffalo) rose into the air, but they ran to safety. Then they camped on a little hill and planted a turquoise walking stick on the East side, a white bead walking stick on the South side, a white shell walking stick on the West side, and a black jet walking stick on the North side. That night they heard chanting and the sound of a basket being pounded. These were the words of the chant:

I am the White Corn Boy.
I walk in sight of my home.
I walk in plain sight of my home.
I walk on the straight path which is towards my home.
I walk to the entrance of my home.
I arrive at the beautiful goods curtain which hangs at the doorway.
I arrive at the entrance of my home.
I am in the middle of my home.
I am at the back of my home.
I am on top of the pollen foot print.
I am on top of the pollen seed print.
I am like the Most High Power Whose Ways Are Beautiful.
Before me it is beautiful,
Behind me it is beautiful,
Under me it is beautiful,
Above me it is beautiful,
All around me it is beautiful.

The man planted a forked stick to find the source of the chant. There he found one kernel of white corn. He planted it and it grew, aided by four chants and prayers. On his right grew six white ears, and on his left grew six yellow ears: twelve ears on the one cornstalk, all standing up. He cut and husked them, the white corn alone and the yellow corn alone. He planted them, white and yellow, in a field, and they grew—although because of someone's laughter, some of the kernels were split open. The place where the man had been when he first heard the corn chant was to be a sacred hill, and the people were to pray there from time to time. The beggar's son left his mother there with all the beautiful goods he had brought magically in a small bundle, while he got even with other men who had tormented him, by visiting their wives. Using snares made of his own hair, he caught little gray birds, strung them together, and roasted them for his meat.

San'hode'di heard of two maidens in the village of Ken Tiel, who were well guarded. These maidens were sacred; all their suitors were sent away. Seeing that many villagers were away, gathering wood, he held a multi-colored flower and chanted. In the coat of the bluebird, he flew over the people. Then he put on rock wren feathers, and then another little rock bird's feathers, and flew to the opening in the roof where the two maidens sat, their legs angled next to one another. The hole let in sunlight. He looked down and there they sat, trimming a dress of antelope skin, spread across their knees. The man laughed, and the younger of the maidens said, "What a beautiful laugh." The man said, "What a beautiful laugh down below," and named the one who had laughed. They looked up to him, and he introduced himself, naming himself.

After this he took the form of the butterfly, a large one with many beautiful colors. The elder marveled at its beauty and suggested that they use its pattern for their design. The younger sister said, "No. Leave it alone. It might not be good for us." But they both tried to catch the butterfly, and as it flew this way and that, the colorful dust from its wings filled the room. The sisters knocked over their water and food, then chased the butterfly outside after he flew through a crack in the door. But outside they couldn't find it; instead, they followed a little yellow bird, hopping through a pumpkin field. The elder sister was sorry at the butterfly's disappearance. So now he took the form of the ripener, a small green insect with a pretty, high song. The sisters chased this, and when they were among the pumpkin vines, he resumed his own form and stood up. The maidens were ashamed, and stood looking down and twisting their bodies and feet, for he asked them why they had followed him. The elder said they should go back, and the younger recalled her earlier admonitions. "But now that we are here," she said, "we will stay and see what comes of it."

The man took them to his camp, fed them on the meat of the little birds he had caught with his own hair. The elder sister spit it out, but the younger swallowed it and said it was not bad. That night the sisters slept hugging each other. The man jumped in water and rolled in the feathers of the little birds, sleeping that way. He told the maidens that he lived that way; they had made a sorry mistake coming after him.

In the morning he started off for his mother's house, telling the maidens not to break the hair snares, should they wish to catch birds. But the snare broke when the bird got tangled in the hair. He returned to find them cold and hungry, which he attributed to their lack of fear. On the fourth night he lay with each of them, chewed his blue gum, and sang his chant. At once he had a beautiful home and he covered the sisters with beautiful robes. When they woke, the elder sister said that this strange new home was "better than our old home ever was."

San'hode'di sent the maidens back to their parents, whom he called cruel. He gave the elder a feather from the Sun's mother, and to the younger he gave a cattail rush—telling them that these would help them in trouble. He transported them home on a rainbow. When they arrived, they decided to hide their treasures under their arms, since they were sure to be stripped and punished. As they expected, they were stripped and led about in a circle, while the village men whipped them. When they could stand it no longer, the elder called for their talismans. The younger threw her cattail rush down and blew four times at the people surrounding her. Immediately the sisters found themselves standing before San'hode'di in his home.

He was sorry for having put them through this punishment, so he shot an arrow toward the village; lightning and rain destroyed all the people. However, the girls mourned their villagers, despite the punishment; thus the man made a medicine that restored the people to life. Then the chief, the father of the two sisters, said, "My son-in-law, you have strong medicine. You are a great man. All the houses are yours."

But San'hode'di lived at his home with his wives, coming to the village only now and then. One day when the three had been to the village, he sent them home and he took the rainbow path to his mother. When she saw him, she asked immediately the whereabouts of his wives. His mother told him, "Quick, quick, my son, the White Butterfly will steal your wives if you are not careful." He returned home, and not finding his wives there, he searched for them. He found three sets of tracks going East, with evidence of flowers kicked off along the way. He came to the edge of the water, where he noticed smoke coming from the top of a little house. He asked aged, red Spider Woman—who lived there—if she had seen his wives. She reported seeing two beautiful maidens with White Butterfly only recently. She warned him of White Butterfly's danger, but he vowed to follow him: "I will eat his brains when I find him."

The young man ran on and found old Frog Man hoeing in a garden. The old man reported having seen White Butterfly and the two beautiful maidens. The young man thought about the old man's funny leg, his popping eyes, his bodily humps, and as he thought, the old man voiced his observations; then invited his "Grandchild" inside, saying that he wanted to ask San'hode'di's father to make all the sacred places known to the young man, to protect him against White Butterfly. The Frog Man got the rainbow path from the young man, then seemed to walk out of his home and return. "I thought that you were going to take my story to my father," said the young man. The Frog said, "Yes, yes, Grandchild, every place is made known. Your Father and the rest of the Holy Beings said that it was time for the White Butterfly to die."

The Frog had shortened the day, and the young man was necessitated to spend the night at the old man's house. He could not use his Sun medicines after sunset. The next morning Spider Woman brought all the people from the sacred places to Frog's garden, and Wind informed San'hode'di of White Butterfly's attire: a headdress of a hummingbird plant. So they made one like it for the young man. With Spider Woman and Wind's help, the people reached White Butterfly's land before he knew it. They chanted against him so that when they reached his home, the flowers on the headdress were wilted and the hummingbirds were almost dead. But the young man's headdress looked its best.

The younger of San'hode'di's wives was grinding corn. With tears in her eyes, she said, "Did I not tell you that this person (the White Butterfly) was not our husband? There is our husband who has come for us. You have thought that there was no one like the White Butterfly."

San'hode'di and White Butterfly went through the same games, the same contests against each other, that the Great Gambler had used. The young man won each of the games: from the bat to the foot races. During these races the White Butterfly threw black magic against the young man; however, the beggar's son recovered and threw it back into White Butterfly's body, stiffening his legs so that the young man passed him by and won the races. All of his friends were dancing and singing; White Butterfly's people wept.

White Butterfly brought forth his ax, telling the young man to kill him while he was still warm. With his own weapon the young man split White Butterfly's head in two. Instead of brains, out flew different colored butterflies. The young man caught one in his hand, saying, "Though you came out of the head of the White Butterfly, you will not enter the brain of a man hereafter. You will be of little use to the people. Only when they catch you and put your pollen on their legs and arms and say:

> May I run swiftly,
> May my days be long,
> May I be strong in arm.

Then the same person will live to see old age. But he must let the butterfly go without harm."

Then all of White Butterfly's wives wept, but San'hode'di asked them why they were crying, since White Butterfly had either killed their husbands, or made slaves of them. He discovered the house where the bodies of the murdered husbands had been thrown. Then he told the people that they were free to go wherever they wished.

San'hode'di was bringing his own two wives, and the two daughters of Spider Woman, home with him; however, at the side of a lake he noticed his two wives crying. Seeing their unhappiness, he pushed them head first into the water, and all he saw was an animal with horns coming out of the water. He told their father to offer a prayer to the water. Spider Woman's two daughters, however, he brought home, and the Navajos adopted them. Their descendants are many to this day; their hair turns gray early and they tend to lose their teeth. It was for this purpose that the young man was born, and the White Butterfly stole the wives and lured their husbands across the water and killed them.

When San'hode'di arrived home, a messenger informed him of two more maidens who were calling for suitors: "Go try your luck." On four successive days, the man caused his body to be covered with sores, from poison ivy and other sources. Only on the fourth day did the girls' mother allow him entry. Then he succeeded in a series of tests, and took the maidens home, despite his sores. Now all this happened so that medicine might be made known that would cure poison ivy and the other diseases of the skin. Since then the medicine of the young man—with which he cured himself—is known for these sores. People chew the leaves of the poison ivy mixed with powder of ground chips of stones. Afterwards they can travel around poison ivy and other poisonous plants.

After the fourth day, San'hode'di was well and he lay with the two maidens. They told their father that they found themselves sleeping under beautiful robes in a home with all they could ever desire. His father-in-law was pleased. Then the man returned to his mother, at a hill between Gallup and Shiprock, where he told her she should stay: "You will have the power over the cornfields of the People called Navajo," he said. "The people will bring precious stones as offering when they come to pray for rain. I will return to you from time to time."

Then he returned to his wives on his flute. There is a peak this side of San
Francisco Mountain, called Tocho whee tso. He is there. His home and those
of his mother are considered sacred places. They say that the beggar woman
worked for the Navajos while her son, afterward, went to another tribe.

This Navajo hero, the beggar's son, is a man whose sacred parentage
and protection offset and complement his reckless energy. It is the narrative of a youth come of age, left apparently fatherless and without human
community beyond his mother, who is ridiculed by others, receives the
blessings of love, game magic, and medicine from the gods, achieves sexual
conquests, is attacked, challenged, and given up for dead, but whose res-
torations by the supernaturals increase his powers, make him even more
potent sexually, and make possible his triumph over adversaries. Other
versions (Haile 1978:1–81; Kluckhohn 1968:158–74; Pepper 1908;
Spencer 1957:137–48. Deerway *Ajiłee*, Luckert 1978:23–166, is quite
another legend) contain other episodes, but by and large our version is
a complete one.

The story emphasizes sexual conquests in a context of rivalry and revenge. In another version his grandmother (rather than his mother)
achieves as much sexual gratification as does the hero. It is said that "he
finally cleaned up all the women in Walpi and his grandmother all the
young boys" (Kluckhohn 1968:163). In addition, sexual and hunting
powers are linked, since he pays for his wives with the antelopes he kills
with his magic hunting prowess. The narrator of another version says,
"That's the reason we call this story Prostitution Way" (Kluckhohn
1968:165).

Beyond his sexual and hunting triumphs, the beggar's son creates a
curative ceremonial, fashioned after his own cures by the holy persons
and his indication of medicinal plants. Although "in no version is mention
made of teaching this love and hunting ritual to earth people" (Spencer
1957:136), the myth clearly portrays the procedure of the Chantway
established by San'hode'di'begaeye and his guardians. As the first sentence
of the myth states, this is a story about medicine, initiated by the holy
persons and now in human use through the mediatory help of the hero.
The myth provides copious information about the healing properties and
locations of numerous curative herbs, but even more important, the myth
gives a rationale for the causation and cure of sickness. It is a story in
which devastation is turned into revival, sacrilege into sacrality, trash
into medicine and food, and disease into strength.

It is also a story that emphasizes the overpowering force of the gods.
Even though the protagonist is a (half-) human hero, his fortune comes
through the benevolence of the all-powerful deities. The myth shows

that human willfulness is not an end in itself, but rather it must seek to gain the power of the holy persons. The hero cannot cure himself, sleeping under medicinal bushes whose deep-rooted secrets he cannot fathom. He can not do what his divine relatives can: overcome disease. It is the hero's duty, therefore, to appropriate divine power to effect cures.

Observers have already commented on the prevalance of mediation in Navajo curing rites. The Navajos lack a strong visionary tradition; in order to attain revelation and draw the holy persons near, a specialist—or rather, a row of specialists—is required. Diagnosticians mediate between the patient and the causes of illness. A relative of the patient approaches a singer and his retinue to perform the chant. The ceremonial itself uses the healers, the physical and enunciated prayers, and especially the sand-paintings, to work the will of health, all mediating between the patient and the effectual cure.

Beyond these, however, stands the hero of the Chantway myth, the folkloric seeker who undergoes suffering and revivification to the ultimate effect of introducing medicine to his tribal descendants. The hero suffers so others may live and be cured. He performs roles of both suffering servant and triumphant avenger, for the eventual, implicit benefit of his people, the Navajos.

It matters not whether these heroes of the many Chantway myths were historical personages, elevated after their death to legendary status. The Navajo hero is significant as hero: paradigm of vitality and the ability to recover from the shock of attack and sickness, model of life-seeking force in the face of death. The Navajo hero as hero serves not only as originator of a life-bringing ceremonial but also as ideal man whose way of living, his process of behavior, affirms health. The Navajo hero is the archetype of the willful healer who finds justice and revenge through the aid of the holy persons. Part god, part human, son of the Sun and son of a beggar woman, he is a model whose exploits the Navajos interject to themselves. It is significant that his mother's seed cakes and rabbits please the palate of a god, who says, "This is my food also," indicating the commonality between the beggar woman, her son, and the deities. The humans and the gods enjoy the same life substance.

Yet the hero must bathe before he can meet the gods, and even so, he smells to the holy people of the mountain. In another version, his stench is caused by a rabbit, tucked under his hair (Kluckhohn 1968:162), a sequence that might remind us of the Ojibwas' Nanabozho in the guise of a hare, stealing into the aliens' camp to obtain fire. San'hode'di'begaeye is still a human in the eyes of the gods, just as later his fellow humans regard him as a kind of divine person. He is midway between gods and humans.

THE HERO AND THE IMPOSSIBLE

Numerous typologies exist regarding the characteristics of folkloric heroes, for example, "conquering," "clever," "cinderella," and "martyr" types (Klapp 1949). It does not serve us to distinguish one type from another, especially when we see that our solitary beggar's son easily fits all of the four preceding characterizations, said to be mutually exclusive. Neither does it help much to recount the usual sequences of hero tales in world folklore, set down in detail, for instances, by Lord Raglan (1956) and Otto Rank (1914). More often than not, the distinguishing features laid out by these important European theorists apply better to nontribal peoples from whose narratives the outlines are drawn. Raglan sets down twenty-two narrative features of hero stories; Rank has nine. Both agree that hero narratives recount the illustrious exploits of a child grown to a man, born of exceptional parentage and in unusual circumstances, attendant with prophecies. With timely aid, he achieves success as an adult. Raglan continues with other characteristics that follow the hero's ascendancy: his decline, death, and remembrance. No matter. What joins the two theorists—one of historical, the other of pyschological bent—is their consensus that the tales of heroes, be they ancestors, prophets, holy men, law-bringers, founders of cults, or subliminal reflections, tell of a child's development to adulthood (Rank 1914:61–68). Whatever their outer paraphernalia, hero narratives are accounts of growing up, of universally applicable human development. Katherine Spencer's (1957:26–30) valuable study of Navajo Chantway myths has corroborated this social and psychological interpretation.

In this context, Joseph Campbell's *The Hero with a Thousand Faces* (1970) has its greatest application. For Campbell, hero myths are essentially accounts of rites of passage, analogous to the periodic ceremonies which tribal youths undergo to mark their coming of age, their achievement of completeness as human beings. An example of a rite of passage is the Navajo girl's puberty ritual, *kinaaldá,* in which she undergoes seclusion, tests, and ceremonial molding of her body, in order for her to become like Changing Woman, the society's ideal of female maturity and fecundity, who in mythic times underwent her own *kinaaldá.* Such rites of passage mark clearly for the youths their stage of human growth and indicate for them their proper roles in their society.

Campbell's "monomyth" of the hero includes three stages of development: first, separation, in which the hero is called, attempts to refuse, but with supernatural aid crosses thresholds into bizarre and foreign territory, is swallowed up by or submerges in the "womb"; second, an initiation occurs, in which the hero undergoes trials, encounters temptations, meets with divinities, and attains atonement with his source, for example, his father, upon which an apotheosis—a mediation of opposites—is attained, and the hero receives a fabulous boon, although not immortality; third, there is a return, in which the hero makes magical flight, is rescued from without, and crosses back, spanning the crucial threshold, and in effect becomes master of two worlds, his own and the one beyond, the source from which power flows. His return is seen as the freedom to live, but not the gift to live forever.

The three steps of Campbell's monomyth match roughly the stages analyzed by van Gennep (1960:20–21ff.) in his *The Rites of Passage.* Each tribal child passes through ritual stages of separation, transition, and incorporation: first, being expelled from regular society; second, coming into contact with liminal danger and power; and finally, reintegrating to the community with a bestowal of gifts. The community puts its children through these passages in order that they should make progress, grow up, and become fruitful compatriots, full human beings. The Navajo hero faces danger and thus secures the power of healing sickness. But on a more personal level, the hero shows how to become a willful, conscious adult, an ideal human type for Navajos to emulate and admire. He undertakes the passage to human maturity to serve as a paradigm of human maturity.

The Navajo hero is a model; he is not a "real" person. He is a cultural creation, like other heroes, a character whose story has been created and propelled through time because it meets the needs of Navajo individuals and society alike. The culture-hero is a product of culture who is said to have brought products to culture. We see that even as a boy the beggar's son is said to be a good builder, a prolific provider of food. His mother says, "I would starve to death without him." Later in the story he receives the power over game for the benefit of humans, and thus the hero is a cultural provider. In particular, the hero brings a health-bestowing Chantway.

Paradoxically, the Navajo hero—a cultural artifact—is suprasocial. In a tribal society where highest importance adheres to kinship ties, he refuses to adhere normally to his human kin. Instead he travels to greater heights, seeking the communion of the immortals. He lives among the foreigners, giving birth to children of his antagonists, the Pueblos, and finally going off to live with people other than the Navajos. He is a breaker of taboos, even though at the end "his home and those of his mother are considered sacred places."

When he sets out, he does not go as conscious provider for future generations of Navajos or anyone else. He is not a do-gooder; he cares not for the products of his restlessness. Rather, he seems to move in order to move, grow in order to grow, seek in order to seek. His movement, growth, and search serve their own desires. Like the Navajos who have created their hero of myth, the beggar's son is more concerned with his vitality and action than he is with static accomplishment to brag of and look upon with pride. In short, he does not plan to help his people, his descendants; his goal is a life-seeking process, not a community-minded ethic of concern. He leaves his mother, and later his families, and seeks to make his own life. There is nothing antisocial in his act; he grows as every child must. Yet the process by which he reaches his potent manhood—his magical, sexual, and food-bringing maturity—belies his extranormal, suprasocial stature. Even after his first encounter with the gods, he changes so markedly that he is unrecognizable to his mother, whom he had hugged so closely the previous nights. Later he cares little for the human bonds of his own creation. His attitude of indifference to his wives and other consorts contrasts strongly with the Navajo Orpheus. The beggar's son thinks more of power and search and vengeance than of family love. He attains communion with the holy persons by himself, for himself. In a society that discourages visions and shamanism, he acts the shamanistic visionary. He travels as the ordinary Navajo cannot. Even in his role as heroic seeker of lasting life in the face of death, the paradigm of Navajo health and healthy-mindedness, he surpasses the Navajo median of achievement. He overachieves and leaps beyond the parameters of acceptable Navajo expectations. This tendency to surpass the norm is probably typical of all heroes; however, in a land of willfulness, the Navajo hero seems especially strongheaded, even aggressive and threateningly dangerous, to be avoided as well as admired.

It is common in the Chantway myths for the hero to overstep his bounds with self-assertion, bringing diseases upon himself, and requiring supernatural aid. San'hode'di'begaeye, too, overasserts himself in his constant search for sex and conquest. He is excessive and reckless, consumed with lust and jealousy; in short, he is out of control and thus in need of healing, just like the patient who needs to undergo Prostitution (Excess) Way. The myth reminds the listeners that no matter how powerful and blessed by gods, humans can still be attacked and defeated by more potent foes—Coyote, for example—if they act foolishly: engaging in rampant sexuality, for instance. The myth reminds the Navajos that the hero is not the source of healing—only supernaturals hold that power. Rather, he is a patient in need of healing, who receives the cure, and consequently makes the cure available to other humans. The myth demonstrates to Navajos the extent as well as the power of human willfulness.

San'hode'di'begaeye's two main rivals in the story, Coyote and White

Butterfly, are instructive clues regarding the hero's personality and excesses. Coyote, the Navajo trickster, will stop at nothing to get his desires. He is irresponsible, angry, and lascivious. His thoroughly uncontrolled nature makes him frightening, if amusing, to the Navajos; his sexuality, although akin to that of other deities, is smutty and embarrassing. Symbol of overassertion, insatiable energy, confusion, and crossed boundaries, "Coyote functions . . . as a symbol of that chaotic Everything within which man's rituals have created an order for survival" (Toelken 1969:231). He is very much like the beggar's son in many of these regards, primarily in that both the hero and the trickster are driven by unquenchable passion to live, grow, and move. The "were-coyote episode" common to Navajo myth, in which a hero or god is hit by a coyote skin, reduced to pitiful conditions, and is revived with Hoop Transformation, reveals not only the dangers to the hero but also the dangers within the hero. The hero and the trickster exchange skins, and they resemble each other so much that San'hode'di'begaeye's wives cannot clearly tell the difference between the two. It seems plausible that the hero of this myth, like the heroes of other myths, must struggle with his own nature. His thirst for attainment must combat his Coyote nature, with its "lust and indolence" (Sandner 1979:148).

Equally, the hero's rivalry with White Butterfly indicates the lustful, uncontrolled nature of the beggar's son. To the Navajos, Butterfly and Moth are symbols of "temptation and foolishness, so despicable that their behavior . . . has come to stand for insanity, the punishment for breaking taboos" (Reichard 1974:405). Like White Butterfly, the hero is a breaker of taboos, a seducer who tempts the non-sunlight-struck maidens by appearing in the guise of a butterfly.

At the point where the hero approximates trickster Coyote and foolish Butterfly, he ceases being heroic and becomes threatening. But at the same time as the hero is pushing to the bounds of acceptable behavior, there is still hope for recovery. As long as he possesses the will to live, thrive, procreate and heal—passions analogous to that which makes him grasp more than he can hold—his ability to be cured persists. In this way, the hero undercuts the regular Navajo patterns, accruing both danger and power, serving as model and potential antimodel, with the final effect of drawing the supernatural to create health anew.

The psychological depth of the myth appears in the recklessness and kinetic bravado of the hero. By stealing offerings, the beggar and her son seem to deserve the persecution they encounter. By antagonizing his enemies, the hero almost presages his later defeat by Coyote. By constantly pressing upwards against the bounds of humanity, the hero seems to strive both to succeed and to falter and die. Perhaps in the shadow of Orpheus, in the face-to-face realization of death's supremacy, the hero—however unconsciously—moves toward death as well as life. He takes dangerous risks; he meddles in taboo; he consorts with his adversaries. It may be too strong to say that he desires death as passionately as he does life, but he certainly flirts with his shadowy destiny.

Like Orpheus, who sought death in order to grasp more fully the expanse of his life and love, the beggar's son probes the exterior limits of life, approaching the teeth of death, in order to grow in complete consciousness. He takes on the qualities of Coyote and Butterfly to push humanity to its limits. He stretches the limits of cultural possibilities and he expands his awareness of life to include death. He experiences death's appearance—it is said of him, "he was almost dead at this time"—and having returned from his coma he is now master, if not of life and death, then at least of health and disease. He combines the instincts toward Thanatos and Eros, in order to complete himself. His journey has its inward, psychological dimension, as well as its outer, geographical and cultural aspects. He rises to consciousness as he falls and recovers, through illness and healing, to curative power and willfulness.

If the myth of the beggar's heroic offspring contains a subtle death wish, it is decidedly secondary in comparison to the myth's vitality, its ceaseless motion and dynamism. The hero is described as a "great runner," even before his divine aid, and with his "big" feet he travels far, both geographically and sexually. His racing prowess, like that of many a Navajo hero, matches keenly the leitmotif of movement in Navajo language, folklore, and life. The Navajo language is composed abundantly of verbs— the words themselves possess movement and strength. The verb "to go," it is estimated, is employed with such variety and frequency that 356,200 conjugations are not only possible but actually in use (Witherspoon 1975:12). The Navajo origin myth records constant upward motion like that of the Hopi emergence myth from which it derives. The Chantway origin myths most often tell of travelers who encounter danger and receive power on their restless journeys. The Navajos' art and music are characterized also by a dynamic, even acrobatic motion. Just as the Navajos traditionally moved between summer and winter camps in a cyclic transhumance; just as today Navajos journey far in their ever-present pickups, their Chantway myths recount and retrace the peripatetic activity of pulsing heroes like San'hode'di'begaeye.

Observers have commented on "the almost obsessive preoccupation with the details of travel, the minute specification of an endless series of place names in Navajo legends" (Kluckhohn 1968:246, n. 4). Parts of the beggar's son's story are little more than a topographical litany. Through the myth, mention is made of geographical locations throughout Navajoland, each filled with descriptive, historical, natural, social, and emotional weight connected to events that took place there. We counted as many as 150 place-names in the different Prostitution Way versions. The land is a littered reliquary of past deeds and significant signposts of present realities. The hero is placed in a real context, through which he travels incessantly. The geographical references tend to emphasize the movement and vivacity of the hero. He is like the Navajos' two most prominent deities: the Sun, and Changing Woman, both of whom have the salient quality of motion. The Sun in his eternal arc, in search of plants to impregnate, and Changing Woman, "ever-renewing, ever-regenerating, ever-benign" (Collier 1962:49) in her seasonal metamorphoses—both refuse stillness. So does San'hode'di, taking after his father the Sun.

It is fitting that the Chantway myths, whose purpose is to recall the origin of life-bestowing rituals, should possess the characteristic of movement, symbolic of life and power. It is also significant that the myth should concentrate its attention not on the results of the hero's quest, that is, the Chantway itself, but rather its subject is the process by which the Chantway developed. It would seem that for the Navajos, the movement itself contains more import than the final product of motion. We are reminded of the motion picture Navajos made of their weaving. The bulk of the film records the frolicking of sheep, the tending to their needs, the shearing of the wool, and the circular motions of the weavers in the process of creation. Almost off-handedly at the end, the rug itself comes into view (Worth and Adair 1972). In the same way the mythic text cares little for products of heroism; instead it sings the praises of the heroic journey, setting an example for the patient to be healed by the resultant Chantway, when he like his heroic paradigm becomes "a person who travels far and wide," and thereby becomes restored in health through his own motion (Henderson 1956:125, 138).

The beggar's son travels to the brink of his own death, recovers, and returns in glory, undergoing an initiation born of movement. He is like Orpheus in that he faces death and survives to pass down the lessons he has learned, the rituals of health he has acquired. The Chantway myths present a philosophy of willfulness (without excess) for the Navajos to follow, a meaning to life which grows out of an encounter with death. Like the Orpheus tradition, the story of the beggar's son and other hero stories of its kind are narratives of personal symbolization and catharsis to the Navajos, truly, "myths to live by" (Campbell 1972), that grow from the realization of death.

The hero cannot attain immortality, however; Orpheus tried and failed. He cannot deliver the eternal to his loved ones, to his kinsmen. Instead he crosses the crucial threshold and brings back a ritual of curing, a promise of rejuvenation for members of the Navajo society. The Navajo hero returns from his liminal, initiatory journey with the next best thing to immortality—eternal hope for health. The Chantway he establishes promises all Navajos the will to live in the hope of consistent, compulsive revivification when health falters. Through persistent recovery, Navajo society can hope to continue and reproduce itself indefinitely, so long as the Chantways and their myths are remembered, narrated, and celebrated.

It is medicine, not immortality, that the Navajo hero delivers to his people. The Navajos know that no easy accommodation can exist between their all too human desire for eternity and their acceptance of death's rule. But knowing that every sickness is a foretaste of death, and every cure heralds the rejuvenating life instincts, they have their hero battling and fluctuating between the two realms. The Navajo hero balances the two complementary drives: to live and accumulate, join and love, and to separate, dissipate, and die. He is at the same time healthy and diseased, demolished and cured.

The polar extremes of human existence are life and death, immortality and mortality. The Navajos know that they cannot achieve eternal life; however, their heroic narratives show the possibility of attaining death's symbol—sickness—and at the same time achieving the symbol of immortality. That is, if

SICKNESS : MORTALITY : : HEALING : IMMORTALITY,

then the hero performs a partially successful, symbolic mediation of death and eternality.

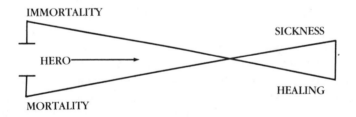

Unable to achieve a satisfactory balance between the desire for immortality and the realization of mortality, the hero moves through the narrative, attaining an apotheosis (from beleaguered, poor, profaning, unblessed orphan boy, to honored, jewel-bedecked, semidivine, charmed hero), an inversion of fortune and identity, during which he becomes deathly ill and recovers triumphantly. Thereby he reaches a successful syzygy between sickness (death's symbol) and healing (life's symbol).

In so doing, the hero story defines the human condition for the Navajos. By crossing the threshold from health to moribund disease and back again, bringing with him the promise of eternally renewable health, if not immortality itself, the hero utters the Navajo ontology: to be human is to be sick and to be cured of sickness. Hence no traditional Navajo until recent times went through life without undergoing a curing ceremonial at least once. Such rituals were—and continue to be—rituals of passage into full Navajo humanity.

The Navajo hero approaches death through sickness. Like Orpheus, he faces death and tells of it. He crosses the threshold and brings back medicine, and a reminder of inevitable death, symbolized by his sickness. His heroic gifts to his people—not just San'hode'di, but all Navajo heroes— are both medicine and consciousness of sickness. Both are essential ingredients of human existence.

But even the limited promise—health, not immortality—is impossible for humans to achieve. The Navajo heroes—the beggar woman's son and the others, including Orpheus—seek to accomplish the impossible. They rise above their circumstances, their misfortunes, their humanity, and achieve a divine rapport and supranormal potency beyond the reach of real humans. They function as models of projected wish fulfillment for the Navajos who chant their praises, who know in reality the impossibility of the heroic achievements. Ordinary humans, even singers and diagnostic specialists, cannot do what the heroes are said to have done. But it is wonderful to imagine oneself in the role of the hero, overcoming one's foes, defeating disease, returning from sure death, speaking with the gods at face-to-face séances. The fact is that the heroes have done what the Navajos cannot. Their mythic heroes have received ceremonials that can surmount illness perpetually, if applied properly and willfully. Supposedly other Navajos can repeat the performances of the beggar's son, after he receives gifts from the gods: "Then the young man was made so that nothing in heaven or on earth could harm him." But of course that is impossible for humans. Moreover, the hero remains young, calling his mother "Grandmother" as she ages and he endures in his prime. The implication of eternal life, youth-in-age, applies for other Navajos besides the hero, but the Navajos know that the promise is impossible for normal humans.

The nobility of their heroes, then, is not in their securing foolproof curatives—they work but they do not always work, and they will not continue to work to ensure immortality—but rather in their quest to do so, even in their failure to achieve impossible goals. The heroes struggle against the impossible, and ultimately "lose." The people still die of sickness and old age, despite cures and willpower. But by struggling, seeking, moving, the heroes and the Navajos who emulate them let shine forth their vitality and noble heroism.

The Navajo heroes promise the impossible. In spite and because of the impossible nature of the heroic quest, the Navajos have chosen to live by and through their Chantway heroics. There is a cathartic quality of the Navajo hero myths—their ability to let Navajos identify their own longings and dread through the heroic narratives. The stories have the power of apotheosis, therapy, and purgation for the people who believe (in) them. The audience can feel along with the beggar's son the smarting resentment at being an outsider, ridiculed and taunted by enemies. With the hero the listeners can exult in his divine blessings, his coming to power, and his glorious achievements. Through the hero, the Navajos can symbolize their own feelings, just as through all myths humans symbolize themselves. They may promise what they cannot deliver—forever successful cures and indefinitely prolonged youth—but as myths of healthy-mindedness, myths that proclaim the nobility and competence of humans living in a difficult world, they offer eminent paradigms to idealize.

But by themselves they are not enough. They lay down the basework of rejuvenation and willful health; however, for the Navajos they need to be made actual through the ceremonials whose origins they describe. The corpus of hero myths needs to be made physical; it demands bodily participation. It is not enough to a patient in need of a cure to hear of the noble will of the hero. Rather, the patient must will himself or herself to become that hero, to take on the mantle of heroism and achieve ritual catharsis in the company of one's tribesfolk.

Both patient and audience share in the cure. With the patient the audience has heard the cause and meaning of the disease. They have turned to the myth that explains illness and promises health, the narrative of their hero, and with the patient the audience gains comfort and understanding from the story. We would go too far to portray the Chantway ceremonial as a group psychotherapy; however, we must assert that the audience and patient relive sacred history in hearing their heroic texts, and as in psychotherapy they ponder through the narrative the origin and nature of disease, in order to effect knowledgeable cures.

Both myths and rituals reassure their people by repeating the familiar, the significant, the fixed points of causation and explanation. They both deal with the most threatening of human problems—the points of crucial danger and fulfillment. In addition, they both arise from and are shared by a community. They are social events that mean to touch everyone within reach and sight. The Navajo cures occur with a full contingent of helpers and hopers, gathered together to effect and witness the healing. They all share the myth, the ritual, and the cure.

But it is the patient who deserves the most prominent attention. On him the congregated wills are focused. In her rests the duty to relive the heroic feats of the myth. Ultimately he must exert will, share in heroic courage, tap divine power, and seize human health. She must relive the heroic myth of healing in order to achieve salvation from death's symbol, disease, making actual the ideals of mythology.

6

An American Indian Monomyth: Narratives of Peyote's Origins

INTRODUCTION

Over the past century, scholars and the public at large have observed the development of a religious complex among American Indians in the United States and Canada, the central feature of which is the partaking of, and reverence toward, a consciousness-altering cactus called peyote *(Lophophora williamsii)*. Peyotism (or the peyote cult or religion, or the Native American Church, as it is variously called) has inspired many book-length accounts, hundreds of articles, and numerous government investigations.

Archaeology reveals the Indian use of peyote in ancient times, as early as A.D. 1000 near Laredo, Texas, where peyote grows wild. Peyote use was the subject of reports by Europeans in Mexico as early as the 1560s, and by 1620 Indians used it widely in New Spain, despite inquisitional prohibitions. Tonkawa and Carrizo Indians of the Gulf area were recorded users by the mid-eighteenth century, and visits from Apache soldiers with Spanish missionaries served to spread peyote use north of its natural growth areas.

Comanche and Kiowa raiders among these Indians, as well as among mestizo and, perhaps, even Tarahumaran and Huichol populations throughout the nineteenth century, encountered peyote use, and carried it back to their home areas in Texas, and then to Indian Territory (now Oklahoma). By 1885 a coalesced peyote complex existed among the Comanche, Kiowa, Kiowa Apache, and perhaps other Indians, and it was observed in some detail by James Mooney (24 January 1892; 1892; 1896b; 1897; n.d.).

In the twentieth century peyotism spread from Oklahoma by means of missionaries, boarding schools, and other intertribal contacts, reaching beyond the limits of the Plains into Utah, Wyoming, Wisconsin, to Canada,

PEYOTIST LOCATIONS AND AREAS WHERE PEYOTE GROWS

and to some degree everywhere (including metropolitan areas on the East and West coasts) Indians lived, and even spread to some non-Indians.

Although the use of peyote dates to ancient times, many researchers have concerned themselves with peyotism's status as a "new religion," born of the crises of American Indian existence in the nineteenth and twentieth centuries. Some modern scholars have emphasized conditions of "deprivation" and "acculturation" surrounding the growth of peyotism in Indian Territory in the late nineteenth century, and its spread onto the Plains and beyond. Following Mooney's (1896a) interpretation of the Ghost Dance of 1890, scholars have described peyotism (and similar religious phenomena) as a "religion of the oppressed" (Lanternari 1965), a "crisis cult" (La Barre 1971), a "revitalization movement" (Wallace 1956), or a type of "nativism" (Linton 1943).

Aberle's (1966) work on Navajo peyotism correlates the growth of the religion to U.S. government-imposed livestock reduction among Navajo herders, in order to demonstrate that peyotism is an attempt to provide a "set of compensations for their most pressing deprivations" (337). Others, like Barber (1941:673–75) and Slotkin (1975:20–21) have said that peyotism's survival as a movement derives from its accommodationist attitude toward white culture. Still others have focused on the chemical effects of peyote—the euphoria it produces—to show that peyotism helps Indians accept their inferior position in American life through a kind of drug-induced escapism. Hoebel writes (1949:126) that peyote is "a compensation for the defeat of the red man and the destruction of his old religion and life." For Plains Indians, where the peyote religion has been most prominent, "constant warfare, insecurity, competition, new diseases, disappearance of buffalo" (La Barre 1947:296) all have created an Indian anxiety of sociological and psychological proportions that peyotism is designed to cure. Peyote membership, it is said, is for those who have found white contact "traumatic" (L. Spindler 1952:595): transitional people who demonstrate a "definite breakdown of emotional control" and "diffuse anxiety." Thus "the cult sanctions schizoid-like behavior by the emphasis placed upon vision seeking and autism" (596).

Omer C. Stewart (1944:89–90; 1972:27–29; 1979b; 1982b) and Åke Hultkrantz (1983) have tried to overcome the thrust of these theories, in order to indicate peyote's more general historical and religious dimensions. The following analysis is an attempt to explicate some of these dimensions.

Although it is correct to view peyotism north of Mexico as a "new" religion, this chapter tries to move beyond the (all too often reductionist) theories of peyotism as "crisis cult," and the like, and interpret it as a bona fide religion, with all the complexities of religious life worldwide.

Attention is directed to the narratives that American Indian peyotists tell regarding the origin of peyote use, or peyotism. By observing these narratives—one might call them myths or legends—one can gain insight to the multifaceted nature of peyotism, a "new" religious matrix that illuminates the study of religious history and phenomenology. In short, the analysis attempts to understand what these peyote myths tell us about peyotism as a religious complex.

The corpus of peyote origin narratives is potentially huge. Stewart writes (1986) that "each of the fifty Peyotist tribes in the U.S. and Canada today could supply at least two origin myths." That is, peyotists narrate a variety of stories to recount the origin of peyote use, and this variety exists not only in different versions of the same basic story, but in manifestly divergent narratives altogether. In a religious tradition without a fixed priesthood, without officially promulgated dogma or absolutely specified ritual form, there exists no one authoritative myth. Rather, peyotists tell a variety of narratives, and accept the validity of all the types.

At the same time, peyotists rarely draw attention to these narratives as particularly significant vehicles for religious knowledge. Peyote origin stories may be told during a peyote ritual—perhaps in the morning, after the official all-night service, when peyotists tell tales of diseases cured, deaths solaced, powers gained, and tasks accomplished.

The attitude of peyotists toward these narratives should be noted. Stewart writes: "I think it is general for a Peyotist to emphasize 'learning from peyote' not carrying on ancient traditions contained in myths" (1986), and ethnographers have remarked that peyotists care little about analyzing, discussing, telling, or even knowing the peyote myths. This is especially true of Indians outside of the Oklahoma core of peyote use.

Nevertheless, an analysis of the peyote origin narratives—sixty stories from over twenty Indian tribes of the Plains and adjacent areas (see Versions at the end of this chapter)—finds that they communicate important data regarding peyotism's history, the experience of peyote ingestion, the ethics of peyotist teachings, the ritual patterns of the peyote meeting, and the theological world view basic to peyotism as a religion.

THE NARRATIVES

Type I

In the first type of peyote origin narrative, peyote reveals itself to Indians. Some of these stories begin with a battle, after which a person or persons—mother and child, sister and brother—become separated from their people and are lost. Or, a member of a hunting or war party is missing, wounded, or assumed dead. In other cases there is a drought or other physical disaster such as an epidemic, that causes death among the people. The initial situation, therefore, is one of difficulty in the extreme, to the point of death. Only rarely does the story fail to present a crucial problem at its outset. Even in its briefest versions, the pattern of Type I is consistent.

Given the situations of life-threatening difficulty, peyote reveals itself. Sometimes the spirit of peyote—(occasionally said to be Jesus) appears or speaks to the individual in distress—the warrior, the relative mourning or seeking the missing tribesman, the lost mother or child—and indicates the lifesaving powers of the peyote plant, if only the person will eat the cactus. In some cases the person is transported to a spirit world, or the distressed individual stumbles upon or lies down in a peyote field, tastes the cactus, and is saved. Immediately, in any case, the person's strength and life are miraculously restored because of the discovery and revelation.

After peyote reveals itself, or is discovered, peyote instructs the individual in various ways. It tells the lost individuals where to find their people; it informs the mourning relative that the missing hunter is alive and can be saved. Lives that were thought lost are reclaimed for the living. The person to whom peyote has revealed itself receives knowledge about peyote's powers, and returns to the people with a message regarding ritual use of peyote, a moral code, a new religious complex that can be identified as peyotism.

The variations within the general pattern of Type I can be described as follows:

I. Peyote is revealed or discovered.
  A. Peyote is desperately needed, but unsought by a person in distress.
    1. Persons are separated from their tribe, and lost.
    2. A person mourns or searches for a missing or dead relative.
  B. A person searches for power, usually to solve a desperate situation.

In order to illustrate Type I, I shall summarize a few of the more complete versions. Joe Blackbear, a Kiowa Apache from Oklahoma, told Brant (1963:180–81) the following story:

There is a story long ago about the origin of peyote, when Indians were fighting one another. On the other side of New Mexico a camp of Indians was attacked and they were scattered in the mountains. There was just one woman and her boy left.

These were Lipan Apaches, and it was very hot and dry there; all the water had dried up. They had no food or water and there was none around them. The woman told her boy that she was tired, hungry, thirsty, maybe she would die there when she rested. She told him to go on and perhaps die elsewhere.

It was early in the morning. The boy went out in the mountains. His mother had told him to look for anyone he could find. He walked around. Then something spoke to him, saying, "I know you are hungry. Look down ahead of you. You will see something green. Eat it."

He saw a green plant, dug it up, and began to eat it. Soon his hunger was gone, as if he had eaten a lot of meat. He dug up more and took them to his mother and told her of the voice. She ate some of the plants and recovered as he had.

In the afternoon it was very hot. She said that she didn't know who gave them the plant, but she would pray to whomever it was. She prayed for water, and to find their people again. Later on, a cloud came; it thundered, rain fell, and there was water. They drank and rested there that night.

She dreamed that someone came to her and told her to look at a certain mountain. She looked and saw her people moving along the hills in her dream. In the morning she told her son of her dream, and she and her boy started off in the direction the dream had indicated. Finally, they were met by a man who recognized them as the lost ones, and they were glad to see each other.

When they reached camp, they told the people what had happened. The boy had some peyote. After they got settled, the boy asked his mother to fix him a secluded tipi, where he would go at night and eat peyote, and then he would go into the mountains and lie down. Inside the tipi he put the peyote on the ground, "just as it looked when he first saw it." He prayed to the spirit who had shown him the peyote. "You have helped me. When I eat peyote tonight I want you to help me to find a way for it." He drummed and sang all night long and stayed in the mountains during the day. Several times he did this.

The old men wondered what he was doing. One old man asked to enter; the young boy invited him in and the man sat beside him. Each night for four nights another man joined them, and was given duties, until the tipi was full. The boy made a cane to pray with, and to walk with when he got old. He made a rattle, a waterdrum and drumstick, saying, "The sound of this drum reminds me of the thunder I heard, the water in it reminds me of the rain that came." The men learned songs of their own and the meetings evolved.

Later, another man learned of peyote and brought it to us. It went north to the Dakotas. To this day it is our religion. Even today man adds new things to make it better. Nowadays the meetings are held on holidays such as Thanksgiving and Easter, and a feast has been added to it.

In Stenberg (1946:139–40), the Northern Arapaho peyotist John Goggles from Wyoming narrates a slightly different story:

Down in old Mexico there were Caddo Indians who were first to discover and use peyote. They were on the warpath, lost their way, became hungry, and had no water. They scattered, each trying to find a way back to the tribe. One man became so weak, he lay down to die. He saw a green herb that looked nourishing. He found it cool, refreshing, and restoring; he felt stronger immediately, so he ate four in all, then fell asleep, feeling light.

When asleep, someone said to him: "My friend, I come to you. I want to tell you something. I am Peyote.... The light means that we have called the Great Father up in the sky. This medicine that you found is blessed by the man that created everything. Great Father put Peyote on earth for the Indian, who knows nothing."

The voice told him to fill his bag with peyote, then showed him the way to water, and to his people, facing east toward the rising sun, symbolizing the Creator's power. "Take it to your people," said the voice. "Don't go round and make enemies any more.... We have to all live as brothers and sisters from one man. Before they go ahead and use this medicine in their lodge tell them to smoke as they would mean peace, peace to everybody." From then on, this medicine opened Indians' eyes; they began to know there was a man above here, their father; they came to touch the earth, their mother; they came to pray to the Creator and mother earth, no one else. They found that this medicine was powerful; it cured people who were ill. And they began to make friends with other tribes.

Goggles continues that from the Caddos, peyote use traveled to the Comanches, the Kiowas, the Arapahos, and other Indians of Oklahoma. Then he tells how a Northern Arapaho drifting through Oklahoma became ill and was cured at a peyote meeting. He goes on with a story of peyote's healing powers on the Northern Arapaho reservation in Wyoming, and he closes with a story regarding his own first use of peyote when he was hurt by a horse falling on him. After being cured, he traveled to Oklahoma and learned the proper ritual use of peyote, and became a peyote priest (see Stenberg 1946:140–45).

A slightly different pattern emerges from versions of Type IA2, illustrated by the earliest recorded peyote origin story in Mooney (1897:330), from the Kiowas, who regard the Mescaleros as the "high priests" of the peyote ritual and the first to discover peyote.

Two young men went on a war expedition to the far south. They did not return at the expected time. After long waiting, their sister retired to the hills to bewail their death, according to custom. Worn out with grief and weeping, she was unable to get back to camp at night. She lay down where she was, and a peyote spirit came to her in her dreams. It told her that although she wailed for her brothers, they were still alive; in the morning she should look where her head now rests and she would find that which will restore her. The spirit gave her further instructions and was gone.

At daylight she found the peyote, dug it up, and took it with her to camp. Here she called the tribal priests, told her vision, and gave instructions she had received from the spirit. Under her direction, the sacred tipi and crescent mound were built. Old men entered, said prayers, sang songs, and ate peyote—"which seems to have been miraculously multiplied"—and at daylight they saw a vision of the two young warriors, wandering on foot and hungry in far off passes of the Sierra Madre. A strong party was organized to rescue the men in enemy country, and after many days they were found and "restored to their people." Since then peyote has been eaten with song and prayer to see visions and receive inspiration. The young girl is venerated as the Peyote Woman.

A Delaware version told by James C. Webber to Petrullo (1934:34–37) combines Types IA 1 and 2, by having the lost Indian searching and mourning for yet another Indian in distress:

About seventy-five years ago the Comanches were at war with some Mexican Indians. After a successful raid, they were pursued so closely that they had to leave behind a sick woman and a little boy, with provisions for them, trusting the Mexicans not to harm the helpless pair. The little boy ran away, however, trying to catch up to his tribe, and the woman worried about his safety and searched for him. "Weak from sickness and age, she sought him, praying and pleading with the Great Spirit to spare him. She told the Great Spirit, even the Creator, that she herself would be willing to die if the child were spared." She fell unconscious.

While in this "pitiful state," an unknown being dressed like a great chief, spoke to her in her language, saying that the child was safe, and instructing her to save her own life by eating an herb that she would find where he was standing. He told her that if she would "eat this herb, you will discover the greatest medicine in this world for the Indians. After you have eaten it, the Great Spirit, even the Creator, will teach you the songs, the rules and regulations of a new Indian religion."

She ate the plants as he instructed and her strength returned immediately. The herb itself took the form of a chief and medicine man and spoke to her, describing the tipi, the half moon altar, the fireplace, the songs, and the rules that shall make up the peyote ritual. "This is the way Peyote was revealed to the Indians."

In Type IB peyote reveals itself to an Indian who seeks it to help himself or his people. One example of this type shall suffice.

The Mescalero Apaches (Opler 1945:211–12) say that peyote eating all began with a Lipan Apache. Peyote had never been known before. When the Lipans began to die out, their ceremonial people did no good, and no kind of medicine could be found to help them. A Lipan man was on a raid for horses, thinking about his people's troubles. He was a good man, eager to help his people, and he began to look around for something that would do them good. He prayed to anything pretty that might help, going from one plant to another.

He came to where peyote happened to be growing; they bore flowers, and stood in the midst of them, saying that they were so beautiful and plentiful that there must be some use for them. "I'd like to see my people as thick as you are. I'd like to hear you speak if you can. You are the prettiest thing I have ever seen." He got one of the plants to speak to him: "Pull me. Pull as many of me as you can. Take us home. Make a tipi. Have the doors toward the east. Then eat me. Then give me to anyone who takes an interest in me and wants to eat me."

His people were dying day and night, so he hurried home with this peyote, told the chief and all the people in his camp, explaining what he had learned, doing everything he had been told. The people all wanted it. He thought his supply would diminish, but it didn't; the pile of them remained the same, and he fed them all. He had been told to take the big one home and put it in the center, to pray to it and talk to it; he did so, and it has been that way always at peyote meetings. "Everyone was feeling good. The different kinds of sickness went away." This is where peyote belief began.

Type II

In the second type of peyote origin narratives Indians acquire the peyote ritual. An Indian warrior leaves his war party to seek out the source of mysterious drumming. He comes upon a ceremony in a tipi, conducted by his enemies who are clairvoyantly aware of his approach. Leaving aside his weapons, he is invited into the meeting and learns the ritual through repeated participation. After the completion of his instruction, he either uses his new power to find horses, or returns to his people—who have already mourned his presumed death—and instructs them in this new ritual knowledge. His people become friends with their former enemies.

In 1938 Ralph Kochampanaskin a Ute, married to a Washo, living in Nevada, told the following version—learned from a Sioux in South Dakota—to Omer C. Stewart in order for him to have the history of peyotism, "complete from the beginning":

Years ago the Sioux, Comanches, the Utes fought and "liked to kill each other. They got along in hardship." They always moved around and were brave. In one camp enemies came and killed most of the Indians and took horses. Only two or three families were left, and they kept lookout and were frightened by every noise.

Finally, the men decided to go a long way off. Their wives prepared for the trip. Three days into the journey, one night, a man was awakened by a noise, like a drum, far away. The next night he decided to follow the sound, and told his friends to reconnoiter at a certain place. He found a big camp and readied his weapons for a fight.

In the middle of the camp he saw a big tipi with light in it. He sneaked up to it to listen. Inside, the man in charge felt someone approaching and sent the fire chief out to investigate; he found the intruder. They didn't speak the same language, but the fire chief used sign language to invite him in, bringing his knife and his food, prepared to fight. The man in charge told him through sign language that the "meeting was to make the Indians good, to make them friends, and to make them stop fighting."

That Indian ate as much peyote as the chief told him, and drank water from the bowl at midnight and thought it was good. In the morning the chief signed to him: "Indians are few. We eat this medicine to keep us going, to keep us alive and allow our children to grow up." He gave him a peyote outfit, a drum, medicine, a gourd, songs, and told him to "carry these things away with you." Officials conducted him safely to his kinsmen. He showed them a drum that had made the noise he had followed, and they tried it out. He told about the medicine, and they decided to head home to hold a meeting. "Those Indians forgot their war trip," returned home, made a fire in their tipi, and passed around the drum, eating the medicine, three men and three women. The Indian couldn't remember the songs at first, but the medicine helped him recall them. He passed on the message of medicine and peace to his friends.

When the medicine ran out, they went back to the first tribe and were welcomed into camp and given a buckskin suitcase full of peyote. The chief told them, "A woman got this Medicine from God, who planted it here. We are glad you are our friends. All Indians are friends. We are glad you came for more medicine."

The Indians went back home, "ate the peyote, had children and increased. Then all the Indians started using it, became friends, and were happy."

An instructive variant that combines Types IA1 and II comes from a Taos narrator, citing a Cheyenne friend (Parsons 1936:63–64):

A long time ago a band of Kiowas went on the warpath. They traveled for several days, when one of the men got sick, and sicker. There were enemies nearby, so they didn't want to stop and tend the sick man, so they left him. He was lying there on the ground, thinking he was going to die. Pretty soon he heard someone singing, shaking a rattle, a small voice near him. He looked around and saw only a peyote plant. From the top of the plant, a place like a blossom was opening and closing, and the singing came from within. The Kiowa spoke to the plant, who invited him inside. The opening expanded to be a big square hole in the ground. He went down the hole and found a kiva-like structure beneath. There were lots of men wearing buckskin, sitting around the wall. They told him to sit in the center and they told him about the plant and how they would make him well, and sent him home to his people with the plant.

"Then they told him about the Plains Indians—they don't believe in *anything*, no God, nothing—how they live just like animals, always going around killing and stealing." After their instruction, he took the plant home and found his relatives, who thought he was dead. They were mourning for him, having cut their hair and killed his horses. They saw him come back alive. He reported what he had seen and heard about the plant. "He told them to use it and to believe in it. . . . Now when they have this they believe in something; they believe in God through this." Thus came the peyote meetings, the all-night singing, the peyote eating, and the belief in God.

Another variant (Beck and Walters 1977:242) comes from Ron Barton, a Navajo peyotist. It begins as Type IB but undergoes a change:

My mother told me the origin legend of peyote, "like a creation myth." Twelve warriors got ready for war, far away. They didn't take women with them back then, but one woman begged to go along. They refused, but she persisted, promising to cook, mend their clothes, and care for them. She belonged to them, so they relented. It was a long way, and she fulfilled her promises; however, all twelve died after fighting a long time.

She cried for them, then started for home, having no purpose in staying where she was. She was taking her time, thinking about her loss, when Coyote met her, understood her sorrow, and told her of a prayer meeting. Wanting to help her, he told her to attend this meeting, in a tipi on a hill, where a man was waiting for her. He had something to teach her, to bring to her people. She went in and saw her twelve warriors. All night she looked and learned. "To give her respect, the men asked her to bring in water in the morning and pray." When it was over, her brothers turned into twelve peyote buttons. She was told to take them home and teach her people, which she did.

It appears as if the story will move from Type IB to Type II, as she enters the meeting; then it appears that it will return to Type IB, because she finds her brothers alive; however, they turn into peyote buttons, a new motif altogether, as is the appearance of Coyote as her guide.

Type III

From the Kiowa Apache (Bittle 1954:71–72) comes a peyote origin narrative that begins as Type IA:

A very long time ago, when a war was raging between the Lipan Apaches and the American army, the Indians were dying and an old woman and young girl got lost in the mountains. The woman in distress received the peyote revelation, and they ate the peyote and were revived.

Then they heard a drum beating in the mountains. Taking up great amounts of peyote, they set out for it. Along the way they met a friendly Coyote, who led them to the drum, and to their people's encampment, which they reached after four days travel. After being welcomed home, she said, "I am a woman, and you are my relatives. This is a good thing. Someone spoke to me in the mountains, and I learned all of this. It is good for all of you." They set up a tipi for a meeting, and after four ceremonies a further event occurred.

This event consists of Type III, found separately in Opler (1940:56–58), as well as in Bittle:

One night they could hear someone coming toward the tipi. They could hear the jingling of little metal spangles on the moccasins. Everyone stayed quiet until the stranger entered the tipi. He carried a war club. Some people ran from the tipi in fear; the braver ones stayed within. The stranger looked at everyone, and walked around slowly behind them. At each person he swung his war club, but each was able to duck his head and avoid the blow. Finally, he came to a young man sitting next to the peyote leader, and him he hit on the head. The young man bled profusely and fell forward. The stranger quietly left the tipi.

The peyote leader didn't know what to do. Everyone consulted and decided to sit there all night to see what would happen to the young man. The chief called for those who had run away to return. All night they ate peyote and sang. When morning came, the young man regained consciousness and sat up, unhurt. The chief gave a corn husk cigarette to the lad, his nephew, and asked him to smoke and relate the events of the night.

The boy said that he didn't understand what had happened. He had followed the stranger out of the tipi. They had walked a long way, to a high bluff, where another tipi stood, like this one. The stranger entered, and the lad followed. Inside, the stranger said, "Here is your brother, the man all of you wanted." The men inside were Indians, with long hair, in a circle, around a fire. The peyote leader said to the young man that he was glad that he came. "This is our way from a long time ago. The Lord made this way just for the Indians, and I want you to learn to use it, and to take it back to your people, and tell them how the Lord made it and how He wants us to use it . . . tell them that this is to be the Indian religion." The peyote leader told the boy that the blood that flowed from his head would produce variously colored flowers in the spring. These beautiful flowers, made by the Lord, should be used to color your face, to show that the Lord gave them to him. Then the boy returned to his people and told them what had happened and what he had learned. This was the origin of face painting at peyote meetings, and this is how the Lipan Apaches came to know "what peyote meant."

In M. E. Opler's (1940) version the peyote people taught the brutally initiated young man magic tricks and granted him their powers to protect him in battle. The man told his companions: "The Peyote people eat themselves. They went through their own bodies like a snake and went through each other. They were in the form of humans and they ate each other just like that. They did all kinds of magical tricks" (58). After returning, he learned more about peyote's rules, until at length he learned all of them, becoming an adept peyotist.

Type IV

Type IV, which exists in only one published version, narrated by the Comanche Tekwakï to McAllester (1949:14–17), continues the violent imagery of Type III and replicates the intertribal acquisition of peyote introduced in Type II:

It was from the Carrizo Apaches that we acquired peyote in the beginning. They were enemies of our people. There was a Comanche so brave that he went on raids by himself. On one occasion, however, he raided with around ten others. In a fight with the Carrizos all his companions were killed, and he was wounded. He used up all his arrows and left his battle paraphernalia. The Carrizos surrounded him, killed him and his mule, and took his belongings.

Some time later they held a peyote meeting and brought all the booty of his, placed behind the leader on the ground. His bow was used as a cane, as at a peyote meeting today, one holds a bow in the left hand as a brace. While this meeting was going on, about midnight, they heard a sound outside. The young Comanche who had been killed lifted the flap, held his hand to his forehead (one could see he had been scalped), groaned, and crawled into the tipi, placing himself in front of the fire, just inside the door. The people on his left and right were frightened and moved to the back of the tipi. The leader told them to behave, and keep their seats, that he had come for a reason. The Carrizos sat in silence.

The Comanche spoke: "You people do not understand peyote power. I . . . know its powers." He reminded them what they had done to him, and that it was now midnight. He told them to smell the smoke of seven Comanches who would arrive in four days. Hold a peyote meeting and give them my bow and this peyote. They will take these things from you with them. One of the Carrizos said in good Comanche that they would do what he told them. As he left, he taught them to sing the song that opens peyote meetings: "I was lost. . . . My arrow, . . . my pipe, . . . long knife. . . ."

In four days the Comanches arrived, and a peyote meeting was set up. The Comanches took the north, shady side; the Carrizos took the south. No woman had ever attended a peyote meeting; now there was one. The Carrizo leader told her to tell "our cousins" the procedure of the meeting. The woman spoke Comanche, calling them "Relatives," which startled them. She told them to watch the performance. When the Carrizos were about to roll cigarettes, the Carrizo leader told her to instruct the Comanches: "I want them to go through these motions: to place their hands on the ground, to extend them upwards toward the sky, toward our Father, and then to smoke with us. Then we will become as one, because our Father has said so."

They did so, and the leader prayed for peace. They had a real meeting. They passed around sage to be chewed and rubbed on everyone, circle sunwise. They passed around peyote to be eaten. The chief asked the woman to invite the Comanches to join the singing as they caught the songs. The meeting went on all night. The leader told them about the young Comanche and his instructions, using the woman as translator. The Comanches received the bow, the peyote, the songs, to pass on to Indian tribes to the north and northeast. In the morning the chief instructed the Comanches about the proper peyote meetings. "This is what peyote says: 'When our Father made you he made me here on earth to grow with you.' " The leader told them that no matter what peyote looks like now, it can take on many different appearances in visions. "Peyote says: 'I am the power of our Father. Here on earth I do as I please because of my power.' " Peyote can appear as a man or woman, as grass growing on the ground, to be cut but to multiply by its roots. Then the leader asked the woman to tell the Comanches that the meeting was over, but that wherever they take peyote, it must come back to us.

Tekwakï concludes his story: "That is the female part of the peyote. It stands for regrowth. The girl who spoke for the leader was a Comanche who had been captured by the [Carrizos]. That is why in stories about the happenings of peyote a woman can appear. This woman brought us our knowledge of peyote. This happened a long time ago. I know this because I heard people talking about it."

Type V

Like its predecessor, Type V exists in only one published version, told by an Omaha Indian, George Phillips, in Lincoln, Nebraska, to Howard (1951a:1–4). Whereas the other types focus on individuals, this narrative describes a band of Tonkawas who discover peyote:

Once the Tonkawas were very many, so many that there were seven rings of lodges when they camped together. They were hated and feared by all the other tribes of the Southern Plains, because of the raiding, plundering wars the Tonkawas waged. All the other tribes called a council, where spokesmen told what had happened to their people; they decided to unite and exterminate the Tonkawas.

At the same time one of the Tonkawa chiefs had a dream: he must take his people to the west, or they will all be killed. When he told his people of his dream, the other chiefs laughed, saying that they were too populous to be threatened. The chief was disappointed; he went through the village, warning everyone. Most were against his plan, so he took his family and a small band of followers, and marched to the setting sun, traveling all night and the next day.

One of his people chanced to look back, and saw a black column of smoke rising where the village had been. Scouts were sent back, and returned with the news that the Tonkawas had been attacked and destroyed: men, women, and children. The scouts said that the band had to hurry, for enemies were trailing them.

They traveled many days and nights, followed by the other tribes close behind. Finally the Tonkawa band reached a cliff where they could go no further. They could see the dust raised by the pursuing warriors. Desperately looking for an escape, one warrior noticed a small cave entrance. They all entered through a tiny opening, and "followed a small passageway back into the earth," to a large room where all the women, children, and old people could hide, while the warriors defended the cave entrance.

The enemies attacked several times but were clubbed back. Tiring of this, the enemies laid seige to the cave. They built fires and danced to taunt the Tonkawas inside, who quickly exhausted all their food. Babies died, and also the weak. The dead were eaten by others.

Finally, one delirious, starved man staggered into a small room of the cave and fell against the wall. When he opened his eyes again he noticed something green. He ate it, for he was starving and willing to eat anything. He ate others he found, then called his people to eat the green plant, too. It had water in it and nourished them.

Then they fell to sleep and slept for seven years. One day a warrior awoke; everyone else was asleep around him. He went to the cave entrance and found only the ashes of fires from years ago. He shook his people awake and they went home again. These Tonkawas say that the green plant was the first peyote, and they claim to be the first peyote users, and all others got it from them. Sometimes you hear the Tonkawas called cannibals by other tribes. This is because of what they did in that cave.

Although the five types and their variations appear disparate in many details, some underlying themes emerge in consistent patterns. Most basically, the stories commence with life-threatening situations, for which peyote provides redemption. The actions of the stories move from warfare to friendship, separation to reunion, starvation to satisfaction, with peyote granting the power to persevere and prosper. There are numerous other features that shall be observed and analyzed: their historicity; evidence of syncretism; Christian influence; their multiple promises, that might appeal to a multiplicity of persons in many situations; their depiction of vivid experiences, grounded in ordeals and heightened by sensory, visionary events; their description of the powers of peyote to promote human life; ethical messages, in particular regard to intertribal relations; their prescriptions of ritual propriety and detail, as well as religious authority and organization. In short, they describe dimensions of religious life that surpass the notion of peyotism as an "escapist," "accommodationist," "acculturationist" "crisis cult."

These narratives of peyote's origin, with their core action of peyote's resolution of life-and-death situations, are replicated by peyotist stories about particular peyote leaders, who invented or passed down ritual elements, or individual Indians who were cured or aided in some way by peyote's powers (Stewart 1975b:7). In Stenberg (1946:139–45), the Northern Arapaho peyotist John Goggles narrates the story of peyote's origin, then traces its diffusion through Oklahoma, to a Northern Arapaho wandering through that state, to the Wyoming Indian communities, to himself personally as recipient of peyote's powers and ritual knowledge. Throughout the episodes of diffusion, curing plays the significant role.

The same is true for the stories told by the Comanches about their famous leader Quanah Parker, who helped introduce and protect peyotism in Indian Territory. Parker's introduction to peyote through a Mexican Indian curandera contains many of the mythical, historical, experiential, ethical, and ritual elements of the narratives already recounted. Brito (1975:131–40) and Marriott and Rachlin (1968:205–11) tell essentially the same story of Parker's conversion to peyote use. Brito heard his story from his Comanche peyote teacher, Michael; Alice Marriott received the story from Marie Cox, Parker's granddaughter-in-law. It lacks complete historical accuracy, but possesses mythical weight:

Quanah Parker's mother, Cynthia Anne Parker, was captured by Texas Comanches when she was a little girl, around age ten. She became a Comanche, married a Comanche, and had Comanche children, including Quanah. He was an outstanding Comanche warrior, who participated in Comanche raids in Texas and Mexico: capturing horses, women, children, and killing men and burning houses.

After the Civil War, the United States put an end to the Comanche raiding and encouraged cattle ranching among the Indians. When Parker's father died, his mother traveled with him to Texas to visit her family, and perhaps for him to learn the cattle business. Around 1870 he journeyed with his mother, who died after reuniting with her parents.

Shortly after her death, Parker became deathly ill—from tuberculosis, or grief, or an infection in his leg, and none of the white doctors were able to cure him. His condition worsened, until his grandmother called upon a Mexican Indian curandera. Suspecting that he was an Indian, she asked about his background, and upon learning of his Comanche blood, she effected a cure by bringing him outside under an arbor and doctoring him with peyote tea. "The drink was as bitter as the death Quanah had been awaiting" (Marriott and Rachlin 1968:209), but he drank, and when he finally awoke, he was cured; "Quanah was given back his life" (Brito 1975:133).

He asked about the medicine that cured him. The curandera told him the origin story of peyote (Marriott and Rachlin 1968:209–10–Type IA), and gave him a Catholic rosary that she told him was a complement to the peyote. "She also told him how to live a good life, a life of peace— not doing any bad to other Indian people" (Brito 1975:134). She took him to a peyote ceremony and told him to teach his people "this way of living" (Marriott and Rachlin 1968:210). When he got home, he taught his people to lead good, generous, kind, clean lives, to "help and comfort their neighbors when they can" (Marriott and Rachlin 1968:211). Peyotism may have already been current among the Comanches; however, Parker introduced Christian elements into it, tried to weed out shamanistic elements from its ritual, and protected it for years from the attacks of the Indian Bureau.

Like many of the peyote origin narratives, the story of Quanah Parker depicts a person separated from his Indian kinsmen, facing death, who is saved by peyote, and then brings it back to his people along with a ritual and ethical code attached to it. Parker goes on a search for mundane knowledge (how to raise cattle), and returns with lifesaving medicine, around which a religion is woven. And like the narratives of Types II and IV, a supposed enemy is the one who teaches peyotism to the hero, thus cementing friendship among Indian peoples.

HISTORICAL DIMENSION: RELIGION AND CHANGE

Although some of the narratives claim to describe events long ago, "way before the United States was discovered" (Beals 1971:433), there is clearly a potential for historicity in the stories. Most of the storytellers attempt to locate peyote's origin in specific places and among specific populations, and particularly the narrators from tribes in Oklahoma—Kiowa Apaches, Comanches, Delawares, and so on—name the same range of tribal discoverers, all from areas within, adjacent to, or within striking distance of the natural peyote fields. Most often mentioned as the discoveries of peyote are the various Apaches, Tonkawas, Caddos, northern Mexican tribesmen, the Kiowas, and the Comanches.

Some authors credit these accounts with historical accuracy (e.g., Opler 1945:210) or at least intent (e.g., McAllester 1949:18), and one can easily recognize conditions that existed in the eighteenth and nineteenth centuries on the Southern Plains, as peyotism was developing as a religious complex: the horse raids, war parties, the shifting alliances and sign language communication, the droughts and wanderings. The stories also have an ecological understanding of peyote's whereabouts, perhaps learned during pilgrimages to the peyote fields.

Nevertheless, Slotkin (1975:30–32) has pointed out the conflicting testimony that peyote narratives bring to peyote's origins and diffusion, and we should not expect these many divergent legends to establish some single, original peyote revelation. The farther the narratives recede from Oklahoma and the U.S. Southwest, the less specificity there is in regard to peyotism's place or tribal origin. The Crows, the Paiutes, the Menominis, and the Chippewas are among the most vague in these respects. Moreover, historians recognize that peyotism has many sources, and its diffusion has followed circuitous routes. The fact that peyotists accept the truth-content of diverse narratives indicates that these stories are not meant as strict historical guides, although they probably do provide a decent clue into some of the paths peyote use took on the way to creating the complex called peyotism. The narratives serve instead as demonstrations of the essential ingredients of the peyote matrix.

The stories cannot provide the kind of documentary evidence regarding, for instance, the conditions that facilitated and obstructed the spread of peyotism, the many individual prophets and missionaries of peyotism's diffusion; the details of the peyote trade; the opposition to peyotism from Christian churchmen, traditionalist and acculturated Indians, and government officials; the ebbing and flowing of enthusiasm for peyotism throughout this century. In short, there are myriad dimensions of peyotism's history that transcend the subject matter of the myths or legends.

Nonetheless, the narratives do point to the fact that peyotism is an historical set of phenomena; they show that religions have a history. From them one can glean some significant factors (if not facts) about peyotism as a cumulative, historical tradition, a coalescing of various elements—some old and new, tribal, pan-Indian, and Christian—into a religious complex that can be identified as peyotism.

The stories indicate peyotism's fluid, syncretistic nature, alternating and combining elements of traditional Indian and Christian world views, ethics, and rituals, as well as incorporating some features of specific tribal cultures. Peyotism is often said to be a combination of ancient Mexican elements, combined with various tribal and pan-Indian traditions of the Plains, with a Christian overlay, a "product of recent history, built upon a traditional cultural foundation" (Spindler and Spindler 1971:99), a "synthesis with limited aspects of Whiteman culture" (Ibid.: 93). Studies have shown the incorporation of peyotism into a few tribal religious systems, as well as the ability of individual peyotists to participate whole-heartedly in traditional tribal religions, mainstream Christianity, and peyotism. As the narratives point out, peyotism is a mixture of elements from diverse sources, a fact in the history of all religions. At the same time peyote myths and peyotism as a complex are discretely identifiable.

If we are to look to Mexico for the origin of peyote mythology, we are bound for disappointment. Marriott and Rachlin (1971:14) state that Type IA comes from northern Mexican Indians, including the Tarahumara, who tell it to this day. The authors also claim that this story has long been told by the Aztecan peoples of Mexico's central Great Valley; however, I cannot verify either of these claims. La Barre (1970:111) suggests that Type II derives not only from the Mescalero and Lipan Apaches but also from the Tamaulipecos of the Mexican Gulf Coast. We have hints

(Lumholtz 1898:4; Petrullo 1934:16) that Type V bears some resemblance to Huichol or other Mexican Indian stories in which peyote takes pity on a tribe, fleeing from an enemy, without water, lost underneath the earth. These suggestive and plausible connections fail to provide the kind of proven continuity between Mexican and U.S. forms of peyotism in regard to ritual activity. To the contrary, an examination of the mythology of Mexican peyote users—Huichol and Tarahumara Indians—uncovers a large corpus of stories that bear little or no resemblance to the narratives of the Native American Church. Indeed, Myerhoff writes that the Huichol peyote-deer-maize "symbol complex should be distinguished from the North American peyote cult with which it has nothing in common" (1970:68).

On the other hand, the peyote narratives fit the generalized patterns of North American Indian (particularly Plains) religiousness: the search for supernatural power to solve crucial dilemmas; the face-to-face relations with persons other than human; the heroic origin of curing rituals; the personification of plants and of nature-beings in general; the special power associated with death; the value of ordeals in attaining power and wisdom. More specifically, however, individual tribes have stamped their own motifs on the peyote narratives: the Apache following of the drum; the Navajo reliance on Coyote for guidance; the Taos entry to a kiva-like structure beneath the earth to receive instruction; the Winnebago reference to Earthmaker as the creative force behind peyote; the Sioux association of the peyote woman with the Buffalo Calf Woman of their own mythology. Radin (1971:376) remarks that the Winnebago peyote origin story, while deriving from other Indians, "has already assumed all the characteristics of a Winnebago fasting experience and ritualistic myth, similar to those connected with the founders of the old Winnebago cult societies." Similarly, the Kiowa story of the origin of Tai-me, the Sundance Doll, resembles Type IB, in which long ago in bad times the Kiowas were hungry. A man searched for food to feed his crying children, but he became exhausted. A voice asked him what he wanted, and upon hearing of the Kiowas' plight, said, "Take me with you, . . . and I will give you whatever you want" (Momaday 1968:96). I do not imply that Type IB derives from the Kiowas; rather, peyotism and its mythology appear to spring from the religious culture of particular tribes, as well as from generalized religious patterns. As Stewart (1948:31) has noted, each culture makes peyotism seem natural, at home, even though peyotists know that it was taught to them by other Indians and is a "new" religion. Even though peyotism appeared to some tribal traditionalists as a foreign abomination to be opposed vigorously, other Indians interpreted peyotism as an outgrowth of, or successor to, their tribal traditions.

The peyote narratives do not make a claim to be the ancient tribal stories. An examination of the hundreds of major motifs from North American Indian mythology finds very little similarity to peyote motifs. These stories are regarded by peyotists and nonpeyotists as narratives peculiar to the peyote complex, and as such they can be incorporated to tribal myths, alternated with them, or rejected. Furthermore, staunch peyotists, including one Winnebago storyteller, have sometimes regarded their peyote beliefs as replacements for old ways: "Before I joined the Peyote sect, [before I ate medicine,] all these things ... I believed to be absolutely true. Not any of it is true (I now know); it is all a falsehood and deception" (Radin 1913:310).

Part of the stridency of the Winnebago peyotist's statement may derive from the Christian influence on peyotism's history. If the ancient Mexican elements are only vaguely represented in peyotism and its narratives, and if tribal patterns are more generalized than specific within the religious complex, Christian elements in the stories are undeniable, although perhaps (some might argue) superficial. They include a disparagement of aboriginal Indian religiousness in the Taos version: "they don't believe in *anything,* no God, nothing—how they live just like animals, always going round killing and stealing" (Parsons 1936:64). One might mention the "missionary spirit" (*The Independent* 1909:431) of peyotists to spread their new faith beyond their tribal boundaries to other Indian tribes, as another Christian influence on peyotism.

In many of the narratives, the name of Jesus appears, identified usually as the voice who reveals peyote's whereabouts, the Savior in white clothes who says, "take that plant and eat it ... it will be food and drink" and "you will find peace in a Savior" (Carlton 1969:2). As the spirit of peyote, Jesus calls to his "Father" and refers to his "gospel" (Radin 1971:351); he tells the pitiful, visionary woman to look for peyote in the imprint of a cross made by her sleeping body (Siskin 1983:187). Indeed, Type IA is referred to in one text as the " 'miracle' story" of a young girl who learns "Christ's message to the red man" (Levine 1968:15). In at least two versions, the recipient of peyote's revelation brings a limited number of plants back home, to have them "miraculously multiplied" (Mooney, 1897:330), like the loaves and fishes of the gospel story. Not only do we find the rosary beads in Quanah Parker's initiation to peyotism, but we find in one version of Type II that, when the hero asks what is this ritual he has stumbled upon, the chief host says, "We are here to worship God. We repent because of our sins" (Skinner 1923:234).

That is, the peyote narratives recognize a place not only for the personage of Jesus and the ritual paraphernalia of Christianity but also for the Christian concept of sinfulness and need for human redemption. There is a place, too, for an ethic of universalized brotherhood that seems to carry a Christian imprint, apparent in the frequent narrative messages of intertribal harmony.

The same is found in peyote ritual and belief: there are numerous references to Christian symbols and statements of Christian ethos. Readings from the Bible, recitations of the Lord's Prayer, the equation of peyote and the Eucharist, trinitarian symbolism, the shape of the cross and the presence of a prominent crucifix, the references to the body of Jesus, the self-accusatory confessions, the representations of Jesus on "Father (or Chief) Peyote" fetishes and gourd rattles, the peyote songs that state: "It is through the name of Jesus and of his father that we go to the place that we go, that is heaven" (Huot 1936:118)—these are unmistakable signs of Christian content. As one peyotist says, "We say we have the Peyote, the Creator, and Jesus. That's how we believe" (d'Azevedo 1978:2).

Christian elements abound in peyotism's narratives, rituals, and beliefs; however, what can be said to be the relationship between Christianity and peyotism? One possibility is that the narratives and peyotism itself are interpretive, inculturated Indian versions of Christian myth and religion. Rachlin states: "Objectively, the Native American Church should be included as a Christian belief" (1968:103).

Another analysis states that Christian elements are a form of superficial "window-dressing" (La Barre 1946:633, n.2) upon an Indian religious complex, "so incorporated that fundamentally the worship is not dependent on Christianity" (Kroeber 1983:398). La Barre (1970:165) has argued this interpretation most cogently in saying that "the layer of Christianity on peyotism is very thin and superficial indeed."

A third possibility is that peyotists have compared their religious complex with Christianity—"It's just like Testament, you know, to lead you towards the Creator" (Slotkin 1952:632)—and found similarities enough to convince them that the two religions are essentially the same, although they have different origins.

Other peyotists interpret their religion as a form of Christianity designed specifically for Indians. They make references to biblical passages regarding a future "Comforter" (Kneale 1950:212; Page 1915:195; Pierson 1915:202) and salvific "herbs" (Snyder 1969:30–31) to justify peyotism against attacks by Christians. Indeed, the Christian elements, including references to the Bible, may be means of blunting criticism of their religion. In such presentations the Christian critics become "the Pharisees and Scribes, . . . the doubters" (Radin 1971:352) of a religion given to Indians by the Christian God himself, partially because non-Indian Christians did not properly understand the biblical message. Thus a Winnebago peyotist says that his religion is Christianity, but he does not want non-Indians participating in it (Cash and Hoover 1971:37–38).

Another analysis is suggested by Stewart (1980a:192–94), who remarks that Indians practice several "distinct and separate religions simultaneously" (Stewart 1982c:181). In such a view, the relationship between Christianity and peyotism in one in which both are available to Indians as religious complexes to be combined, alternated, or rejected in various situations, but are usually kept apart. In some cases, individual Indians create their own complexes of religious elements, and they draw upon Christian, peyotist, and other elements in so doing. In such a view, there is no necessary exclusivity between the two traditions, as they are combined according to the personal patterns of an individual Indian. Given the long interpretation of Christian and Indian religious complexes, and given the fact that virtually all peyotists in the past century have Christian training and identify themselves at least nominally as Christians, it would be virtually impossible to keep Christian and peyotist elements separated in theory or practice. Many peyotists not only express Christianity in terms of Indian symbol systems but also accept the Christian message to a large degree. Densmore (1941:77) has characterized the Christian-native syncretism in peyotism most succinctly, by concluding that in peyotism, "The American Indian is making his own religion," even when the two complexes seem objectively at odds with one another. Even La Barre (et al. 1951:582) has admitted that peyotism is "Christianity adapted to traditional Indian beliefs and practices."

A final word is necessary regarding peyotism's syncretism with Christianity. Brito's Comanche peyotist instructor stated that Quanah Parker used a rosary in his peyote cures; however, "This doesn't mean that he learned to pray with it like Catholics do" (1975:135). On the other hand, when asked: "Are you saying that Quanah applied the idea of the supplication of the passion of Christ to the use of peyote?" (135), he answered yes. When the Winnebago peyote leader John Rave said, "God, his holiness," in "baptizing" members with an infusion of peyote, younger, more christianized members translated the prayer as "God, the Son, and the Holy Ghost" (Radin 1971:341). One Ute community incorporated Christian elements into peyotism; another eschewed them (Marvin Opler 1940:470–71). In short, peyotists have interpreted their Christian elements in various ways, at various times, and in various contexts. Under pressure from agents, missionaries, courts, and other forces against the aboriginal Indian religious elements, the historical trend over the past century has probably been toward greater christianization. The Kiowa Apaches, for example, rooted out the shamanistic rivalries and displays that characterized their peyotism before Christian inroads. These elements are demonstrated by some of the features in the stories of Type III. As one Kiowa Apache says, "They abolished those bad things in there. They put the White Man's God in, and made it like a church" (Beals 1971:51). The Winnebago Albert Hensley, a christianized peyotist, decried the shamanistic uses of peyote in his origin narrative (Radin 1971:352). For him, and it appears for most of the narrators, Christian elements are integrated in peyotism, and have supplanted any purely native complex.

Peyotism, like any other religious tradition, has contained a diversity of beliefs, deriving from diverse sources, appealing to diverse individuals in diverse ways. Over the past century, numerous changes have occurred in peyote practices, including the frequency of meetings, the amount of peyote consumption, the degree of curing, the tendency toward secrecy or nativism, the participation by women and the young, and the incorporation of Christian elements, among many other features. The appeal of peyotism to Indians has varied with circumstances. To some its pan-Indian features were attractive; to others the visionary features, or the promise of curing, or the preaching against alcohol use, or the Christian ethics were appealing. Peyote doctrines have always been variable, and continue to be today. Even in the peyote narratives, one can find the promises of more horses, brotherhood, medicine, success against enemies and ritual propriety. That is, the myths participate in peyotism's multiple appeal, its historicity, as it has repeatedly transcended the label of "crisis cult." It should also be noted, however, that the religion, peyotism, has a much more diverse history than its origin narratives suggest. The religion has transcended the myths, even though the myths contain the core elements of peyotism as a historical religious complex.

EXPERIENTIAL DIMENSION: RELIGION AND POWER

The peyote stories, for all their diversity of content, all describe vivid personal experiences, ordeals and earthly salvations, that illustrate the experiential dimension of peyotism. In the narratives there is direct contact with the miraculous power of peyote and its rituals. Peyote is something to be experienced; on this matter all peyotists agree.

Peyotists say that the physical effect of peyote is characterized by a thrilling sense of "personal significance of external and internal stimuli. The user is prompted to ask of everything, 'What does this mean for me?'" (Aberle 1966:6) There is the feeling in using peyote of being taken over, overwhelmed, by a force greater than oneself, or receiving power directly and personally from something grand. The result of the peyote experience is "an absolute conviction that we do not invent what we learn and know, that those things come from God through peyote" (Laney 1972:129). In these ways peyote use triggers religious experience, a per-ceived contact with an awe-inspiring holiness.

Peyotists say that without using, experiencing peyote directly, you can know nothing, you can receive no power. Slotkin (1952) regards this feature as one of the basic elements in peyotism: "The doctrine and rites of Peyotism can be learned only through taking Peyote oneself. Much emphasis is placed upon the necessity of direct revelation" (571). Pe-yotists tell interviewers that they cannot explain peyotism; one can only experience it, and for this reason the spirit voice in narrative Type I and the hosts in Type II state: "Don't just look at it. Eat it!" (Hoebel 1949:128) Significantly, the heroes of the stories bring back to their people not only a story of their experiences, but more importantly, the peyote itself, so their people can duplicate the original event for themselves. In their per-sonal peyote experiences, Indians can receive revelation from the su-pernatural world; they can come to understand their individual life situations; they can grasp the meanings of seemingly meaningless peyote song lyrics, as truths are revealed through peyote use. Such experiences are predogmatic, preethical, indicating that the experiential dimension of religion need not have an ethical or credal content (although a religious complex usually includes these). The myths suggest that religion begins with the experience of supernatural power; all else is accretion.

Indeed, in peyotism the myths themselves are secondary to the personal experiences, and peyotists are much more likely to tell stories of peyote's effect on their own lives or the lives of their relatives, than they are to tell the origin narratives. Thus, it matters not that most tribes credit pey-ote's discovery to other tribal members, since the real importance of peyote lies in its direct, personal contact through ingestion. In their per-sonal stories peyotists tend to replicate the major themes of the peyote narratives (Opler 1936:148–49); however, without the personal stories the origin narratives mean little. Hence John Wilson, one of the peyote prophets "was not particularly concerned with how the Comanche had Peyote revealed to them because it was upon his own revelation that he wished to lay stress" (Speck 1933:556).

Peyotists often contrast their experiential dimension of religion to the credal, ethical, book-learned knowledge of Christianity. They emphasize that peyote is direct access to God, without dogma, authority, or formal priesthood, or abstractions:

There ain't no preaching in our ceremony. We get our knowledge from the Almighty direct. We don't need nobody telling us what the word is. That's what peyote is for. You take that, and the medicine will do the rest.

God will talk to you himself. You don't need no bible. [Spindler and Spindler 1971:96]

Furthermore, criticisms of peyotism without experience of peyote are considered invalid by peyotists. Experience is the test of validity.

What characterizes the peyote experience? The stories emphasize its power, its concern for Indian welfare, the feeling of relief, of physical redemption, of accomplishment. Nevertheless, the stories also describe the ordeals that lead to peyote use and that are part of the peyote experience. This twofold effect in the myths—the ordeal and the exhilaration—may derive from the nature of narratives in general: the problems that beset storied heroes and the plots that lead to the solution of the initial problems. In stories heroes are lost and need to be found, or they are almost dead and need to be brought back to life. The twofold effect may also point out the structure of vivid religious experiences: the enormous disquiet, followed by enormous relief and fulfillment.

In addition, however, the twofold effect is also consistent with, and perhaps grounded in, the chemical makeup of peyote itself. Composed of two main types of alkaloids (among others), one resembling strychnine, the other resembling morphine, peyote tends to produce two phases in humans who ingest it. First is the nausea, dizziness, choking, the pains and shortness of breath, the hunger, cramps, and tremors, accompanied by restlessness, anxiety, depression, agitation, fear of death and dissolution. Then there is the euphoria, peace, contentment, contemplation, exhilaration and pleasant fantasies that can last for many hours.

In the origin stories the ordeal precedes, sets the stage for, the euphoric ending. In Type IA the ordeal consists of abandonment, hunger, thirst, and despair, producing a "pitiful" state that elicits the compassion of the peyote spirit (Petrullo 1934:35). In one version (Radin 1971:351) the spirit tells the pitiful Indian: "I have caused you to go through all this suffering, for had I not done it, you would never have heard of the proper (religion)." In Type III the bloody beating delivered to the peyotist represents his initiation to the secrets of the peyote people. In the Navajo combination of Type I and Type II, the twelve brothers die in order to become twelve peyote buttons, the medicine serving as the fruit of warfare. In Type IV the Comanche warrior is killed and scalped before bringing his message regarding the peyote ritual, and in Type V there is the ordeal of the siege in the cave that leads to the discovery of salvific peyote. Even in the Quanah Parker story there are the hero's separation from his people, the deaths of his parents, and the malignant illness that introduce him to the curandera and her medicine.

In the peyote religion Indians come to experience peyote in order to solve their problems, as a relief to the ordeals of their lives; moreover, the very taking of peyote is a type of ordeal, as is apparent in the Quanah Parker story: "The drink was as bitter as the death Quanah had been awaiting" (Marriott and Rachlin 1968:209). Peyotists all attest: taking peyote is a test, an ordeal; "they do not make peyote consumption a simple hedonic gratification" (Aberle 1966:9). The Indians say, "You must suffer to peyote" (Long 1941:234), and only because it is absolutely indispensable, is it eaten, so distasteful is the cactus. As a result, peyotists regard their peyote meetings as tough, suffering, almost self-torture, a sort of stationary pilgrimage that replicates the bitter road of the heroes of the peyote origin stories: the roads of war, starvation, loneliness and death, at the end of which lies the redemptive peyote.

Peyote meetings are hard work, much harder than a Christian service, peyotists attest: "That Peyote ain't easy on you like that Bible is. . . . and it will be hard on you if you ain't ready for it. . . . It can kill you or bring you life. It all depends on you" (d'Azevedo 1978:37–38). If it is used in a trifling manner, it can backfire, peyotists say. Such carelessness is called "shooting" yourself because peyote is "loaded" and can cause paranoia and sickness in the person improperly prepared for its power (Simmons 1918:7). Thus peyotists cleanse themselves, go without alcohol, and place themselves in an attitude of benevolence and humility before receiving peyote, and violent nausea is sometimes regarded as a sign of incorrect preparation.

Some scholars suggest that the arduous aspect of the peyote experience is part of its appeal, fitting the patterns of Plains religiousness with its tradition of vision fasting, self-torture, suffering and bravery; however, the ordeal comprises only part of the peyote experience. Euphoria and fulfillment mark the long stretches of an all-night peyote meeting, as illustrated in the happy endings of the peyote origin narratives.

The physical and mental exhilaration that peyote produces is surely the reason that Mexican Indians used peyote in races, at war, during pilgrimages and dances, in order to allay thirst and hunger, and permit extended periods of concentration and exercise. The peyotist feels no hunger, no fatigue, even after a whole night of prayer, singing and drumming. As one Chiricahua Apache says of his peyote experience, the world looked "very pretty" to him; the singing sounded "very, very lovely" during the ritual; "The Indians' dresses looked beautiful," and the sunrise he witnessed was "very, very beautiful"; indeed, the sun rose "on the best world you ever saw. It's going to make you feel young and good in every way" (Opler 1939:437). The exhilarating effect of peyote helps reaffirm for the peyotist the world as it is, a world with peyote at hand to redeem life's ordeals. In this regard, the peyote narratives reaffirm the world order for peyotists, since they present a world of ordeals that are resolved by peyote's power.

The experiences of the mythic heroes parallel the experiences of peyote in ritual use; in no case is this parallel more apparent than in regard to the visionary themes. In both myth and ritual there is a face-to-face religiousness, a heightened awareness of the holy, a revelation of peyote's power, producing a knowledge that works.

Bernardino Sahagun, writing in the 1560s (Safford 1915:294), stated that peyote caused Mexican Indians to "see visions either frightful or laughable." In 1720 at Taos an Indian drank a peyote tea "to see fantasies in his imagination" (Slotkin 1951:421), and was so convinced of his visions' truth that he gathered his people to act upon his visionary revelation. In 1888 an Indian agent decried peyote use among the Comanches, Apaches, and Kiowas: "While under its influence they are in dreamland and see the most beautiful visions. One of the strange hallucinations which it produces is the belief that everything seen in the visions is real" (United States 1888:98). Thus peyote's production of visions has been observed for centuries by non-Indians.

Some observers have contended that peyote's ability to produce visions in a pattern similar to aboriginal Plains vision questing added to its appeal, especially in the early years of the cult. The process of emptying oneself, becoming pitiful through ordeal, in order to receive protection and fulfillment from the supernaturals, was salient in peyotism's myth and ritual, and thus Plains and other vision-seeking cultures felt at home in the new religious complex, especially in the late nineteenth and early twentieth centuries, when U.S. authorities were forbidding traditional means of vision seeking (e.g., the Sundance). La Barre (1941:41) has written that "The supernatural vision is the 'psychic authority' for the Plains Indians' life-activities and beliefs, much as the pragmatic or scientific laboratory method is our own culture's touchstone for truth," and thus peyote's visions have carried authenticity and authority. It is significant that many of the old-time visions were actually auditory, rather than (or in addition to) visual—the supernaturals speak or sing or drum messages to the visionary—and in the peyote narratives it is the auditory vision that prevails, as it does in peyote pilgrimages when peyotists say the plants sing to the devoted searcher in order to reveal their whereabouts.

Many scholars have rejected undue attention to the visions in peyotism, arguing that peyotists distinguish between revelation and visions—seeking the former and rejecting the latter. Over time visions have become less important to many peyotists, and in many tribal patterns visions never played a role in peyotism. In addition, peyotism became popular among

Indians with little or no visionary traditions—Navajos, most prominently—
and what visions take place more often derive from drumming and exhaustion, not from peyote itself. Despite the fact that visions are part of
Plains and peyote religiousness and often "lead to deep psychological
transformations" (Steinmetz 1980:97), there has been perhaps a tendency
to overemphasize their importance in peyotism.

Nevertheless, the peyote origin legends bear witness most emphatically
to peyote's visionary quality. Type I narratives contain auditory visions
in virtually every version: the peyote spirit appears or speaks to the pitiful
Indian and brings him or her to the salvific peyote fields, guiding him or
her to safety, and giving instructions regarding the proper ritual use and
worship of the cactus. If a vision is a direct visit from the supernaturals,
a sensory contact with the powers upon whom human life depends, the
peyote narratives are visionary, and they set a pattern for the visions—
the sensory revelations—of the peyote experience in ritual. Although
visions do not play a salient role in Type II stories—these, after all, are
descriptions of ritual acquisition rather than peyote's revelation—the visit
from the supernaturals at a peyote meeting in Type III continues the
vision pattern.

Moreover, one of the powers granted by peyote to Indians is the ability—as described in the narratives—to attain visionary states in ritual. As
the visionary woman instructs her people in ritual, she says, "We will
find out things from peyote at night, just like seeing things in the daytime"
(Navajo Tribal Council 1954:23), and in at least one version the first
vision is of horses to be discovered. Numerous other peyote stories of
personal experiences stress the vision-granting powers of the plant: for
instance, the Washos' tale of how they found an important, hidden
treaty through visionary revelation (d'Azevedo 1973), or in John Wilson's
visions that led to his creation of one standard ritual pattern (Speck
1933:541–43).

The visions that peyotists receive while under peyote's influence usually
concern instruction, revelation, the attainment of power, protection, inspiration, prophecy, and salvation. Many peyote dreams act as means of
solving personal problems; are often of "concrete personal achievement,"
representing the visionary as a "successful hunter, farmer, trader, orator,
lover" (Laswell 1935:237); and are means by which visionaries validate
recent decisions they have made. They serve to defend peyote practice,
as in the following Navajo peyotist's visions:

> And then Jesus spoke to me. I asked him, "What is this peyote?" And Jesus
> Christ said to me, "Today when many are against this, and many are for it,
> Me, too, those who hated Me crucified Me on the cross. And then after My

blood dropped to the earth from My heart, and there grew up from the earth vegetation, and that was peyote, and peyote is My blood," He said. [Aberle 1966:166]

They are also a means of gaining new songs and the powers adhering to them, as well as realizing moral progress.

The Winnebago peyotist John Rave (Radin 1950:262) overcame his dread of the living thing inside him during his first peyote experience and realized that peyote was the cause of his vision:

> Throughout all the years that I had lived on earth, I now realized that I had never known anything holy. Now, for the first time, I knew something holy. . . . O, would that some of the other Winnebago might also learn about it.

Part of the fulfillment of his and other peyotists' visions consisted of their sense that they were sharing in a common visionary experience with their cohorts and that the effects of peyote visions would be felt by a whole community, to whom benefit would come. As a result, some peyotists interpret each other's visions for one another, and in so doing make reference to the peyote origin narratives.

Some peyotist visionaries "meet with the stranger who appears in the origin myth, while still others meet with Jesus, or relive the suffering on the cross" (Bittle 1954:76). Another peyotist recalls:

> After I revived—that medicine revived me—well, then I started to think back, who created this medicine? And then I see a vision too. . . . I recognized Him, gradually . . . Jesus Christ. . . . And then, about that time, then the old leader told that [origin] story. It seemed like I lived right through it; in order so that I understand it, I had to live through that story. [Slotkin 1952:609]

The visionary experience of peyote does not exist for its own sake. Peyotism is not primarily a form of mysticism, in which contemplation of, and absorption in the godhead are goals in and of themselves. Rather, the visionary experience of peyote—in the stories and in actuality—serves as a conduit and proof of peyote's powers. The holy in peyotism is a life-sustaining, protective, curative, spiritual substance for use by pitiful humans.

Peyotism's theology is varied—including Jesus Christ, various tribal gods, a Creator in various combinations—but the peyote spirit symbolized by the plant is central and unvarying. In the peyote origin narratives people ingest peyote and they are cured; their hunger and thirst are allayed; they feel no fatigue; they can endure; they gain courage and a sense of direction; they are granted wisdom and leadership, the ability to produce peaceful accord and overcome apparent death, as well as the ability to send rain and provide the depth of health itself; they can foretell the future or see at a distance; they cure others. That is, the full complement of life-promoting powers derive ultimately and immediately from the supernatural-natural powers of peyote. As the peyote spirit says in one narrative, "I am the power of our Father. Here on earth I do as I please because of my power" (McAllester 1949:17). A Navajo peyotist affirms the message of the myths: "Peyote is a power. There is a power in there. That power, he has many names. You don't know how much power is there. It will take all your lifetime and you will know only a small part of the power" (Beck and Walters 1977:233).

Indians have regarded peyote as a power to be experienced for centuries. Sahagun wrote in the 1560s: "It is a common food of the Chichimecas, for it sustains them and gives them courage to fight and not to feel hunger nor thirst; and they say that it protects them from all dangers" (Schleiffer 1973:30). Probably because of the actual physical effects of peyote, it has been used as a panacaea, not only in situations of illness, but in situations of any conceivable danger and need; it is a source of strength; it is power, "derived from nature—the giver of all things" (Bromberg and Tranter 1943:524). Fox peyote songs speak of it as a medicine that is "supposed to help us" (Huot 1936:118). Crow peyotists say that a "tremendous power pervades the tipi during a meeting" (Kiste 1962:103), a power that can be felt by all. A Navajo says, "Peyote has always been a religion. It is used mainly to gain power" (Beck and Walters 1977:233).

Although the narratives do not emphasize peyote's medicinal powers (the stories are more concerned with starvation, thirst, abandonment, and warfare), some of the myths point to the curative power of the plant. The peyote spirit tells the pitiful woman in Type IA: "It will heal all their ills and sorrows" (Marriott and Rachlin 1968:210); and in Type IB it is stated explicitly that a man seeks out a new medicine because the old ones are failing; his people are dying. When peyote reveals itself and he learns the rituals, it is said: "Everyone was feeling good. The different kinds of sickness went away" (Opler 1945:212). In the stories about Quanah Parker, the medicinal power of peyote is especially prominent.

The evidence is abundant that Indians have been drawn to peyotism at least in part for its supposed power to heal, and peyotism has functioned to some degree as a curing ritual. Peyotism has drawn upon traditional notions that religion and medicine are interrelated, and in the demise of some traditional curing practices peyotism has taken their place, or combined with aboriginal curing rites. Indian peyotists often tell of their personal experiences of curing ("I was just like a skeleton," said one Ponca who was cured by peyote: Curtis 1930, vol. 19:213). Peyote missionaries stressed the plant's power to cure, not only physical but also psychological ills, granting Indians a chance at a long, well-adjusted, healthy life. Non-Indian doctors have objected to the medical features of peyotism, because they interfere with other modes of therapy, and although some have suggested that peyote may contain elements that resist bacteria, there has been a reduced emphasis on peyote's curative prowess in recent years among some peyotists. Still, for the stretch of peyotism's history, curing has stood as one of the primary symbols of peyote's power.

More basic to the legends is peyote's power to nourish. Peyote is a food, having the qualities of meat, of vegetation, and of water as it is described in the stories. It is not unknown for Indians and non-Indians alike to survive on peyote while starving in the Texan and Mexican desert, and the stories speak eloquently of its powers and sustenance. Thus a Washo peyotist speaks of peyote: "This little green thing grows in the desert. There ain't no water where It grows, but It's got plenty water in It. When you eat It you ain't thirsty. It fills you up. You ain't hungry" (d'Azevedo 1978:1). At peyote meetings the participants eat the cactus as an experience of peyote's power to sustain. As such, it symbolizes the human dependence on the natural and supernatural world for survival. It is the transubstantial food, just as the corn, fruit, and meat of the ritual peyote meal are symbols of mundane sustenance. "All of the important elements for man's sustenance are woven into the ceremony," state two Crow peyotists; "thus the entire ceremony is symbolic of man's dependence on and use of things in his environment, fire, water, plants, and animals—all things necessary to his survival and continuance" (Old Coyote and Old Coyote 1969:4). However, the most powerful food of all is the peyote itself: "The Medicine is the main thing of all. It's our life. None of them other things here can do much without the Herb the Creator give us" (d'Azevedo 1978:13).

In addition to peyote's powers as medicine and food, its ability to produce clairvoyant, divinatory visions is also a feature in the peyote origin stories. In Type II tales, the host peyote chief is able to see the hero approaching his ceremonial tipi, and advises his fellows accordingly. In other cases the discoverer or initiate receives the ability to divine the location of horses, using the power of peyote. Throughout peyotism's history, including the early Spanish records, peyote's power to produce visions has been associated with its power of clairvoyance. Francisco Hernandez reported in the sixteenth century that Mexican Indians used it to foretell events, including attacks by enemies or the weather, or to see what is hidden, for example, who has stolen something (Safford 1915:295; Schleiffer 1973:31). An Indian agent in 1888 (United States: 98) said that Oklahoma Indians considered peyote as "an oracle, endowed with the power of revelation." These uses have continued among some peyotists, and Navajo names for peyote include the notions that nothing is hidden from it, horizon to horizon, not even in a storage crypt, because it stands in the middle of the earth (Aberle 1966:377). A Washo peyotist states: "The whole world is in there. . . . It shows you everything there is to see . . . all the people in the world . . . all the different animals . . . all the places" (d'Azevedo 1978:1).

Peyote's powers have included its use as a talisman in war, as a counteractive agent to witchcraft, as a love-medicine, through whose power "you can ask to have every good-looking girl fond of you" (Opler 1939:436). In Type IB stories there is a series of variants that concern a chief's son who has inherited the chieftaincy, but has no real power with which to lead and serve. Once receiving the revelation of peyote, he could become a real chief, because now, "he had power from Peyote" (Slotkin 1952:572). In short, peyote's powers are multifaceted.

As a power, peyote fit the shamanistic patterns of Indian religiousness; it was a power to be used for the benefit of one's group. It also fit the patterns of witchcraft as a power to be used for oneself, even at the expense of others. Peyotists claimed shamanstic powers, and opponents accused peyotism as a vehicle for witchcraft. Peyotism is so associated with an ethic of humility, worship, and universal brotherhood and peace that it is necessary to note that, especially in its early years in the nineteenth century, the religious complex emphasized the manipulation of power for good or evil.

The Type III narratives reveal this "magical" dimension to the peyote experience. The bloodily initiated peyotist visits the peyote people, and finds them eating one another, performing transformative and other magical tricks, and they grant him their power to repeat their actions. There is no curing, no redemption, no ethical content, to this version of peyote's discovery, and one might suspect that it represents an earlier aspect of peyotism that has been eclipsed over time. Potawatomi shamans carried peyote in their medicine bundles in the late nineteenth century, before the peyote complex came to them. The Mescaleros used peyote in shamanistic services until the early twentieth century, in which shamans competed with one another to prove their individual powers. There was no Christian element in Mescalero peyotism during this period, and it was associated with warfare against Indians and non-Indians alike. Its use was by individuals, not by a society or church, and magic tricks were the sign of peyote's power. Thus we cannot deny the shamanistic dimension of peyotism, not only because both shamanism and peyotism are socioreligious curing complexes that seek supernatural power and employ visions, but because such a dimension uncovers a pre-Christian aspect of the religious complex.

Nevertheless, the history of peyotism has seen a struggle against shamanism and witchcraft, in which the experience of power has been subordinated to the ethical dimension. Peyote's early reputation was that of a power: to protect, to cure, to manipulate. By the turn of the century, under Christian influence, peyotism came to emphasize the leading of a moral life. Thus we find stories of Quanah Parker in moral combat with a Kiowa shaman who tried to use peyote for self-aggrandizement and witchcraft. Parker defeated him and preached the ethical content of peyotism. Shamanstic curing has remained in tandem with the peyote religious complex, since there always remains a need for power in any religion; however, shamanistic practices have been subordinated to ethical exhortations as part of a broad religious complex.

ETHICAL DIMENSION: RELIGION AND COMMUNITY

Shamanism should not be placed in a position antagonistic to ethics; indeed, shamanism consists of manipulation of supernatural power, with the aid of forces similar to the peyote spirit, for the good of the community. Shamanism, like peyotism, is power not for its own sake, but for the aid of one's people. Congruent with traditional Indian values, peyotism (like shamanism) has been concerned with goodness as well as success in this world, with less concern for an afterlife.

In this context one should note that in the origin stories peyote is almost never intended for the individual alone; it is to be brought home to the visionary's people, to the seeker's people, for the benefit of the group. Peyotism possesses a social context in which its ethical dimension is prominent. The narratives and the history of peyotism illustrate the function of religion as a means of maintaining and improving community relations and conditions, for the benefit (at least theoretically) of individuals and the group.

The stories emphasize the social nature of peyotism in a most consistent manner. The most regular pattern of the narratives is for the hero to be separated from the kin group, to receive the gift of peyote, and to return with peyote to the group. In Type IA the separation of individual from the community is equated with starvation, thirst, being lost in a desert without means of support; to be separated from the group is to die. In this situation the stories often stress the loyalty of the hero to a relative, for instance, the mother who watches after her child when the two are lost, or the sister who mourns and searches for the missing brother. People perform their proper ritual obligations to those presumed dead, and in general the societal bonds are maintained. In Type II legends, these bonds are evidenced by the joyful reunions with the hero presumed dead. In both types the hero brings back peyote to be shared with the kinship group and life is reaffirmed at the happy end of the tale. In Type IV a small band of Tonkawas are separated from the rest of their people, who are then destroyed, but after being saved by peyote the band returns home. In the stories about Quanah Parker, the hero is separated from his Comanche kin, and then falls ill. In the end he returns to them with the gift of peyote. We often hear that peyotism in North America is an individualist religion, distinct from the tribal peyotism of Mexican Indians; however, the mythic message—that separation from the community equals death, and reunion spells life—seems to define peyotism as a religion of the community, held together by a community ethic.

The ethics of peyotism find their voice during the peyote meeting, sometimes before the ritual breakfast, when the chief or another respected person may deliver moral lectures in solemn manner. These lectures ask how peyotists should conduct themselves in this life; how to use God and peyote as a guide to behavior; how to adjust to non-Indians; how to abstain from alcohol; how to fulfill obligations to family, kin, and tribe. At the same time there may be confessions made by peyotists, accompanied by violent sobbing and requests to the community for forgiveness, or personal tales of moral transformation. These self-exposures are "a conversion in the conventional sense—that is, recognition of sin, repentance, faith in a new religion, and a desire for a new way of life" (Stewart 1944:72). One Winnebago recalls that when he first used peyote,

> he became deathly sick and ejected from his stomach "several bottles of whiskey, several plugs of tobacco, and two bull dogs"; that this accumulation of filth represented all the sins he had ever committed and that, with its expulsion, he became "pure and clean in the sight of God"; that, by a continued use of peyote he would remain in that condition ... and he was transformed—a new man. [Kneale 1950:212]

John Rave says that when he first took peyote,

> my heart was filled with murderous thoughts. I wanted to kill my brother and sister. ... All my thoughts were fixed on the warpath ..., some evil spirit possessed me. I was suffering from a disease. I even desired to kill myself. ... Then I ate this medicine (peyote) and everything changed. The

brother and sister whom I wanted to kill, to them I now became deeply attached. I wanted them to live. This, the medicine had accomplished for me. [Radin 1950:258]

The moral transformation wrought by peyote is often associated with cures and the reception of power for success. The killer becomes the lover; the sick becomes well; the evil becomes good. Thus the powerful and ethical dimensions of peyotism are interconnected in the minds of the peyotists. In particular, the transformative peyote stories portray peyote as a cure from alcoholism, as part of a larger pattern of ethical redemption.

Peyote ethics are usually not expressed in absolute forms; however, peyotists emphasize certain kinds of behavior considered preferable or moral. In peyote ethics it is good to be restrained, abstinent, faithful, truthful. One should be generous and help others, be a good neighbor and have respect for others, without coercion. One should be reticent to assume leadership and one should value past traditions. One should be humble in the presence and use of peyote, especially since a humble mien produces compassion on the part of the peyote spirit.

The most all-encompassing ethic of peyotism is that "The Peyotists are supposed to have a feeling of brotherly love for one another" (Slotkin 1952:571), as well as for all people. All members are regarded as close kin and should be treated accordingly in order to live the ethical peyote road. Part of this ethic may derive from the physical effects of peyote: its overcoming of the subject-object dichotomy, its euphoric tendency. One non-Indian who ate peyote with Apaches and Comanches while journeying through the desert noted that, after four days of eating peyote, "we felt so light and happy that we loved everybody and wanted to fly away" (Jones 1899:95). And there is a peyote joke about an Indian who goes "girling" in the city and meets an old-time Indian who treats him as an uncle treats a nephew, promising him what he wants. When the nephew asks for some love medicine, the old man pulls out four peyote buttons, saying, "Here, take these and love *everybody!*" (Howard 1962a:14) On the other hand, some observers assume that peyote ethics are essentially Christian in origin, with a special regard to Indian kinship groups. In any event, Larry Etsitty, a vice president of Navajoland Native American Church, states, "The Peyote to me is my bible. I know what I should be doing and shouldn't be doing. To me, when I take that Peyote, I feel humble (respectful) all the time" (Beck and Walters 1977:233). Thus peyotism fosters an ethical religiousness, an attitude of respect and communion, that constitutes one dimension to the religious complex as a whole.

So striking in the attitude of friendliness proposed by the peyote ethic is the degree to which it is universalized. Peyotism proposes more than the kinship obligations that one would expect in a tribal society. Peyotism proposes more than respect for allies and neighbors. Rather, the peyote narratives and peyote ethics make an explicit call for peaceful relations with all Indians, and even with all peoples.

Many of the myths close with the following sort of advice: "Now you should love one another," says Jesus as the vision visitor (Radin 1971:351). In Stenberg (1946:139) the vision visitor says, "Don't go round and make enemies any more. . . . live as brothers and sisters." A Menomini legend concludes, "that now they all shake hands, each with the other. They are also brothers and sisters of the white man" (Slotkin 1952:572). A Northern Arapaho comments on the legend: "Peaceful living with alien and un-friendly groups is an obligation placed upon the people by the original peyote revelation" (Stenberg 1946:131).

In the narratives the message of peaceful relations is stated explicitly; moreover, the very structure of the stories demonstrates that peyotism has existed as a movement with a political goal of uniting as allies the American Indians of the Plains and beyond, and ending intertribal wars and raids. First, the stories of Type IA almost all begin with warfare as the initial situation, the cause of the distress for which peyote is the cure. If war among Indians is the cause of the problem, and peyote is its res-olution, the underlying message is to devalue warfare as a mode of activity.

In story Types IV and V we find the same structure; however, in Type IV two details add to the cogency of the peace message. First, the war paraphernalia of the killed Comanche are transformed into the utensils of peyotism. His bow becomes the staff of authority and peace at peyote meetings. Second, the female captive—taken in warfare—becomes the translator and mediator who joins the former enemies into allies, "cousins" and "relatives" (16). McAllester (1949:18) comments on this transformation by stating that the woman represents regrowth as the feminine alternative to the masculine warrior. It would be possible to say that the stories so far merely balance war and peace as alternative possibilities; however, the explicit message of peaceful ethics belies such an interpretation. The Carrizo chief says, "Then we shall become as one, because our Father has said so" (16).

In Type II the initial situation is also a hostile raid, not explicitly con-demned; however, the hero leaves the war party behind, leaves behind his booty, in order to follow the different drumming. He comes upon his enemies in a peyote meeting and they treat him with hospitality and friendliness, even though they know through clairvoyance that he is an enemy bent on fighting them. In some Plains cultures there exists a motif in which a man in a tipi senses the approach of an enemy; he readies his weapon and kills the intruder with dispatch. Here the story is transformed. The hosts tell the intruder to "go hang up his weapons" (Beals 1971:46), or he takes a chance on being killed and leaves his weapons behind, trusting in his enemies' hospitality. The peyote chief tells him that the "meeting was to make the Indians good, to make them friends, and to make them stop fighting" (Kochampanaskin 1938), and after participating, it is said of the hero: "Because of the peyote he had eaten, he felt a warm glow in his heart as toward brothers" (Ball 1966:7). The peyote chief confesses, "We, too have killed and murdered many people, and it is not good. You came tonight looking for trouble. Maybe you are a scout for a war-party" (Skinner 1923:234). The hero falsely denies his original intent, but after his conversion to peyotism, he too confesses: "I left on the war-path and got into a religious assembly. I was caught by the Great Spirit Himself" (Ibid.: 237). The message could not be more consistent: peyotism is to replace the wars and raids that characterized part of southern Plains life in the eighteenth and nineteenth centuries.

In the Quanah Parker stories and peaceful ethic is replicated through the same structure. The stories both stress the constant raiding that comprised part of Comanche existence, in which Parker participated. They both end with Parker's peaceful message. He overcomes witchcraft and hostility at a peyote meeting, and teaches his people through peyote use to be generous, kind, good, clean, to let others see their religion is good because they are good. Today, the narrative concludes, Native American Church worshipers lead moral lives, and "help and comfort their neighbors when they can " (Marriott and Rachlin 1968:211). As in the other myths we have discussed, the Quanah Parker stories proceed from warfare to the point of death to medicine, and then to the ethics of leading a good life of peace.

Only in Type III is peace among tribes not one of the central statements. One can guess that these stories represent an older, unreformed, shamanistic ethic of power by bloody initiation; whereas the other types, while perhaps as old, have been fashioned—seemingly through some christianization—into a new ethic to overcome the old uses of peyote. No longer shall the plant be used to predict victories or to give courage and endurance in war; no longer shall it be used to gain wealth through raids. Peyote reveals a new, peaceful consciousness. A christianized Winnebago peyotist once told Radin (1971:351–52) that the original discoverer of peyote—a Mescalero Apache—did not use peyote in an ethical way; rather, he and his tribe used its powers for warfare and horse thefts. It took another revelation, he said, this time to the Comanches, to bring the peaceful use of peyote. Radin comments that this judgment was idiosyncratic; however, it appears to be a partially accurate historical summary, consistent with the thrust of almost all the peyote origin stories, except those of Type III. The Apaches used peyote shamanistically, without a christianized ethic of brotherhood; it took Quanah Parker and other peyotists beginning in Indian Territory to fashion the peaceful peyote ethics that have prevailed to the present day.

The message of intertribal peace is underscored by the common pattern in the stories of attributing peyote's discovery to another tribe; this is the case with most of the legends. There is the understanding in the narratives that this is a religion for, and of, Indians, not just one's particular tribal unit. In many versions of Type II, but even in some Type IA versions, the hero must overcome tribal loyalty before peyote is discovered or ingested. Most prominently, the mother tells her daughter to seek any Indians and go with them, even "not our tribe" (Beals 1971:44). In a Chippewa version, only one man is left from a tribe after terrible wars. The Creator tells him that another tribe consists of his brothers and sisters (Slotkin 1952:632).

This tendency of Indians to consider themselves related to Indians of other tribes is often referred to as pan-Indianism. A phenomenon brought to flower by reservations like those in Oklahoma that gathered different Indians together; by advanced modes of communication (mails, railroads) that fostered interreservation contacts; by boarding schools that joined diverse Indians; by the use of English as a common language; by Christian teachings that broadened tribal perspectives; by intermarriage, a common sense of being wronged by non-Indians, and other factors, pan-Indianism has been "the expression of a new identity and the institutions and symbols which are both an expression of that new identity and a fostering of it. It is the attempt to create a new ethnic group, the American Indian." (Thomas 1968:77).

The peyote religion has been perhaps a major expression of pan-Indianism over the past century, and pan-Indianism has been one of the major dimensions of peyotism. Peyotists commonly hold meetings with members of diverse tribes, and "the view is frequently expressed that peyote's power has brought all the tribes into friendly association and has mitigated old hostilities and hatreds" (Brant 1950:212). A Menomini peyotist attests: "Before I use this medicine, I never know much different tribe. Now this American Church come here, I know lots of them, different Indians. . . . They come here and shake hands with us, friends with us. . . . I like that" (Slotkin 1952:607). Indeed, it is said that some peyotists "feel closer, and are more friendly" (Newcomb 1955:1042) to fellow peyotists from other tribes, than they are to nonpeyotists of their own tribe. Unlike most forms of Indian-initiated religiousness, peyotism is truly pan-Indian in ideology, myth, ritual and organization, "the largest intertribal organization of American Indians in existence" (Rachlin 1964:262). With Oklahoma regarded as the "origin place and hearth" (Hayes 1940:35), with pilgrimages made to the peyote fields, with the euphoric effects of the cactus dissolving tensions, peyotism has "received the most enduring loyalty" (Hertzberg 1971:284) of all forms of pan-Indianism and has functioned as a civil religion for Indian cultural nationalism. Some have argued that peyotism's pan-Indianism is a cause of tribal disintegration, or a stepping stone toward acculturating to the American mainstream; however, peyotists see their religion differently. As members of their tribal communities as well as American Indians, they regard the religion as a means of persisting: "This here Church is holding up all Indians. It's the main thing keeps us from being wiped out" (d'Azevedo 1978:3).

As for the notion that peyotism is the cause of pan-Indianism, it should be pointed out that the religious complex grew out of intertribal contacts that already existed. Perhaps the period of peyotism's coalescing was one of intertribal warfare; however, intermarriage, trade, alliances, gift exchange, and a shared religious consciousness served as preconditions for the particular pan-Indianism of the peyote religion. Peyotism was but one in an endless series of new religious complexes that have passed from tribe to tribe over the centuries, and such exchanges, it would seem, have always promoted some sort of pan-Indianism. In particular, the great mobility of Plains life engendered by the acquisition of the horse fostered not only warfare but also an increased pan-Plains commonality, symbolized by sign language (note its presence in Ball 1966:7; Beals 1971:46; Kochampanaskin 1938; Skinner 1923:236) and the Sundance—a pan-Indian ritual to which peyotism has been partial successor. In short, peyotism was as much a fruit of pan-Indianism as it was a seed, and it flowered on the Plains because Plains culture was already homogenized to a large degree. Peyotism should thus be considered a Plains religion growing out of an areal culture, coalescing many Plains features, although carried beyond the Plains by missionaries.

As a pan-Indian movement, peyotism should be compared to the Drum Dance, or Pow-wow religion, since the myth of the Pow-wow drum—as told among the Chippewas and Sioux—bears a striking resemblance to story Type IA. In 1877, the story is told (Armstrong 1892:156–60; Barrett 1911:256; Works Progress Administration 1936–40, 1942: envelope 2, no. 10), the U.S. army defeated a Sioux force, and a young girl was separated from her people. She hid in a river until she was about to collapse of hunger and exhaustion. In that distressed and pitiful condition, she received a visitation from the Great Spirit, who restored her and gave

instructions for her to bring back to her people to construct the Pow-
wow drum, the dance of which would foster intertribal peace and unity
(see Wilson 1973:405, 421, n. 19). The two parallel myths seem to have
arisen independently; however, they both express the same ethical message of pan-Indian peace. Significantly—although it has lost its religious
basis—the Pow-wow is today perhaps equal to the peyote religion in
creating pan-Indian cohesion on a cultural level.

Peyotism has functioned to produce an Indian consciousness partially
through an assertion, expressed through myth and ritual, of Indian identity
apart from non-Indians. The myths provide peyotists with an identity
grounded in significant, revelatory, past events, the patterns of which
continue in Indians' lives today, and the rituals provide the opportunity
for Indians to express themselves openly among fellow Indians, normally
without the presence of unfamiliar whites. This has occurred as so many
other Indian traditions were dissolving, and peyotism has given hundreds
of thousands of Indians an opportunity to express not only their religiousness but also their Indianness. As one Crow Indian puts it, "This
religion is the one thing left that's really Indian, and not borrowed from
our white brothers" (Berquist 1957:40).

The origin narratives play an important role in reinforcing peyotists'
Indian identity. The stories are all about Indians, for whom the supernaturals feel compassion, and for whom the Creator placed peyote on
the earth. A Kiowa Indian was quoted as saying:

> In the first creation God himself used to talk to the people and tell them
> what to do. Way after, Christ came among the white people and told the
> people what to do. White [people] have everything. The Indian got nothing.
> But in a little while, toward the last, God gave us peyote; that's how we
> happened to find God." [Snyder 1969:16]

The rituals reenact traditional forms—both tribal and generalized—and
even the new forms are often interpreted in terms of the Indian past. An
Omaha Indian calls the peyote altar "the flesh of our grandfathers and
grandmothers" (Howard 1956:433), and worship around such an altar
implies a veneration for Indian ancestry in general.

In some of the narratives, symbols of Indian identity, for example, the
wearing of buckskin, blankets, or long hair, make it clear that peyotism
"is to be the Indian religion" (Bittle 1954:72). A 1902 Tonkawa peyote
meeting (Opler 1939:433–35) required the men to dress in long hair,
"Indian" shirt, buckskin leggings, blanket, face paint, and herbs, without
any non-Indian perfume, and even in the 1960s certain peyote chiefs
were insisting on the wearing of at least a blanket to express Indianness.

In other cases, peyotists wear specially fashioned peyote jewelry, and the paraphernalia used at the peyote meetings are meant to symbolize Indian heritage. A Crow peyotist remarks: "In old days we used the peace pipe. Today we use corn husks. In the corn itself, the corn represents the Indian. In order to get away from the white man—use corn husks" (Kiste 1962:50).

Some scholars have termed such self-conscious expressions of identity "nativism"; however, peyotism, like any other religious complex, comprises one of the means that a population employs to identify itself and create a means of cohering to one another by establishing ways of acting that can be called normative or ethical. Call the process civil religion, or the sociological function of religion, it is not a process unique to American Indians.

Nevertheless, given the attempts by Christians to gather Indians under non-Indian theology, myths, rituals, and leadership, and given the long-standing Christian antagonism to peyote use, it is no wonder that peyotists have emphasized the discretely Indian nature of their religious complex. One might consider peyotism as an "independent church movement" that has incorporated Christian elements, but has insisted on its separateness for Indians, as a rival to Christianity.

Peyotism took on this quality of a "racial" religion between 1910 and 1920, during a period of virulent attacks on peyote use by non-Indians, and it was at this time that peyotism gained organizational status as a church. Since that time, peyotists have spoken of the ways in which their religion differs from (and compares favorably to) Christianity. Peyotists have asserted that every group of people receives its particular relgious form from God, and peyotism is the divinely created Indian worship, not to be mixed with Christianity. Other peyotists have argued that white people need Christianity because they crucified Christ and must be redeemed for their sins; Indians, on the other hand, committed no such crime, and thus could receive revelation directly through the peyote spirit.

The pattern of conversion to peyotism often includes a previous association and disenchantment with Christianity, and peyotism is perceived as a favorable alternative to the non-Indian religion. In some cases peyotists have served as activists for Indian rights and claims. In short, peyotism has included the ethic of Indian specialness, apart from non-Indian institutions, and "the widespread acceptance of the peyote religion says something to the widespread rejection of Christianity" (Tippett 1967:89).

The stories of Quanah Parker's conversion underscore the Indianness of peyotism, even though he has been credited with the introduction of Christian traits to the peyote complex. Not only do white medicines among white people fail to cure him, and not only does the curandera make sure that he is an Indian before she applies the peyote cure, but the plot of the story can be read as follows: Quanah Parker travels to his white relatives to learn white ways, but he returns with the Indian religion of peyotism.

RITUAL DIMENSION: RELIGION AND STRUCTURE

The peyote "meeting" provides the opportunity for Indians to experience the holy directly by eating and drinking peyote substances. The ritual also serves as a means for Native American Church members to encourage moral behavior, either through exhortations or confessions, and the event functions to reinforce the sense of commonality among peyotists. Moreover, the meeting acts upon the symbols and messages of the origin narratives. The peyote ritual is a meeting in which is met the divine, the related community, the proper way of life, and the sacred history of the religious complex called peyotism.

As in other religions, the peyote ritual is intricately symbolic. Expressed by a Menomini, "Everything represents" (Slotkin 1952:582). Many of the representations point to the origin stories, which often make explicit descriptions and validations of the normative peyote meeting. Not all peyotists agree on the exact meanings of each ritual item, and many do not care to analyze their ceremonial activity; however, the myths refer to and explain much within the events at peyote meetings.

Without delineating the ritual details, the following summary of the peyote meeting can suffice. A peyote chief conducts an all-night ritual in a tipi, with the help of assistants (drum chief, fire chief, cedar chief, water woman) and specialized paraphernalia (staff of authority, gourd rattle, feather fan, bone whistle, drum, cedar, tobacco, etc.). In the center of the tipi is an altar, made of a crescent or moon—a mound of earth—with a line running along its tip. A fire is to the east of the altar, and the tipi opens to the east. On the top of the crescent sits the "chief peyote," a large, well-formed cactus. Everyone sits around the inner circumference of the tipi, facing the altar and fire, the chief sitting in the far west. After speeches, the chief passes around tobacco to be smoked, sage to be rubbed on the body, and chewed, and peyote to be eaten. Then the chief passes around the drum and rattle, and the participants sing for most of the night, while consuming the peyote. At midnight the chief calls a recess, during which the ashes from the fire are formed into a cresent lying between the altar and the fire. Water is brought in, and all drink. The meeting continues as before, until just before dawn, when the water woman brings in more water, followed by a ritual breakfast, usually of corn, fruit, meat, and candy. Then the peyotists greet the morning sun and return to the tipi to talk informally, until later in the morning, when the meeting is concluded with a feast. The bulk of the meeting is taken up with singing, praying, contemplating, and eating peyote.

For whatever reasons the meetings are held—to cure or bless, to commemorate holidays or weddings, to fulfill a vow, to pray for rain, to prophesy or divine, to show hospitality to guests, to name a child, to give thanks, or "just because we feel good" (Stenberg 1946:118)—they are "remarkably homogeneous" (Anderson 1985:41), and have been for the past century, possessing a "uniformity . . . comparable to the sameness of the Catholic Mass wherever performed" (Stewart 1983:4). The present ritual structure—which has many variants within certain parameters—was based on Lipan models, but took its "Basic Plains" (Bittle 1954:70) or "Kiowa-Comanche" (Howard 1967:2) shape around 1880, in Oklahoma. If one compares the descriptions given by Mooney (24 January 1892; 1897), a century ago, to those of the 1980s, one sees that they have changed very little.

Within this structure peyotists express a great deal of emotion and conviction. They beg and pray for pity; they sing their thanks; they confess their sins and their desires. With great "fervor," with "tears streaming down their faces and voices choked with emotion," they make their "supplication," their "reiterated expressions of humility" (Stenberg 1946:132–33). Their prayers express their plight and their hope: "Look to me. Poor me. Pity me. Help me. Help me to know the spirit way" (Underhill 1952:147). The "overt emotionalism" (Spindler and Spindler 1971:104) of the peyote meeting contrasts markedly with many traditional Plains ceremonies, which insist upon composure and restraint. This "intense emotion and reverence" may derive from the expectation that "any individual may come face to face with supernatural powers during the course of the ceremony" (Newcomb 1956b:208), or it may be that peyotists are there "because they feel a hurtful need" (Laney 1972:115) and are filled with anxiety about themselves and their earthly predicaments. Often the result of the meeting is "emotional catharsis" (La Barre 1947:303), in psychological terms, or an experience of religious resolution.

The stories of peyote's origin often refer to the rituals—for instance (Brant 1963:181), when the visionary boy prays to the peyote spirit: "You have helped me. When I eat peyote tonight I want you to help me to find a way for it"—or describe the meetings in great detail: the tipi, the crescent altar, the officials, the peyote passing, the drum, rattle, staff and fire, the water ceremonies, and the like. In narrative Types IA, III, and IV initiation into knowledge about the cactus is almost always followed by ritual instruction, in order to employ peyote correctly.

In addition, elements from the myths are carried out in the ritual actions at peyote meetings, making the myths and rituals explanations for one another. Some examples:

The crescent altar is sometimes said to represent the motion made by the starving visionary, lying in the desert, moving her arms in a crescent above her head; or, where a cross is present on the altar, it may represent the visionary's body as it lay, arms outstretched, on the desert sand (Slotkin 1952:573; Siskin 1983:187).

The fasting that peyotists undergo before a meeting and the eating of the peyote replicate precisely the starvation and salvation of peyote food, found in the desert. Vomiting the peyote at first only increases the fact of emptying, before peyote provides its spiritual nourishment.

When water is passed around at midnight and just before dawn; it repeats the way in which peyote saved the pitiful visionary of thirst; thus some peyotists pray: "At long last the holy water is passed around just in time to save us from dry and dusty death" (Laney 1972:123).

The chief peyote, placed on the crest of the crescent "represents the spirit of peyote and the first peyote which was revealed to peyote woman" (Kiste 1962:34). In a myth (Carlton 1969:2) it is said that the peyote fetish should be placed in the center of the altar, "like it was growing out of the ground."

From these examples it should be clear that story Type I serves as the paradigm for the peyote meeting, and the participants take the role of the pitiful hero, when they eat the peyote and seek to meet the holy face to face. The meeting takes place in a tipi that recreates the sacred geography of the peyote fields, where the plant first revealed itself to Indians, and the altar is the prominent ground of a sacred geography (see chart opposite, following La Barre 1970:44; Laney 1972:114).

Along the crest of the altar is a line that is called the peyote road; however, the term "peyote road" also refers to the way of life a peyotist aspires to live, inspired by peyote experiences. The circular path around the inside of the tipi, between the sitting participants and the central geography of altar, fire, and ashes, is also a road that must be walked in sunwise direction, and only with the guidance of the peyote chief, or "roadman." These roads mark the passage of a person's lifetime, the footprints of the supernaturals and ancestral spirits, as well as the borderland between humans and the divine, and it is the duty of the peyote officials to keep the peyotists on the right path, the correct road of life. The roads also represent the processions that peyotists formerly made while eating

TYPICAL PEYOTE MEETING TIPI

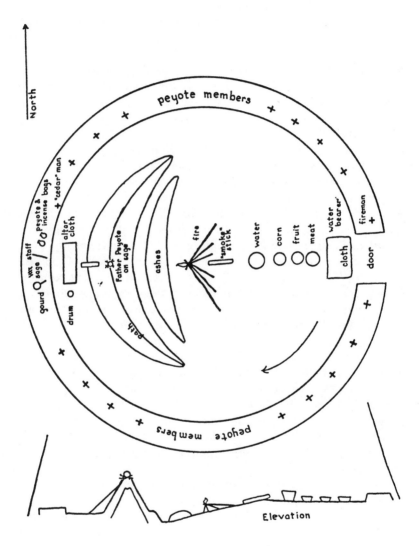

peyote, before they discovered that visions were better obtained in sitting position. But the roads also replicate the path taken by the pitiful visionary in the desert, the warpath that became the peyote way, and the pilgrimages that have been made to the peyote fields for centuries and are continued by Indians today. In short, the peyote meeting represents a mythic pilgrimage that has reached the holy land and has become stationary.

For the past century, and today still, peyote dealers have shipped dried peyote from the area of the peyote fields in south Texas to Indians across America. In addition, the plant is "easily cultivated" (Anderson 1985:153), if one has the patience to provide it with the proper growing conditions. Nevertheless, some peyotists have preferred, if at all possible, and often at great personal expense, to travel directly to the peyote fields in pilgrimage. Peyotists say that the cactus should come from "God's garden (nature) rather than from the controlled hand of man" (Morgan 1976:118). The pilgrims fast, purify themselves, pray, smoke cigarettes, and seek the peyote by listening for its song: "You can hear them singing— they tell you where they are—they really sing to you" (Kiste 1962:65). That is, peyote reveals itself to the pilgrims as it once revealed itself to the pitiful, lost, starving Indian. The myth, the pilgrimage, and the regular peyote meeting are bound in a knot of symbolic reenactment.

Significant in the ritual recreation of the origin stories of Type I is the devotion paid to the peyote woman, represented by the water woman at the meetings: "It was a woman who first found Peyote and this woman who comes in with the water in the morning represents that first woman" (Dustin 1960:45). In former days, peyotists say, you could hear the voice of the first peyote woman, singing high above the men's songs during the meetings, although today such experiences are rare; indeed, women are usually not allowed to sing at peyote meetings.

Mooney (1892) described a "mescal rattle," that is, a peyote rattle, among the Kiowas in Indian Territory, the central figure on which is a woman whom the Kiowas said represents the peyote woman, the presiding goddess of the ceremony. The Indians said that she also represents the interior of the peyote meeting place. On her body are placed signs of the crescent altar, the chief peyote, the fire, ashes, and the devotees themselves (see Slotkin 1975: plate 22). The peyote tipi, therefore, symbolizes not only the actual peyote fields, the desert where the visionary of story Type I discovered peyote, but also the peyote woman herself, in whose body peyotists seek their way, their road of life, their life itself. A Crow peyotist states: "The tipi itself is a man's second mother. . . . The tipi is a home. When you enter it, [it's] like coming back home—home to the ways of your people. When you come out—[it's] like being reborn" (Kiste 1962:52).

While the narratives of Types II and III, as well as the Quanah Parker stories, recognize the original revelation of peyote in Type I, they remind peyotists that the ritual has come down to the present day through proper channels, either through human (Type II) or supernatural (Type III) provenience. The story Type II is distinctly about the proper passing down of ritual. The drum calls the hero to the peyote meeting; the chief invites him to observe the procedure in order to learn it and bring it back to his people. One version (Parsons 1936:64) suggests that the peyote plants themselves are calling the hero to ritual initiation (a reminder of the pilgrimage); however, in the other versions the hosts are authorized humans. The drum that calls the hero to learn the ritual calls peyotists to worship today at the all-night meeting (a reminder of the songs peyote sings to pilgrims). In story Type III the supernaturals initiate the hero to peyote's power, giving him the ability to learn the ritual procedure. The basic peyote songs are also said to originate in myth (McAllester 1949:15). The peyote legends may begin with revelation, but they invariably proceed to the foundations of ritual.

More profound within the structure of the myths is the repeated theme of the hero, separated, emptied, initiated, and reunited—a paradigm associated redundantly with rituals of initiation. In its structure, therefore, the peyote meeting is not only a pilgrimage but also an initiation into experiential communion with God and the way of the peyote community, through the sacramental incorporation of a living symbol of nature.

The myths establish the necessity and rules for the peyote rituals, and they encourage peyotists to participate in the communal meetings with the proper attitude. After a Comanche visionary and her mother bring peyote to their people, they travel to the nearest tribe of peyote eaters and ask permission to "learn their rites" (Skinner 1923:238). The neighbor chief tells her, "Just eating it alone will save no one" (239), and that "it must be taken in the right way, with a good heart, for it can save no one by itself" (239). Other narratives repeat the formula that peyote ritual requires a "right way," which consists not only of ritual exactness but also an attitude of humility, reverence, and religiousness; peyotism must be a "worship" (Brant 1950:213).

Peyotism tends to be sacramental, rather than hierarchical, as a religion, with its emphasis on the ritual, the experience, the ethics, rather than the organization. Nevertheless, the origin stories do describe and validate a ritual leadership: the peyote chief and his assistants. Type II narratives find this leadership in place when the hero arrives at the ceremonial tipi to learn the peyote ritual; there is already a structure for authority. In stories of Type I the visionary woman or her child returns to the people and passes on the ritual knowledge to chiefs, priests, and elders. In other words, the nonauthoritative female or child—who has had the visionary, revelatory experience—defers to the male and adult authorities in the tribe; hence, the stories serve as ideology for the present male, adult leadership to uphold its power within the peyote religion. One might regard Type I as the intuitive, and Type II as the ritual story; however, both function as part of a hierarchy, however limited. Of course Type III myths present a situation in which an organization is already functioning, with an established leadership, when the peyote supernaturals initiate a boy (or man) into a special knowledge, thus bypassing human authority, for direct contact of the supernatural—as peyotists can do today.

Peyotism's national organization—the Native American Church—is a bureaucratic institution not described in the myths, and not in keeping with the tribal origins of the complex. To an extent, it is an outgrowth of the pan-Indian aspect of peyotism; however, it arose more as a means to defend peyotism against the attacks of its enemies, than as a vehicle for common experience, ethics, or rituals. Peyotism became a type of church, with state charters and national officers, only in response to state and national legislative attempts to destroy the religion. The charter movement began in 1914 in Oklahoma, and with the help in 1918 of anthropologist James Mooney, who clearly regarded the church structure as a legal ploy to gain systematic protection of religious liberties for peyotists. By the 1950s there were twenty-eight charters in thirteen states, and one in Canada under the title of Native American Church; however, the national organization possesses no regulations for ordination, no official creed. The Montana NAC was incorporated in 1925 for the specific purpose of lobbying against antipeyote legislation in the state, and in 1957, when it was finally successful, the NAC organization dissolved, having fulfilled its purpose. Thus peyotism has remained congregational in its church polity, with no bishops, no dogma, no heresy accusations, and no synods, despite its legal superstructure. Of this aspect of peyotism's history, a feature of the life of many religions, the myths remain silent, they remain more concerned with peyotism as sacrament, not bureaucracy.

By their focus on the peyote ritual, the stories suggest that peyotism may have begun, not as a complex religious matrix, but as a ritual in which Indians experienced the power of peyote. When Stewart states (1982b:1) that peyotists participate in Christian liturgy, shamanistic cures, the Sundance, one might conclude that Indians practice many religions simultaneously; however, another interpretation might shed more light on peyote's experiential, ritual dimensions.

Pre-Columbian peyote use was as a rite, a cult, part of a larger religious complex among the Indians of Mexico, part of a larger religious system. Peyote was one medicine among many, one means of religious revelation among many, one cultic focus among many. Even in the mid-nineteenth century, peyote use consisted of individual use (the experience of power) and tribal use in ritual. Peyote use was adapted by Apaches, Oklahoma Indians, and others, not as a religious complex—with its own organization, world view, ethics, and so on—but as a ritual which they added to their own religious patterns. Peyote use continued to be a rite, and little more than a rite. When an Indian accepted peyote use, it was as a new power, a new medicine, a focus for a new ritual in which one experienced the supernatural or joined one's fellows in common practice. One did not "convert to peyotism," as one might incorrectly state it. Indians who attended Mass, who performed in a Sundance, who gave or received shamanistic cures, were simply participating in different rituals—each with its own mythological background, theology, and practitioners. The use of one did not exclude the use of others; each was a separate rite to be fitted into the individual's (or the tribe's) more general religious framework, however compartmentalized.

Under Christian influence, however, as traditional religious complexes dissolved, Indians attached to peyote use a matrix of religious dimensions—ethics, world view, even a bureaucracy—so that "Around Peyote developed a religion" (Slotkin 1975:23); hence, today, in its "modern form," the peyote ritual is the centerpiece for a "religious complex of its own, considered to promote health, happiness, and welfare among its adepts" (Hultkrantz 1981:283). The experiential ritual is still central—more directly at the core of the complex than are the myths, for example—but as a "total configuration" that "produces in the person attending the all-night ceremony, a feeling of security, warmth, and communion with God" (Howard 1967:2), the peyote ritual expresses the same beliefs, using the same symbols, as the origin narratives.

THEOLOGICAL DIMENSION: RELIGION AND BELIEF

Over time the peyote religion has undergone some changes and variations, as it has evolved from an experience of power to a cultic focus, from a ritual to a way of acting in community, and then to an organizational structure. In its evolution, it has sometimes lost elements and gained others, and incorporated them in various ways, giving peyotism a polyvalent character: sometimes appearing as offshoot of shamanism, sometimes as a version of Christianity, sometimes as a rejection of tribal rituals, sometimes as a device for visions. Like other religions, its myriad features have attracted various adherents for different reasons, and those adherents have in turn fashioned their own varieties of peyote religiousness. Hence "peyotism should be considered as a movement in itself in which many factors, including curing, visionary, apologetic tendencies, etc., are all functionally interrelated and have all contributed to its widespread acceptance or rejection" (Malouf 1942:101).

Peyotism is a full-fledged religion, with a bearing on every aspect of its participants' lives. It promotes morality, sobriety, work, charity, brotherly love. Its leaders conduct weddings and funerals. Its members lend each other money, intermarry, and work together. At peyote meetings peyotists discuss problems of sickness, mental illness, marital relations, and politics. In such a religion, in such a church, the narratives of peyote's origin may become lost in the details of everyday life; however, they still contain and express the theological foundation for peyotism; they continue to state the ethos, the world view, the set of beliefs that characterize peyotism.

The peyote origin stories vary, but they all point to a supernatural world that has pity and compassion for the Indians, and communicates spiritual power through the peyote plant.

Peyotism's theology is nondogmatic, variable, and syncretistic. One can hear prayers to "God, Jesus, Mother Mary, Peyote" (Stewart 1948:18), and one can find the presence of tribal deities alongside the homogenized Great Spirit or Creator. Nevertheless, peyotism's theology, as set forth in the myths and as stated by peyotists, contains as much consistency as found in the rituals.

There is a belief in a supernatural world, a part of the cosmos, that interacts with the material world. There is a Creator or Great Spirit—virtually indistinguishable from the Christian God—who controls all destiny. There are other spiritual beings—in this there is great variation—who are subservient to the Creator, as well as powers in the world that are the creations of the Great Spirit. Peyote is the supernatural, natural creation designated as the special guide and helper to Indians, whose existence makes possible a communication between humans and the Creator.

Peyotists regard humans as weak beings, dependent upon the Creator's will for their very existence. It is human frailty, as well as human need to be reminded of moral direction, that provides the conditions for which peyote was created. God created peyote to help Indians live, and for them to live correctly.

The supernatural is the precondition, and the human is the condition, by which peyote is created. The peyote myths consistently express a belief in a supernatural world that has power, and a human world that lacks it; a supernatural world that possesses answers, and a human world that needs them and often seeks them.

Peyote serves as the means by which the Creator shares power and answers; it is the means by which humans can seek these things. And it is the means by which God and humans can communicate; it is "pre-eminently a mediator between God and man" (Laney 1972:127), that provides humans with life and with understanding. The myths make it clear that peyote has supernatural powers that save human lives, and they demonstrate that toward Indians peyote is "compassionate" as it brings Indians to redemption and "spiritual unity with the Supreme Being" (Petrullo 1940:57).

The narratives that have helped provide this theology have kept the Indian use of peyote religious for centuries:

> The legends of its effectiveness as a supernatural medicine have kept peyote from being used hedonistically as a narcotic and have helped to maintain its exalted role as a near-divinity—a place it holds to this day, even among highly acculturated Indian groups in the United States. [Schultes 1972:14]

It would be possible—as non-Indians have done—to eat peyote and hallucinate. Even in a ritual setting in a community the partaking of peyote would not in and of itself make for religiousness. The stories, and the theological world view they express about a supernatural world with compassion for Indians, have granted the crucial element of belief to make peyotism religious. Belief has made peyote use a religion.

In one of the versions of story Type IA, a passage reads (Radin 1971:351): "His being lost in the hills seemed to symbolize to him the condition of his people before they had eaten the peyote; they would be lost and then find their way again." In another version (Stenberg 1946:144), it is said that "suffering and hard times would bring them to find peyote." It would be possible to interpret these statements as proofs that peyotism is a "revitalization" movement or a "crisis cult" that has met the needs of poor and suffering Indians over the past century. The pitiable condition of the mythic hero, however, represents not only a specific situation (loss of buffalo, loss of autonomy, loss of health, etc.) but the human condition. The peyote myths have the qualities to be universalizable, and peyote theology is universalized. When John Wilson sought peyote's revelation, and *"Peyote took pity on him"* (Speck 1933), the compassion was for his humility and sincerity as a religious seeker (albeit an Indian one), not for his socioeconomic situation. In the peyotists' world view, and in the origin stories, peyote cares for Indians (and for all humans, by extension) because peyote's nature is to be compassionate. Religionists worldwide have posited the effective existence of compassionate spirits; peyote is one of them, in peyotism's world view.

As presented in the narratives, peyote's compassion reveals itself not in trivial situations but in conditions of life-and-death importance. The myths propose that peyote's powers make the most crucial difference between starvation and survival, abandonment and reunion, death and continuance. According to the myths, Indians' lives depend on peyote. In virtually every version of Type IA, the visionaries are said to be next to death, "almost dead, but that plant saved her life" (Carlton 1969:2). In some cases the mother announces to her child: "I think that I'm going to die" (Beals 1971:44). The stories make it clear that peyote rescues the desperate Indians from death, and continues to do so: "Out of it life starts all over again" (Denman 1957:6). In story Type IB the hero seeks peyote specifically because his people are dying and he wishes to save them with a new medicine power. In narratives of Type II the hero's people give him up for dead and begin to mourn him. In their view he is a dead man, when he returns with the life-giving powers and rituals of peyote. In the Navajo variant (Beck and Walters 1977:242) the twelve dead brothers become the twelve peyote buttons, to be carried to the people by their sister. In Type III the peyote supernaturals club the peyotist until he is bloody and appears dead to his fellows; only then is he initiated to peyote's secrets and powers. In Type IV the dead and scalped Comanche instructs his enemies in correct peyote use, to be given in turn to his own people; thus life for his kin comes through his death. In Type V the bulk of the Tonkawas are killed, and those in the cave are already practicing cannibalism, before peyote saves them with their seven-year sleep. Finally, in the Quanah Parker stories (Type VI), the death of Parker's father and mother, and his own closeness to death bring him to peyote's curing abilities. That is to say, in every type, death is the doorway to the supernatural compassion of peyote, and in every type peyote overcomes death, reverses death, transforms death into life-promoting power, and brings a message of life-sustaining ethics. The myths define peyotism as a religious experience, ritual, ethic, and belief—a religious complex with a history—that attempts to transcend death and promote life.

One might say, as many have done, that such a belief is a flight from reality, a divorce from the real world, an opiate and fantasy, a drug-produced form of autism. Not only antipeyotist activists but also scholars have produced such a charge, noting the narcotic effects of the cactus and the disorienting crisis-beset condition of modern Indians. La Barre (1972:265) has compared the peyotist to a "paranoid schizophrenic" who "pretends to be talking about the grandiose outside cosmic world, but ... is really talking grandiosely in symbolic ways only about his narcissistic self and his inner world." The peyote origin stories might be interpreted as products and examples of wishful thinking (that a Creator cares about Indians), and certainly the experience of peyote might be termed an opiate. The peyote complex might be called—like any religion—"the defense mechanism of a society in confused and crisis-torn times" (La Barre 1972:265).

If one were to make these claims about all religions and their myths (as La Barre does), the point would be moot; however, to single out Indian religions like the peyote complex as "crisis cults" is to neglect the more inclusive dimensions of peyotism. Surely its myths—like the myths of religions worldwide—carry an imprint of the nonrational, the impossible; however, to regard the whole of peyotism as a "flight from reality" is to reduce a richly complex religious tradition to only one of its many dimensions. As often as peyotism masks the more materialist (sociological, political, economic, etc.) understandings of human problems, it forces its members to face their life-and-death matters in serious and penetrating ways, by making references to a theological world view that tries to comprehend not only the Indian situation but the human condition. The origin stories help establish that world view.

It is true that peyotism became a means of reestablishing Indian world views when traditional complexes were falling into ruin or disuse. In times of religious crisis, in which Indians did not know what to believe, or how to make their beliefs effective, peyotism was an answer and a comfort. But to call peyotism a "revitalization movement" or a "crisis cult" is to forget that people—including the Indians of the Plains and surrouding areas—have a long history of religious renewals, in which they have rethought and refashioned their relations to what they have considered ultimate. Peyotism is one such example, and its myths present the process of reformulation. Second, peyotism has become more than a "revitalization" or "crisis" complex, and it is because its myths describe a human condition—not just a limited situation applicable to a few Indians in a specific time and place—that peyotism has continued to develop, guided by a comprehensive world view. Supporting the religious complex known as peyotism is an ethos, a meaning-laden set of theological beliefs, expressed in the peyote origin stories—narratives that constitute in their entirety an American Indian monomyth.

Versions of the Peyote Origin Narratives

Source	Tribe of Narrator	Type
Ball 1966:7	Comanche	II
Barnard 1963:580		I
Beals 1971:43–44	Kiowa Apache	IA1
Beals 1971:45–46	Kiowa Apache	II
Beck and Walters 1977:242	Navajo	I-II
Bittle 1954:71–72	Kiowa Apache	I-III
Boyd 1983:277	Kiowa	IA2
Brant 1963:180–81	Kiowa Apache	IA1
Brito 1975:4–6	Comanche	IA1
Brito 1975:131–40	Comanche	VI
Bromberg and Tranter 1943:524	Paiute	IA1
Carlton 1969:2	Navajo	IA1
Conn 1982:n.p.		IA1
Curtis 1930:Vol. 19. 211–12	Comanche	II
Curtis 1967:23	Cheyenne	IA1
Denman 1957:5–6	Kiowa	IA2
Howard 1951a:1–4	Omaha	V
Kiste 1962:49	Crow	IA1
Kochampanaskin 1938:n.p.	Ute	II
La Barre 1970:111	Kiowa	II
Marriott and Rachlin 1968:205–11	Comanche	VI-IA1
Marriott and Rachlin 1971:14–15	Comanche	IA1
McAllester 1949:14–17	Comanche	IV
Mooney 1897:330	Kiowa	IA2
cf. Gerber 1980:31–32		
Navajo Tribal Council 1954:22–23	Kiowa Apache	IA1
cf. Dustin 1960:7–9		
Old Coyote and Old Coyote n.d.	Crow	I
M. E. Opler 1938:272–74	Lipan Apache	II
M. E. Opler 1940:56–58	Lipan Apache	III
M.E. Opler 1945:210–12	Mescalero Apache	IB
Parsons 1936:63–64	Taos	II
cf. Waters 1942:83–84		
Parsons 1936:64	Taos	I
Parsons 1969:535	Caddo	IA1
Petrullo 1934:34–37	Delaware	IA1–2
Petrullo 1934:37–38	Delaware	IA1
Petrullo 1934:38–40	Delaware	IA2
Petrullo 1934:40–41	Comanche?	IA2
Radin 1971:350–52	Winnebago	IA1
Ruby 1962:30	Sioux	IA1

Simmons 1918:1		IB
Simmons 1918:1–2		IB
Simmons 1918:n.p.		I
Siskin 1983:187	Washo	IB
Skinner 1923:232–37	Prairie Potawatomi	II
Skinner 1923:237–39	Prairie Potawatomi	IA1
Skinner 1923:239–41	Prairie Potawatomi	IA2
Slotkin 1952:572	Menomini	IA1
Slotkin 1952:573	Menomini	IA2
Slotkin 1952:573	Menomini	IB
Slotkin 1952:573–74	Menomini	IB
Slotkin 1952:572	Menomini	IB
Slotkin 1952:632	Chippewa	IA1
Speck 1933:554–55	Delaware	IA2
Speck 1933:555–56	Delaware	IA1
Stenberg 1946:139–40	Northern Arapaho	IA1
Stewart 1938:2		I
Stewart 1975b:7	Comanche/Kiowa	IA2
Tilgham 1938:113–16	Comanche	VI
Underhill 1965:266		IA1
Wallace and Hoebel 1952:334	Comanche	II

7

The Genesis of Phillip Deere's Sweat Lodge

Okemah, Oklahoma, 8 June 1983: this afternoon I helped Phillip Deere gather wood for a fire in which to heat the volcanic stones he had obtained in New Mexico. He required stones that could retain heat, glow red with heat, and throw out steamy heat when splashed with water. Now the score of stones were settled in the coals of the fire, ready.

After supper, ten of us walked to the western edge of the beaver pond, by the side of the woods, undressed by the fire, and prepared to enter Phillip's sweat lodge. An assistant shoveled the seething stones into the center of the lodge—a small cave in the side of a round hill, the bank of the pond, shored up by full timbers and lined internally with wet, muddy clay—as Phillip spoke about the lodge.

It faces east, he said, for that is the direction from which his people came to this place, in Okfuskee County, from their earlier homes in Alabama and Georgia. The lodge itself is a mound, like the pregnant form of a woman's belly, the womb of the Mother Earth from whose mouth the Muskogees emerged in the beginning of human time. The lodge takes the form of the ancient mounds in which Phillip's people—the Muskogee, or Creek Indians (the Muskogees being the "dominant" nation of the old Creek Confederacy which also incorporated the Hitchitees, Natchez, Yuchis, Alabamas, Koasatis, and other tribes, most from the Muskhogean language family [Debo 1979:3])—used to bury their dead, returning them to their earthly womb. Phillip stated that we go naked now, back into the womb, naked as we emerged, naked as animals.

The ten of us drank a sip of mint tea from a gourd, received a sprig of sage, and entered the lodge on all fours through the small opening, circling sunwise to our places around the lodge, with our knees pulled up, our backs to the mud wall. In his position facing east, Phillip began to ladle boiling, scented water from a bucket onto the stones, creating an intensely hot, perfumed, wet sauna for the better part of an hour.

Phillip spoke: when people first came out of the earth, they had no language, no way of teaching each other. The only sound they could make was a wolf-cry, a plaintive cry of need. These humans were dependent upon the earth and so they cried. Babies today cry in the same way when they emerge from their mother, and the mother responds to their cry of need by placing them to the breast, just as Mother Earth forever hears our needs and feeds us, takes care of us. The sweat lodge reminds us of that relationship by returning us to that womb, that hot, dark, wet womb.

He spoke of the Great Mystery, our Grandfather, the Great Spirit, whatever name we choose to use. Nobody has ever seen him directly, but we come to the sweat lodge to seek him and get close to him, as well as Mother Earth. This Creator put everything on earth to sustain life. Nothing was left out. Mother Earth still follows her original instruction to support life, so she provides water, food, and other essentials for sustenance. This was the Creator's plan for us and for all life, and our human lives interact with all other lives on this earth.

Phillip spoke of transgressions. We all do wrong and we come to the lodge to correct ourselves, to set ourselves aright, to gain balance and harmony once again. To the men in this sweat he explained that women need such purification less regularly than men, because women cleanse themselves with the moon, periodically. But for women and for men there is no act so grievous that a sweat lodge cannot purify its effects. If we leave the lodge and do bad things later, we can always come back to the lodge to cleanse ourselves. Forgiveness is continually possible, through the sweat lodge.

Interspersed with Phillip's quiet exhortations were songs, chanted in the full-throated, falsetto style of the Plains, with a leader and chorus. There were also prayers, requested by Phillip: vocal prayers of thanks for the work Phillip was doing, prayers requesting help for Indian activists, for the earth, for Indian children. There were prayers for the Indian and the human commonweal. And there were unvoiced prayers, silent reflections.

As the stones cooled and the steam subsided, the lodge ritual coming to a close, Phillip advised us that everyone who takes a sweat is a relative. We sweat to seek and find our relatives, and no one is lonely who is in the sweat lodge. As we left the lodge to pay our respects to the water in the beaver pond, each exiting in a sunwise circuit, we shouted, "All my relations!" one by one as we crossed the threshold.

We jumped into the water—without whom life would be impossible, he said. The water purifies us further, washing away what the rock and vapor brought to the surface of our skin. Under the moon, we bathed and chatted for a while, then went back to gather our clothes, have a smoke by the dying fire, and dispersed, some to the roundhouse, some to the ballground, some to their campfires and tents to talk and sleep.

This sweat lodge ritual and many other under Phillip's careful guidance took place on his 160 acres, during two meetings held on his property. Phillip hosted the Youths and Elders Conference and the International Indian Treaty Council in his capacity as spiritual advisor to the politically active American Indian Movement (AIM) and as religious leader of the Muskogee, or Creek, traditionalists. Most of the guests—Indians from all across the United States and Canada and even from Latin America—took a sweat with Phillip as a focal aspect of their participation in the meetings. Until his death of cancer in 1985, Phillip Deere was frequent host to Indian gatherings. Along with a handful of other Indian men, he became "influential among Indian peoples throughout the country" (Josephy 1982:89), revered as a thinker who combined spirituality and politics, appealing to Indians across the boundaries of tribe and age. At the sweat I attended there were young and old Indians from Oklahoma, California, South Dakota, New York, North Carolina, and elsewhere—diverse corners of the continent; Phillip's lodge embraced them all, together.

The appeal of Phillip's sweat rite derived partially from its reference to contemporary concerns of widespread Indians, as well as from its co-joining of various tribal (and perhaps Christian) elements. Like other modern "New Age" religious complexes, it combined messages of spirituality, personal adjustment, and communal awareness with cultic activity (see Lindsey 1986). At the same time Phillip grounded his ritual explicitly in Creek myth and cosmology; he performed not as a vaguely pan-Indian guru but as a traditional Creek medicine man. Indeed, the ritual's effect depended largely on his integrity as a genuine, tribally based religious practitioner.

It is my purpose here to seek the genesis of Phillip Deere's sweat lodge: its basis in his tribal traditions, as well as its pan-tribal continuities, its ancient mythological heritage as well as its present-day functions.

Phillip Deere's sweat ritual is part of the continent-wide phenomenon of vapor baths. Sweat lodges "pervaded" (Aaland 1978:160) Indian cultures from the Eskimos to the Mayans, and Indians sweated ritually for the purposes of cleansing, purifying, healing, revitalizing, relaxing, and identifying with their fellows. Hartley Burr Alexander (1953:46) called the sweat bath "one of the most widespread of Indian customs," undertaken not only to purify, heal, and restore, but to bring Indians "intimately and directly into contact with the Powers which uphold [the] world, giving the universal health and sanity of nature." Harold Driver noted

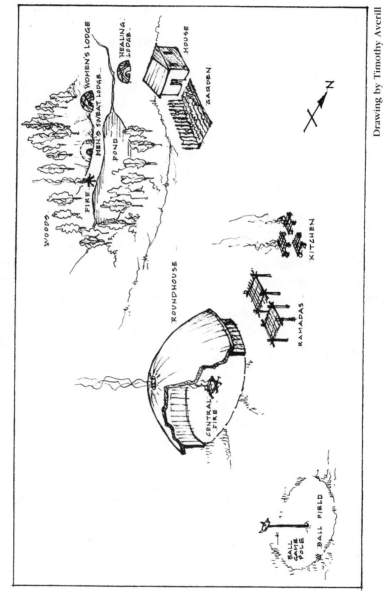

PHILLIP DEERE'S LAND

Drawing by Timothy Averill

that "Special sweathouses were used by the vast majority of North American aborigines" (1972:132, see map 20), and throughout native North America, "Domed shapes are even more widespread because the water vapor sweathouse ... was nearly everywhere of this shape" (129).

Of circumpolar origin, there is archaeological evidence for North American sweat lodges dating from longer than a thousand years ago. In the historical records are descriptions of sweat lodges from the sixteenth century in Mexico, from the seventeenth century in New England, and among eighteenth-century Indians of the Prairies and Plains. These lodges took three basic methods of producing heat. Indians poured water on hot stones, as did Phillip; they lit fires within enclosed spaces; or (among the Mayans) they employed heating ducts from outside the chamber. The hot rock method was used by Indians of the Plains, the Southwest, the Great Basin, and the Eastern Woodlands, whereas direct fire lodges prevailed among the Alaskan Eskimos, Pacific Northwest California Indians, as well as the Pueblos. In addition, Indians sweated without lodges, using kettles, blankets, hot sand, trenches, and by running great distances, as well as by other means of physical exertion. Thus, in its material form, Phillip Deere's lodge followed a long and wide tradition of sweat baths.

In its purpose or meaning, too, his sweat ritual finds analogues across the continent. Sweat lodges were often associated with the gods and myths of creation and sustenance, and were claimed as the primal structure of ritual life. It is often said (e.g., among the Nez Perces) that in the beginning the sweat lodge gave crucial help to needy humans; among the Navajos, the sweat lodge was associated with emergence from the underworld. Commonly the building or preparation of the sweat lodge was part of the overall ritual, part of the work of cosmos building. In the hot stone baths, the stones were usually regarded as sources of power, instruction, and health, means of manifesting the sacred to the Indians. Sweats served the purpose of cleansing, both physically and spiritually, functioning as a "purification rite by those seeking supernatural power or by the sick seeking relief from infirmities" (Driver 1972:133).

Among the twentieth-century Sioux whose sweat lodges are amply depicted, one can find numerous similarities to Phillip's ritual. The Sioux sweat is the oldest of their rites; it purifies; it is related to the goddess of earth and represents her womb; one is reborn in the lodge; one crawls in and out of the lodge, like a naked baby or like an animal; it revivifies people physically and spiritually; it requires a watchful leader; it promotes the relatedness not only of the immediate participants but of all beings on this Mother Earth. Hence the Sioux cry out, "All my relations!" upon leaving the sweat lodge (e.g., Weil 1982:42).

Considering the facts that (1) sweat lodges are pan-Indian in heritage;

(2) Phillip's ritual is greatly similar to those found on the Plains and elsewhere today; (3) his participants—and colleagues in general—are pan-tribal; (4) sweat lodges are springing up wherever Indians meet across tribal borders, at universities, prisons, even Christian revivals; and considering that numerous non-Indians have written about their experiences in the sweat, to the point of tedium, it might be argued that Phillip's sweat lodge can have little to reveal. What can be learned from such a paradigmatic Indian ritual, so familiar as to be banal?

Indeed, what can we learn from any ritual? Easy to observe, difficult to interpret, rituals make cumbersome tools with which to unpack the messages of American Indian cultural expression. "Like 'myth,' when it is used as a synonym from 'false belief,' 'ritual' has a bad reputation," writes one theorist. "In popular usage it connotes 'boring, empty routine' " (Grimes 1982:55). Moreover, numerous participants in the same ritual may differ widely in their interpretation of it. Phillip explained to us what he thought his ritual meant, and he may have brought the others around him to his understanding; however, there were surely divergent meanings gained by the participants. Given the different tribal backgrounds, interpretations would vary. Moreover, we cannot expect that this one ritual should express the fullness of possibilities for which Phillip would celebrate such a rite. The sweat I witnessed might differ from one for healing, and Phillip did indeed conduct healing sweats in a separate lodge for two people with serious ailments: cancer and paralysis of the legs. Sweats for women would surely differ from those for men, although any sweat conducted by Phillip would express his character as a fatherly, protective, gentle, forgiving leader.

Nevertheless, if we view the sweat ritual from Phillip's viewpoint, and we view him as a Muskogee, or Creek, religious leader grounded in a tribal tradition, albeit with a pan-Indian, contemporary audience and interest, then we can gain insight to the ritual. Robert Lowie (1915:234–56) once wrote that ritual diffusion is so common among American Indians that the best place to begin an analysis of a particular ritual is with the immediate context of a specific event, including the tribal background of the ritual actors. He said that rites have been borrowed and shared for millennia, and neighboring tribes often express different meanings through the same apparent ceremony. Hence in this chapter we shall seek the genesis of Phillip's sweat lodge not only in contemporary Indian yearnings for spirituality and identity, but within the long historic development of the Creek religious complex.

We shall observe that sweats have long been part of Creek ritual life, taking place in many Creek cultural contexts. The primary purpose of Creek sweats—and indeed, of Creek ritual in general over the centuries—

has been the purification and forgiveness of wrongdoing. Thus we shall interpret the sweat as a means of purgation (sweating out impurities), ordeal (the intense heat), withdrawal, quietude, reflection, all aimed at receiving forgiveness from the Creator and Mother Earth. The moral dimension to Phillip's sweat lodge, the emphasis on forgiveness, reflects the long-held focus of Creek religiousness. It is consistent, we shall find, with the main patterns of Creek ceremonialism: the yearly cleansing and ritualized vomiting, the general principles of Creek medicine. It is consistent with Creek theology and mythology; indeed, Phillip's explanation derives directly from the Creek account of emergence and migration, the foundational accounts of Creek tribal existence.

We might interpret his ritual at first as an expression of nativistic neo-philosophy, a concoction for a pan-Indian audience, even with Christian influences. Phillip's exhortations resembled those of a thoughtful Christian preacher. On closer inspection, however, we see his sweat lodge more firmly in the tradition of American Indian religiousness, combining as he does the northern (circumpolar, hunting) and southern (Mexican, agricultural) traditions of America. He used a sweat lodge (northern) according to a mythic world view of emergence (southern) from the underground. More specifically, his sweat lodge derives from a pattern of Southeast ceremonialism dating from the Mississippian period, the thirteenth century, the time of the Southern Cult, when Southeast pan-Indian religiousness coalesced. There have been changes in Creek religion over the centuries, and we shall see that the former roles of the sweat in promoting warfare and achieving prestige have taken a lesser place in comparison to the modern roles of healing and moral cleansing. Phillip's own role as a religious leader was in keeping with the contemporary pattern of individualized Creek authority. Yet Phillip employed his sweat lodge as part of a ritual structure that addressed the concerns of his pan-Indian clientele in the language of Creek tradition, thus revealing the relevance, the viability, of the ancient Creek cosmology to present-day Indians across America.

SWEATS AMONG SOUTHEASTERN INDIANS

Ritual sweating has long been a prominent part of religious, medicinal, and social life among the Indians of the Southeast in general, and in particular among the Muskogees and other Creek Confederacy Indians. Beverly (1968:218–19) said of the Indians of seventeenth-century Virginia:

They take great delight in Sweating, and therefore in every Town they have a Sweating-House, and a Doctor is paid by the Publick to attend it. They commonly use this to refresh themselves, after they have been fatigu'd with Hunting, Travel, or the like, or else when they are troubl'd with Agues, Aches, or Pains in their Limbs. Their method is thus, the Doctor takes three or four large Stones, which after having heated red hot, he places 'em in the middle of the Stove, laying on them some of the inner Bark of Oak beaten in a Mortar, to keep them from burning. This being done, they creep in six or eight at a time, or as many as the place will hold, and then close up the mouth of the Stove, which is usually made like an oven, in some Bank near the Water side. In the mean while, the Doctor, to raise a Steam, after they have been stewing a little while, pours cold Water on the Stones, and now and then sprinkles the Men to keep them from fainting. After they have sweat as long as they can well endure it, they sally out, and (tho it be in the depth of Winter) forthwith plunge themselves over Head and Ears in cold Water, which instantly closes up the Pores, and preserves them from taking cold. The heat being thus suddenly driven from the extreme parts to the Heart makes them a little feeble for the present, but their Spirits rally again, and they instantly recover their Strength, and find their Joynts as supple and vigorous as if they never had travell'd, or been indispos'd.... All the Crudities contracted in their Bodies are by this means evaporated and carry'd off.

Similar descriptions were made of Chickasaw, Natchez, Timucua, and other Southeastern Indians in the Colonial period, noting that such a ritual procedure was thought to cure fevers, colds, rheumatic disorders, as well as cases of sluggishness, exhaustion, rashes, cramps, and internal ailments. In some cases sweats were administered to individuals rather than groups, and one illustration shows the patient lying face down on a bench, with face over a fiery pot with steam coming into the mouth and nose (Swanton 1911:85; 1946:790–91, plate 105).

In the eighteenth century Adair said of the Creeks, that in the coldest weather "men and women turn out of their warm houses or stoves, reeking with sweat, singing their usual sacred notes, Yo Yo, etc., at the dawn of day." Plunging into a river, even through ice, the Indians were happy to have performed this religious duty, which was a "crime" to neglect, "and thus purged away the impurities of the preceding day by ablution" (Swanton 1928c:366). Creek sweat baths were used primarily for cures, and whether they took place in permanent huts, caves in riverine banks, dome-shaped huts covered with hides or mats, or under blankets, they were followed invariably by water baths. The use of steam and water constituted a regular aspect of Southeastern Indian "hydrocentric" healing ritualism (Albanese 1984:364, n. 60).

Creeks used the "vapor-bath efficaciously" (Eakins, 1851:274) as a means of curing; however, there were other uses. Warriors took sweats before the battle, hunters before the chase; in general, the rituals preceded many important undertakings. In order to "inculcate their mysteries" (Swanton 1928c:366) to apprentices, Creek healers led their pupils away from the village and prepared them with fasting and sweat bathing. The graduates of these programs possessed the authority to heal, tell myths, and give moral advice. Sweats were also employed in rites of passage and in the taking of titles. When Louis Le Clerc Milfort became a Creek war chief in the late eighteenth century, part of his installation consisted of a sweat. He recalled that

> the whole assembly undressed completely and went, absolutely naked, into a circular cabin, where the priests had gone to await us. Each one of them had carried there a brass kettle in which they had boiled the war medicine. Shortly afterwards, the subordinate chiefs brought pebbles which they had heated red hot . . . , and the priests, while singing, threw on them the water which was contained in . . . two gourds. . . . This caused terrible heat and steam. The whole assembly was perspiring profusely, and I was perspiring so freely through every pore in my body that, although I was in very good health, I thought that it would be impossible to endure it. We remained in this condition about half an hour, then some of the chiefs went out of the cabin, the priests gathered around me and we all left and went immediately to plunge into a river which was a short distance from the cabin. It was not without a great deal of fear that I made up my mind to follow the example of the entire assembly; it appeared to me extremely dangerous, perspiring as I then was, to jump at once into the cold water; but it was impossible for me to do otherwise, and I suffered nothing more than fright. . . . On coming out of the water, where we remained only a short time, each one dressed, and we returned to the grand cabin (Milfort 1972:101, see 99–102).

Finally, Indians of the Creek Confederacy used sweat rituals "for the purpose of enhancing supernatural power" (Swanton 1928a:710), and warding off illness as well as curing it. Among the Yuchis, "It is done also to right one's self with the Sun deity" (Speck 1909:136), as well as for the other purposes we have mentioned. That is, Creek sweat lodges functioned not only physically and socially, but also spiritually, as a way of making things right with the gods. For various purposes, in various contexts, Creek sweats were still common in the early twentieth century.

The "cabin" where Milfort took his sweat was most likely the common Creek roundhouse, also referred to as the rotunda, hothouse, warm house, winter council house, assembly room, or mountain house. Resembling

Prairie earthlodges and the semisubterranean men's clubhouses of the Pacific Coast where direct-fire, communal sweats were common, and no doubt deriving from the circular, earth-covered hothouses from archaeological sites such as Ocmulgee National Monument in Georgia, this structure has been one of the most important ceremonial buildings among the Creeks. A sign on the road in front of Phillip Deere's land advertised his roundhouse, or *cokopolokse.*

The Creek town plans (see page 216) consisted, usually, of three main areas, in addition to homes (which had their own small hothouses), earthen mounds resembling Mexican pyramids, and surrounding fields: the roundhouse, an enclosed or semienclosed octagon or circle, twenty to a hundred feet in diameter, twenty to fifty feet high, with a spiral fire at the center and benches around the periphery; the square grounds or big house, made up of four sheds or beds at right angles to each other, surrounding a central fire; and the chunky yard or ball field, with central ball-game pole, with skull or fish atop. In the summer most public events were held in the public square grounds. The chiefs and elders, warriors and matrons, entire villages and their guests, gathered for council and ceremony, deliberating and dancing around the central fire. It is said that "Every person knew his place in the Square" (Hewitt 1939:132). Possibly "the square-ground developed from the large rectangular 'town house' surmounting the great central platform mounds on the later sites east of the Mississippi" (Waring 1968:53), but it is certain that over the historical period the square ground served as public arena for crucial Creek rituals. In addition, the ceremonially significant ball games took place on the ball fields that were also permanent structures. These three elements— roundhouse, square, and ball field—were persistent elements from the seventeenth to the early twentieth century, despite "considerable changes both in evolution and subsequent devolution" (Swanton 1928c:191). The construction of all three was considered a ceremonial event in its own right.

Within this town design, the roundhouse played the more important role during the winter and other inclement weather. Harold Driver comments (1972:133) that, "In the Southeast, the winter dwellings, called hothouses, were reminiscent of direct-fire sweathouses. Men, women, and children slept together in them with a fire burning all night, arose together in the morning dripping with perspiration, and rushed out the door to the nearest stream for a cold bath." Patients went there for cures; celebrants danced around its fire; secret councils met there; and old men gathered there for talk, smoke, and sleep. But sweating seems to have been its most consistent ritual activity, until the roundhouses went into decline in the early twentieth century.

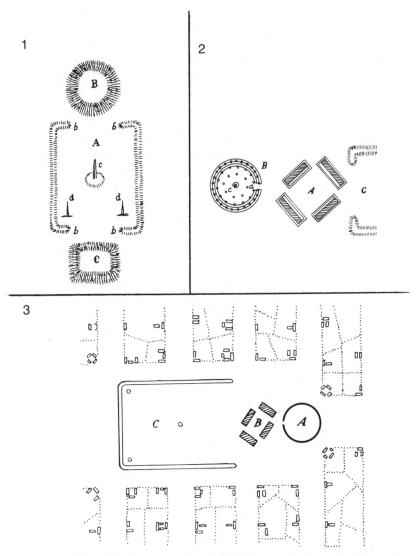

CREEK CEREMONIAL GROUNDS AFTER BARTRAM 1853 (Howard 1968: 132). Fig. 1 shows: A) ball field; B) roundhouse; C) public square; b,b,b,b) rim of ball field; c) ballgame pole; d,d) slave posts. Fig. 2 shows: A) public square; B) roundhouse; C) ball field; a) opening of roundhouse door; c) spiral fire. Fig. 3 shows: A) roundhouse; B) public square; C) ball field—all surrounded by village habitations.

POLLUTION AND PURIFICATION

Whether in the roundhouses or in small sweat lodges, Creek sweating was suffused with the notion of purification, the exorcising of pollution, the overcoming of guilt, and the correcting of relations with the divine, in particular, the attaining of forgiveness. It is said that the Indians of the Southeast lived in a "morally intense community" (Hudson 1976:174), one in which purification and forgiveness were necessary, recurrent features.

In reading Adair's 1775 firsthand observations of Southeast Indians, *History of the American Indians,* one is struck by the constant attention paid by the natives to the problem of pollution. One is perhaps skeptical of Adair, because of his interest in proving the Hebraic heritage of the Indians; nevertheless, purification does appear as a salient leitmotif in Creek religion, carried down to Phillip Deere's sweat lodge. Southeast Indian women took their newborns to a creek or spring for a bath or sprinkling, even before the first suckling took place, as a "ceremonial means of overcoming pollution" (Hudson 1976:322, 324), in a manner perhaps reminiscent of men crawling from the sweat lodge womb, down to the pond. A Yuchi chief remarks that, "after the Yuchi people were made, they wished to have some medicine to clean themselves. For ... they wished to keep their bodies clean so Mother, the Sun, and the Breath Master would be pleased with them. So they washed in the creek" (in Mahan 1983:112). In eating the right food, in maintaining menstrual taboos, in constant cleansing, in their major ceremonials, as well as through sweating, "the Southeast Indians went to great lengths to keep themselves in a ritually pure condition" (Hudson 1979:3). Creeks returning from long journeys were not permitted into their homes without first receiving purification by medicine. Creeks blamed droughts and other setbacks on moral failure, especially adultery, which angered the gods, and adulterers were fiercely punished. An Indian agent among the Creeks in the first half of the nineteenth century noted that their narratives were designed for "moral instruction" (Nunez 1958:18), and Creek songs, despite being at times "extravagantly libidinous," were often exceedingly moral, serving the "purpose of religious lectures" (Bartram 1958:321).

Some observers suggested that the Creeks strove for moral elevation in order to achieve heavenly rewards and avoid punishment after death. Others said that Creek socioreligious hierarchies provided rewards and punishment on earth: "The fundamental idea regarding punishment was that it cleansed the culprit from the guilt of

his crime. Criminals carried no guilt with them out of the world"
(Hewitt 1939:147). James H. Howard asserts (1968:87) specifically of
the Creeks:

Apparently the only techniques which were regarded as moving the will
of the Master of Breath were fasting, abstinence, purification with medicines,
and the observance of religious formulae. . . . Perhaps the strong emphasis
on peace and the high moral tone of the ceremonies were not so much
virtue for virtue's sake but rather were designed to oblige the Master of
Breath to insure good crops.

Whether for its own sake, or for a further end, purification was an obsession within Creek Indian religion.

The Creek emphasis on purification may have revealed a societal sense
of unworthiness or wrongdoing; however, it also signaled a cosmology
that was, at core, "forgiving" (see Driver 1972:413–18). The Creek world
view can be seen as an example of "a very human effort to relate the
changing requirements of action to a permanent and unchanging order
of things," expressing "the underlying notion that there is a relationship
between origins and ethics." Within the Creek tradition, "ritual actions"
constitute one of the "modes in which its moral beliefs may be expressed"
(Lovin and Reynolds 1985:1, 2–3, 4).

A prominent ritual means by which the Creeks expressed their desire
for moral purification was the ceremonial use of the Black Drink. Con-
cocted of the yaupon holly, *Ilex vomitoria,* the Black Drink had a long
history among the Creeks and other Southeastern Indians, and was thoroughly integrated into their daily lives and councils. Indians from coastal
North Carolina to coastal Texas near the Rio Grande, right up to the area
of peyote use—that is, within the natural range of the plant—were known
to drink the Black Drink (Hudson 1979: maps 1 and 2). One of the Creeks'
four major medicinal teas, the Black Drink was not an especially strong
emetic, chemically. Maybe on an empty stomach, maybe mixed with
snakeroot, maybe by suggestion, but not chemically on its own; however,
the Creeks drank the Black Drink in order to vomit ritually and cleanse
themselves.

In particular, Creek men—warriors, chiefs, priests, and elders—drank
and vomited the drink, "in order to attain ritual purity" (Hudson 1979:2).
Caleb Swan reported (1855:267) that, "After drinking copiously, the warrior, by hugging his arms across his stomach, and leaning forward, dis-
gorges the liquor in a large stream from his mouth, to the distance of six
or eight feet," while the men talked, smoked and socialized. He remarked

that among the Creeks, "it is thought a handsome accomplishment in a young fellow to be able to spout well." Although in fact the Creeks drank the pleasant-tasting tea for stimulation and pleasure, the prevalent Creek belief was that the Black Drink "purifies them from all sin, and leaves them in a state of perfect innocence; that it inspires them with an invincible prowess in war; and that it is the only solid cement of friendship, benevolence, and hospitality" (Swan 1855, quoted in Fairbanks 1979:123). Creek men took the brew in the morning before breakfast, before undertaking any important decisions, before warring or hunting, before constructing a roundhouse, or square, or ball-game pole, before dancing, and again in the evening, before bed. In short, it served the same function as a sweat: to purify a person regularly and ritually.

Like the sweat, Black Drink seems to have been primarily—perhaps exclusively—a male perogative and purgative. One scholar suggests that the men drank the liquid "before meeting in council with other men . . . to separate them ritually from women. And it is likely that they induced vomiting to rid themselves of any possible contamination by impure food" (Hudson 1979:3). Another scholar suggests that "It thus served as an identification of adult male status in a society otherwise strongly emphasizing female power and authority" (Fairbanks 1979:138), in a strongly matrilineal and matrilocal context. It may also be that men took the Black Drink because they required purification more than did the women, and represented a male discharge analogous to menstruation.

If swallowing and vomiting the Black Drink was a means by which Creek men cleansed themselves, the entire Creek society reached ritual purity as a unit every summer during the annual Busk ceremonial. The term "Busk" derives from the Creek word *boshita*, meaning "a fast." Begun during the mythical migrations of the first Creek peoples, the Indians knew that it was initiated by the divine for the yearly benefit of the Creeks:

> The busk with its fire, its medicines, and its ceremonial was a great unifying element between the several members of the Creek confederacy, all the tribes which united with it either adopting such a ceremonial or altering their own to agree with it. And further than that it was a special unifying institution within each town, bringing all together for a definite purpose in which the good of each and the good of all were bound up. All transgressions, except some forms of murder, were then forgiven, all disturbances adjusted, and thus the unity and peace of the state reestablished. [Swanton 1928b:548]

The Creek Busk served many functions. Taking place when the corn crop was green, or just ready to be eaten, it was held for agricultural fertility and prosperity. Held in mid-summer, it was the central axis around which the Creek ceremonial season (April–October) revolved. It fostered social unity and tribal health, promoted intra-Confederacy peace, and honored the clans and their totemic animals. It was an opportunity for intertribal visiting and feasting, and brought the Master of Breath within the community, to dwell in the fire. But above all, the Busk existed in order for the Creeks to empty themselves of the old year and its food, fire, and deeds, and to commence a new year, a new moral existence, a new purity. Thus at Busk the Creeks extinguished the old fire in the square and kindled a new fire. They sought expiation of old sins, forgiveness from the community and the gods. They fasted until their bodies had given off the food of the old year and then feasted on the new, green corn.

The ritual of the fire had special import, since "the most basic ceremonial concept in the entire Southeast is that of the sacred fire, identified with the sun, fed by four oriented logs, and symbolizing the supreme sky being" (Howard 1968:25). The cross and circle motif found in Southeast sites dating from the Mississippian period of the thirteenth century symbolized the four ceremonial logs and the ceremonial area called the "fire" (Howard 1968:19; Waring 1968:33–35). By extinguishing and rekindling the sacred fire at Busk, the Creeks wiped clean the slate of their relationship with the deities and began the new year purified.

At this, the Creeks' "most solemn celebration" (Bartram 1958:323), the Indians cleaned their yards, drank the Black Drink and released the contents of their stomachs, bathed repeatedly in the river, swept out their hearths, rubbed themselves in ashes and medicines, and took sweats in lodges and under blankets. They observed a "strict rule of penance" (Nunez 1958:131), the men refusing to touch women or even shake hands with an "unpurified" (131) person during the ceremonial time, for fear of being "polluted" (41). Only at the close of the ceremonial, perhaps eight days, did the Creeks celebrate their newfound purity "promiscuously," with festive "conviviality" (Swan 1855:258).

An eighteenth-century observer concluded that "This happy institution of the *Boos-ke-tub,* restores man to himself, to his family and to his nation. It is a general amnesty, which not only absolves the Indians from all crimes, murder only excepted, but seems to bury guilt itself in oblivion" (Hawkins 1971:78). For some contemporary Muskhogeans, including Florida Seminoles, the Green Corn ceremonial continues to be "a time for *cleansing,* [emphasis theirs] for renewal. The men take sweatbaths, fast, and drink . . . a boiled drink which makes them vomit" (Beck and Walters 1977:260). In short, Busk continues to be a ritual means by which

Creeks and others express their belief in a moral cosmos that requires and accepts atonement for wrongdoing.

In his perceptive essay "The Forgiving Creeks," Harold Driver (1972:413–18) stated that "Perhaps the most distinctive feature of Creek religion and magic was the forgiving of every wrong short of murder at the greatest ceremony of the year, the Green Corn Dance." For the Creeks, for whom blood wars and revenge were a way of life and death (see, e.g., the blood revenge upon a singer whose relatives had committed a murder, in Nunez 1958:133–35), and whose reprisals against adulterers included excised noses and ears, beatings, gang rapes, enforced sentences of prostitution, under intense moral judgment, the forgiveness of wrongdoers by the community as well as by the gods constituted an act of great forbearance.

Nevertheless, it should be noted that Busk also included elaborate initiations of Creek men into the military class, as well as mock killings of enemies. That is, Busk fostered intratribal forgiveness and peace, along with preparations for war against enemies. Only with the weakening of Creek Confederacy military powers in the nineteenth century did Busk— and Creek ritualism in general—take on a more wholly pacific nature, empasizing even more strongly the themes of forgiveness and purification so evident in Phillip Deere's sweat lodge.

Forgiveness also lay at the foundation of Creek medicinal ideas. In the myth recounting the origin of diseases, the Creeks told how humans once offended animals either by overkilling them or by mistreating their bodily remains. In revenge, the animals created sicknesses—constipation (caused by beaver), aching teeth and gums (snake), nausea and diarrhea (bird, bear), headache (deer, sun), boils (deer), swollen joints and stiff muscles (yearling deer), sleeplessness (fish), and others—but in the spirit of forgiveness they also created the cures. Hence in their medicinal songs the Creeks thanked the animals for their help and imitated the animals said to be the cause of the ailment. These songs also strengthened a human identification with the animal world, as did Creek wall paintings and tattoos of humans with animal heads and members, as did animal clan totems, and as did crawling, naked, into sweat lodges; but their main purpose was to recall and complete the forgiveness provided to humans by animals in primordial times. It was the task of the Creek curers and knowers to pass down not only information of herbal remedies and surgical procedures but also the mythic knowledge of forgiveness and the ritual means of purification. As a modern medicineman, Phillip Deere promulgated these themes in his sweat lodge, and it is significant that incarcerated Indians responded gratefully to the forgiving sweats he conducted in prisons in Oklahoma.

THE MYTHOLOGICAL CONTEXTS

He also set forth the principles of traditional Creek theology. He focused attention on the Creator—Master of Life, Breath, and Death—and the Earth Mother, and posited divinities who care deeply about humans in general, Indians in particular, and are receptive to entreaties for atonement. Eighteenth-century observers said that the Creeks worshiped the Great Spirit and paid homage to the sun, moon, planets, and culture heroes, mediators to the Great Spirit, and dispensers of comfort and well-being (Bartram 1853:20). Creeks in the early twentieth century told Frank Speck (1911:163) that the Master of Breath originated all dances and ceremonies, and "conditioned prosperity upon their continuance. Most of the dances are propitiatory, influencing the spirits of various animals and supernatural agencies which are capable of inflicting trouble," he wrote. Creeks conducted such rituals because they were confident of divine favor and gifts.

The Creeks, like other Southeastern Indians, may have believed in an underworld of disorder and change, inversions and madness, as well as of invention, potential, and fertility; however, their "Upper World represented structure, expectableness, boundaries, limits, periodicity, order, stability" (Hudson 1976:127–28), and the assurance of past events, and the Indians could count on prevailing order if they performed their rituals properly. Theirs was a cosmos upon which they could rely.

Creek reliance on helpful deities finds evidence in the myths of emergence and migration, and sacred histories of the Creek Confederacy and its component peoples. It is the emergence myth upon which Phillip Deere based his understanding of his sweat lodge and its ritual.

Numerous sources attest that the Muskogees and other Creeks "believe their original predecessors came from the west, and resided Underground" (Adair, in Swanton 1928c:40). The Yuchis, Hitchitis, Alabamas, Coasatis and Natchez all told stories greatly resembling those of the dominant Muskogees, and indeed the entire Southeast possessed a remarkable similiarity in regard to cosmology and myth, creating in terms of folklore "one fairly homogenous group" Speck 1909:138; 1907:145; Swanton 1929:267). It is possible to find Southeast stories that ascribe human origin not to emergence, but rather to the sun, sky, moon, sea, ashes, eggs, and plants; most prominently, the Yuchis call themselves the "Offspring of the Sun" (Speck 1909:105), and even some Muskogees will mention a human origin other than the earth. Some Creeks even tell of the various origins of different Confederacy tribes in order to highlight the unifying power of the Master of Breath in creating the Confederacy: "Now the people had come upon the earth. The Shawnee came from above. The Creeks came from the ground. The Choctaw came from the water. The Yuchi came from the sun" (Speck 1909:143). Despite these variations, one can find a "harmony between the various versions" (Swanton 1928c:33) of the Creek origin stories, perhaps solidified by the unity of the Creek Confederacy. This harmony draws upon the imagery of emergence from the earth.

The context for the Creek origin myth is difficult to ascertain. The great warrior leader was known to recite the "traditional history of the people" (Hewitt 1929:151) during Busk, emphasizing the founding and importance of the festival and other societal customs that "tended to preserve their health and prolong their lives." However, among the Yuchis, such myths could be told at any time of year. One Creek storyteller and chief said that the emergence and migration traditions "must be repeated in a certain manner word for word, for a mistake would cost blood" (Swanton 1928c:63); however, such myths were and are passed down in families, keeping them "alive for generations" (Robinson n.d.:3), and within medicine societies. Milfort (1972:102) said that old Creek men told of their first ancestors, the Muskogees, through stories which they recalled by strings of beads. In any event, a few Creek myths are extant in the literature on the Creeks.

In recent telling (Robinson n.d.:4), a female Creek narrates a "legend," "The Origin of the Clans":

> Our Elders say that in the beginning the Muscogee people were born out of the earth itself. They crawled up out of the ground through a hole like ants. In those days, they lived in a far western land beside tall mountains that reached the sky. They called the mountains the backbone of the earth. Then a thick fog descended upon the earth, sent by the Master of Breath, *Hesakitumesee.* The Muscogee people could not see. They wandered around blindly . . . calling out to one another in fear. They drifted apart and became lost. The whole people were separated into small groups and the people in these groups stayed close to one another in fear of being entirely alone.
>
> Finally the Master had mercy on them. From the eastern edge of the world, where the sun rises, he began to blow away the fog. He blew and blew until the fog was completely gone. The people were joyful and sang a hymn of thanksgiving to the Master of Breath. And in each group the people turned to one another and swore eternal brotherhood. They said that from then on these groups would be like large families. The members of each group would be as close to each other as brother and sister, father and son.

The story closes with the formation of the clans: Wind, Bear, Deer, Alligator, Raccoon, and Bird—and Wind most prominent. An illustration for the legend, made by a Creek artist and derived from a style found on ancient, engraved Muskogee shells (perhaps the shells out of which Black Drink was taken), illustrates two Indians crawling out of a cavelike hole in a mound of the earth, shaped and situated exactly like Phillip Deere's sweat lodge.

A second version, dating from a speech given in 1735 by Chekilli, a Creek chief (Brinton 1870:7–10), states that, "At a certain time, the Earth opened in the West, where its mouth is. The earth opened and the Cussitaws came out of its mouth, and settled near by. But the earth became angry and ate up their children." Some moved further west, but most remained there at their emergence place, out of a sense of propriety. "Their children, nevertheless, were eaten by the Earth, so that, full of dissatisfaction, they journeyed toward the sunrise." On their eastward migration, the people crossed a slimy river, a bloody river, to a thunderous mountain with fire spewing from it, making a "singing noise." They learned herbal knowledge and other things there. They mingled this fire with one from the north, making the fire they use today, "and this, too, sometimes sings." On the mountain was a pole, shaped like a wooden tomahawk, with which they killed a child. The tomahawks of today are made of its wood, and the mountain is regarded as a primal mound of creation.

A third version comes from Ispahihtoa, a Creek chief, who narrated (Swanton 1928c:55–63):

> Far off toward the west many people came out of the ground.... At that time the people were without clothing or fire. And they sewed together leaves of trees with which to cover themselves. And while they were there the Breath-holder (*Hisakita immsi si*) spoke to them and said: "The earth which lies here is the foundation of all things." And he said: "The earth being created, the second thing is water, the third the trees and grass, and the fourth the things having life." Even down to the smallest things they were created. [55–56]

The Kasihtas, Cowetas (two Creek town groups), and Chickasaws came from the emergence place to the east because in the west "they became so evil that they could find nothing pure in the world except the sun, and they determined to travel eastward to find the place from whence it came" (54).

Along the migration route, the Kasihtas "raised a mound, leaving a great chamber in the center in which to fast and purify their bodies. They left their women, children, and other noncombatants there and went on toward the east" (54). The Cowetas later used the mound for purification, and when they were attacked by Cherokees, the Coweta warriors "poured up from the bowels of the earth" (54–55) and defeated them. The Kasihtas reached the sea, but could not see for a fog. In the morning the sun rose out of the sea, and they could see; they "concluded that that was why it was so bright and pure" (55). Both groups purified themselves once again in two mounds by the sea:

> They said that this action would give them help. When they were ready they caused a wind to blow on the people covered with fog living there, and the fog was cleared away. [57]

Then they killed part of a population living there, took many captives, and exterminated the town. They built a town there on their own.

The Kasihtas and Cowetas had been vying for position on the seacoast; however,

> the Kasihta said "We came out of the center of the earth." The Coweta answered "We came out at the same place but the root of a tree extending in front of us, we emerged only after a delay." Then they learned that they had been created one people. [59]

They erected the four sheds to make the village square; they constructed the roundhouse and ball field according to a plan, and after purifying themselves established the Busk in the middle of the summer, with its dances, vomiting, purifications, and fasting. Only then did peace come about.

Other versions express the emergence and subsequent migration in slightly different terms, providing the composite account more texture. Louis Perryman, a Creek chief, remarked: "The Coweta say that they came out from under the earth and found the surface soft and muddy, difficult to travel upon. By and by it became dry and hard" (Swanton 1928c:53). The Alabamas said that when they emerged, they were frightened by an owl, and most returned underground; therefore, the Alabamas are so few in number (Swanton 1922:192). It is common to find it said that "In the beginning the Indians came pouring out of the earth like ants," as Judge Nokosi, a Creek chief told Swanton (1928c:65). One myth states that "people came out from a cavern in the earth, and as they emerged a man standing at the entrance bestowed their various clan designations" (Swanton 1928c:111), and they dressed like animals or took accompanying totemic creatures. It is a common motif that in ancient times "people were sitting about in groups enveloped in darkness"; when light came, they could see animals, and they named themselves by the animals they saw: deer, bear, and others (Swanton 1928c:111). Sometimes they called to each other in the dark, or developed sensitivity of touch and other senses "in their efforts to obtain subsistence" (Swanton 1928c:112). The wind is associated with peace because it was the wind that blew away the enveloping fog, thus revealing the Creeks' clan identities to them. The emergence place is frequently said to be "the navel of the world," near the Rocky Mountains, "the backbone of the earth" (Swanton 1928c:52), and invariably the Creeks moved eastward toward their future homes. In any event, the Creek origin stories "speak of their ancestors as having come up out of the ground at 'the navel of the earth,' the connection of the navel with birth evidently having been responsible for this designation" (Swanton 1928c:63–64). For this reason, no doubt, Indians such as the Chickasaws called the artificial mounds in their old country "navels" (64, n. 43), or wombs.

This imagery of emergence is related to the emergence myths of the Southwest, including those of the Hopis, and is part of a Meso-America tradition. Typically, these emergence myths personify the earth as mother and giver of food, and most important societal rituals are said to have been formed shortly after the event. Clan names, town plans, economic activities, and other social necessities are formed after emergence, and regularly the emergence leads to a migration to the tribes' present locations.

In the Creek versions there is an added emphasis on mounds, caves, and mountains, at which their ancestors stayed, repaired and purified themselves, and found a good life. The Muskogees told Hawkins that they had lived at "two mounds of earth" (1971:19) with other Indians, west of the Mississippi, before coming east. Milfort reports (1972:37, 54, 102–13) that the Creeks were eager to visit "the caves that their ancestors had lived in," fine caves where they had dwelled happily. His expedition to the Red River on the northern prairies seems farfetched, but the fond reference to caves in Creek myth is common, giving depth to Phillip Deere's use of a cave as sweat lodge, and to his depiction of it as a womb from which human life emerged.

There exists a Creek Orpheus tradition, in which four men seek their dead wives. They find themselves in a great cave, where they are surrounded by a cloud. By turning themselves into swift animals, three are able to get beyond the cloud, but the one who remains in human form is crushed by the cloud. Within the cave, the three survivors climb behind the cloud, and find an old woman who feeds them corn, beans, and squash, more than they can eat, and shows them their deceased wives. She protects the men, and helps them to bring three of their wives back to life (Speck 1909:144–46).

Creek emergence often leads to an eastward migration where orderly

Creek life evolved under divine direction. It should be noted that Creek myths find the origin of Busk during the migration, the town design after settling in the east, and there are even myths that tell how emissaries from the Master of Breath deliver medicines, talismans, and other ceremonies to the people (Foreman 1930:123–24; Swanton 1928c:65–66; Waring 1968:48–51). But according to Phillip Deere, the sweat lodge was the first ritual provided for the Indians, an ur-rite preceding all others.

Creek origin myths sometimes describe the earth as a flat, animate substance with a succession of planes below and above (Eakins 1851:271). Others describe the process by which land was created from water (Eakins 1851:266; Speck 1909:138). Still others dwell on the history of the Creeks after settling on the eastern shore, including the coming of the whites from out the eastern sea. One Creek told Swanton (1938c:76) that "Indians were believed to have come out of the earth, and therefore they own it and are to go back into it. The white people, on the other hand, were created later out of the foam of the sea." A common motif has the whites disembarking, and cheating the Indians of their land and livelihood (Swanton 1922:173; 1928c:76). These versions reinforce the Creek opinion that "the Great Spirit brought them from the ground, and that they are the right possessors of this soil" (Eakins 1851:266), or that "they sprang from the earth, the soil, and hence the earth is man's mother and therefore sacred, and man cannot sell his own mother" Swanton (1928b:480).

Creek origin myths sometimes close with predictions regarding the end of the earth, when the Creeks return to the place where they emerged from the earth at the navel. At that time the Busk will begin to suffer, the Creek civil authority will erode. Creeks will sing the Christ song and disappear as a people (Swanton 1928c:77–78). Some of these predictions take a Christian hue, with images of the dead arising, the coming of the Master of Breath, the separation of the good and wicked (Swanton 1928c:45; cf. 78); however, even in their Christian colors they draw upon the imagery of the emergence myth.

The Creek emergence myth expresses either explicitly or implicitly a belief in the earth as mother, and in his explanation of the sweat lodge, Phillip Deere focuses the ritual on Mother Earth. Yet in some of the emergence versions, for example, in Ispahihtoa's narrative, a High God creates the earth and speaks of the earth's uses to humans. Phillip, on the other hand, revered the earth as a goddess in her own right. One might suspect that Phillip's interpretation is a modern, pan-Indian formulation, in line with the ecological neo-romanticism and feminist tendencies of our day. But it is also possible that Ispahihtoa downplayed the feminine aspects of divinity under the influences of patriarchal Christian teachings, or that the white recorder ignored the identification of the earth goddess. A third possibility is that the Creeks, like other Indians, possessed flexible theological concepts, and depending on personality, context, and other factors, a person might emphasize different gods—now the High God, now the earth goddess.

In any event, Phillip's formulation is in keeping with the maincurrents of traditional Indian thought, for as Åke Hultkrantz states, "the belief in a goddess, usually identified with Mother Earth, is found almost everywhere in North America" (1983:202). Hultkrantz notes that "It is possible that the peyote religion, which spread over North America from the 1880s, has contributed to the belief in Mother Earth among hunting tribes" (204); however, among the agricultural Creeks, benevolent goddesses of nature had a long and fitting history. In particular, the Creeks identified corn with a goddess's body; hence they treated the crop with tenderness and respect. In the many Creek versions of corn's origin, Corn Woman invariably feeds individuals from her body. They spy on her, seeing her in the process of scratching off scabs of skin from her thighs or feet. They are revolted and lose their appetite. She realizes that they have learned her secret, and gives them instructions to bury her in a field, or lock her in a corn crib. In either case, corn grows from her deposited corpse. Through all the motifs, one can see the image of the life-supporting, self-sacrificing nature goddess, protecting the Indians, and functioning on her own, without a male consort.

The Creek emergence and womb imagery, in combination with the traditions regarding Corn Woman, make one conclude that Phillip Deere was drawing upon his tribal traditions in his statements about Mother Earth. He may have been further influenced by the Shawnee devotion to "Our Grandmother," a female deity "forever on the lips" (Voegelin 1970:3) of Oklahoma Shawnees. She was a supreme being and creator, living in the sky, but caring for the earth, both the living and the dead, and a source of divinatory inspiration. Devotion to her seems to have been especially strong among Shawnee nativists who tried to turn their people from Christianity in the 1880s, and perhaps as far back as the Shawnee-Creek resistance to white inroads in the early nineteenth century. Given the long history of Shawnee-Creek alliances and intermarriages, and given Phillip's identification with the politico-religious ideology of Shawnee-Creek resistance movements, it is not surprising to find his reverence for a nature goddess of great Nativist importance.

It is also not surprising that Phillip help separate sweats for men and women. During his conferences he made frequent public announcements that menstruating women should not be within the roundhouse, or near the fire, and that they should not bathe in the beaver pond. His observation of menstrual taboos was consistent with Creek (and pan-Indian) tradition. Creek religious thought regarded menstrual discharge as a release of impurity, and thus a dangerous substance. During their periods, Creek women were secluded in menstrual huts; they had no contact with men, bathed downstream, walked downwind, and of course did not enter the ceremonial areas. Perhaps as a result of these concerns for strict separation, "In ancient times," a Creek informant said, "men and women were almost like two distinct peoples" (Swanton 1928c:384). Even in the twentieth century, Creek men and women had separate areas of the home in which they dwelled, even separate buildings where men and women entertained members of their respective sex. Naturally, then, Phillip would separate men and women in the sweat rituals, and for more reason than his statement that women need less purification due to their monthlies. In his attitude toward women, Phillip was acting the traditional Muskogee Creek.

TRADITION AND PERSISTENCE

John R. Swanton once accused (1928c:76) his Creek narrators of interweaving their own traditions with those of "schoolbook and other latter-day elements into a kind of Indian neo-philosophy," and one could say the same of Phillip Deere. Like Swanton's storytellers, and indeed like all religious practitioners in touch with their own times, Phillip was interested not in the antiquarian business of reciting ancient doctrines, but in the task of creating, living, and espousing a relatively consistent world view that would be relevant to those who came to him for direction. Despite the devolution of Creek religious structures—the Creeks had given up many herbal remedies and even the Black Drink when they could not procure the once-familiar plants after Removal; their governmental duties became separated from religious functions after the 1930s; among the Eastern Creeks the language died out and their culture became that of rural Southern folk; some Oklahoma Creek towns gave up rituals altogether; societies of medicinemen fell apart and curers worked individually; village roundhouses ceased to be built—Phillip drew upon his Creek heritage to meet the needs of his pan-Indian followers.

Whereas some Creeks found in Christianity an appropriate and satisfying outlet for their ancient moralism and ritualism; whereas the long history of Christian missions among the Creeks has left its mark even among the traditionalists who espouse the old ways and resist formal Christian identification; and whereas Christian inroads have weakened native Creek religious expression, Phillip's ritual and its underlying mythology were decidedly Indian, and not just generalized Indian, but specifically Creek in genesis.

The heritage from which Phillip gained his world view was, in a sense, pan-Indian, but pan-Indian insofar as Southeastern Indian culture was relatively uniform, from the Mississippian period onward. With few natural barriers to cultural diffusion, in historical times there was a continuity of cultures, world views, myths, and rituals throughout the Southeast, and dislocated Southeastern Indians had little trouble finding homes among other Southeastern Indians, even from varying language groups. When the Natchez were dispersed in the 1730s, they went to live with Creeks, Cherokees, Catawbas, and Chickasaws; the Creek Confederacy itself was composed of different language groups who shared nevertheless a common culture. An effective and widespread system of sign language existed throughout the Southeast that furthered the tendency toward cultural homogeneity.

Southeastern pan-Indianism—a similarity of cultural motifs from Florida to Oklahoma, from the Gulf of Mexico to the Great Lakes—owed part of its uniformity to the centuries of influence from Mexico, coalescing as early as A.D. 1200, and this Southeastern, Mississippian culture influenced Indian culture not only throughout the Mississippi and Ohio river valleys, but "almost all of American Indian culture east of the Rocky Mountains" (Howard 1968:3), including those of the Plains. Phillip Deere's special appeal to Sioux and Chippewa Indians of the northern Plains may have been in no small part due to their shared, ancient pan-Mississippian culture.

The world view underlying Phillip's sweat lodge had its roots, perhaps, in the so-called Southern Cult (Death Cult or Buzzard Cult), a religious complex from A.D. 1200 to 1400 in the Southeast, a movement that helped establish "basic ceremonial beliefs in common over the entire area" (Fairbanks 1952:297). This was perhaps a "messianic" or "revitalization movement," or a "widely shared religious ideology," "wholly pre-Columbian" (Howard 1968:7), "which swept through the Southeast," much as peyotism took the Plains in the past century, "crossing cultural boundaries and imposing a sort of religious unity on the entire region," establishing the "trappings of the state religion throughout the Southeast" (11–12).

Little is known for certain about the Southern Cult. It appears to have gained some impetus from Mexican sources, although it drew at least as much from indigenous Southeastern culture traits. It seems to have been concerned with human transformation, renewal, and rebirth, a cultus of life-support. Its primary message was that of a connection between peace and medicine, possibly in response to a crisis, possibly as an attempt to join politically diverse groups (Waring 1968:66–67). Whatever its specific content, the Cult had as its far-reaching effect the religio-political ideology that produced the Creek Confederacy and its ceremonial structure. Indeed, the Creeks are reputed to be the direct and central descendents of Mississippian, Southern Cult syntheses.

Some say that the contemporary Creek Busk carries that continuity of ancient Mississippian culture (Howard 1968:14), and that "the Creeks used their ceremonial as a political instrument for achieving a peace league of a strongly religious character" (Waring 1968:67). "It should be possible," says one scholar, "to demonstrate the parallelisms between what is preserved of Creek religious ceremonial and the Southern Cult" (Fairbanks 1952:298), not only in the engraved conch shells of Mississippian archaeology employed in holding the Creek Black Drink; not only in stylistically similar glyphs of animal-humans found in thirteenth-century burials and square ground decorations from the historical period; not only in the "numerous circular earthlodges which clearly had a ritual use" (Fairbanks 1979:121) similar to that of the roundhouse and sweat lodge; not only in fire symbolism; not only in town layout—but in the persistent drive to join together diverse Indians by means of religious ritual. For centuries the Creeks have incorporated various tribes into their Confederacy, binding them with the Busk and other rituals, and offering them sanctuary in their towns of peace. Even after the Removal to Indian Territory, they admitted outlanders to their councils—Shawnees and others— and were active in consolidating the interests of the tribes living in what is now Oklahoma. Into the twentieth century the "all-embracing internationalism of the Creeks" (Debo 1979:138) has prevailed, and by sharing his rituals and myths with fellow Indians, Phillip Deere has continued his people's ancient tradition of political consolidation.

A look at his 160 acres of land (diagram on page 209) reveals the layout of the old Creek towns (diagram on page 216), designs dating, perhaps, to the Mississippian period. Lacking the square with its ceremonial sheds—because his land lacks chiefs, elders, warriors, and so on— Phillip's property contained three focal areas: first, a roundhouse, where he held public councils and rituals. A spiral fire burned at its center; eagle heads, floral beaded pouches, feather fans, and dangling fur bedecked the four supporting posts. Benches circled the walls, and ritual decorum was demanded of all who entered. In his roundhouse Phillip combined the old functions of square and rotunda. Second, his ball field surrounded a central pole with a cow's skull at top. His family and friends played the traditional Creek ball game, men against women, according to ancient rules. His ball field lacked the military paraphernalia of eighteenth-century courts—scalps and human skulls—as the Creeks have lost their military power, and as the sweat lodge itself has become divorced from its strong military heritage, but in all else his ball field resembled that of the Old Creek towns. The third focal area for ritual consisted of three sweat lodges: one for men, one for women, and one for those in need of individual curing. In ancient Creek towns these would not have drawn attention; however, on Phillip's land they became prominent fixtures in his attempt to conserve his heritage and embrace other Indians through its integrity. All in all, he lay out his property with the intent of establishing the functional equivalent of a traditional Creek town, which Indians could enter in order to seek and find themselves. His land was sacred territory, a sanctuary in profane America, where Indians could be at home, together, at moral ease. To the Indians who stepped onto his land, sat around his roundhouse fire, played about his ball field, ate his food, slept on his ground, and crawled in and out of his sweat lodge, Phillip Deere offered an old viable Creek message: that all can be forgiven, all can be consolidated, all can be made pure, through ritual effort expressing the images of mythology.

References and Bibliographies

Preface

Momaday, N. Scott
1980   "Commencement Address," Hobart and William Smith Colleges, Geneva, NY.

Chapter 1: Mythography

Aarne, Antti and Stith Thompson
1964   *The Types of the Folktale. A Classification and Bibliography* (Helsinki: Suomalainen Tiedeakatemia, Academia Scientiarum Fennica, FF Communications, 184).

Abrahams, Roger D.
1972   "Personal Power and Social Restraint in the Definition of Folklore," *Toward New Perspectives in Folklore,* ed. Américo Paredes and Richard Bauman (Austin: University of Texas Press, Publications of the American Folklore Society, Bibliographical and Special Series, 23):16–30.

Alexander, Hartley Burr
1925   *Manito Masks. Dramatizations, with Music, of American Indian Spirit Legends* (New York: E. P. Dutton).
1964   *The Mythology of All Races, Vol. X, North American,* ed. Louis Herbert Gray (New York: Cooper Square).

Allen, Paula Gunn
1974   "The Mythopoeic Vision in Native American Literature: The Problem of Myth," *American Indian Culture and Research Journal,* 1:3–11.

Andriolo, Karin R.
1981   "Myth and History: A General Model and Its Application to the Bible," *American Anthropologist,* 83:261–84.

Arlow, Jacob A.
1961   "Ego Psychology and the Study of Mythology," *Journal of the American Psychoanalytic Association,* 9:371–93.

Bär, Eugen
n.d.   "Myth and Primary Process: A Psychoanalytic Approach, " *Ars Semiotica,* unpublished proofs.

Bartsch, Hans Werner, ed.
1961   *Kerygma and Myth. A Theological Debate* (New York: Harper & Row).

Bascom, William R.
1954   "Four Functions of Folklore," *Journal of American Folklore,* 67:333–49.
1955   "Verbal Art," *Journal of American Folklore,* 68:245–52.
1957   "The Myth-Ritual Theory," *Journal of American Folklore,* 70:103–14.
1965   "The Forms of Folklore: Prose Narratives," *Journal of American Folklore,* 78:3–20.

Basson, A. H.
1958   *David Hume* (Harmondsworth, Middlesex: Penguin).

Bateson, Gregory
1976   *Steps to an Ecology of Mind* (New York: Ballantine).

Bauman, Richard
1972   "Differential Identity and the Social Base of Folklore," *Toward New Perspectives in Folklore,* ed. Américo Paredes and Richard Bauman (Austin: University of Texas Press, Publications of the American Folklore Society, Bibliographical and Special Series, 23):31–41.

Becker, Ernest
1973   *The Denial of Death* (New York: Free Press).
1975   *Escape from Evil* (New York: Free Press).

Bedford, Gary S.
1981   "Notes on Mythological Psychology: Reimagining the Historical Psyche," *The Journal of the American Academy of Religion,* 49:231–47.

Beidelman, Thomas O.
1967   "Hyena and Rabbit: A Kagaru Representation of Matrilineal Relations," *Myth and Cosmos,* ed. John Middleton (Austin: University of Texas Press):287–301.
1970   "Myth, Legend and Oral History: A Kagaru Traditional Text," *Anthropos,* 65:74–97.

Ben-Amos, Dan
1972   "Toward a Definition of Folklore in Context," *Toward New Perspectives in Folklore,* ed. Américo Paredes and Richard Bauman (Austin: University of Texas Press, Publications of the American Folklore Society, Bibliographical and Special Series, 23):3–15.

Benedict, Ruth
1968   "Introduction to Zuni Mythology," *Studies on Mythology,* ed. Robert A. Georges (Homewood, IL: Dorsey):102–36.

Benoist, Jean-Marie et al.
1973   "Claude Lévi-Strauss's L'Homme Nu Reviewed in an International Perspective," *The Human Context,* 5:209–37.

Berggren, Douglas
1966   "From Myth to Metaphor," *The Monist,* 50:530–52.

Bettelheim, Bruno
1977   *The Uses of Enchantment. The Meaning and Importance of Fairy Tales* (New York: Random House).

Bidney, David
1950   "The Concept of Myth and the Problem of Psychocultural Evolution," *American Anthropologist,* 52:16–26.
1971   "Myth, Symbolism, and Truth," *Myth. A Symposium,* ed. Thomas A. Sebeok (Bloomington: Indiana University Press):3–24.

Bierhorst, John
1975   "American Indian Verbal Art and the Role of the Literary Critic," *Journal of American Folklore,* 88:401–8.
1976   *The Red Swan. Myths and Tales of the American Indians* (New York: Farrar, Straus and Giroux).

Boas, Franz
1905   "The Mythologies of the Indians," *The International Quarterly,* 11:327–42; 12:157–73.
1912   *Tsimshian Texts* (Leyden: E. J. Brill, Publications of the American Ethnological Society, 3):65–284.
1915   "Mythology and Folk-Tales of the North American Indians," *Anthropology in North America,* Franz Boas et al. (New York: G. E. Stechert):306–49.
1966   *Race, Language and Culture* (New York: Free Press).

Brinton, Daniel G.
1868   *The Myths of the New World* (New York: Leypoldt & Holt).

Brown, Norman O.
1959   *Life against Death. The Psychoanalytic Meaning of History* (New York: Random House).

Brown, Truesdell S.
1946   "Euhemerus and the Historians," *Harvard Theological Review,* 39:259–74.

Buchler, Ira R. and Henry A. Selby
1968   *A Formal Study of Myth* (Austin: University of Texas Press, Center for Intercultural Studies in Folklore and Oral History, Monograph Series, 1).

Bulfinch, Thomas
1967   *Bulfinch's Mythology* (London: Spring).

Bultmann, Rudolf
1958   *Jesus Christ and Mythology* (New York: Charles Scribner's Sons).

Burns, Thomas A.
1977   "Folkloristics: A Conception of Theory," *Western Folklore,* 36:109–34.

Caillois, Roger
1972   *Le Mythe et l'Homme* (n.p.: Gallimard).

Campbell, Joseph
1965   *The Masks of God: Primitive Mythology* (New York: Viking).
1969   "The Historical Development of Mythology," *Myth and Mythmaking,* ed. Henry A. Murray (Boston: Beacon):19–45.

Caponigri, A. Robert
1968   *Time and Idea. The Theory of History in Giambattista Vico* (Notre Dame: University of Notre Dame Press).

Carloye, Jack
1980   "Myths as Religious Explanations," *The Journal of the American Academy of Religion,* 48:175–89.

Carvalho-Neto, Paulo de
1972   *Folklore and Psychoanalysis,* trans. Jacques M. P. Wilson (Coral Gables, FL: University of Miami Press).

Cassirer, Ernst
1953   *Language and Myth,* trans. Susanne K. Langer (New York: Dover).
1955   *The Philosophy of Symbolic Forms, Vol. 2: Mythical Thought,* trans. Ralph Manheim (New Haven: Yale University Press).

Chase, Richard
1969   *Quest for Myth* (New York: Greenwood).

Codère, Hélène
    1974   "La Geste du Chien d'Asdiwal: The Story of Mac," *American Anthropologist,*
                76:42–47.

Cohen, Percy S.
    1969   "Theories of Myth," *Man (The Journal of the Royal Anthropological Institute),*
                n.s., 4:337–53.

Colby, Benjamin N.
    1966   "The Analysis of Culture Content and the Patterning of Narrative Concern in
                Texts," *American Anthropologist,* 68:374–88.
    1973a   "Analytical Procedures in Eidochronic Study," *Journal of American Folklore,*
                86:14–24.
    1973b   "A Partial Grammar of Eskimo Folktales," *American Anthropologist,* 75:645–
                62.

Colby, Benjamin N. and Michael Cole
    1973   "Culture, Memory and Narrative," *Modes of Thought. Essays on Thinking in
                Western and Non-Western Societies,* ed. Robin Horton and Ruth Finnegan
                (London: Faber & Faber):63–91.

Colby, Benjamin N., George A. Collier, and Susan K. Postal
    1963   "Comparison of Themes in Folktales by the General Inquirer System," *Journal
                of American Folklore,* 76:318–23.

Cooke, John Daniel
    1927   "Euhemerism: A Mediaeval Interpretation of Classical Paganism," *Speculum,*
                2:396–410.

Cords, Nicholas and Patrick Gerster, eds.
    1973   *Myth and the American Experience* (Beverly Hills: Glencoe).

Cornford, Francis MacDonald, trans.
    1970–72   *The Republic of Plato* (London: Oxford University Press).

Cox, David
    1961   *History and Myth. The World around Us and the World within* (London:
                Darton, Longman & Todd).

Cox, Howard L.
    1948   "The Place of Mythology in the Study of Culture," *American Imago,* 5:83–
                94.

Culler, Jonathan and Howard Gardner
    1973   "The Impact of Structuralism," *The Human Context,* 5, 35–67.

Cunningham, Adrian
    1973   "Myth, Ideology, and Lévi-Strauss: The Problem of the Genesis Story in the
                Nineteenth Century," *The Theory of Myth. Six Studies,* ed. Adrian Cunningham
                (London: Sheed and Ward):132–76.

Curtin, Jeremiah
    1898   *Creation Myths of Primitive America in Relation to the Religious History
                and Mental Development of Mankind* (Boston: Little, Brown).

Daniélou, Jean
    1969   "The Word Goes Forth," *The Crucible of Christianity,* ed. Arnold Toynbee
                (New York: World):283–98.

Dawson, Christopher
    1958   *Religion and the Rise of Western Culture* (Garden City, NY: Image).

Demetracopoulou, D.
1933   "The Loon Woman Myth: A Study in Synthesis," *Journal of American Folklore,*
        46:101–28.

Demetracopoulou, D. and Cora Du Bois
1932   "A Study of Wintu Mythology," *Journal of American Folklore,* 45:373–500.

Devereux, George
1971   "Art and Mythology: A General Theory," *Art and Aesthetics in Primitive So-
        cieties,* ed. Carol F. Jopling (New York: E. P. Dutton):193–224.

Diamond, Stanley
1974   *In Search of the Primitive. A Critique of Civilization* (New Brunswick, NJ:
        Transaction).

Donaldson, Mara E.
1981   "Kinship Theory in the Patriarchal Narratives: The Case of the Barren Wife,"
        The Journal of the American Academy of Religion, 49:77–87.

Dorson, Richard M.
1969   "Theories of Myth and the Folklorist," *Myth and Mythmaking,* ed. Henry A.
        Murray (Boston: Beacon):76–89.
1971   "The Eclipse of Solar Mythology," *Myth. A Symposium,* ed. Thomas A. Sebeok
        (Bloomington: Indiana University Press):25–63.
1972   *Folklore: Selected Essays* (Bloomington: Indiana University Press).
1976   *Folklore and Fakelore. Essays toward a Discipline of Folk Studies* (Cambridge:
        Harvard University Press).

Doty, William G.
1980   "Mythophiles' Dyscrasia: A Comprehensive Definition of Myth," *The Journal
        of the American Academy of Religion,* 48:531–62.
1986   *Mythography. The Study of Myths and Rituals* (University: University of Al-
        abama Press).

Douglas, Mary
1976   "The Meaning of Myth," *The Structural Study of Myth and Totemism,* ed.
        Edmund Leach (London: Tavistock):49–69.

Douglas, Wallace W.
1952–53 "The Meanings of 'Myth' in Modern Criticism," *Modern Philology,* 22:232–
        42.

Doyle, Arthur Conan
1930   *The Complete Sherlock Holmes* (Garden City, NY: Doubleday).

Drake, Carlos C.
1967   "Jung and His Critics," *Journal of American Folklore,* 80:321–33.
1969   "Jungian Psychology and Its Uses in Folklore," *Journal of American Folklore,*
        82:122–31.

Dundes, Alan
1962a   "Earth-Diver: Creation of the Mythopoeic Male," *American Anthropologist,*
        64:1032–51.
1962b   "From Etic to Emic Units in the Structural Study of Folktales," *Journal of
        American Folklore,* 75:95–105.
1964a   *The Morphology of North American Indian Folktales* (Helsinki: Suomalainen
        Tiedeakatemia Academia Scientiarum Fennica, Folklore Fellows Communi-
        cations, 195).

1964b   "Texture, Text, and Context," *Southern Folklore Quarterly*, 28:251–65.
1965a   "On Computers and Folk Tales," *Western Folklore*, 24:185–89.
1965b   "Structural Typology in North American Indian Folktales," *The Study of Folklore*, ed. Alan Dundes (Englewood Cliffs, NJ: Prentice-Hall):206–15.
1966   "Metafolklore and Oral Literary Criticism," *The Monist*, 50:505–16.
1971   "The Making and Breaking of Friendship as a Structural Frame in African Folk Tales," *Structural Analysis of Oral Tradition*, ed. Pierre Maranda and Elli Köngäs Maranda (Philadelphia: University of Pennsylvania Press):171–85.
1972   "Folk Ideas as Units of Worldview," *Toward New Perspectives in Folklore*, ed. Américo Paredes and Richard Bauman (Austin: University of Texas Press, Publications of the American Folklore Society, Bibliographical and Special Series, 23):93–103.

Dundes, Alan et al.
1971   "An Experiment: Suggestions and Queries from the Desk, with a Reply from the Ethnographer," *Structural Analysis of Oral Tradition*, ed. Pierre Maranda and Elli Köngäs Maranda (Philadelphia: University of Pennsylvania Press):292–324.

Dunne, John S.
1975   *Time and Myth* (Notre Dame: University of Notre Dame Press).

Dupré, Wilhelm
1975   *Religion in Primitive Cultures. A Study in Ethnophilosophy* (The Hague: Mouton).

Durkheim, Émile
1915   *The Elementary Forms of the Religious Life*, trans. Joseph Ward Swain (London: George Allen & Unwin).

Eggan, Dorothy
1971   "The Personal Use of Myth in Dreams," *Myth. A Symposium*, ed. Thomas A. Sebeok (Bloomington: Indiana University Press):107–21.

Ehrlich, Clara
1937   "Tribal Culture in Crow Mythology," *Journal of American Folklore*, 50:307–408.

Eliade, Mircea
1957   *Mythes, rêves et mystères* (n.p.: Gallimard).
1959a   *Cosmos and History. The Myth of the Eternal Return*, trans. Willard R. Trask (New York: Harper & Row).
1959b   *The Sacred and the Profane. The Nature of Religion*, trans., Willard R. Trask (New York: Harcourt, Brace & World).
1961   *Images and Symbols. Studies in Religious Symbolism*, trans. Philip Mairet (London: Harvill).
1963   *Aspects du Mythe* (n.p.: Gallimard).
1969   "The Yearning for Paradise in Primitive Tradition," *Myth and Mythmaking*, ed. Henry A. Murray (Boston: Beacon):61–75.
1970   *Patterns in Comparative Religion*, trans. Rosemary Sheed (Cleveland: World).

Farnell, L. R.
1919–20 "The Value and the Methods of Mythologic Study," *Proceedings of the British Academy*, 9:37–51.

Feldman, Burton and Robert D. Richardson
1972   *The Rise of Modern Mythology 1680–1860* (Bloomington: Indiana University Press).

Findlay, J. N.
1980   "The Myths of Plato," *Myth, Symbol, and Reality,* ed. Alan M. Olson (Notre Dame: University of Notre Dame Press):165–83.

Finley, M. I.
1965   "Myth, Memory, and History," *History and Theory,* 4:281–302.

Finnegan, Ruth
1970   *Oral Literature in Africa* (Oxford: Clarendon).
1973   "Literacy Versus Non-Literacy: The Great Divide?," *Modes of Thought. Essays on Thinking in Western and Non-Western Societies* (London: Faber & Faber).

Fischer, J. L.
1963   "The Sociopsychological Analysis of Folktales," with comments, *Current Anthropology,* 4:235–95.

Fisher, John F.
1975   "An Analysis of the Central Eskimo Sedna Myth," *Temenos,* 11:27–42.

Flint, Robert
1884   *Vico* (Edinburgh: William Blackwood and Sons).

Fontana, Bernard L.
1969   "American Indian Oral History: An Anthropologist's Note," *History and Theory,* 8:366–70.

Fontenrose, Joseph
1966   *The Ritual Theory of Myth* (Berkeley: University of California Press, Folklore Studies, 18).

Fortes, Meyer
1960   "Oedipus and Job in West African Religion," *Anthropology of Folk Religion,* ed. Charles Leslie (New York: Random House): 5–49.

Frankfort, Henri et al.
1967   *Before Philosophy. The Intellectual Adventure of Ancient Man* (Baltimore: Penguin).

Frazer, James George
1913   *The Belief in Immortality and the Worship of the Dead,* 3 vols. (London: Macmillan), 1.
1926   *The Worship of Nature,* 3 vols. (London: Macmillan), 1.
1927   *Man, God and Immortality. Thoughts on Human Progress* (London: Macmillan).
1930   *Myths of the Origin of Fire* (London: Macmillan).
1933   *The Fear of the Dead in Primitive Religion* (London: Macmillan).
1964   *The New Golden Bough,* ed. Theodor H. Gaster (New York: New American Library).

Freilich, Morris
1975   "Myth, Method, and Madness," *Current Anthropology,* 16:207–26.

Freud, Sigmund
1927   *The Future of an Illusion,* trans. W. D. Robson-Scott (Garden City, NY: Doubleday).
1931   *Totem and Taboo. Resemblances between the Psychic Lives of Savages and Neurotics,* trans. A. A. Brill (New York: New Republic).
1962   *Civilization and Its Discontents,* trans. James Strachey (New York: W. W. Norton).
1970   *Character and Culture,* ed. Philip Rieff (New York: Collier).

1977   *Introductory Lectures on Psychoanalysis,* trans. and ed. James Strachey (New
          York: W. W. Norton).

Fried, Morton H.
1975   *The Notion of Tribe* (Menlo Park, CA: Cummings).

Fulbright, James William
1964   *Old Myths and New Realities* (New York: Random House).

Gadamer, Hans-Georg
1980   "Religious and Poetical Speaking," *Myth, Symbol, and Reality,* ed. Alan M.
          Olson (Notre Dame: University of Notre Dame Press): 86–98.

Gaster, Theodor H.
1954   "Myth and Story," *Numen,* 1:184–212.
1966   *Thespis. Ritual, Myth, and Drama in the Ancient Near East* (New York: Harper
          & Row).

Gennep, Arnold van
1910   *La formation des légendes* (Paris: E. Flammarion).

Georges, Robert A.
1968   *Studies on Mythology* (Homewood, IL: Dorsey).
1969   "Toward an Understanding of Storytelling Events," *Journal of American
          Folklore,* 82:313–28.

Gibbs, Lee W. and W. Taylor Stevenson, eds.
1975   *Myth and the Crisis of Historical Consciousness* (Missoula, MT: Scholars
          Press).

Gilsenan, Michael
1972   "Myth and the History of African Religion," *The Historical Study of African
          Religion,* ed. T. O. Ranger and I. N. Kimambo (London: Heinemann): 50–70.

Godelier, Maurice
1971   "Myth and History," *New Left Review,* 69:93–112.

Goldfrank, Esther Schiff
1926   "Isleta Variants: A Study in Flexibility," *Journal of American Folklore,* 39:
          70–78.

Goodman, Lisl M.
1981   *Death and the Creative Life* (New York: Springer).

Graves, Robert
1959   "Introduction," *Larousse Encyclopedia of Mythology* (London: Paul Hamlyn):
          v–viii.

Graves, Robert and Raphael Patai
1964   *Hebrew Myths: The Book of Genesis* (New York: McGraw-Hill).

Greenway, John
1964   *Literature among the Primitives* (Hatboro, PA: Folklore Associates).

Greimas, A. J.
1973   "Comparative Mythology," *Mythology,* ed. Pierre Maranda (Harmondsworth,
          Middlesex: Penguin): 162–70.

Grimal, Pierre
1965   "Introduction: Man and Myth," *Larousse World Mythology,* trans. Patricia
          Beardsworth (London: Paul Hamlyn): 8–15.

Guerra, Francisco
1971   *The Pre-Columbian Mind* (London: Seminar).

Hadas, Moses and Morton Smith
1965   *Heroes and Gods. Spiritual Biographies in Antiquity* (New York: Harper & Row).

Hamilton, Edith
1942   *Mythology* (New York: New American Library).

Harnack, Adolf
1962   *The Mission and Expansion of Christianity in the First Three Centuries* (New York: Harper & Brothers).

Harrison, Jane Ellen
1969   *Themis. A Study of the Social Origins of Greek Religion* (Cleveland: World).

Hassan, Ihab H.
1952   "Towards a Method in Myth," *Journal of American Folklore,* 65:205–15.

Heidegger, Martin
1968   *What Is Called Thinking?,* trans. J. Glenn Gray and F. Wieck (New York: Harper & Row).

Henige, David P.
1974   *The Chronology of Oral Tradition. Quest for a Chimera* (Oxford: Clarendon).

Herskovits, Melville J.
1946   "Folklore after a Hundred Years: A Problem in Redefinition," *Journal of American Folklore,* 59:89–100.

Herskovits, Melville J. and Frances S. Herskovits
1958a   *Dahomean Narrative. A Cross-Cultural Analysis* (Evanston, IL.: Northwestern University Press, African Studies, 1).
1958b   "Sibling Rivalry, the Oedipus Complex, and Myth," *Journal of American Folklore,* 71:1–15.

Heusch, Luc de
1975   "What Shall We Do with the Drunken King?," *Africa,* 45:363–72.

Hewitt, J. N. B.
1959   "Mythology," *Handbook of American Indians North of Mexico,* ed. Frederick Webb Hodge, 2 vols. (New York: Pageant), 1:964–72.

Hocart, A. M.
1916   "The Common Sense of Myth," *American Anthropologist,* 18:307–18.
1952   *The Life-Giving Myth and Other Essays* (London: Methuen).

Honko, Lauri
1968   "Genre Analysis in Folkloristics and Comparative Religion," *Temenos,* 3:48–66.
1972   *The Problem of Defining Myth* (Helsinki: Finnish Society for the Study of Comparative Religion, Studies on Religion, Articles and Reprints, 2).

Hooke, S. H., ed.
1933   *Myth and Ritual: Essays on the Myth and Ritual of the Hebrews in Relation to Culture Patterns of the Ancient Near East* (London: Oxford University Press).
1958   *Myth, Ritual, and Kingship. Essays on the Theory and Practice of Kingship in the Ancient Near East and in Israel* (London: Oxford University Press).

Hubbard, Caroline
1973   "Lévi-Strauss: An Anthropological Critique," *The Theory of Myth. Six Studies,* ed. Adrian Cunningham (London: Sheed and Ward): 79–103.

Hudson, Wilson M.
   1966   "Jung on Myth and the Mythic," *The Sunny Slopes of Long Ago,* ed. Wilson
            M. Hudson and Allen Maxwell (Dallas: Southern Methodist University Press,
            Publications of the Texas Folklore Society, 33): 181–97.

Hultkrantz, Åke
   1956   "Religious Tradition, Comparative Religion and Folklore," *Ethnos,* 21:11–29.
   1960   "Religious Aspects of the Wind River Shoshoni Folk Literature," *Culture in
            History. Essays in Honor of Paul Radin,* ed. Stanley Diamond (New York:
            Columbia University Press): 552–69.
   1969   "Review of Mythologiques: Origine des manières de tables, by Claude Lévi-
            Strauss," *American Anthropologist,* 71:734–7.
   1972   "An Ideological Dichotomy: Myths and Folk Beliefs among the Shoshoni Indians
            of Wyoming," *History of Religions,* 11:339–53.
   1977   "History of Religions in Anthropological Waters: Some Reflections against the
            Background of American Data," *Temenos,* 13:81–97.
   1979   "Myths in Native North American Religions," *Native Religious Traditions,*
            ed. Earle H. Waugh and K. Dad Prithipaul (Waterloo, Ontario: Wilfred Laurier
            University Press, Studies in Religion, 8): 77–97.

Hume, David
   1947   *Dialogues Concerning Natural Religion,* ed. Norman Kemp Smith (London:
   [1779]   Thomas Nelson and Sons).
   1956   *The Natural History of Religion,* ed. H. E. Root (London: Adam & Charles
   [1757]   Black).

Huntington, Richard and Peter Metcalf
   1979   *Celebrations of Death: The Anthropology of Mortuary Ritual* (Cambridge:
            Cambridge University Press).

Hyman, Stanley Edgar
   1971   "The Ritual View of Myth and the Mythic," *Myth. A Symposium,* ed. Thomas
            A. Sebeok (Bloomington: Indiana University Press):136–53.
   1974   *The Tangled Bank. Darwin, Marx, Frazer and Freud as Imaginative Writers*
            (New York: Atheneum).

Hymes, Dell
   1971   "The 'Wife' Who 'Goes Out' Like a Man: Reinterpretation of a Clackamas Chi-
            nook Myth," *Structural Analysis of Oral Tradition,* ed. Pierre Maranda and
            Elli Köngäs Maranda (Philadelphia: University of Pennsylvania Press):49–80.

Jacobs, Melville
   1952   "Psychological Inferences from a Chinook Myth," *Journal of American Folk-
            lore,* 65:121–37.
   1960   *The People Are Coming Soon. Analyses of Clackamas Chinook Myths and
            Tales* (Seattle: University of Washington Press).
   1971   *The Content and Style of an Oral Literature. Clackamas Chinook Myths and
            Tales* (Chicago: University of Chicago Press).

Jacobs, Melville and John Greenway, comps. and eds.
   1966   *The Anthropologist Looks at Myth* (Austin: University of Texas Press, Pub-
            lications of the American Folklore Society, Bibliographical and Special Series,
            17).

James, E. O.
   1938   *Comparative Religion. An Introduction and Historical Study* (London: Me-
            thuen).

1957   "The Nature and Function of Myth," *Folk-Lore,* 68:474–82.

Jason, Heda
1973   "The Genre in Oral Literature: An Attempt at Interpretation, *Temenos,* 9:156–60.

Jaspers, Karl and Rudolf Bultmann
1958   *Myth and Christianity. An Inquiry into the Possibility of Religion without Myth* (New York: Noonday).

Jensen, Adolf E.
1973   *Myth and Cult among Primitive Peoples,* trans. Marianna Tax Choldin and Wolfgang Weissleder (Chicago: University of Chicago Press).

Jones, Ernest
1965   "Psychoanalysis and Folklore," *The Study of Folklore,* ed. Alan Dundes (Englewood Cliffs, NJ: Prentice-Hall):88–102.

Jung, Carl Gustav
1963   *Memories, Dreams, Reflections,* ed. Aniela Jaffe (New York: Random House).
1964   "Approaching the Unconscious," *Man and His Symbols,* ed. Carl Gustav Jung (Garden City, NY: Doubleday):18–103.
1969   *Psychology and Religion* (New Haven: Yale University Press).

Jung, Carl Gustav and C. Kerényi
1969   *Essays on a Science of Mythology. The Myth of the Divine Child and the Mysteries of Eleusis,* trans. R. F. C. Hull (Princeton, NJ: Princeton University Press, Bollingen Series, 22).

Kellogg, Robert
1973   "Oral Literature," *New Literary History,* 5:55–66.

Kirk, G. S.
1973   *Myth. Its Meaning and Functions in Ancient and Other Cultures* (Cambridge: Cambridge University Press).

Kluckhohn, Clyde
1968   "Myths and Rituals: A General Theory," *Studies on Mythology,* ed. Robert A. Georges (Homewood, IL: Dorsey):137–67.
1969   "Recurrent Themes in Myths and Mythmaking," *Myth and Mythmaking,* ed. Henry A. Murray (Boston: Beacon):46–60.

Koehl, Richard
1966   "Symbolism and Myth," *The Monist,* 50:611–25.

Köngäs, Elli Kaija
1960   "The Earth Diver (Th. A 812)," *Ethnohistory,* 7:151–80.

Kroeber, A. L.
1908   "Catch-words in American Mythology," *Journal of American Folklore,* 21:222–27.
1951   "A Mohave Historical Epic," *Anthropological Records,* 11:71–176.

Kroeber, Karl
1979   "Deconstructionist Criticism and American Indian Literature," *Boundary 2,* 7:73–89.

La Barre, Weston
1948   "Folklore and Psychology," *Journal of American Folklore,* 61:382–90.

Lafitau, Joseph François
1974   *Customs of the American Indians Compared with the Customs of Primitive*

[1724]   *Times*, ed. and trans. William N. Fenton and Elizabeth L. Moore, 2 vols. (Toronto: Champlain Society Publications, 48).

Lambing, Andrew Arnold
1885   "Supposed Vestiges of Early Christian Teaching in the New World," *Catholic Historical Researches*, 2:41–54.

Lang, Andrew
1887   *Myth, Ritual, and Religion*, 2 vols. (London: Longmans, Green).

Langer, Susanne K.
1951   *Philosophy in a New Key. A Study in the Symbolism of Reason, Rite, and Art* (New York: New American Library).

Lantis, Margaret
1953   "Nunivak Eskimo Personality as Revealed in the Mythology," *Anthropological Papers of the University of Alaska*, 2:109–74.

Law, R. C. C.
1973   "Traditional History," *Sources of Yoruba History*, ed. S. O. Biobaku (Oxford: Clarendon):25–40.

Lawson, E. Thomas
1978   "The Explanation of Myth and Myth as Explanation," *The Journal of the American Academy of Religion*, 46:507–23.

Leach, Edmund
1961   "Lévi-Strauss in the Garden of Eden: An Examination of Some Recent Developments in the Analysis of Myth," *New York Academy of Sciences, Transactions*, 2:386–96.
1969   *Genesis as Myth and Other Essays* (London: Jonathan Cape).
1976a   *Culture and Communication: The Logic by Which Symbols Are Connected* (Cambridge: Cambridge University Press).
1976b   "Introduction," *The Structural Study of Myth and Totemism*, ed. Edmund Leach (London: Tavistock):vi–xix.

Leo, John
1968   "Analyst Calls Death of Myths a Healthy Sign," *New York Times*, 25 November:49.

Lessa, William A.
1965   "On the Symbolism of Oedipus," *The Study of Folklore*, ed. Alan Dundes (Englewood Cliffs, NJ: Prentice-Hall):114–25.
1973   " 'Discoverer-of-the-Sun': Mythology as a Reflection of Culture," *Mythology*, ed. Pierre Maranda (Baltimore: Penguin):71–110.

Levin, Harry
1969   "Some Meanings of Myth," *Myth and Mythmaking*, ed. Henry A. Murray (Boston: Beacon):103–14.

Lévi-Strauss, Claude
1962   *La pensée sauvage* (Paris: Plon).
1963   *Structural Anthropology*, trans. Claude Jacobson and Brooke Grundfest Schoepf (New York: Basic Books).
1967   "Four Winnebago Myths: A Structural Sketch," *Myth and Cosmos*, ed. John Middleton (Austin: University of Texas Press):15–26.
1969   *The Raw and the Cooked. Introduction to a Science of Mythology: 1*, trans. John Weightman and Doreen Weightman (New York: Harper & Row).
1971   "The Science of the Concrete," *Art and Aesthetics in Primitive Societies*, ed. Carol F. Jopling (New York: E. P. Dutton):225–49.

1974   *From Honey to Ashes. Introduction to a Science of Mythology: 2*, trans. John Weightman and Doreen Weightman (New York: Harper & Row).

1975   *Le voie des masques*, 2 vols. (Genève: Albert Skira).

1976   "The Story of Asdiwal," *The Structural Study of Myth and Totemism*, ed. Edmund Leach (London: Tavistock):1–47.

Lifton, Robert Jay

1979   *On Death and the Continuity of Life* (New York: Simon and Schuster).

Littleton, G. Scott

1965   "A Two-Dimensional Scheme for the Classification of Narratives," *Journal of American Folklore*, 78:21–27.

Lord, Albert B.

1973   *The Singer of Tales* (New York: Atheneum).

Lowie, Robert H.

1908a   "Catch-Words for Mythological Motives," *Journal of American Folklore*, 21:24–27.

1908b   "The Test-Theme in North American Mythology," *Journal of American Folklore*, 21:97–148.

1942   *Studies in Plains Indian Folklore* (Berkeley: University of California Press).

Luomala, Katherine

1940   *Oceanic, American Indian, and African Myths of Snaring the Sun* (Honolulu: Bernice P. Bishop Museum, Bulletin 168).

Malinowski, Bronislaw

1925   "Complex and Myth in Mother-Right," *Psyche*, 5:194–216.

1954   *Magic, Science and Religion* (Garden City, NY: Doubleday).

Manuel, Frank E.

1959   *The Eighteenth Century Confronts the Gods* (Cambridge: Harvard University Press).

Maranda, Pierre, ed.

1973   *Mythology* (Baltimore: Penguin).

Maranda, Pierre and Elli Köngäs Maranda, eds.

1971a   *Structural Analysis of Oral Tradition* (Philadelphia: University of Pennsylvania Press).

1971b   *Structural Models in Folklore and Transformational Essays* (The Hague: Mouton, Approaches to Semiotics, 10).

Marx, Karl

1977   *Capital. A Critique of Political Economy*, 3 vols, trans. Ben Fowkes (New York: Random House), 1.

McElwain, Thomas

1978   *Mythological Tales and the Allegany Seneca* (Stockholm: Acta Universitatis Stockholmiensis, Stockholm Studies in Comparative Religion, 17).

Middleton, John

1967   "Some Social Aspects of Lugbara Myth," *Myth and Cosmos*, ed. John Middleton (Austin: University of Texas Press):47–61.

Miller, Robert J.

1952   "Situation and Sequence in the Study of Folklore," *Journal of American Folklore*, 65:29–48.

Moon, Sheila

1974   *A Magic Dwells. A Poetic and Psychological Study of the Navaho Emergence Myth* (Middletown, CT: Wesleyan University Press).

Moore, Tim
    1973   "The Analysis of Stories," *The Theory of Myth. Six Studies,* ed. Adrian Cunningham (London: Sheed and Ward):22–39.

Müller, F. Max
    1867   *Chips from a German Workshop,* 2 vols. (London: Longmans, Green), 2: *Essays on Mythology, Traditions, and Customs.*
    1885   *Lectures on the Science of Language,* 2 vols. (London: Longmans, Green).

Munz, Peter
    1973   *When the Golden Bough Breaks. Structuralism or Typology?* (London: Routledge & Kegan Paul).

Murray, Henry A.
    1969   "The Possible Nature of a 'Mythology' to Come," *Myth and Mythmaking,* ed. Henry A. Murray (Boston: Beacon): 300–353.

Nathhorst, Bertel
    1970   *Formal or Structural Studies of Traditional Tales* (Stockholm: Acta Universitatis Stockholmiensis, Stockholm Studies in Comparative Religion, 9).

Noss, Philip A.
    1977   "The Performance of the Gbaya Tale," *Forms of Folklore in Africa. Narrative, Poetic, Gnomic, Dramatic,* ed. Bernth Lindfors (Austin: University of Texas Press):135–43.

Olcott, William Tyler
    1914   *Myths of the Sun (Sun Lore of All Ages)* (New York: Capricorn).

Oliver, Harold H.
    1980   "Relational Ontology and Hermeneutics," *Myth, Symbol, and Reality,* ed. Alan M. Olson (Notre Dame: University of Notre Dame Press):69–85.

Olson, Alan M.
    1980a.   "Introduction," *Myth, Symbol, and Reality,* ed. Alan M. Olson (Notre Dame: University of Notre Dame Press):1–12.
    1980b   "Myth, Symbol, and Metaphorical Truth," *Myth, Symbol, and Reality,* ed. Alan M. Olson (Notre Dame: University of Notre Dame Press):99–125.

Parrinder, Geoffrey
    1962   *Comparative Religion* (London: George Allen & Unwin).

Patai, Raphael
    1972   *Myth and Modern Man* (Englewood Cliffs, NJ: Prentice-Hall).

Peck, William Jay
    1968   "Structure and History in Myth Interpretation," *Paideuma,* 14:148–54.

Peek, Philip M.
    1978   "Attitudes towards the Creation of Verbal Art," New York State African Studies Association Meeting, New York.

Perry, W. J.
    1973   *The Primordial Ocean. An Introductory Contribution to Social Psychology* (London: Methuen).

Pettazzoni, Raffaele
    1954   *Essays on the History of Religions,* trans. H. J. Rose (Leiden: E. J. Brill).

Powell, John Wesley
    1881   *Sketch of the Mythology of the North American Indians* (Washington, DC: Government Printing Office).

Propp, Vladimir
1973   *Morphology of the Folktale* (Austin: University of Texas Press).

Radcliffe-Brown, A. R.
1968   "The Interpretation of Andamanese Customs and Beliefs: Myths and Legends," *Studies on Mythology,* ed. Robert A. Georges (Homewood, IL: Dorsey):46–71.

Radin, Paul
1926   "Literary Aspects of Winnebago Mythology," *Journal of American Folklore,* 39:18–52.
1973   *Literary Aspects of North American Mythology* (Norwood, PA: Norwood).

Raglan, Fitzroy Richard Somerset
1971   "Myth and Ritual," *Myth. A Symposium,* ed. Thomas A. Sebeok (Bloomington: Indiana University Press):122–35.

Rahner, Hugo
1963   *Greek Myths and Christian Mystery,* trans. Brian Battershaw (London: Burns & Oates).

Rahv, Philip
1953   "The Myth and the Powerhouse," *Partisan Review,* 20:635–48.

Ramsey, Jarold
1978   "From 'Mythic' to 'Fictive' in a Nez Perce Orpheus Myth," *Western American Literature,* 13:119–32.

Randle, Martha Champion
1952   "Psychological Types from Iroquois Folktales," *Journal of American Folklore,* 65:13–21.

Reichard, Gladys A.
1921   "Literary Types and Dissemination of Myths," *Journal of American Folklore,* 34:269–307.
1944   "Individualism and Mythological Style," *Journal of American Folklore,* 57:16–25.
1947   *An Analysis of Coeur D'Alene Indian Myths* (Philadelphia: American Folklore Society).

Reik, Theodor
1957   *Myth and Guilt. The Crime and Punishment of Mankind* (New York: George Braziller).

Reinach, Salomon
1931   *Orpheus. A History of Religions* (London: George Routledge).

Reinitz, Richard
1969   "Cubism and the Writing of History," *University of Denver Quarterly,* 4:7–16.

Reno, Stephen J.
1973   "Myth in Profile," *Temenos,* 9:38–54.

Ricoeur, Paul
1967   *The Symbolism of Evil,* trans. Emerson Buchanan (New York: Harper & Row, Religious Perspectives, 17).

Rivers, W. H. R.
1968   "The Sociological Significance of Myth," *Studies on Mythology,* ed. Robert A. Georges (Homewood, IL: Dorsey):27–45.

Robertson, John M.
1910   *Christianity and Mythology* (London: Watts).

Róheim, Géza
1922   "Psycho-analysis and the Folk-tale," *International Journal of Psycho-analysis,* 3:180–86.
1930   *Animism, Magic, and the Divine King* (London: Kegan Paul, Trench, Trubner).
1941   "Myth and Folk-tale," *American Imago,* 2:266–79.
1950   *Psychoanalysis and Anthropology. Culture, Personality and the Unconscious* (New York: International Universities).

Rossi, Ino
1973   "The Unconscious in the Anthropology of Claude Lévi-Strauss," *American Anthropologist,* 75:20–48.

Rowe, William L.
1966   "Tillich's Theory of Signs and Symbols," *The Monist,* 50:593–610.

Ruthven, K. K.
1976   *Myth* (London: Methuen, The Critical Idiom, 31).

Saliba, John A.
1974   "The New Ethnography and the Study of Religion," *Journal for the Scientific Study of Religion,* 13:145–59.
1975   "The Virgin-Birth Debate in Anthropological Literature: A Critical Assessment," *Theological Studies,* 36:428–54.
1976   "Religion and the Anthropologists: 1960–1976," Paper presented at American Academy of Religion Annual Meeting, St. Louis.

Santillana, Giorgio de and Hertha von Dechend
1969   *Hamlet's Mill. An Essay on Myth and the Frame of Time* (Boston: Gambit).

Scheub, Harold
1972   "The Art of Nongenile Mazithathu Zenani, a Gcaleka Ntsomi Performer," *African Folklore,* ed. Richard M. Dorson (Garden City, NY: Doubleday):115–42.
1977   "The Technique of the Expansible Image in Xhosa Ntsomi-Performances," *Forms of Folklore in Africa. Narrative, Poetic, Gnomic, Dramatic,* ed. Bernth Lindfors (Austin: University of Texas Press):37–63.

Seznec, Jean
1953   *The Survival of the Pagan Gods* (New York: Pantheon, Bollingen Series, 38).

Sharpe, Eric J.
1971   *Fifty Key Words. Comparative Religion* (Richmond, VA: John Knox).

Simmons, Donald C.
1961   "Analysis of Cultural Reflection in Efik Folktales," *Journal of American Folklore,* 74:126–41.

Smith, Jonathan Z.
1972   "I Am a Parrot (Red)," *History of Religions,* 11:391–413.

Smith, Robert Jerome
1969   "The Concept of Equivalence: A Polemical Analysis," *Journal of American Folklore,* 82:329–41.

Snyder, Gary
1979   *He Who Hunted Birds in His Father's Village. The Dimensions of a Haida Myth* (Bolinas, CA: Grey Fox).

Sontag, Frederick
1966   "A Metaphysics of Mythical Meaning," *The Monist,* 50:565–76.

Spence, Lewis
1931   *An Introduction to Mythology* (London: George G. Harrap).
1961   *The Outlines of Mythology* (Greenwich, CT: Fawcett).
1975   *Myths and Legends of the North American Indians* (Blauvelt, NY: Multimedia).

Spencer, Katherine
1947   *Reflection of Social Life in the Navaho Origin Myth* (Albuquerque: University of New Mexico Publications in Anthropology, 3).

Sproul, Barbara Chamberlain
1972   "Prolegomena to the Study of Creation Myths," unpublished Ph.D. dissertation, Columbia University.

Stern, Theodore
1963   "Ideal and Expected Behavior as Seen in Klamath Mythology," *Journal of American Folklore,* 76:21–30.

Stevenson, W. Taylor
1969   *History as Myth. The Import for Contemporary Theology* (New York: Seabury).

Strenski, Ivan
1973   "Mircea Eliade: Some Theoretical Problems," *The Theory of Myth. Six Studies,* ed. Adrian Cunningham (London: Sheed and Ward): 40–78.

Stross, Brian
1972   "Serial Order in Nez Percé Myths," *Toward New Perspectives in Folklore,* ed. Américo Paredes and Richard Bauman (Austin: University of Texas Press, Publications of the American Folklore Society, Bibliographical and Special Series, 23): 104–13.

Susman, Warren I.
1964   "History and the American Intellectual: Uses of a Usable Past," *American Quarterly,* 16:243–63.

Swanton, John R.
1907   "A Concordance of American Myths," *Journal of American Folklore,* 20:220–22.
1910   "Some Practical Aspects of the Study of Myths," *Journal of American Folklore,* 23:1–7.

Taylor, A.E.
1927   *David Hume and the Miraculous* (Cambridge: Cambridge University Press).

Tedlock, Dennis
1972a   *Finding the Center. Narrative Poetry of the Zuni Indians* (New York: Dial).
1972b   "On the Translation of Style in Oral Narrative," *Toward New Perspectives in Folklore,* ed. Américo Paredes and Richard Bauman (Austin: University of Texas Press, Publications of the American Folklore Society, Bibliographical and Special Series, 23): 114–33.
1972c   "Pueblos Literature: Style and Verisimilitude," *New Perspectives on the Pueblos,* ed. Alfonso Ortiz (Albuquerque: University of New Mexico Press): 219–42.
1980   "The Spoken Word and the Work of Interpretation in American Indian Religion," *Myth, Symbol, and Reality,* ed. Alan M. Olson (Notre Dame: University of Notre Dame Press): 129–44.

Thomas, L. L., J. Z. Kronenfeld, and D. B. Kronenfeld
1976   "Asdiwal Crumbles: A Critique of Lévi-Straussian Myth Analysis," *American Ethnologist,* 3:147–73.

Thompson, Stith
1946   *The Folktale* (New York: Holt, Rinehart and Winston).
1955–58 *Motif-Index of Folk-Literature,* 6 vols. (Bloomington: Indiana University Press).
1968   *Tales of the North American Indians* (Bloomington: Indiana University Press).
1971   "Myth and Folktales," *Myth. A Symposium,* ed. Thomas A. Sebeok (Bloomington: Indiana University Press): 169–80.

Thousendfriend, Gigi
1971   "Christ as a Symbol of the Self in the Psychology of Carl Gustav Jung," unpublished M.A. thesis, Northwestern University.

Tillich, Paul
1967   *Systematic Theology* (Chicago: University of Chicago Press).
1969   *What Is Religion?,* ed. James Luther Adams (New York: Harper & Row).

Titiev, Mischa
1952   "Folklore as an Expression of Araucanian Culture," *Journal of American Folklore,* 65:371–78.

Topitsch, Ernst
1969   "World Interpretation and Self-Interpretation: Some Basic Patterns," *Myth and Mythmaking,* ed. Henry A. Murray (Boston: Beacon): 157–73.

Tucker, Robert C., ed.
1972   *The Marx-Engels Reader* (New York: W. W. Norton).

Turner, Victor
1968   "Myth and Symbol," *International Encyclopedia of the Social Sciences,* ed. David L. Sills (New York: Macmillan), 10:576–81.

Tylor, Edward Burnett
1958   *Religion in Primitive Culture* (New York: Harper & Brothers), chaps. 11–
[1871]   19.

Underhill, Ruth M.
1965   *Red Man's Religion. Beliefs and Practices of the Indians North of Mexico* (Chicago: University of Chicago Press).

Van Baal, J.
1971   *Symbols for Communication. An Introduction to the Anthropological Study of Religion* (Assen: Koninklijke Van Gorcum).

Van Baaren, Th. P.
1955   "Primitive Anthropology," *Anthropologie religieuse. L'homme et sa destinée à la lumière de l'histoire des religions,* ed. C. J. Bleeker (Leiden: E. J. Brill, History of Religion Supplements to *Numen,* 2): 4–13.
1969   "Are the Bororo Parrots or Are We?," *Liber Amicorum. Studies in Honor of Professor Dr. C. J. Bleeker* (Leiden: E. J. Brill, Studies in the History of Religions, Supplements to *Numen,* 17): 8–13.

Vansina, Jan
1965   *Oral Tradition. A Study in Historical Methodology,* trans. H. M. Wright (Chicago: Aldine).
1970   *Kingdoms of the Savanna* (Madison: University of Wisconsin Press).
1978   *The Children of Woot* (Madison: University of Wisconsin Press).

Vecsey, Christopher
 1977   "Tribal Texts and Contexts," *Parabola Guide,* 1:4–6.
 1980   "American Indian Environmental Religions," *American Indian Enrivonments. Ecological Issues in Native American History,* ed. Christopher Vecsey and Robert W. Venables (Syracuse, NY: Syracuse University Press):1–37.
 1981   "Introduction," *Belief and Worship in Native North America,* Åke Hultkrantz, ed. Christopher Vecsey (Syracuse, NY: Syracuse University Press).
 1983   *Traditional Ojibwa Religion and Its Historical Changes* (Philadelphia: American Philosophical Society).

Verene, Donald
 1966   "Cassirer's View of Myth and Symbol," *The Monist,* 50:553–64.

Vickery, John B.
 1973   *The Literary Impact of "The Golden Bough"* (Princeton, NJ: Princeton University Press).

Vico, Giovanni Battista
 1968   *The New Science,* trans. Thomas Goddard Bergin and Max Harold Fisch (Ithaca,
 [1725]   NY: Cornell University Press).

Vivas, Eliseo
 1970   "Myth: Some Philosophical Problems," *The Southern Review,* 6:89–103.

Voegelin, Erminie W.
 1950   "Myth," *Standard Dictionary of Folklore, Mythology, and Legend,* 2 vols. (New York: Funk & Wagnalls), 2:778.

Waardenburg, Jacques
 1973–74 *Classical Approaches to the Study of Religion. Aims, Methods and Theories of Research,* 2 vols. (The Hague: Mouton, Religion and Reason, 3 and 4).
 1980   "Symbolic Aspects of Myth," *Myth, Symbol, and Reality,* ed. Alan M. Olson (Notre Dame: University of Notre Dame Press): 41–68.

Wach, Joachim
 1963   *The Comparative Study of Religions,* ed. Joseph M. Kitigawa (New York: Columbia University Press).

Ward, D. J. H.
 1909   *The Classification of Religions. Different Methods, Their Advantages and Disadvantages* (Chicago: Open Court).

Waterman, T. T.
 1914   "The Explanatory Element in the Folk-Tales of the North-American Indians," *Journal of American Folklore,* 27:1–54.

Watts, Alan W.
 1970   *Myth and Ritual in Christianity* (Boston: Beacon).

Wiesel, Elie
 1980   "Myth and History," *Myth, Symbol, and Reality,* ed. Alan M. Olson (Notre Dame: University of Notre Dame Press): 20–30.

Wieting, Stephen G.
 1972   "Myth and Symbol Analysis of Claude Lévi-Strauss and Victor Turner," *Social Compass,* 19:139–54.

Willis, R. G
 1967   "The Head and the Loins: Lévi-Strauss and Beyond," *Man,* n.s., 2:519–34.

Wissler, Clark
1936   *Star Legends among the American Indians* (New York: American Museum of Natural History).

Young, Arthur M.
1964   *Echoes of Two Cultures* (Pittsburgh: University of Pittsburgh Press).

Young, Frank W.
1970   "A Fifth Analysis of the Star Husband Tale," *Ethnology,* 9:389–413.

Chapter 2: The Emergence and Maintenance of the Hopi People

Abrahams, Roger D. and Richard Bauman
1978   "Ranges of Festival Behavior," *The Reversible World. Symbolic Inversion in Art and Society,* ed. Barbara A. Babcock (Ithaca, NY: Cornell University Press): 193–208.

Adams, David Wallace
1979   "Schooling the Hopi: Federal Indian Policy Writ Small, 1887–1917," *Pacific Historical Review,* 48:335–56.

Alexander, Hartley Burr
1964   *The Mythology of All Races, Vol. X, North American,* ed. Louis Herbert Gray (New York: Cooper Square).

Anderson, Frank G.
1955   "The Pueblo Kachina Cult: A Historical Reconstruction," *Southwestern Journal of Anthropology,* 11:404–19.

Babcock, Barbara A.
1978   "Introduction," *The Reversible World. Symbolic Inversion in Art and Society,* ed. Barbara A. Babcock (Ithaca, NY: Cornell University Press):13–36.

Baxter, Sylvester
1882   "The Father of the Pueblos," *Harper's New Monthly Magazine,* 65:72–91.

Beck, Peggy V. and A. L. Walters
1977   *The Sacred Ways of Knowledge, Sources of Life* (Tsaile, AZ: Navajo Community College Press).

Benedict, Ruth
1959   *Patterns of Culture* (Boston: Houghton Mifflin).

Boas, Franz
1915   "Mythology and Folk-Tales of the North American Indians," Franz Boas et al., *Anthropology in North America* (New York: G.E. Stechert):306–49.
1917   "The Origin of Death," *Journal of American Folklore,* 30:486–91.

Bouissac, Paul
1976   *Circus and Culture. A Semiotic Approach* (Bloomington: Indiana University Press).

Bourke, John G.
1920   *The Urine Dance of the Zuni Indians of New Mexico* (n.p.).
1934   *Scatologic Rites of All Nations* (New York: American Anthropological Society).

Bradfield, Richard Maitland
1973   *A Natural History of Associations. A Study in the Meaning of Community,* 2 vols. (London: Gerald Duckworth), 2.

Brandt, Richard B.
1954   *Hopi Ethics. A Theoretical Analysis* (Chicago: University of Chicago Press).

Branson, Oscar T.
1976   *Fetishes and Carvings of the Southwest* (Santa Fe: Treasure Chest).

Budnik, Dan
n.d.   "Black Mesa: Progress Report on an Ecological Rape," unpublished ms.

Burns, Tom
1953   "Friends, Enemies, and the Polite Fiction," *American Sociological Review,* 18:654–62.

Chapman, Antony J. and Hugh C. Foot, eds.
1977   *It's a Funny Thing, Humour* (Oxford: Pergamon. International Conference on Humour and Laughter, Cardiff, Wales, 1976).

Charles, Lucile Hoerr
1945   "The Clown's Function," *Journal of American Folklore,* 58:25–34.

Clements, Forrest E.
1932   "Primitive Concepts of Disease," *University of California Publications in American Archaeology and Ethnology,* 32:185–252.

Clemmer, Richard O.
1978   "Black Mesa and the Hopi," Joseph Jorgensen et al., *Native Americans and Energy Development* (Cambridge, MA: Anthropology Resource Center):17–34.

Colton, Harold S.
1959   *Hopi Kachina Dolls. With a Key to Their Identification* (Albuquerque: University of New Mexico Press).

Corlett, William Thomas
1935   *The Medicine-Man of the American Indian and His Cultural Background* (Baltimore: Charles C. Thomas).

Courlander, Harold
1971   *The Fourth World of the Hopis* (New York: Crown).

Coze, Paul
1957   "Kachinas: Masked Dancers of the Southwest," *National Geographic Magazine,* 112:218–36.

Crumrine, N. Ross
1969   "Čapakoba, the Mayo Easter Ceremonial Impersonator: Explanations of Ritual Clowning," *Journal for the Scientific Study of Religion,* 8:1–22.

Cunningham, Adrian
1973   "Myth, Ideology, and Lévi-Strauss: The Problem of the Genesis Story in the Nineteenth Century," *The Theory of Myth. Six Studies,* ed. Adrian Cunningham (London: Sheed and Ward):132–76.

Cushing, Frank Hamilton
1923   "Origin Myth from Oraibi," *Journal of American Folklore,* 36:163–70.

Desai, Mahesh M.
1939   *Surprise. A Historical and Experimental Study* (London: Cambridge University Press, British Journal of Psychology, Monograph Supplements, 22).

Disher, M. Willson
1925   *Clowns and Pantomimes* (Boston: Houghton Mifflin).

Douglas, Mary
1968   "The Social Control of Cognition: Some Factors in Joke Perception," *Man,* 3:361–76.

Dozier, Edward P.
1956   "The Role of the Hopi-Tewa Migration Legend in Reinforcing Cultural Patterns and Prescribing Social Behavior," *Journal of American Folklore*, 69:176–80.

Earle, Edwin and Edward A. Kennard
1938   *Hopi Kachinas* (New York: J. J. Augustin).

Eggan, Dorothy
1971   "The Personal Use of Myth in Dreams," *Myth. A Symposium*, ed. Thomas A. Sebeok (Bloomington: Indiana University Press):107–21.

Elmendorf, William W.
1967   "Soul Loss Illness in Western North America," *Indian Tribes of Aboriginal America*, ed. Sol Tax (New York: Cooper Square):104–14.

Fewkes, Jesse Walter
1891   "A Few Summer Ceremonials at Zuñi Pueblo," *Journal of American Ethnology and Archaeology*, 1:1–62.
1892a   "A Few Summer Ceremonials at the Tusayan Pueblos," *Journal of American Ethnology and Archaeology*, 2:1–160.
1892b   "A Few Tusayan Pictographs," *American Anthropologist*, 5:9–26.
1893   "A-Wá-To Bi: An Archeological Verification of a Tusayan Legend," *American Anthropologist*, old series, 6:363–76.
1894   "Dolls of the Tusayan Indians," *Internationales Archiv für Ethnographie*, 7:45–73.
1896   "The Tusayan Ritual: A Study of the Influence of Environment on Aboriginal Cults," *Smithsonian Institution Annual Report* (Washington, DC):683–700.
1897a   "Tusayan Katchinas," *Bureau of Ethnology, Fifteenth Annual Report* (Washington, DC):245–313.
1897b   "The Sacrificial Element in Hopi Worship," *Journal of American Folklore*, 10:187–201.
1900a   "The New-Fire Ceremony at Walpi," *American Anthropologist*, 2:80–138.
1900b   "A Theatrical Performance at Walpi," *Proceedings of the Washington Academy of Sciences*, 2:605–29.
1900c   "Tusayan Migration Traditions," *Bureau of American Ethnology, Nineteenth Annual Report* (Washington, DC):573–633.
1903   "Hopi Katcinas Drawn by Native Artists," *Bureau of American Ethnology, Twenty-First Annual Report* (Washington, DC):3–126.
1910   "The Butterfly in Hopi Myth and Ritual," *American Anthropologist*, 12:576–94.

Fewkes, Jesse Walter and A. M. Stephens [sic]
1892   "The Nā-Ác-Nai-Ya: A Tusayan Initiation Ceremony," *Journal of American Folklore*, 5:189–217.

Frank, Larry and Francis H. Harlow
1974   *Historic Pottery of the Pueblo Indians 1600–1880* (Boston: New York Graphic Society).

Freud, Sigmund
1962   *Civilization and Its Discontents*, trans. James Strachey (New York: W. W. Norton).
1963   *Jokes and Their Relation to the Unconscious*, trans. and ed. James Strachey (New York: W. W. Norton).

Goldfrank, Esther S.

1948   "The Impact of Situation and Personality on Four Hopi Emergence Myths," *Southwestern Journal of Anthropology*, 4:241–62.

Gordon, Suzanne

1973   *Black Mesa. The Angel of Death* (New York: John Day).

Gruner, Charles

1978   *Understanding Laughter. The Workings of Wit and Humor* (Chicago: Nelson-Hall).

Haeberlin, Herman Karl

1916   "The Idea of Fertilization in the Culture of the Pueblo Indians," *Memoirs of the American Anthropological Association*, 3:1–55.

Harris, David

1980   "Last Stand for an Ancient Indian Way," *New York Times Magazine*, 16 March:38–41, 63ff.

Harvey, Byron III

1970   *Ritual in Pueblo Art. Hopi Life in Hopi Painting* (New York: Contributions from the Museum of the American Indian, Heye Foundation, 24).

1972   "An Overview of Pueblo Religion," *New Perspectives on the Pueblos*, ed. Alfonso Ortiz (Albuquerque: University of New Mexico Press):197–217.

Hieb, Louis Albert

1972a   "The Hopi Ritual Clown: Life as It Should Not Be," unpublished Ph.D. dissertation, Princeton University.

1972b   "Meaning and Mismeaning: Toward an Understanding of the Ritual Clown," *New Perspectives on the Pueblos*, ed. Alfonso Ortiz (Albuquerque: University of New Mexico Press):163–95.

Hodge, F. W.

1896   "Pueblo Snake Ceremonials," *American Anthropologist*, 9:133–36.

Honigmann, John J.

1942   "An Interpretation of the Social-Psychological Functions of the Ritual Clown," *Character and Personality (Journal of Personality)*, 10:220–26.

Ivins, Molly

1979   "Hopi Spirits Dance Again on the Mesa," *New York Times*, 30 July, by-line article.

James, William

1958   *The Varieties of Religious Experience. A Study in Human Nature* (New York: New American Library).

Kennard, E. A.

1937   "Hopi Reactions to Death," *American Anthropologist*, 39:491–96.

Koenig, Seymour H.

1972   *Sky, Sand and Spirits. Navajo and Pueblo Indian Art and Culture* ([Yonkers]: Hudson River Museum).

1976   *Hopi Clay. Hopi Ceremony* (Katonah, NY: Katonah Gallery).

Leach, Edmund

1976   *Culture and Communication. The Logic by Which Symbols Are Connected* (Cambridge: Cambridge University Press).

Levine, Jacob

1961   "Regression in Primitive Clowning," *Psychoanalytic Quarterly*, 30:72–83.

Lewis, I. M.
1971   *Ecstatic Religion. An Anthropological Study of Spirit Possession and Sha-manism* (Harmondsworth, Middlesex: Penguin).

Long, Charles H.
1963   *Alpha. The Myths of Creation* (New York: George Braziller).

Maier, Norman R.
1932   "A Gestalt Theory of Humor," *British Journal of Psychology,* 23:69–74.

Makarius, Laura
1970   "Ritual Clowns and Symbolical Behavior," *Diogenes,* 69:44–73.

Marriott, Alice and Carol K. Rachlin
1972   *American Indian Mythology* (New York: New American Library).

Matthews, Washington
1902   "Myths of Gestation and Parturition," *American Anthropologist,* 4:737–42.

Mills, George
n.d.   *Kachinas and Saints. A Contrast in Style and Culture* (Colorado Springs, CO: Taylor Museum).

Mindeleff, Cosmos
1900   "Localization of Tusayan Clans," *Bureau of American Ethnology, Nineteenth Annual Report* (Washington, DC): 635–53.

Mindeleff, Victor
1891   "A Study of Pueblo Architecture: Tusayan and Cibola," *Bureau of Ethnology, Eighth Annual Report* (Washington, DC): 3–298.

Monro, D. H.
1951   *Argument of Laughter* (Melbourne: Melbourne University).

Moon, Sheila
1974   *A Magic Dwells. A Poetic and Psychological Study of the Navaho Emergence Myth* (Middletown, CT: Wesleyan University Press).

Nequatewa, Edmund
1967   *Truth of a Hopi* (Flagstaff: Museum of Northern Arizona).

Ortiz, Alfonso
1972   "Ritual Drama and the Pueblo World View," *New Perspectives on the Pueblos,* ed. Alfonso Ortiz (Albuquerque: University of New Mexico Press): 135–61.
1973   *The Tewa World. Space, Time, Being, and Becoming in a Pueblo Society* (Chicago: University of Chicago Press).

Parsons, Elsie Clews
1917   "Notes on Zuni," 2 parts, *Memoirs of the American Anthropological Association,* 4. 149–327.
1923a   "The Hopi Wöwöchim Ceremony in 1920," *American Anthropologist,* 25:156–87.
1923b   "The Origin Myth of Zuñi," *Journal of American Folklore,* 36:135–62.
1925   *A Pueblo Indian Journal 1920–1921* (Menasha, WI: Memoirs of the American Anthropological Association, 32).
1936   *Hopi Journals of Alexander M. Stephen,* 2 vols. (New York: Columbia University Press, Contributions to Anthropology, 23).
1939   *Pueblo Indian Religion,* 2 vols. (Chicago: University of Chicago Press).

Parsons, Elsie Clews and Ralph L. Beals
1934   "The Sacred Clowns of the Pueblo and Mayo-Yaqui Indians," *American Anthropologist,* 36:491–514.

Peet, Stephen Denison
1905   *Myths and Symbols; or, Aboriginal Religions in America* (Chicago: Office of the American Antiquarian).

Piddington, Ralph
1963   *The Psychology of Laughter. A Study in Social Adaptation* (New York: Gamut).

Qoyawayma, Polingaysi (Elizabeth Q. White)
1978   *No Turning Back*, as told to Vada F. Carlson (Albuquerque: University of New Mexico Press).

Roediger, Virginia More
1941   *Ceremonial Costumes of the Pueblo Indians. Their Evolution, Fabrication, and Significance in the Prayer Drama* (Berkeley: University of California Press).

Rogers, Spencer L.
1944   "Disease Concepts in North America," *American Anthropologist,* 46:559–64.

Rooth, Anna Birgitta
1957   "The Creation Myths of the North American Indians," *Anthropos,* 52:497–508.

Scully, Vincent
1975   *Pueblo/Mountain, Village, Dance* (New York: Viking).

Sekaquaptewa, Emory
1979   "One More Smile for a Hopi Clown," *Parabola,* 4:6–9.

Sekaquaptewa, Helen
1981   *Me and Mine. The Life Story of Helen Sekaquaptewa,* as told to Louise Udall (Tucson: University of Arizona Press).

Sidis, Boris
1913   *The Psychology of Laughter* (New York: D. Appleton).

Simmons, Leo W., ed.
1971   *Sun Chief. The Autobiography of a Hopi Indian* (New Haven: Yale University Press).

Simpson, Ruth DeEtte
1951–53   "The Hopi Indians," *The Masterkey,* 25:109–24, 155–66, 177–85; 26:5–12, 87–94, 122–29, 149–60, 179–91; 27:11–14.

Spicer, Edward H.
1972   *Cycles of Conquest. The Impact of Spain, Mexico, and the United States on the Indians of the Southwest, 1533–1960* (Tucson: University of Arizona Press).

Sproul, Barbara Chamberlain
1972   "Prolegomena to the Study of Creation Myths," unpublished Ph.D. dissertation, Columbia University.

Stephen, Alexander
1929   "Hopi Tales," *Journal of American Folklore,* 42:1–72.

Steward, Julian H.
1931a   "The Ceremonial Buffoon of the American Indian," *Papers of the Michigan Academy of Science, Arts and Letters, 1930,* 14:187–207.
1931b   "Notes on Hopi Ceremonies in Their Initiatory Form in 1927–1928," *American Anthropologist,* 33:56–79.

Stewart, Susan
1979   *Nonsense. Aspects of Intertextuality in Folklore and Literature* (Baltimore: Johns Hopkins University Press).

Tedlock, Barbara
1975   "The Clown's Way," *Teachings from the American Earth*, ed. Dennis Tedlock and Barbara Tedlock (New York: Liveright): 105–18.

Thompson, Laura
1945   "Logico-Aesthetic Integration in Hopi Culture," *American Anthropologist*, 47:540–53.

Thompson, Laura and Alice Joseph
1965   *The Hopi Way* (New York: Russell & Russell).

Titiev, Mischa
1941   "A Hopi Visit to the Afterworld," *Papers of the Michigan Academy of Science, Arts and Letters, 1940*, 26:495–504.
1944   *Old Oraibi. A Study of the Hopi Indians of the Third Mesa* (Cambridge: Papers of the Peabody Museum of American Archaeology and Ethnology, Harvard University, 22).
1948   "Two Hopi Myths and Rites," *Journal of American Folklore*, 61:31–43.
1950   "The Religion of the Hopi Indians," *Forgotten Religions*, ed. Vergilius Ferm (New York: Philosophical Library): 365–78.
1971   "Some Aspects of Clowning among the Hopi Indians," *Themes in Culture (Essays in Honor of Morris E. Opler)*, ed. Mario D. Zamora, J. Michael Mahar, and Henry Orenstein (Quezon City, Philippines: Kayumanggi): 326–36.
1972   *The Hopi Indians of Old Oraibi. Change and Continuity* (Ann Arbor: University of Michigan Press).

Turner, Victor W.
1969   *The Ritual Process. Structure and Anti-Structure* (Chicago: Aldine).
1978   "Comments and Conclusions," *The Reversible World. Symbolic Inversion in Art and Society*, ed. Barbara A. Babcock (Ithaca, NY: Cornell University Press): 276–96.

Tyler, Hamilton, A.
1964   *Pueblo Gods and Myths* (Norman: University of Oklahoma Press).

Vogel, Virgil J.
1973   *American Indian Medicine* (New York: Ballantine).

Vogt, Evon
1976   "Rituals of Reversal as a Means of Rewiring Social Structure," *The Realm of the Extra-Human. Ideas and Actions*, ed. Agehananda Bharati (The Hague: Mouton): 201–11.

Voth, H. R.
1905   *The Traditions of the Hopi* (Chicago: Field Columbian Museum, Anthropological Series, 8).
1912   "The Oraibi Marau Ceremony," *Field Museum of Natural History*, Publication 156, Anthropological Series, 2:1–88.

Wallis, Wilson D.
1936   "Folk Tales from Shumopovi, Second Mesa," *Journal of American Folklore*, 49:1–68.

Waters, Frank and Oswald White Bear Fredericks
1970   *Book of the Hopi* (New York: Ballantine).

Welsford, Enid
1961   *The Fool. His Social and Literary History* (Garden City, NY: Doubleday).
Wheeler-Voegelin, Erminie and Remedios W. Moore
1957   "The Emergence Myth in Native North America," *Studies in Folklore in Honor of Distinguished Professor Stith Thompson* (Bloomington: Indiana University Press, Folklore Series, 9): 66–91.
Whorf, Benjamin Lee
1956   *Language, Thought, and Reality* (New York: John Wiley & Sons).
1975   "An American Indian Model of the Universe," *Teachings from the American Earth. Indian Religion and Philosophy,* ed. Dennis Tedlock and Barbara Tedlock (New York: Liveright): 121–29.
Willeford, William
1969   *The Fool and His Scepter. A Study in Clowns and Jesters and Their Audience* (Evanston, IL: Northwestern University Press).
Williams, Benjamin S.
1978   "Hopi Classification System as Evidenced through Myth and Text," unpublished Honors paper, Hobart and William Smith Colleges.
Wittfogel, Karl A. and Esther S. Goldfrank
1943   "Some Aspects of Pueblo Mythology and Society," *Journal of American Folklore,* 56:17–30.
Wright, Barton
1973   *Kachinas: A Hopi Artist's Documentary* (Flagstaff, AZ: Northland).
Zucker, Wolfgang
1954   "The Image of the Clown," *Journal of Aesthetics and Art Criticism,* 12:310–17.
1967   "The Clown as the Lord of Disorder," *Theology Today,* 24:306–17.

Chapter 3: The Ojibwa Creation Myth

Anonymous
1930a   "Thunderbird Legend of the Post," *Wisconsin Archeologist,* 9:128–29.
1930b   "Winneboujou," *Wisconsin Archeologist,* 9:130.
Armstrong, Benj. G.
1892   *Early Life among the Indians* (Ashland, WI: A. W. Bowron).
Barnouw, Victor
1950   *Acculturation and Personality among the Wisconsin Chippewa* (Menasha, WI: American Anthropological Association, 72).
1955   "A Psychological Interpretation of a Chippewa Origin Legend," *Journal of American Folklore,* 68:73–85, 211–23, 341–55.
Blackbird, Andrew J.
1887   *History of the Ottawa and Chippewa Indians of Michigan, and Grammar of Their Language* (Ypsilanti, MI: Ypsilantian Job Printing House).
Blackwood, Beatrice
1929   "Tales of the Chippewa Indians," *Folk-Lore,* 40:315–44
Blessing, Fred K.
1963   "Birchbark Mide Scrolls from Minnesota," *Minnesota Archaeologist,* 25:91–142.

Bloomfield, Leonard
    1957   *Eastern Ojibwa Grammatical Sketch, Texts and Word List* (Ann Arbor: University of Michigan Press).

Bottineau, J. B.
    1878   "Chippewa Mythology," Smithsonian Institution, Bureau of American Ethnology Archives, Chippewa Manuscripts, no. 3605.

Brinton, Daniel Garrison
    1885   "The Chief God of the Algonkins, in His Character as a Cheat and Liar," *American Antiquarian,* May:137–39.

Brown, Charles E.
    1902–13   "Chippewa Indians," Papers, 1902–45, Box 3, State Historical Society of Wisconsin Manuscripts, HB.

Carson, William
    1917   "Ojibwa Tales," *Journal of American Folklore,* 30:491–93.

Carver, Jonathan
    1784   *Three Years Travels, through the Interior Parts of North-America* (Philadelphia: n.p.).

Chamberlain, Alexander F.
    1890   "The Thunder-Bird amongst the Algonkins," *American Anthropologist,* 3:51–54.
    1891   "Nanibozhu amongst the Otchipwe, Mississagas, and Other Algonkian Tribes," *Journal of American Folklore,* 4:193–213.
    1900   "Some Items of Algonkian Folk-Lore," *Journal of American Folklore,* 13:271–77.
    1906   "Cree and Ojibwa Literary Terms," *Journal of American Folklore,* 19:346–47.

Coleman, Bernard, Sr., Ellen Frogner, and Estelle Eich
    1962   *Ojibwa Myths and Legends* (Minneapolis: Ross and Haines).

Cooper, John M.
    1933   "The Cree Witiko Psychosis," *Primitive Man,* 6:20–24.
    1934   *The Northern Algonquian Supreme Being* (Washington, DC: Catholic University of America Press, Anthropological Series, 2).
    1946   "The Culture of the Northeastern Indian Hunters: A Reconstructive Interpretation," *Man in Northeastern North America,* ed. Frederick Johnson (Andover, MA: Papers of the Robert S. Peabody Foundation for Archaeology, 3):272–305.

Copway, George (Kah-Ge-Ga-Gah-Bowh)
    1858   *Indian Life and Indian History, by an Indian Author* (Boston: Albert Colby).

Densmore, Frances
    1910,   *Chippewa Music,* 2 vols. (Washington, DC: Smithsonian Institution, Bureau
    1913   of American Ethnology, Bulletins 45, 53).
    1929   *Chippewa Customs* (Washington, DC: Smithsonian Institution, Bureau of American Ethnology, Bulletin 86).

Dewdney, Selwyn
    1975   *The Sacred Scrolls of the Southern Ojibway* (Toronto: University of Toronto Press).

Dixon, Roland B.
1909   "The Mythology of the Central and Eastern Algonkins," *Journal of American Folklore,* 22:1–9.

Dorson, Richard M.
1952   *Bloodstoppers and Bearwalkers. Folk Traditions of the Upper Peninsula* (Cambridge: Harvard University Press).

Dundes, Alan
1962   "Earth-Diver: Creation of the Mythopoeic Male," *American Anthropologist,* 64:1032–51.

Fisher, Margaret W.
1946   "The Mythology of the Northern and Northeastern Algonkians in Reference to Algonkian Mythology as a Whole," *Man in Northeastern North America,* ed. Frederick Johnson (Andover, MA: Papers of the Robert S. Peabody Foundation for Archaeology, 3):226–62.

Flannery, Regina
1946   "The Culture of the Northeastern Indian Hunters: A Descriptive Analysis," *Man in Northeastern North America,* ed. Frederick Johnson (Andover, MA: Papers of the Robert S. Peabody Foundation for Archaeology, 3):263–71.

Gabaoosa, George
1900   "Story of Nanabosho's Mother," Smithsonian Institution, Bureau of American Ethnology Archives, Chippewa Manuscripts, no. 1640.
1921   "Nanabosho Myth, with Occasional Notes by J. N. B. Hewitt, Smithsonian Institution, Bureau of American Ethnology Archives, Chippewa Manuscripts, no. 1637.
1925   "The Myth of the Daymaker," 2 parts, Smithsonian Institution, Bureau of American Ethnology Archives, Chippewa Manuscripts, no. 1645.

Gatschet, Albert S.
1889   "Ojibwe (Ojibwa) Texts, from Ka'spash, at Turtle Mountain Reservation, N.D.," Smithsonian Institution, Bureau of American Ethnology Archives, Chippewa Manuscripts, no. 1999.

Gilfillan, Joseph Alexander
1908–9   "Ojibway (Chippewa) Legends," Smithsonian Institution, Bureau of American Ethnology Archives, Chippewa Manuscripts, no. 1476.

Hallowell, A. Irving
1934   "Some Empirical Aspects of Northern Saulteaux Religion," *American Anthropologist,* 36:389–404.
1939   "Some European Folktales of the Berens River Saulteaux," *Journal of American Folklore,* 52:155–79.
1942   *The Role of Conjuring in Saulteaux Society* (Philadelphia: University of Pennsylvania Press, Publications of the Philadelphia Anthropological Society, 2).
1946   "Concordance of Ojibwa Narratives in the Published Works of Henry R. Schoolcraft," *Journal of American Folklore,* 59:136–53.
1947   "Myth, Culture and Personality," *American Anthropologist,* 49:544–56.
1955   *Culture and Experience* (Philadelphia: University of Pennsylvania Press).
1960   "Ojibwa Ontology, Behavior, and World View," *Culture in History: Essays in Honor of Paul Radin,* ed. Stanley Diamond (New York: Columbia University Press):19–52.

Hamilton, James Cleland
1898–99 "Famous Algonquins; Algic Legends," *Transactions of the Canadian Institute*, 6:285–312.
1903   "The Algonquin Manabozho and Hiawatha," *Journal of American Folklore*, 16:228–33.

Hewitt, J. N. B.
1926   "Ethnological Researches among the Iroquois and Chippewa," *Explorations and Field-Work of the Smithsonian Institution in 1925* (Washington, DC: Smithsonian Miscellaneous Collections, 78):114–17.
n.d.   "Transliteration of Nanabosho Myth into the B.A.E. Alphabet of Chippewa Text, no. 1637," Smithsonian Institution, Bureau of American Ethnology Archives, Chippewa Manuscripts, no. 1638.

Hickerson, Harold
1960   "The Feast of the Dead among the Seventeenth Century Algonkians of the Upper Great Lakes," *American Anthropologist*, 62:81–107.
1962a   *The Southwestern Chippewa. An Ethnohistorical Study* (Menasha, WI: American Anthropological Association, 92).
1962b   "Notes on the Post-Contact Origin of the Midewiwin," *Ethnohistory*, 9:404–26.
1963   "The Sociohistorical Significance of Two Chippewa Ceremonials," *American Anthropologist*, 65:67–85.

Hilger, M. Inez, Sr.
1951   *Chippewa Child Life and Its Cultural Background* (Washington, DC: Smithsonian Institution, Bureau of American Ethnology, Bulletin 146).

Hindley, John I.
1885   *Indian Legends. Nanabush, the Ojibbeway Savior* (n.p.).

Hoffman, W. J.
1891   "The Midē'wiwin or 'Grand Medicine Society' of the Ojibwa," *Bureau of Ethnology, Seventh Annual Report to the Secretary of the Smithsonian Institution 1885–86*:143–300.

Jenks, Albert Ernest
1902   "The Bear-Maiden, an Ojibway Folk-Tale from Lac Courte Oreille Reservation, Wisconsin," *Journal of American Folklore*, 15:33–35.

Jenness, Diamond
1935   *The Ojibwa Indians of Parry Island, Their Social and Religious Life* (Ottawa: Canada Department of Mines, Bulletin 78, Anthropological Series, 17).

Johnson, Frederick
1929   "Notes on the Ojibwa and Potawatomi of the Parry Island Reservation, Ontario," *Indian Notes*, 6:193–216.

Jones, Peter (Kahkewaquonaby)
1861   *History of the Ojebway Indians; with Especial Reference to Their Conversion to Christianity* (London: A. W. Bennett).

Jones, William
1917,   *Ojibwa Texts*, 2 vols., ed. Truman Michelson (Leyden and New York: Pub-
1919   lications of the American Ethnological Society, 7, parts 1 and 2).

Josselin de Jong, J. P. B. de
1913   "Original Odzibwe-Texts," *Beiträge zur Völkerkunde* (Leipzig and Berlin: Herausgegeben aus Mitteln des Baessler-Instituts, 5): 1–54.

Kinietz, Vernon
1939   "Birch Bark Records among the Chippewa," *Proceedings of the Indiana Academy of Science,* 49:38–40.
1940   *The Indians of the Western Great Lakes 1615–1760* (Ann Arbor: Occasional Contributions from the Museum of Anthropology of the University of Michigan, no. 10).
1947   *Chippewa Village, The Story of Katikitegon* (Bloomfield Hills, MI: Cranbrook Institute of Science).

Kinnaman, J.O.
1910   "Chippewa Legends," *American Antiquarian,* 32:96–102, 137–44.

Knight, Julia
1913   "Ojibwa Tales from Sault Ste. Marie, Mich.," *Journal of American Folklore,* 26:91–96.

Köngäs, Elli Kaija
1960   "The Earth Diver (Th. A 812)," *Ethnohistory,* 7:151–80.

Kohl, J. G.
1860   *Kitchi-Gami. Wanderings Round Lake Superior,* trans. Lascelles Wraxall (London: Chapman and Hall).

Landes, Ruth
1937   *Ojibwa Sociology* (New York: Columbia University Press).
1968   *Ojibwa Religion and the Midéwiwin* (Madison: University of Wisconsin Press).
1971   *The Ojibwa Women* (New York: W. W. Norton).

Leekley, Thomas B.
1965   *The World of Manabozho. Tales of the Chippewa Indians* (New York: Vanguard).

Makarius, Laura
1973   "The Crime of Manabozho," *American Anthropologist,* 75:663–75.

Mallery, Garrick
1972   *Picture-writing of the American Indians,* 2 vols. (New York: Dover).

McKenney, Thomas L.
1927   *Sketches of a Tour to the Lakes, of the Character and Customs of the Chippeway Indians, and of Incidents Connected with the Treaty of Fond du Lac* (Baltimore: Fielding Lucas, Jun'r).

Michelson, Truman
1911   "Ojibwa Tales," *Journal of American Folklore,* 24:249–50.
n.d.   "Chippewa Legend and Ethnology," Smithsonian Institution, Bureau of American Ethnology Archives, Chippewa Manuscripts, no. 2821.

Miscogeon, John L.
1900a   "The Legend of Nanabozho," Smithsonian Institution, Bureau of American Ethnology Archives, Chippewa Manuscripts, no. 1639.
1900b   "Ojibwa (Ottawa) Text; Note, Correction and Occasional Translation by J. N. B. Hewitt," Smithsonian Institution, Bureau of American Ethnology Archives, Chippewa Manuscripts, no. 1641.
1900c   "The Story of the South (Summer) and the North (Winter) in Ojibwa (or Ottawa) Text," Smithsonian Institution, Bureau of American Ethnology Archives, Chippewa Manuscripts, no. 1642.
1900d   "Story of Nanabozho's Mother," Smithsonian Institution, Bureau of American Ethnology Archives, Chippewa Manuscripts, no. 2077.

Miscogeon, John L. and George Gabaoosa
   1900   "A Visit to Skyland, in Ojibwa (or Ottawa) Text," Smithsonian Institution,
           Bureau of American Ethnology Archives, Chippewa Manuscripts, no. 2334.

Morriseau, Norval
   1965   *Legends of My People,* ed. Selwyn Dewdney (Toronto: Ryerson).

Osborn, Chase S. and Stellanova Osborn
   1942   *Schoolcraft-Longfellow-Hiawatha* (Lancaster, PA: Jaques [sic] Cattell).

Parker, Seymour
   1960   "The Wiitiko Psychosis in the Context of Ojibwa Personality and Culture,"
           American Anthropologist, 62:603–23.
   1962   "Motives in Eskimo and Ojibwa Mythology," *Ethnology,* 1:516–23.

Quimby, George Irving
   1960   *Indian Life in the Upper Great Lakes, 11,000 B.C. to A.D. 1800* (Chicago:
           University of Chicago Press).

Radin, Paul
   1914   *Some Myths and Tales of the Ojibwa of Southeastern Ontario* (Ottawa: Canada
           Department of Mines Geological Survey, Memoir 48, Anthropological Series,
           2).

Radin, Paul and A. B. Reagan
   1928   "Ojibwa Myths and Tales," *Journal of American Folklore,* 41:61–146.

Reagan, Albert B.
   1921   "The Flood Myth of the Chippewa," *Proceedings of the Indiana Academy of
           Science 1919,* ed. F. Payne: 347–52.
   1928   "The Magic Pots," Wisconsin Archeologist, 7. 227–28.

Redsky, James (Esquekesik)
   1972   *Great Leader of the Ojibway: Mis-quona-queb,* ed. James R. Stevens (Toronto:
           McClelland and Stewart).

Reid, Dorothy M.
   1963   *Tales of Nanabozho* (New York: Henry Z. Walck).

Ritzenthaler, Robert E.
   1945   "Totemic Insult among the Wisconsin Chippewa," *American Anthropologist,*
           47:322–24.

Ritzenthaler, Robert E. and Pat Ritzenthaler
   1970   *The Woodland Indians of the Western Great Lakes* (Garden City, NY: Natural
           History).

Rogers, Edward S.
   1962   *The Round Lake Ojibwa* (Toronto: Royal Ontario Museum—University of
           Toronto Press, Art and Archaeology Division, Occasional Paper, 5).

Rooth, Anna Birgitta
   1962   *The Raven and the Carcass. An Investigation of a Motif in the Deluge Myth
           in Europe, Asia and North America* (Helsinki: Academia Scientiarum Fennica,
           Folklore Fellows Communications, 186).

Schmidt, Wilhelm
   1948   "The Central-Algonkin Floodmyth," *Actes du XXVIIIe Congrès International
           des Americanistes, Paris 1947* (Paris: Musée de l'Homme): 317–19.

Schoolcraft, Henry Rowe
   1839   *Algic Researches,* 2 vols. (New York: Harper & Brothers).
   1848   *The Indian in His Wigwam, or, Characteristics of the Red Race of America*
           (Buffalo: W. H. Graham).

1853–57   *Information, Respecting the History, Condition and Prospects of the Indian Tribes of the United States,* 6 vols. (Philadelphia: Lippincott, Grambo).

Shimpo, Mitsuru and Robert Williamson
1965   *Socio-cultural Disintegration among the Fringe Saulteaux* (Saskatoon: University of Saskatchewan Press).

Sieber, S. A.
1950   *The Saulteaux Indians* (Techny, IL: Mission House).

Skinner, Alanson
1914   "Some Aspects of the Folk-Lore of the Central Algonkin," *Journal of American Folklore,* 27:97–100.
1916   "European Tales from the Plains Ojibwa," *Journal of American Folklore,* 29:330–40.
1919   "Plains Ojibwa Tales," *Journal of American Folklore,* 32:280–305.

Smith, Harlan I.
1894   "Ojibwa Legends," Smithsonian Institution, Bureau of American Ethnology Archives, Chippewa Manuscripts, no. 37.
1897   "The Monster in the Tree: An Ojibwa Myth," *Journal of American Folklore,* 10:324–25.
1906   "Some Ojibwa Myths and Traditions," *Journal of American Folklore,* 19:215–30.

Speck, Frank G.
1915   *Myths and Folk-Lore of the Timiskamins Algonquin and Timagami Ojibwa* (Ottawa: Canada Department of Mines Geological Survey, Memoir 71, Anthropological Series, 9).

Teicher, Morton I.
1960   *Windigo Psychosis. A Study of a Relationship between Belief and Behavior among the Indians of Northeastern Canada* (Seattle: University of Washington Press).

Underhill, Ruth M.
1948   *Ceremonial Patterns in the Greater Southwest* (New York: J. J. Augustin, Monographs of the American Ethnological Society, 13).

United States Works Progress Administration
1936–40 "Chippewa Indian Historical Project Records," 2 reels, microfilm.
1942

Verwyst, Chrysostom
n.d.   "Notes on Chequamegon Bay, Including Several Indian Legends," The State Historical Society of Wisconsin Manuscripts, F902C51/VE.

Walker, Louise Jean
1959   *Legends of Green Sky Hill* (Grand Rapids, MI: Eerdmans).
1961   *Red Indian Legends. Tribal Tales of the Great Lakes* (London: Odhams).
1964   *Woodland Wigwams* (Hillsdale, MI: Hillsdale School Supply).

Warren, William Whipple
1885   "History of the Ojibways, Based upon Traditions and Oral Statements," *Collections of the Minnesota Historical Society,* 5:21–394.

Wilson, Edward F.
1886   *Missionary Work among the Ojebway Indians* (London: Society for Promoting Christian Knowledge).

Young, Egerton R.
1903   *Algonquin Indian Tales* (New York: Revell).

n.d.   *Stories from Indian Wigwams and Northern Campfires* (Toronto: William Briggs).

Chapter 4: The Story and Structure of the Iroquois Confederacy

Akweks, Aren (Ray Fadden)
1948   *The Formation of the Ho-de-no-sau-ne or League of the Five Nations* (St. Regis Mohawk Reservation, Hogansburg, NY: Akwesasne Counselor Organization.
1972   *Migration of the Iroquois* (Akwesasne, Mohawk Nation: White Roots of Peace).

Beauchamp, William M.
1892   *The Iroquois Trail* (Fayetteville, NY: H. C. Beauchamp, Recorder Office).
1921   *The Founders of the New York Iroquois League and Its Probable Date* (Rochester, NY: Researches and Transactions of the New York State Archeological Association 3, no. 1).
1926   "The Principal Founders of the Iroquois League and Its Probable Date," *Proceedings of the New York State Historical Association,* 24:27–36.
1962   *A History of the New York Iroquois Now Commonly Called the Six Nations* (Port Washington, NY: Ira J. Friedman, Inc.).

Boice, L. Peter
1979   "The Iroquois Sense of Place: Legends as a Source of Environmental Imagery," *New York Folklore,* 5:179–88.

Boyce, Douglas W.
1973   "A Glimpse of Iroquois Culture History through the Eyes of Joseph Brant and John Norton," *Proceedings of the American Philosophical Society,* 117:286–94.

Brant-Sero, John Ojijatekha
1901   "Dekanawideh; the Law-giver of the Caniengahakas," *Man,* 1:166–70.

Canfield, William W.
1902   *The Legends of the Iroquois Told by "The Cornplanter"* (New York: A. Wessels Company).

Clark, Joshua V. H.
1849   *Onondaga,* 2 vols. (Syracuse: Stoddard and Babcock).

Colden, Cadwallader
1964   *The History of the Five Indian Nations Depending on the Province of New-*
[1727,   *York in America* (Ithaca, NY: Cornell University Press).
1747]

Converse, Harriet Maxwell
1974   *Myths and Legends of the New York Iroquois* (Albany: State University of New York Press).

Dunlap, William
1839   *History of the New Netherlands, Province of New York, and State of New York, to the Adoption of the Federal Constitution,* 2 vols. (New York: Carter and Thorp).

Elm, Lloyd M., Sr.
1976   "The Hodinonshonni," *The Conservationist,* 30/4:3–5.

Fenton, William N.
1947   "Iroquois Indian Folklore," *Journal of American Folklore,* 60:383–97.
1949a   "Seth Newhouse's Traditional History and Constitution of the Iroquois Confederacy," *Proceedings of the American Philosophical Society,* 93:141–58.

1949b   "Collecting Materials for a Political History of the Six Nations," *Proceedings of the American Philosophical Society,* 93:233–38.

1960   "The Hiawatha Wampum Belt of the Iroquois League for Peace: A Symbol for the International Congress of Anthropology," *Men and Cultures,* ed. Anthony F. C. Wallace (Philadelphia: University of Pennsylvania Press): 3–7.

1962   " 'This Island, the World on the Turtle's Back,' "*Journal of American Folklore,* 75:283–300.

1971   "The New York State Wampum Collection: The Case for the Integrity of Cultural Treasures," *Proceedings of the American Philosophical Society,* 115:437–61.

1975   "The Lore of the Longhouse: Myth, Ritual and Red Power," *Anthropological Quarterly,* 48:131–47.

1978   "Problems in the Authentication of the League of the Iroquois," *Neighbors and Intruders: An Ethnohistorical Exploration of the Indians of Hudson's River,* ed. Laurence M. Hauptman and Jack Campisi (National Museum of Man Mercury Series, Canadian Ethnology Service Paper No. 39. Ottawa: National Museums of Canada): 261–68.

Fenton, William N. and Gertude P. Kurath
1951   "The Feast of the Dead, or Ghost Dance, at Six Nations Reserve, Canada," *Symposium on Local Diversity in Iroquois Culture,* ed. William N. Fenton (Washington, DC: Smithsonian Institution, Bureau of American Ethnology, Bulletin 149):143–65.

Gibson, John Arthur
1899   "The Deganawiídah Legend: A Tradition of the Founding of the League of the Five Iroquois Tribes," as told to J. N. B. Hewitt, ed. Abram Charles, John Buck, Sr., and Joshua Buck (1900–14), trans. William N. Fenton and Simeon Gibson (1941), Smithsonian Institution, Bureau of American Ethnology Archives, no. 1517C.

Goldenweiser, Alexander A.
1916   Review of Arthur C. Parker, *The Constitution of the Five Nations, American Anthropologist,* 18:431–36.

Hale, Horatio
1882   "A Lawgiver of the Stone Age," *Proceedings of the American Association for the Advancement of Science,* 30:324–41.

1883   *The Iroquois Book of Rites* (Philadelphia: D. G. Brinton).

Henning, Ch. H.
1898   "The Origin of the Confederacy of the Five Nations," *Proceedings of the American Association for the Advancement of Science,* 47:477–80.

Henry, Thomas R.
1955   *Wilderness Messiah. The Story of Hiawatha and the Iroquois* (New York: William Sloane Associates, Inc.).

Hertzberg, Hazel W.
1966   *The Great Tree and the Longhouse. The Culture of the Iroquois* (New York: Macmillan).

Hewitt, J. N. B.
1892   "Legend of the Founding of the Iroquois League," *American Anthropologist,* old series, 5:131–48.

1894   "Era of the Formation of the Historic League of the Iroquois," *American Anthropologist,* old series, 7:61–67.

1902   "Orenda and a Definition of Religion," *American Anthropologist*, 4:33–46.
1915   "Some Esoteric Aspects of the League of the Iroquois," *International Congress of Americanists, Proceedings*, 19:322–26.
1917   Review of Arthur C. Parker, *The Constitution of the Five Nations*; Campbell Scott, *Traditional History of the Confederacy of the Six Nations*; and William M. Beauchamp, *Civil, Religious and Mourning Councils and Ceremonies of Adoption of the New York Indians*, *American Anthropologist*, 19:429–38.
1920   "A Constitutional League of Peace in the Stone Age of America," *Annual Report, Smithsonian Institution, 1918*:527–45.
1927   "Ethnological Studies among the Iroquois Indians," *Smithsonian Miscellaneous Collections*, 78:237–47.
1929   "The Culture of the Indians of Eastern Canada," *Explorations and Field-Work of the Smithsonian Institution in 1928*:179–82.
1930   "The 'League of Nations' of the Iroquois Indians in Canada," *Explorations and Field-Work of the Smithsonian Institution in 1929*: 201–6.
1931   "Field Studies among the Iroquois Tribes," *Smithsonian Institution Explorations and Fieldwork*: 175–78.
1937   "Field Studies of the Iroquois in New York State and in Ontario, Canada," *Explorations and Field-Work of the Smithsonian Institution in 1936*:83–86.
1944   "The Requickening Address of the Iroquois Condolence Council," ed. William N. Fenton, *Journal of the Washington Academy of Sciences*, 34:65–79.

Howard, Helen Addison
1971   "Hiawatha: Co-Founder of an Indian United Nations," *Journal of the West*, 10:428–38.

Jennings, Francis
1984   *The Ambiguous Iroquois Empire* (New York: W. W. Norton).

Johansen, Bruce E.
1982   *Forgotten Founders. Benjamin Franklin, the Iroquois and the Rationale for the American Revolution* (Ipswich, MA: Gambit Incorporated, Publishers).

Laing, Mary E.
1920   *The Hero of the Longhouse* (Yonkers-on-Hudson, NY: World Book Company).

Morgan, Lewis Henry
1972   *League of the Iroquois* (Secaucus, NJ: Citadel Press).
[1851]

Müller, Werner
1968   "North America," Walter Krickeberg et al., *Pre-Columbian American Religions* (New York: Holt, Rinehart and Winston). "Twin Gods and a Dual World: The Iroquois of Lake Ontario": 180–93.

Newhouse, Seth (Dayodekane)
1885   "Traditional History and Constitution of the Iroquois Confederacy," American Philosophical Society Library, microfilm.
1897   "Constitution of the Confederacy by Dekanawidah," trans. J. N. B. Hewitt (1937), Smithsonian Institution, Bureau of American Ethnology Archives, no. 3490.

Norton, John
1970   *The Journal of Major John Norton 1816*, ed. Carl F. Klinck and James J. Talman (Toronto: Champlain Society).

Parker, Arthur C.

1918   "The Constitution of the Five Nations: A Reply," *American Anthropologist,* 20:120–24.

1968   *Parker on the Iroquois,* ed. William N. Fenton (Syracuse, NY: Syracuse University Press).

Randle, Martha Champion

1952   "Psychological Types from Iroquois Folktales," *Journal of American Folklore,* 65:13–21.

Richter, Daniel K.

1983   "War and Culture: The Iroquois Experience," *The William and Mary Quarterly,* 40:528–59.

Schoolcraft, Henry R.

1846   *Notes on the Iroquois* (New York: Barlett & Welford, Astor House).

1847   *Notes on the Iroquois* (Albany: Erastus H. Pease & Co.).

Scott, Duncan C.

1912   "Traditional History of the Confederacy of the Six Nations," *Transactions of the Royal Society of Canada,* 5:195–248.

Snyderman, George S.

1954   "The Functions of Wampum," *Proceedings of the American Philosophical Society,* 98:469–94.

1961   "The Functions of Wampum in Iroquois Religion," *Proceedings of the American Philosophical Society,* 105:571–608.

1979   *Behind the Tree of Peace. A Sociological Analysis of Iroquois Warfare* (New York: AMS Press).

1982   "An Ethnological Discussion of Allegany Seneca Wampum Folklore," *Proceedings of the American Philosophical Society,* 126:316–26.

Tooker, Elisabeth

1978   "The League of the Iroquois: Its History, Politics, and Ritual," *Handbook of North American Indians,* 15, Northeast, ed. Bruce G. Trigger (Washington, DC: Smithsonian Institution): 418–41.

Venables, Robert W.

1980   "Iroquois Environments and 'We the People of the United States,' " *American Indian Environments. Ecological Issues in Native American History,* ed. Christopher Vecsey and Robert W. Venables (Syracuse, NY: Syracuse University Press): 81–127.

Wallace, Anthony F. C.

1958a   "Dreams and the Wishes of the Soul: A Type of Psychoanalytic Theory among the Seventeenth Century Iroquois," *American Anthropologist,* 60:234–48.

1958b   "The Dekanawideh Myth Analyzed as the Record of a Revitalization Movement," *Ethnohistory,* 5:118–30.

1972   *The Death and Rebirth of the Seneca* (New York: Random House, Vintage Books).

Wallace, Paul A. W.

1946   *The White Roots of Peace* (Philadelphia: University of Pennsylvania).

1948   "The Return of Hiawatha," *New York History,* 29:385–403.

Weinman, Paul L.

1969   *A Bibliography of the Iroquoian Literature* (Albany: State University of New York Press).

Wolf, Morris
1919   *Iroquois Religion and Its Relation to Their Morals* (New York: Columbia University Press).

Chapter 5: A Navajo Heroic

Astrov, Margot
1950   "The Concept of Motion as the Psychological Leitmotif of Navaho Life and Literature," *Journal of American Folklore*, 63:45–56.

Boas, Franz
1897   "Northern Elements in the Mythology of the Navaho," *American Anthropologist*, old series, 10:371–76.

Brinton, Daniel G.
1882   *American Hero-Myths* (Philadelphia: H. C. Watts).

Campbell, Joseph
1970   *The Hero with a Thousand Faces* (Cleveland: World).
1972   *Myths to Live by* (New York: Bantam).

Collier, John
1962   *On the Gleaming Way* (Chicago: Sage).

Dyk, Walter
1938   *Son of Old Man Hat* (Lincoln: University of Nebraska).
1951   "Notes and Illustrations of Navaho Sex Behavior," *Psychoanalysis and Culture*, ed. George B. Wilbur and Warner Muensterberger (New York: International Universities): 108–19.

Edinger, Edward F.
1976   "The Tragic Hero: An Image of Individuation," *Parabola*, 1:66–73.

Frisbie, Charlotte Johnson
1967   *Kinaaldá. A Study of the Navaho Girl's Puberty Ceremony* (Middletown, CT: Wesleyan University Press).
1978   *Navajo Mortuary Practices and Beliefs* (Hurst, TX: American Indian Quarterly, 4).

Gayton, A. H.
1935   "The Orpheus Myth in North America," *Journal of American Folklore*, 48:263–93.

Gennep, Arnold van
1960   *The Rites of Passage*, trans. Monika B. Vizedom and Gabrielle L. Caffee (Chicago: University of Chicago Press).

Gill, Sam D.
1977   "Prayer as Person: The Performative Force in Navajo Prayer Acts," *History of Religions*, 17:143–57.

Goodwin, Grenville
1945   "A Comparison of Navaho and White Mountain Apache Ceremonial Forms and Categories," *Southwestern Journal of Anthropology*, 1:498–506.

Guthrie, W. K. G.
1966   *Orpheus and Greek Religion. A Study of the Orphic Movement* (New York: W. W. Norton).

Haile, Berard
1933   "Navaho Games of Chance and Taboo," *Primitive Man*, 6:35–40.

1938	"Navaho Chantways and Ceremonials," *American Anthropologist,* 40:639–52.
1940	"A Note on the Navaho Visionary," *American Anthropologist,* 42:359.
1942	"Navaho Upward-Reaching Way and Emergence Place," *American Anthropologist,* 44:407–20.
1943	"Soul Concepts of the Navaho," *Annali Lateranensi,* 7:59–94.
1947a	*Head and Face Masks in Navaho Ceremonialism* (St. Michaels, AZ: St. Michaels Press).
1947b	*Navaho Sacrificial Figurines* (Chicago: University of Chicago Press).
1947c	*Starlore among the Navaho* (Santa Fe: Museum of Navaho Ceremonial Art).
1978	*Love-Magic and Butterfly People. The Slim Curly Version of the Ajilee and Mothway Myths,* ed. Karl Luckert (Flagstaff: Museum of Northern Arizona).
1979	*Waterway. A Navajo Ceremonial Myth Told by Black Mustache Circle* (Flagstaff: Museum of Northern Arizona).

Henderson, Joseph L.
1956   "A Psychological Commentary," *The Pollen Path,* ed. Margaret Schevill Link (Stanford: Stanford University Press): 125–40.

Hill, W. W.
1935a   "The Hand Trembling Ceremony of the Navaho," *El Palacio,* 38:65–69.
1935b   "The Status of the Hermaphrodite and Transvestite in Navaho Culture," *American Anthropologist,* 37:273–9.
1936   "Navaho Rites for Dispelling Insanity and Delirium," *El Palacio,* 41:71–74.
1938a   *The Agricultural and Hunting Methods of the Navaho Indians* (New Haven: Yale University Press Publications in Anthropology, 18).
1938b   "Navajo Use of Jimsonweed," *New Mexico Anthropologist,* 3:19–21.
1940   "Navajo Salt Gathering," *The University of New Mexico Bulletin,* Anthropological Series, 3:5–25.
1944   "The Navaho Indians and the Ghost Dance of 1890," *American Anthropologist,* 46:523–7.

Hill, W. W. and Dorothy W. Hill
1945   "Navaho Coyote Tales and Their Position in the Southern Athabaskan Group," *Journal of American Folklore,* 58:317–43.

Hodge, William H.
1964   "Navaho Pentecostalism," *Anthropological Quarterly,* 37:73–93.

Hultkrantz, Åke
1957   *The North American Indian Orpheus Tradition* (Stockholm: Ethnographical Museum of Sweden, Monograph Series, 2).

Klapp, Orrin E.
1949   "The Folk Hero," *Journal of American Folklore,* 62:17–25.
1972   *Heroes, Villains, and Fools. Reflections of the American Character* (San Diego: Aegis).

Kluckhohn, Clyde
1938a   "Participation in Ceremonials in a Navaho Community," *American Anthropologist,* 40:359–69.
1938b   "Navaho Women's Knowledge of Their Song Ceremonials," *El Palacio,* 45:87–92.
1968   *Navaho Witchcraft* (Boston: Beacon).

1969   "Navaho Categories," *Primitive Views of the World,* ed. Stanley Diamond (New York: Columbia University Press): 95–128.

Kluckhohn, Clyde and Dorothea Leighton
1962   *The Navaho* (Garden City, NY: Doubleday).

Kluckhohn, Clyde and Katherine Spencer
1940   *A Bibliography of the Navajo Indians* (New York: J. J. Augustin).

Kluckhohn, Clyde and Leland C. Wyman
1940   *An Introduction to Navaho Chant Practice* (Menasha, WI: Memoirs of the American Anthropological Association, 53).

Ladd, John
1957   *The Structure of a Moral Code. A Philosophical Analysis of Ethical Discourse Applied to the Ethics of the Navaho Indians* (Cambridge: Harvard University Press).

Leighton, Alexander H. and Dorothea C. Leighton
1941   "Elements of Psychotherapy in Navaho Religion," *Psychiatry,* 4:515–23.
1942   "Some Types of Uneasiness and Fear in a Navaho Indian Community," *American Anthropologist,* 44:194–209.

Luckert, Karl W.
1972   "Traditional Navaho Theories of Disease and Healing," *Arizona Medicine,* 29:570–73.
1975   *The Navajo Hunter Tradition* (Tucson: University of Arizona Press).
1978   *A Navajo Bringing-Home Ceremony. The Claus Chee Sonny Version of Deerway Ajiłee* (Flagstaff: Museum of Northern Arizona).
1979   *Coyoteway. A Navajo Holyway Healing Ceremonial* (Tucson: University of Arizona Press; Flagstaff: Museum of Northern Arizona).

Matthews, Washington
1897   *Navaho Legends* (New York: G. E. Stechert, Memoirs of the American Folk-Lore Society, 5).
1898   "Ichthyophobia," *Journal of American Folklore,* 11:105–12.
1899   "The Study of Ethics among the Lower Races," *Journal of American Folklore,* 12:1–9.
1902   *The Night Chant, A Navaho Ceremony* (New York: Memoirs of the American Museum of Natural History, 6).

Miller, David L.
1970   "Orestes: Myth and Dream as Catharsis," *Myths, Dreams, and Religion,* ed. Joseph Campbell (New York: E. P. Dutton): 26–47.

Morgan, William
1931   "Navaho Treatment of Sickness: Diagnosticians," *American Anthropologist,* 33:390–402.
1932   "Navaho Dreams," *American Anthropologist,* 34:390–405.
1936   *Human-Wolves among the Navaho* (New Haven: Yale University Press Publications in Anthropology, 11).

Morris, Ivan
1975   *The Nobility of Failure. Tragic Heroes in the History of Japan* (New York: Holt, Rinehart & Winston).

Newcomb, Franc Johnson
1938   "The Navajo Listening Rite," *El Palacio,* 45:46–49.
1939   "How the Navajo Adopt Rites," *El Palacio,* 46:25–27.
1940   *Navajo Omens and Taboos* (Santa Fe: Rydal).
1964   *Hosteen Klah. Navaho Medicine Man and Sand Painter* (Norman: University of Oklahoma Press).

Newcomb, Franc Johnson, Stanley Fishler, and Mary C. Wheelwright
1956   *A Study of Navajo Symbolism* (Cambridge: Papers of the Peabody Museum of Archaeology and Ethnology, Harvard University, 32).

Norman, Dorothy
1969   *The Hero. Myth/Image/Symbol* (New York: World).

O'Bryan, Aileen
1956   *The Dine. Origin Myths of the Navaho Indians* (Washington, DC: Smithsonian Institution, Bureau of American Ethnology, Bulletin 163).

Pepper, George H.
1908   "Ah-jih-lee-hah-neh, a Navajo Legend," *Journal of American Folklore,* 21:173–83.

Raglan, Fitzroy Richard Somerset
1956   *The Hero. A Study in Tradition, Myth, and Drama* (New York: Vintage).

Rank, Otto
1914   *The Myth of the Birth of the Hero (A Psychological Interpretation of Mythology)* (New York: Nervous and Mental Disease Monograph Series, 18).

Rapoport, Robert N.
1954   *Changing Navajo Religious Values. A Study of Christian Missions to the Rimrock Navahos* (Cambridge: Papers of the Peabody Museum of American Archaeology and Ethnology, Harvard University, 41).

Reichard, Gladys A.
1944   *Prayer: The Compulsive Word* (New York: J. J. Augustin, Monographs of the American Ethnological Society, 7).
1948   "Navajo Classification of Natural Objects," *Plateau,* 21:7–12.
1949   "The Navaho and Christianity," *American Anthropologist,* 51:66–71.
1974   *Navaho Religion. A Study of Symbolism* (Princeton: Princeton University Press, Bollingen Series, 18).

Sandars, N. K., ed.
1964   *The Epic of Gilgamesh* (Baltimore: Penguin).

Sandner, Donald
1979   *Navaho Symbols of Healing* (New York: Harcourt Brace Jovanovich).

Sapir, Edward
1936   "Internal Linguistic Evidence Suggestive of the Northern Origin of the Navaho," *American Anthropologist,* 38:224–35.

Spencer, Katherine
1947   *Reflection of Social Life in the Navaho Origin Myth* (Albuquerque: University of New Mexico Press, Publications in Anthropology, 3).
1957   *Mythology and Values. An Analysis of Navaho Chantway Myths* (Philadelphia: Memoirs of the American Folklore Society, 48).

Thompson, Stith
  1946   *The Folktale* (New York: Holt, Rinehart and Winston).

Toelken, J. Barre
  1969   "The 'Pretty Language' of Yellowman: Genre, Mode, and Texture in Navaho Coyote Narratives," *Genre,* 2:211–35.
  1976   "Seeing with a Native Eye: How Many Sheep Will It Hold?," *Seeing with a Native Eye. Essays on Native American Religion,* ed. Walter Holden Capps (New York: Harper & Row): 9–24.
  1977   "The Demands of Harmony. An Appreciation of Navajo Relations," *Parabola,* 2:74–81.

Tozzer, Alfred Marston
  1909   "Notes on Religious Ceremonials of the Navaho," *Putnam Anniversary Volume, Anthropological Essays* (New York: G. E. Stechert): 299–343.

Travers, P. L.
  1976   "The World of the Hero," *Parabola,* 1:42–51.

Tyler, Hamilton A.
  1964   *Pueblo Gods and Myths* (Norman: University of Oklahoma Press).

Underhill, Ruth M.
  1948   *Ceremonial Patterns in the Greater Southwest* (New York: J. J. Augustin, Monographs of the American Ethnological Society, 13).

Van Deursen, Arie
  1931   *Der Heilbringer. Eine Ethnologische über den Heilbringer bei den Nord-Americkanischen Indianern* (Groningen, Den Haag: Bij J. B. Wolters' Uitgevers-Maatschappij).

Van Valkenburgh, Richard
  1945   "The Government of the Navajos," *Arizona Quarterly,* 1:63–73.

Vogt, Evon Z. and Ethel M. Albert, eds.
  1970   *People of Rimrock. A Study of Values in Five Cultures* (New York: Atheneum).

Witherspoon, Gary
  1975   *The Central Concepts of Navajo World View* (Lisse: Peter de Ridder).
  1977   *Language and Art in the Navajo Universe* (Ann Arbor: University of Michigan Press).

Worth, Sol and John Adair
  1972   *Through Navajo Eyes. An Exploration in Film and Anthropology* (Bloomington: Indiana University Press).

Wyman, Leland C.
  1936   "Navaho Diagnosticians," *American Anthropologist,* 38:236–46.
  1950   "The Religion of the Navaho Indians," *Forgotten Religions,* ed. Vergilius Ferm (New York: Philosophical Library): 341–61.
  1957   *Beautyway: A Navaho Ceremonial* (New York: Bollingen Foundation Series, 53).
  1962   *The Windways of the Navaho* (Colorado Springs: The Taylor Museum of the Colorado Springs Fine Arts Center).
  1970   *Blessingway* (Tucson: University of Arizona Press).

Wyman, Leland C. and Flora L. Bailey
  1943a   "Navaho Girl's Puberty Rite," *New Mexico Anthropologist,* 6–7:3–12.
  1943b   *Navaho Upward-Reaching-Way. Objective Behavior, Rationale and Sanction* (Albuquerque: University of New Mexico Bulletin, Anthropological Series, 4).

1945   "Idea and Action Patterns in Navaho Flintway," *Southwestern Journal of Anthropology*, 1:356–77.

Wyman, Leland, C., W. W. Hill and Iva Ósanai

1942   *Navajo Eschatology* (Albuquerque: University of New Mexico Bulletin, Anthropological Series, 4).

Wyman, Leland C. and Clyde Kluckhohn

1938   *Navaho Classification of Their Song Ceremonials* (Menasha, WI: Memoirs of the American Anthropological Association, 50).

Chapter 6: An American Indian Monomyth: Narratives of Peyote's Origin

Aberle, David F.

1966   *The Peyote Religion among the Navaho* (Chicago: Aldine).

Aberle, David F. and Omer C. Stewart

1957   *Navaho and Ute Peyotism: A Chronological and Distributional Study* (Boulder: University of Colorado Press).

Albaugh, Bernard J. and Philip O. Anderson

1974   "Peyote in the Treatment of Alcoholism among American Indians," *American Journal of Psychiatry*, 131:1247–50.

American Review of Reviews

1922   "The Problem of Peyote" (editorial), 65:437–38.

Anderson, Edward F.

1985   *Peyote. The Divine Cactus* (Tucson: University of Arizona Press).

Arizona News

1956   "Peyote Users Lose Round as Navajo Council Strengthens Anti-Peyotism Measure," 6 July:1, 4.

Armstrong, Benj. G.

1892   *Early Life among the Indians* (Ashland, WI: A. W. Bowron).

Arth, Malcolm J.

1956   "A Functional View of Peyotism in Omaha Culture," *Plains Anthropologist*, 7:25–29.

Ball, Eve

1966   "Peyote Priest," *Frontier Times*, 40:28–30.

Barber, Bernard

1941   "A Socio-Cultural Interpretation of the Peyote Cult," *American Anthropologist*, 43:673–75.

Barber, Carroll, G.

1959   "Peyote and the Definition of Narcotic," *American Anthropologist*, 61:641–46.

1960   "Rejoinder to Maurer," *American Anthropologist*, 62:685–87.

Barnard, Mary

1963   "The God in the Flowerpot," *American Scholar*, 32:578–86.

Barrett, S. A.

1911   *The Dream Dance of the Chippewa and Menominee Indians of Northern Wisconsin* (Milwaukee: Bulletin of the Public Museum of the City of Milwaukee).

Barron, Frank, Murray E. Jarvik, and Sterling Bunnell, Jr.

1964   "The Hallucinogenic Drugs," *Scientific American*, 210:29–37.

Baugh, Timothy G.
    1970   "Revitalization Movements among the Kiowa and Kiowa-Apache," *Papers in Anthropology*, 2:66–83.

Beals, Kenneth
    1971   "The Dynamics of Kiowa Apache Peyotism," *Papers in Anthropology*, 12:35–89.

Beals, Ralph L.
    1932   "Comparative Ethnology of Northern Mexico before 1750," *Ibero-Americana*, 2:93–225.

Beck, Peggy V. and A. L. Walters
    1977   *The Sacred Ways of Knowledge, Sources of Life* (Tsaile, AZ: Navajo Community College Press).

Bee, Robert L.
    1965   "Peyotism in North American Indian Groups," *Transactions of the Kansas Academy of Science*, 68:13–61.
    1966   "Potawatomi Peyotism: The Influence of Traditional Patterns," *Southwestern Journal of Anthropology*, 22:194–205.

Benedict, Ruth
    1930   "Psychological Types in the Cultures of the Southwest," *Proceedings of the 23rd International Congress of Americanists, 1928:* 572–81.

Benítez, Fernando
    1975   *In the Magic Land of Peyote* (Austin: University of Texas Press).

Bennett, Wendell C. and Robert M. Zingg
    1935   *The Tarahumara. An Indian Tribe of Northern Mexico* (Chicago: University of Chicago Press).

Benzi, Marino
    1969   "Voisins des Huichols sous l'effet du peyotl," *L'Hygiene Mentale*, 58:61–97.
    1972   *Les derniers adorateurs du peyotl. Croyances, coutumes et mythes des indiens Huichol* (Paris: Gallimard).

Bergman, Robert L.
    1971   "Navajo Peyote Use: Its Apparent Safety," *American Journal of Psychiatry*, 128:695–99.

Berquist, Laura
    1957   "Peyote. The Strange Church of Cactus Eaters," *Look*, 21:36–41.

Bittle, William E.
    1954   "The Peyote Ritual: Kiowa-Apache," *Bulletin of the Oklahoma Anthropological Society*, 2:69–78.
    1960   "The Curative Aspects of Peyotism," *Bios*, 31:140–48.

Boyd, Maurice
    1983   *Kiowa Voices. Myths, Legends and Folktales*, 2 vols. (Fort Worth: Texas Christian University Press), 2.

Boyer, L. Bryce, Ruth M. Boyer, and Harry W. Basehart
    1973   "Shamanism and Peyote Use among the Apaches of the Mescalero Indian Reservation," *Hallucinogens and Shamanism*, ed. Michael J. Harner (London: Oxford University Press): 53–66.

Braasch, W. F., B. J. Branton, and A. J. Chesley
    1949   "Survey of the Medical Care among the Upper Midwest Indians," *Journal of the American Medical Association*, 139:220–26.

Brand, Stewart
1967   "The Native American Church Meeting," *Psychedelic Review,* 9:20–35.
Brant, Charles S.
1950   "Peyotism among the Kiowa-Apache and Neighboring Tribes," *Southwestern Journal of Anthropology,* 6:212–22.
1963   "Joe Blackbear's Story of the Origin of the Peyote Religion," *Plains Anthropologist,* 8:180–81.
Brito, Silvester John
1975   "The Development and Change of the Peyote Ceremony through Time and Space," unpublished Ph.D. dissertation, Indiana University.
Bromberg, Walter and Charles L. Tranter
1943   "Peyote Intoxication: Some Psychological Aspects of Peyote Rite," *Journal of Nervous and Mental Disease,* 97:518–27.
Campbell, T. N.
1958   "Origin of the Mescal Bean Cult," *American Anthropologist,* 60:156–60.
Carlton, Henry
1969   "Peyote History Told by Member," *Navajo Times,* 6 November, 10:2.
Cash, Joseph H. and Herbert T. Hoover, eds.
1971   *To Be an Indian. An Oral History* (New York: Holt, Rinehart and Winston).
Cazeneuve, J.
1959   "Le peyotisme au Nouveau-Mexique," *Revue Philosophique,* 149:169–82.
Christian Century
1962   "Navajos Sentenced for Using Peyote" (editorial), 79:1506.
Church and State
1964   "Religious Use of Peyote Upheld," 17:3.
Clark, David
1967   "The Peyote Religion," *Navajo Times,* 22 June, 8:4.
Clark, Walter Houston
1969   *Chemical Ecstacy. Psychedelic Drugs and Religion* (New York: Sheed and Ward).
Clifton, James A.
1968   "Factional Conflict and the Indian Community: The Prairie Potawatomi Case," *The American Indian Today,* ed. Stuart Levine and Nancy Oestreich Lurie (Deland, FL: Everett / Edwards, Inc.): 115–32.
Cohen, Alan
1976   "The Small Grey Bird. A Study of Forms and Patterns in Shamanism and Ecstatic Experience," unpublished B. Litt. thesis, Oxford University.
Collier, Donald
1937   "Peyote, a General Study of the Plant, the Cult, and the Drug," *Survey of Conditions of Indians in United States,* United States Congress. Senate Committee on Indian Affairs, 75th Congress (Washington, DC: Government Printing Office): 18234–57.
Collins, John James
1967   "Peyotism and Religious Membership at Taos Pueblo, New Mexico," *The Southwestern Social Science Quarterly,* 48:183–191.
1968   "A Descriptive Introduction to the Taos Peyote Ceremony," *Ethnology,* 7:427–49.

Conn, Richard, ed.
    1982   *Circles of the World. The Traditional Art of the Plains Indians* (Seattle: University of Washington Press).

Curtis, Edward S.
    1907–30   *The North American Indian,* 20 vols. (Cambridge: Harvard University Press and Edward S. Curtis).

Curtis, George
    1967   "Dear Editor," *Navajo Times,* 9 February, 8:23.

Davis, Leslie B.
    1961   *Peyotism and the Blackfeet Indians of Montana. An Historical Assessment* (Browning, MT: Museum of the Plains Indians).

d'Azevedo, Warren L.
    1973   "The Delegation to Washington: A Washo Peyotist Narrative," *The Indian Historian,* 6:4–6.
    1978   *Straight with the Medicine. Narratives of Washoe Followers of the Tipi Way* (Reno: University of Nevada).

Denman, Leslie Van Ness
    1957   *The Peyote Ritual. Visions and Descriptions of Monroe Tsa Toke* (San Francisco: Grabhorn Press).

Densmore, Frances
    1941   "Native Songs of Two Hybrid Ceremonies among the American Indians," *American Anthropologist,* 43:77–82.

Devereux, George
    1969   *Reality and Dream. Psychotherapy of a Plains Indian* (Garden City, NY: Doubleday).

Dittmann, Allen T. and Harvey C. Moore
    1957   "Disturbance in Dreams as Related to Peyotism among the Navaho," *American Anthropologist,* 59:642–49.

Downs, James F.
    1966   *The Two Worlds of the Washo, An Indian Tribe of California and Nevada* (New York: Holt, Rinehart and Winston).

Dustin, C. Burton
    1960   *Peyotism and New Mexico* (Farmington, NM: C. Burton Dustin).

Easterlin, Malcolm
    1941   "Peyote—Indian Problem No. 1," *Scribner's Commentator,* 11:77–82.

Everett, Michael W.
    1967   "Peyotism and the Pueblo Indians of the Southwestern United States," Centre for New Religious Movements, Selly Oak Colleges, Birmingham, England.

Fenton, William N.
    1957   "Factionalism at Taos Pueblo, New Mexico," *Bulletin, Bureau of American Ethnology,* 164:297–344.

Feraca, Stephen E.
    1963   *Wakinyan. Contemporary Teton Dakota Religion* (Browning, MT: Bureau of Indian Affairs Blackfeet Agency).

Fernberger, Samuel W.
    1923   "Observations on Taking Peyote *(Anhalonium Lewinii),*" *American Journal of Psychology,* 34:267–70.

1932 "Further Observations on Peyote Intoxication," *Journal of Abnormal and Social Psychology,* 26:367–78.

Fintzelberg, Nicholas M.
1969 *Peyote Paraphernalia* (San Diego: San Diego Museum of Man).

Fortune, Reo Franklin
1932 *Omaha Secret Societies* (New York: Columbia University Press).

Furst, Peter T.
1972 "To Find Our Life: Peyote among the Huichol Indians of Mexico," *Flesh of the Gods. The Ritual Use of Hallucinogens,* ed. Peter T. Furst (New York: Praeger): 136–84.

Furst, Peter T. and Barbara G. Myerhoff
1966 "Myth as History: The Jimson Weed Cycle of the Huichols of Mexico," *Anthropologica,* 17:3–39.

Gerber, Peter
1980 *Die Peyote-Religion. Nordamerikanische Indianer auf der Suche nach einer Identität* (Zürich: Völkerkundemuseum der Universitat Zürich).
1982 "On the Theoretical Explanation of the Peyote Religion," Centre for New Religious Movements, Selly Oak Colleges, Birmingham, England.

Gilles, Albert S., Sr.
1970 "The Southwestern Indian and His Drugs," *Southwest Review,* 55:196–203.

Gilmore, Melvin R.
1919 "The Mescal Society among the Omaha Indians," *Publications of the Nebraska State Historical Society,* 19:163–67.

Goggin, John M.
1938 "A Note on Cheyenne Peyote," *New Mexico Anthropologist,* 3:26–30.

Harrington, M. R.
1944 "Peyote Outfit," *The Masterkey,* 18:143–44.

Hayes, Alden
1940 "Peyote Cult on the Goshiute Reservation at Deep Creek, Utah," *New Mexico Anthropologist,* 4:34–36.

Hertzerg, Hazel W.
1971 *The Search for an American Indian Identity. Modern Pan-Indian Movements* (Syracuse, NY: Syracuse University Press).

Hill, Tom and Kenneth Beals
1966 "Some Notes on Kiowa-Apache Peyotism with Special Reference to Ethics and Changes," *Papers in Anthropology,* 7:1–24.

Hoebel, E. Adamson
1949 "The Wonderful Herb. An Indian Cult Vision Experience," *Western Humanities Review,* 3:126–30.

Howard, Frankie
1966 "Peyote Not Religious Herb but Drug, Councilman Says," *Navajo Times,* 7 July, 7:1, 5.

Howard, James H.
1950 "Omaha Peyotism," *Museum News,* 11:3–5.
1951a "A Tonkawa Peyote Legend," *Museum News,* 12:1–4.
1951b "Omaha Peyotism," *Hobbies,* 56:142.
1955 "Pan-Indian Culture of Oklahoma," *Scientific Monthly,* 81:215–20.

1956   "An Oto-Omaha Peyote Ritual," *Southwestern Journal of Anthropology,* 12:432–36.

1957   "The Mescal Bean Cult of the Central and Southern Plains: An Ancestor of the Peyote Cult?," *American Anthropologist,* 59:75–87.

1960   "Mescalism and Peyotism Once Again," *Plains Anthropologist,* 5:84–85.

1962a   "Peyote Jokes," *Journal of American Folklore,* 75:10–14.

1962b   "Potawatomi Mescalism and Its Relationship to the Diffusion of the Peyote Cult," *Plains Anthropologist,* 7:125–35.

1967   "Half Moon Way. The Peyote Ritual of Chief White Bear," *Museum News,* 28:1–24.

Howard, James H. and Peter Le Claire et al.
1965   *The Ponca Tribe* (Washington, DC: Smithsonian Institution, Bureau of American Ethnology, Bulletin 195).

Hultkrantz, Åke
1981   "Conditions for the Spread of the Peyote Cult in North America," *Belief and Worship in Native North America,* ed. Christopher Vecsey (Syracuse, NY: Syracuse University Press): 282–93.

Huot, Martha Champion
1936   "Peyote Songs," *Transition,* 23:117–19.

The Independent
1909   "The New Mescal Religion," 66:430–31.

Indian Voices
1967   "Indians Defend Use of 'Vision Plant,' " February–March: 5–6.

Jones, Jonathan H.
1899   *A Condensed History of the Apache and Comanche Indian Tribes* (San Antonio, TX: Johnson Bros. Printing Co.).

Kamffer, Raúl
1957   "Plumed Arrows of the Huichols of Western Mexico," *Américas,* 9:12–16.

Kiste, Robert C.
1962   "Crow Peyotism," Centre for New Religious Movements, Selly Oak Colleges, Birmingham, England.

Klineberg, Otto
1934   "Notes on the Huichol," *American Anthropologist,* 36:446–60.

Klüver, Heinrich
1966   *Mescal and Mechanisms of Hallucinations* (Chicago: University of Chicago Press).

Kneale, Albert H.
1950   *Indian Agent. An Autobiographical Sketch* (Caldwell, ID: Caxton Printers).

Kochampanaskin, Ralph
1938   "Peyote Origin Myth," as told to Omer C. Stewart, ms.

Kroeber, Alfred L.
1983   *The Arapaho* (Lincoln: University of Nebraska Press).

La Barre, Weston
1939   "Notes on Richard Schultes' 'The Appeal of Peyote,' " *American Anthropologist,* 41:340–42.

1941   "A Cultist Drug-Addiction in an Indian Alcoholic," *Bulletin of the Menninger Clinic,* 5:40–46.

1946   "Review of Omer C. Stewart, *Washo-Northern Paiute Peyotism. A Study in Acculturation,*" *American Anthropologist,* 48:633–35.

1947   "Primitive Psychotherapy in Native American Cultures: Peyotism and Confession," *The Journal of Abnormal and Social Psychology,* 42:294–309.

1957   "Mescalism and Peyotism," *American Anthropologist,* 59:708–11.

1958   "Review of David F. Aberle and Omer C. Stewart, *Navaho and Ute Peyotism. A Chronological and Distributional Study,*" *American Anthropologist,* 60:171.

1964   "The Narcotic Complex of the New World," *Diogenes,* 48:125–38.

1970   *The Peyote Cult* (New York: Schocken Books).

1971   "Materials for a History of Studies of Crisis Cults: A Bibliographic Essay," *Current Anthropology,* 12:3–44.

1972   "Hallucinogens and the Shamanic Origins of Religion," *Flesh of the Gods. The Ritual Use of Hallucinogens,* ed. Peter T. Furst (New York: Praeger): 261–78.

La Barre, Weston et al.

1951   "Statement on Peyote," *Science,* 114:582–83.

Lahurreau, H. L.

1969   "Whitewashed the Peyote Way?," *Navajo Times,* 4 December, 10:4.

Landes, Ruth

1970   *The Prairie Potawatomi. Tradition and Ritual in the Twentieth Century* (Madison: University of Wisconsin Press).

Laney, John H.

1972   "The Peyote Movement: An Introduction," *Spring:* 110–31.

Lanternari, Vittorio

1965   *The Religions of the Oppressed. A Study of Modern Messianic Cults,* trans. Lisa Sergio (New York: New American Library).

Laswell, Harold D.

1935   "Collective Autism as a Consequence of Culture Contact: Notes on Religious Training and the Peyote Cult at Taos," *Zeitschrift für Socialforschung,* 4:232–47.

Laurence, M., Sr.

1953   "A Trip to Quapaw in 1903," *Chronicles of Oklahoma,* 31:142–67.

Leonard, Irving A.

1942   "Peyote and the Mexican Inquisition, 1620," *American Anthropologist,* 44:324–26.

Levine, Stuart

1968   "Forward: The Survival of Indian Identity," *The American Indian Today,* ed. Stuart Levine and Nancy Oestreich Lurie (Deland, FL: Everett/Edwards, Inc.): 1–23.

Lieber, Michael D.

1972   "Opposition to Peyotism among the Western Shoshone: The Message of Traditional Belief," *Man,* 7:387–96.

Linton, Ralph

1943   "Nativistic Movements," *American Anthropologist,* 45:230–40.

Long, Haniel

1941   *Piñon Country* (New York: Duell, Sloan & Pearce).

Lumholtz, Carl
  1894a   "The American Cave-Dwellers: The Tarahumaris of the Sierra Madre," *Bulletin of the American Geographical Society*, 26:299–325.
  1894b   "Tarahumari Dances and Plant-Worship," *Scribner's Magazine*, 16:438–56.
  1898   "The Huichol Indians of Mexico," *Bulletin of the American Museum of Natural History*," 10:1–14.
  1900   "Symbolism of the Huichol Indians," *Memoirs of the American Museum of Natural History*, 3:1–228.
  1902   *Unknown Mexico*, 2 vols. (New York: Charles Scribner's Sons).

MacGregor, Gordon
  1951   *Warriors without Weapons. A Study of the Society and Personality Development of the Pine Ridge Sioux* (Chicago: University of Chicago Press).

Malouf, Carling
  1942   "Gosiute Peyotism," *American Anthropololgist*, 44:93–103.

Marriott, Alice
  1954   "The Opened Door," *The New Yorker*, 30:80–82, 85–91.

Marriott, Alice and Carol K. Rachlin
  1968   *American Indian Mythology* (New York: New American Library).
  1971   *Peyote* (New York: New American Library).

Master, R. E. L. and Jean Houston
  1966   *The Varieties of Psychedelic Experience* (New York: Holt, Rinehart and Winston).

McAllester, David P.
  1949   *Peyote Music* (New York: Viking Fund).
  1952   "Menomini Peyote Music," *Transactions of the American Philosophical Society*, 42:681–700.
  1954   *Enemy Way Music* (Cambridge: Papers of the Peabody Museum of American Archaeology and Ethnology).

McAllister, J. Gilbert
  1966   "Kiowa-Apache Tales," *The Sky is My Tipi*, ed. Mody C. Boatright (Dallas: Southern Methodist University Press): 1–141.

McNickle, D'Arcy
  1943   "Peyote and the Indian," *Scientific Monthly*, 57:220–29.

McRae, William E.
  1975   "Peyote Rituals of the Kiowas," *Southwest Review*, 60:217–33.

Merriam, Alan P. and Warren L. d'Azevedo
  1957   "Washo Peyote Songs," *American Anthropologist*, 59:615–41.

Methvin, J. J.
  1899   *Andele, or, The Mexican-Kiowa Captive* (Louisville, KY: Pentecostal Herald Press).
  1927   "Reminiscences of Life among the Indians," *Chronicles of Oklahoma*, 5:166–79.

Momaday, N. Scott
  1968   *House Made of Dawn* (New York: Harper & Row).

Mooney, James
  1892   "Eating the Mescal," *The Augusta Chronicle*, 24 January: 11.
  1892   "A Kiowa Mescal Rattle," *American Anthropologist*, old series, 5:64–65.
  1896a   "The Ghost-Dance Religion and the Sioux Outbreak of 1890," *Bureau of*

American Ethnology, 14th Annual Report, 1892–93, Part 2 (Washington, DC: Smithsonian Institution, Government Printing Office): 641–1136.

1896b   "The Mescal Plant and Ceremony," *Therapeutic Gazette,* 12:7–11.

1897   "The Kiowa Peyote Rite," *Der Urquell,* 1:329–33.

n.d.   "Peyote," Smithsonian Institution, Bureau of American Ethnology Archives, no. 2537.

Morgan, George Robert

1976   "Man, Plant, and Religion. Peyote Trade on the Mustang Plains of Texas," unpublished Ph.D. dissertation, University of Colorado.

Morgan, George Robert and Omer C. Stewart

1984   "Peyote Trade in South Texas," *Southwestern Historical Quarterly,* 87:269–96.

Murie, James R.

1914   "Pawnee Indian Societies," *Anthropological Papers of the American Museum of Natural History,* 11:543–644.

Myerhoff, Barbara G.

1970   "The Deer-Maize-Peyote Symbol Complex among the Huichol Indians of Mexico," *Anthropological Quarterly,* 43:64–78.

1974   *Peyote Hunt. The Sacred Journey of the Huichol Indians* (Ithaca, NY: Cornell University Press).

Navajo Tribal Council

1954   "Minutes of Meetings, 1–3 June, 1954," mimeograph, Centre for New Religious Movements, Selly Oak Colleges, Birmingham, England.

Newberne, Robert E. L.

1922   *Peyote. An Abridged Compilation from the Files of the Bureau of Indian Affairs* (Washington, DC: Government Printing Office).

Newcomb, William W., Jr.

1955   "A Note on Cherokee-Delaware Pan-Indianism," *American Anthropologist,* 57:1041–45.

1956a   "A Reappraisal of the 'Cultural Sink' of Texas," *Southwestern Journal of Anthropology,* 12:145–53.

1956b   "The Peyote Cult of the Delaware Indians," *Texas Journal of Science,* 8:202–11.

1961   *The Indians of Texas from Prehistoric to Modern Times* (Austin: University of Texas Press).

Old Coyote, Henry and Lloyd Old Coyote

1969   "The Sacramental Use of Peyote," *Absaroka,* March: 1–4.

Opler, Marvin K.

1940   "The Character and History of the Southern Ute Peyote Rite," *American Anthropologist,* 42:463–78.

1942   "Fact and Fancy in Ute Peyotism," *American Anthropologist,* 44:151–59.

Opler, Morris E.

1936   "The Influence of Aboriginal Pattern and White Contact on a Recently Introduced Ceremony, the Mescalero Peyote Rite," *Journal of American Folklore,* 49:143–66.

1938   "The Use of Peyote by the Carrizo and Lipan Apache Tribes," *American Anthropologist,* 40:271–85.

1939   "A Description of a Tonkawa Peyote Meeting Held in 1902," *American Anthropologist*, 41:433–39.
1940   *Myths and Legends of the Lipan Apache Indians* (New York: J. J. Augustin).
1945   "A Mescalero Apache Account of the Origin of the Peyote Ceremony," *El Palacio*, 52:210–12.
1969   *Apache Odyssey. A Journey between Two Worlds* (New York: Holt, Rinehart and Winston).

Page, Elizabeth M.
1915   *In Camp and Tepee. An Indian Mission Story* (New York: Board of Publication and Bible-School Work of the Reformed Church in America).

Parker, Arthur C.
1917   "The Perils of the Peyote Poison," *American Indian Magazine*, 5:12–13.

Parman, Donald L.
1976   *The Navajos and the New Deal* (New Haven: Yale University Press).

Parsons, Elsie Clews
1929   *Kiowa Tales* (New York: G. E. Stechert).
1936   *Taos Pueblo* (Menasha, WI: George Banta Publishing Company).
1969   *Notes on the Caddo* (New York: Kraus Reprint Co.).

Petrullo, Vincenzo
1934   *The Diabolic Root. A Study of Peyotism, the New Indian Religion, among the Delawares* (Philadelphia: University of Pennsylvania Press).
1940   "Peyotism as an Emergent Indian Culture," *Indians at Work*, 7:51–60.

Pierson, (Mrs.) Delavan L.
1915   "American Indian Peyote Worship," *The Missionary Review of the World*, 28:201–6.

Posern-Zielińska, Mirosława
1981   "Native Religions and Ethnic Identity of the American Indians," *North American Indian Studies. European Contributions*, ed. Pieter Hovens (Göttingen: Edition Herodot): 183–99.

Prentiss, D. W. and Francis P. Morgan
1895   "Anhalonium Lewinii (Mescal Buttons)," *Therapeutic Gazette*, 11:577–85.

Rachlin, Carol K.
1964   "Native American Indian Church in Oklahoma," *Chronicles of Oklahoma*, 42:262–72.
1968   "Tight Shoe Night: Oklahoma Indians Today," *The American Indian Today*, ed. Stuart Levine and Nancy Oestreich Lurie (Deland, FL: Everett/Edwards, Inc.): 99–114.

Radin, Paul
1913   "Personal Reminiscences of a Winnebago Indian," *Journal of American Folklore*, 26:293–318.
1914   "A Sketch of the Peyote Cult of the Winnebago: A Study in Borrowing," *Journal of Religious Psychology*, 7:1–22.
1950   "The Religious Experiences of an American Indian," *Eranos-Jahrbuch*, 18:249–90.
1963   *The Autobiography of a Winnebago Indian* (New York: Dover Publications).
1971   *The Winnebago Tribe* (Lincoln: University of Nebraska Press).

Rhodes, Willard

1958   "A Study of Musical Diffusion Based on the Wandering of the Opening Peyote Song," *International Folk Music Journal,* 10:42–49.

Ridgway, James

1965   "More Lost Indians," *The New Republic,* 153:19–22.

Ritzenthaler, Robert E. and Frederick A. Peterson

1956   *The Mexican Kickapoo Indians* (Milwaukee: Milwaukee Public Museum).

Ruby, Robert H.

1955   *The Oglala Sioux. Warriors in Transition* (New York: Vantage Press, Inc.).

1962   "I Witnessed a Service of the Indian Peyote Cult," *Frontier Times,* 36:30–31, 40.

Safford, William E.

1915   "An Aztec Narcotic," *Journal of Heredity,* 6:291–311.

Schleiffer, Hedwig, ed.

1973   *Sacred Narcotic Plants of the New World Indians. An Anthology of Texts from the Sixteenth Century to Date* (New York: Hafner Press).

Schultes, Richard Evans

1938a   "The Appeal of Peyote *(Lophophora Williamsii)* as a Medicine," *American Anthropologist,* 40:688–715.

1938b   "Peyote—An American Indian Heritage from Mexico," *El Mexico Antiguo,* 4:199–208.

1972   "An Overview of Hallucinogens in the Western Hemisphere," *Flesh of the Gods. The Ritual Use of Hallucinogens,* ed. Peter T. Furst (New York: Praeger): 3–54.

Scotch, Norman A. and Freda L. Scotch

1971   "Social Factors in Hypertension among the Washo," *The Washo Indians of California and Nevada,* ed. Warren L. d'Azevedo (Salt Lake City: University of Utah Press): 69–76.

Seymour, Gertrude

1916   "Peyote Worship. An Indian Cult and a Powerful Drug," *Survey,* 36:181–84.

Shimkin, D. B.

1942   "Dynamics of Recent Wind River Shoshone History," *American Anthropologist,* 44:451–62.

Shonle, Ruth

1925   "Peyote, the Giver of Visions," *American Anthropologist,* 27:53–75.

Simmons, C. S.

1918   "The Peyote Road: An Exegesis of the Religious and Mystic Rites of the North American Indians," Smithsonian Institution, Bureau of American Ethnology Archives, no. 2537 (part).

Siskin, Edgar E.

1983   *Washo Shamans and Peyotists. Relgious Conflict in an American Indian Tribe* (Salt Lake City: University of Utah Press).

Skinner, Alanson

1915   "Societies of the Iowa, Kansa, and Ponca Indians," *Anthropological Papers of the American Museum of Natural History,* 11:679–801.

1924   *The Mascoutens or Prairie Potawatomi Indians* (Milwaukee: Public Museum of the City of Milwaukee).

Slotkin, James S.
1951   "Early Eighteenth Century Documents on Peyotism North of the Rio Grande," *American Anthropologist,* 53:420–27.
1952   "Menomini Peyotism. A Study of Individual Variation in a Primary Group with a Homogeneous Culture," *Transactions of the American Philosophical Society,* 42:567–700.
1955   "Peyotism, 1521–1891," *American Anthropologist,* 57:202–30.
1956a   "The Peyote Way," *Tomorrow,* 4:64–70.
1956b   "Peyotism, 1521–1891: Supplement," *American Anthropologist,* 58:184.
1975   *The Peyote Religion. A Study in Indian-White Relations* (New York: Farrar, Straus and Giroux, Octagon Books).

Smith, (Mrs.) Maurice G., communicated by John R. Swanton
1934   "A Negro Peyote Cult," *Journal of the Washington Academy of Sciences,* 24:448–53.

Snyder, Walter W.
1969   "The Native American Church: Its Origin, Ritual, Doctrine, and Ethic," *Bulletin of the Oklahoma Anthropological Society,* 18:13–38.

Speck, Frank G.
1933   "Notes on the Life of John Wilson, the Revealer of Peyote, as Recalled by His Nephew, George Anderson," *The General Magazine and Historical Chronicle,* 35:539–56.

Spindler, George Dearborn
1952   "Personality and Peyotism in Menomini Indian Acculturation," *Psychiatry,* 15:151–59.

Spindler, George Dearborn and Louise Spindler
1971   *Dreamers without Power. The Menomini Indians* (New York: Holt, Rinehart and Winston).

Spindler, Louise
1952   "Witchcraft in Menomini Acculturation," *American Anthropologist,* 54:593–602.

Steinmetz, Paul B.
1980   *Pipe, Bible and Peyote among the Oglala Lakota* (Stockholm: Almqvist & Wiksell International).
1983   "Three Types of Religious Acculturation among the Oglala Lakota," *Traditions in Contact and Change,* ed. P. Slater et al. (Waterloo: Wilfred Laurier Press): 527–41.
1984   *Meditations with Native Americans—Lakota Spirituality* (Santa Fe: Bear & Co.).

Steltenkamp, M. F.
1982   *The Sacred Vision. Native American Religion and Its Practice Today* (New York: Paulist Press).

Stenberg, Molly Peacock
1946   "The Peyote Culture among Wyoming Indians: A Transitional Link between Indigenous Culture and an Imposed Culture," *University of Wyoming Publications,* 12:85–156.

Stewart, Omer C.
1938   "Cactus Christianity," transcript, radio interview, Station KGO, University of California Radio Service.

1939   "Washo-Northern Paiute Peyotism: A Study in Acculturation," *Proceedings of the Sixth Pacific Science Congress,* 4:65–67.
1941   "The Southern Ute Peyote Cult," *American Anthropologist,* 43:303–8.
1944   "Washo—Northern Paiute Peyotism. A Study in Acculturation," *University of California Publications in American Archaeology and Ethnology,* 40:63–142.
1948   *Ute Peyotism. A Study of a Cultural Complex* (Boulder: University of Colorado Press).
1954   "Peyotism: A Modern Indian Religion," *Delphian Quarterly,* 37:7–8, 37.
1956a   "Peyote and Colorado's Inquisition Law," *Colorado Quarterly,* 5:79–90.
1956b   "Three Gods for Joe," *Tomorrow,* 4:71–76.
1961a   "The Native American Church and the Law with Description of Peyote Religious Services," *Westerners Brand Book,* 17:5–18.
1961b   "Peyote and the Arizona Court Decision," *American Anthropologist,* 63:1334–37.
1972   "The Peyote Religion and the Ghost Dance," *The Indian Historian,* 5:27–29.
1974   "Origin of the Peyote Religion in the United States," *Plains Anthropologist,* 65:211–23.
1975a   "Peyote and the Law," Centre for New Religious Movements, Selly Oak Colleges, Birmingham, England.
1975b   "The Peyote Religion of the Plains," Centre for New Religious Movements, Selly Oak Colleges, Birmingham, England.
1979a   "A New Look at Cree Peyotism," *Lifeways of Intermontane and Plains Montana Indians,* ed. Leslie B. Davis (Bozeman: Montana State University Press): 151–55.
1979b   "Anthropological Theory and History of Peyotism," *Ethnohistory,* 26:277–81.
1980a   "The Native American Church," *Anthropology on the Great Plains,* ed. W. Raymond Wood and Margot Liberty (Lincoln: University of Nebraska Press): 188–96.
1980b   "Peyotism and Mescalism," *Plains Anthropologist,* 25:297–309.
1982a   "The History of Peyotism in Nevada," *Nevada Historical Society Quarterly,* 25:197–209.
1982b   "Testing Anthropological Theories about Peyotism with Ethnohistorical Data," paper presented, 44th International Congress of Americanists, Manchester, England.
1982c   "Review of Paul B. Steinmetz, *Pipe, Bible and Peyote among the Oglala,*" *Plains Anthropologist,* May, 27:180–81.
1983   "Peyotism in Montana," *Montana,* 33:2–15.
1984   "Taos Factionalism," *American Indian Culture and Research Journal,* 8:37–57.
1986   Personal correspondence.

Tax, Sol
1972   "The Social Organization of the Fox Indians," *Social Anthropology of North American Tribes,* ed. Fred Eggan (Chicago: University of Chicago Press): 241–82.

Thomas, Robert K.
1968   "Pan-Indianism," *The American Indian Today,* ed. Stuart Levine and Nancy Oestreich Lurie (Deland, FL: Everett/Edwards, Inc.): 77–85.

Thompson, Stith
   1968   *Tales of the North American Indians* (Bloomington: Indiana University).
Tilghman, Zoe A.
   1938   *Quanah. The Eagle of the Comanches* (Oklahoma City: Harlow Publishing Corporation).
Tippett, Alan R.
   1967   "Report on the San Juan Episcopal Mission to the Navajo, Farmington, N.M.," Centre for New Religious Movements, Selly Oak Colleges, Birmingham, England.
Troike, Rudolph C.
   1962   "The Origins of Plains Mescalism," *American Anthropologist,* 64:946–63.
Turner, Harold W.
   1978   *Bibliography of New Religious Movements in Primal Societies. Vol. II: North America* (Boston: G. K. Hall & Co.).
Underhill, Ruth
   1948   *Peyote* (Santa Fe: San Vicente Foundation, Inc.).
   1952   "Peyote," *Proceedings, 30th International Congress of Americanists:* 143–48.
   1965   *Red Man's Religion* (Chicago: University of Chicago Press).
United States, Department of the Interior, Bureau of Indian Affairs
   1886–90   *Annual Reports* (Washington, DC: Government Printing Office).
Vogel, Virgil J.
   1973   *American Indian Medicine* (New York: Ballantine Books).
Wagner, G.
   1932   "Entwicklung und Verbreitung des Peyote-Kultes," *Baessler Archiv,* 15:59–141.
Wagner, Roland Marshall
   1974   "Western Navajo Peyotism: A Case Analysis," unpublished Ph.D. dissertation, University of Oregon.
   1975a   "Pattern and Process in Ritual Syncretism: The Case of Peyotism among the Navajo," *Journal of Anthropological Research,* 31:162–81.
   1975b   "Some Pragmatic Aspects of Navaho Peyotism," *Plains Anthropologist,* 20:197–205.
Wallace, Anthony F. C.
   1956   "Revitalization Movements," *American Anthropologist,* 58:264–81.
Wallace, Ernest and E. Adamson Hoebel
   1952   *The Comanches. Lords of the South Plains* (Norman: University of Oklahoma Press).
Waters, Frank
   1942   *The Man Who Killed the Deer* (New York: Farrar & Rinehart, Inc.).
Whitewolf, Jim
   1969   *The Life of a Kiowa Apache Indian,* ed. Charles S. Brant (New York: Dover Publications).
Wilson, Bryan R.
   1973   *Magic and the Millennium. A Sociological Study of Religious Movements of Protest among Tribal and Third-World Peoples* (New York: Harper & Row).

Works Progress Administration
1936–   "Chippewa Indian Historical Project Records," microfilm, State Historical So-
40, 1942   ciety of Wisconsin, Madison.

Wuttunee, William I. C.
1968   "Peyote Ceremony," *The Beaver,* Summer: 22–25.

Zenner, Walter P.
1960   "Charisma and Peyotism," *Current Anthropology,* 2:501–2.

Zolotarevskaja, I. A.
1961   "Some Materials on the Assimilation of Oklahoma-Indians," *Plains Anthropologist,* 6:1–6.

Chapter 7: *The Genesis of Phillip Deere's Sweat Lodge*

Aaland, Mikkel
1978   *Sweat* (Santa Barbara, CA: Capra Press).

Adair, James
1775   *History of the American Indians,* ed. Samuel Cole Williams (New York:
Promontory Press, reprint, n.d.).

Albanese, Catherine L.
1984   "Exploring Regional Religion: A Case Study of the Eastern Cherokee," *History
of Religions,* 23:344–71.

Alexander, Hartley Burr
1953   *The World's Rim. Great Mysteries of the North American Indians* (Lincoln:
University of Nebraska Press).

Bartram, William
1853   "Observations on the Creek and Cherokee Indians," *Transactions of the
American Ethnological Society,* 3:1–81.
1958   *The Travels of William Bartram. Naturalist's Edition,* ed. Francis Harper
(New Haven: Yale University Press).

Beck, Peggy V. and A. L. Walters
1977   *The Sacred. Ways of Knowledge, Sources of Life* (Tsaile, AZ: Navajo Community
College Press).

Beverly, Robert
1968   *The History and Present State of Virginia,* ed. Louis B. Wright (Charlottesville:
University Press of Virginia).

Brinton, D. G.
1870   *The National Legend of the Chahta-Muskogee Tribes* (Morrisania, NY: n.p.).

Brown, Joseph Epes
1971   *The Sacred Pipe. Black Elk's Account of the Seven Rites of the Oglala Sioux*
(Baltimore: Penguin Books).

Debo, Angie
1979   *The Road to Disappearance. A History of the Creek Indians* (Norman: University of Oklahoma Press).

Deere, Phillip
1983   Personal interviews with the author, Okemah, OK.

Driver, Harold E.
1972   *Indians of North America* (Chicago: University of Chicago Press).

Dusenberry, Verne
    1963   "Ceremonial Sweat Lodges of the Gros Ventre Indians," *Ethnos,* 28:46–62.
Eakins, D. W.
    1851   "Some Information Respecting the Creeks, or Muscogees," *Historical and Statistical Information Respecting the History, Condition and Prospects of the Indian Tribes of the United States,* 6 vols., ed. Henry R. Schoolcraft (Philadelphia: Lippincott, Grambo & Co.), 1:265–83.
Fairbanks, Charles H.
    1952   "Creek and Pre-Creek," *Archeology of Eastern United States,* ed. James B. Griffin (Chicago: University of Chicago Press): 285–300.
    1979   "The Function of Black Drink among the Creeks," *Black Drink. A Native American Tea,* ed. Charles M. Hudson (Athens: University of Georgia Press): 120–49.
Fire, John/Lame Deer and Richard Erdoes
    1972   *Lame Deer. Seeker of Visions* (New York: Simon and Schuster).
Foreman, Grant, ed.
    1930   *A Traveler in Indian Territory. The Journal of Ethan Allen Hitchcock, Late Major-General in the United States Army* (Cedar Rapids, IA: Torch Press).
Gatschet, Albert S.
    1969   *A Migration Legend of the Creek Indians* (New York: AMS Press).
    [1884]
Green, Michael D.
    1979   *The Creeks. A Critical Bibliography* (Bloomington: Indiana University Press).
Grimes, Ronald L.
    1982   *Beginnings in Ritual Studies* (Lanham, MD: University Press of America).
Hatt, Gudmund
    1951   "The Corn Mother in America and in Indonesia," *Anthropos,* 46:853–914.
Hawkins, Benjamin
    1971   *A Sketch of the Creek Country in the Years 1798 and 1799* (New York: Kraus
    [1848]   Reprint Co.).
Hewitt, J. N. B.
    1939   "Notes on the Creek Indians," ed. John R. Swanton, *Bureau of American Ethnology Bulletin* 123, Anthropological Papers, Smithsonian Institution, 10:119–59.
Howard, James H.
    1968   *The Southeastern Ceremonial Complex and Its Interpretation* (n.p.: Missouri Archaeological Society), memoir 6.
Hudson, Charles M.
    1976   *The Southeastern Indians* (n.p.: University of Tennessee Press).
    1979   *Black Drink. A Native American Tea* (Athens: University of Georgia Press).
Hultkrantz, Åke
    1981   *Belief and Worship in Native North America,* ed. Christopher Vecsey (Syracuse, NY: Syracuse University Press).
    1983   "The Religion of the Goddess in North America," *The Book of the Goddess Past and Present,* ed. Carl Olson (New York: Crossroad): 202–16.
Josephy, Alvin M., Jr.
    1982   *Now That the Buffalo's Gone. A Study of Today's American Indians* (New York: Alfred A. Knopf).

Krieger, Alex D.
1945   "An Inquiry into Supposed Mexican Influence on a Prehistoric 'Cult' in the Southern United States," *American Anthropologist,* 47:483–515.

Lewis, Thomas M. N. and Madeline Kneberg
1958   *Tribes That Slumber. Indian Times in the Tennessee Region* (Knoxville: University of Tennessee Press).

Lindsey, Robert
1986   "Spiritual Concepts Drawing a Different Breed of Adherent," *New York Times,* 29 September: A1, B12.

Lopatin, Ivan A.
1960   "Origin of the Native American Steam Bath," *American Anthropologist,* 62:977–93.

Lovin, Robin W. and Frank E. Reynolds, eds.
1985   *Cosmogony and Ethical Order. New Studies in Comparative Ethics* (Chicago: University of Chicago Press).

Lowie, Robert H.
1915   "Ceremonialism in North America," *Anthropology in North America,* Franz Boas et al. (New York: G. E. Stechert & Co.): 229–58.

Mahan, Joseph B.
1983   *The Secret. America in World History before Columbus* (Columbus, GA: published by the author).

Marriott, Alice and Carol K. Rachlin
1972   *American Indian Mythology* (New York: New American Library).

Milfort, Louis Le Clerc
1972   *Memoirs or a Quick Glance at My Travels and My Sojourn in the Creek Nation,* trans. and ed. Ben C. McCary (Savannah, GA: Beehive Press).

Nunez, Theron A., Jr.
1958   "Creek Nativism and the Creek War of 1813–1814," *Ethnohistory,* 5:1–47, 131–75, 292–301.

Paper, Jordan
1983   "The Post-Contact Origin of an American Indian High God: The Suppression of Feminine Spirituality," *American Indian Quarterly,* 7:1–24.

Paredes, J. Anthony
1975   "The Folk Culture of the Eastern Creek Indians: Synthesis and Change," *Indians of the Lower South: Past and Present,* ed. John K. Mahon (Pensacola, FL: Gulf Coast History and Humanities Conference): 93–111.

Piomingo (John Robinson)
1810   *The Savage* (Philadelphia: Thomas S. Manning).

Powers, Marla N.
1980   "Menstruation and Reproduction: An Oglala Case," *Signs,* 6:54–65.

Powers, William K.
1977   *Oglala Religion* (Lincoln: University of Nebraska Press).
1984   *Yuwipi. Vision and Experience in Oglala Ritual* (Lincoln: University of Nebraska Press).

Robinson, Gary
n.d.   *Tales of the Muscogee* (Boulder: Centre Productions Inc.).

Rooth, Anna Birgitta
  1957   "The Creation Myths of the North American Indians," *Anthropos,* 52:497–508.

Speck, Frank G.
  1907   "The Creek Indians of Taskigi Town," *Memoirs of the American Anthropological Association,* 2:99–164.
  1909   *Ethnology of the Yuchi Indians* (Philadelphia: University of Pennsylvania Museum), Anthropological Publications, 1.
  1911   *Ceremonial Songs of the Creek and Yuchi Indians* (Philadelphia: University of Pennsylvania Museum), Anthropological Publications, 1.

Spotted Eagle, Chris
  1983   "The Great Spirit within the Hole," Corporation for Public Broadcasting, movie.

Swan, Caleb
  1855   "Position and State of Manners and Arts in the Creek, or Muscogee Nation in 1791," *Historical and Statistical Information Respecting the History, Condition and Prospects of the Indian Tribes of the United States,* 6 vols., ed. Henry R. Schoolcraft (Philadelphia: J. B. Lippincott & Co.), 5:251–83.

Swanton, John R.
  1911   *Indian Tribes of the Lower Mississippi Valley and Adjacent Coast of the Gulf of Mexico* (Washington, DC: U.S. Government Printing Office). Smithsonian Institution, Bureau of American Ethnology, Bulletin 43.
  1922   *Early History of the Creek Indians and Their Neighbors* (Washington, DC: U.S. Government Printing Office). Smithsonian Institution, Bureau of American Ethnology, Bulletin 73.
  1928a   "Aboriginal Culture of the Southeast," *Forty-Second Annual Report of the Bureau of American Ethnology, 1924–1925* (Washington, DC: U.S. Government Printing Office): 677–726.
  1928b   "Religious Beliefs and Medical Practices of the Creek Indians," *Forty-Second Annual Report of the Bureau of American Ethnology, 1924–1925* (Washington, DC: U.S. Government Printing Office): 473–672.
  1928c   "Social Organization and Social Usages of the Indians of the Creek Confederacy," *Forty-Second Annual Report of the Bureau of American Ethnology, 1924–1925* (Washington, DC: U.S. Government Printing Office):31–472.
  1928d   "The Interpretation of Aboriginal Mounds by Means of Creek Indian Customs," *Annual Report . . . of the Smithsonian Institution . . . for the Year . . . 1927* (Washington, DC: U.S. Government Printing Office):495–506.
  1929   *Myths and Tales of the Southeastern Indians* (Washington, DC: U.S. Government Printing Office). Smithsonian Institution, Bureau of American Ethnology, Bulletin 88.
  1946   *The Indians of the Southeastern United States* (Washington, DC: U.S. Government Printing Office). Smithsonian Institution, Bureau of American Ethnology, Bulletin 137.

Taitt, David
  1916   "Journal of a Journey through the Creek Country, 1772," *Travels in the American Colonies,* ed. Newton D. Mereness (New York: Macmillan):493–565.

Tuggle, William Orrie
  1973   *Shem, Ham & Hapheth,* ed. Eugene Current-Garcia with Dorothy B. Hatfield (Athens: University of Georgia Press).

Vecsey, Christopher
1984   "American Indian Spiritual Politics," *Commonweal,* 111:203–8.

Voegelin, C. F.
1970   *The Shawnee Female Deity* (New Haven: Human Relations Area Files Press). Yale University Publications in Anthropology, 10.

Waring, Antonio J., Jr.
1968   *The Waring Papers,* ed. Stephen Williams (Cambridge: Peabody Museum, Harvard University).

Waring, Antonio J., Jr. and Preston Holder
1945   "A Prehistoric Ceremonial Complex in the Southeastern United States," *American Anthropologist,* 47:1–34.

Weil, Andrew
1982   "The Indian Sweat," *American West,* 19:42–49.

Wheeler-Voegelin, Erminie and Remedios W. Moore
1957   "The Emergence Myth in Native North America," *Studies in Folklore in Honor of Distinguished Service Professor Stith Thompson, ed. W. Edson Richmond* (Bloomington: Indiana University Press). Folklore Series, 9:66–91.

Wilson, Lee Anne
1979   "Human and Animal Imagery on Southern Cult Shell Work, Southeastern United States, A. D. 100 to 1250," unpublished Ph.D. dissertation, Columbia University.

Witthoft, John
1949   *Green Corn Ceremonialism in the Eastern Woodlands* (Ann Arbor: University of Michigan Press). Occasional Contributions from the Museum of Anthropology, 13.

Index